HUMAN VALUES IN MANAGEMENT

Corporate Social Responsibility Series

Series Editor:
Professor David Crowther, London Metropolitan University, UK

This series aims to provide high quality research books on all aspects of corporate social responsibility including: business ethics, corporate governance and accountability, globalization, civil protests, regulation, responsible marketing and social reporting.

The series is interdisciplinary in scope and global in application and is an essential forum for everyone with an interest in this area.

Human Values in Management

Edited by

ANANDA DAS GUPTA
Indian Institute of Plantation Management

ASHGATE

Published by
Ashgate Publishing Limited
Gower House
Croft Road
Aldershot
Hants GU11 3HR
England

Ashgate Publishing Company
Suite 420
101 Cherry Street
Burlington, VT 05401-4405
USA

Ashgate website: http://www.ashgate.com

British Library Cataloguing in Publication Data
Human values in management. - (Corporate social
   responsibility series)
   1.Management - Moral and ethical aspects 2.Management -
   Social aspects 3.Business ethics 4.Social responsibility of
   business
   I.Gupta, Ananda Das
   174.4

Library of Congress Cataloging-in-Publication Data
Human values in management / edited by Ananda Das Gupta.
      p. cm. -- (Corporate social responsibility series)
   Includes bibliographical references and index.
   ISBN 0-7546-4275-5
   1. Management--Moral and ethical aspects. 2. Management--Social aspects. 3.
Business ethics. 4. Corporate responsibility. I. Das Gupta, Ananda,
1955- II. Series.

   HF5387.H858 2004
   174'.4--dc22

2004013251
ISBN 0 7546 4275 5

Printed and bound in Great Britain by Antony Rowe Ltd, Chippenham, Wiltshire

Contents

List of Figures, Tables and Exhibits

Figures

Tables

Exhibits

List of Contributors

R.P. Banerjee, Professor, Eastern Institute of Integrated Learning in Management, Calcutta, India.

C. Panduranga Bhatta, Associate Professor, Indian Institute of Management, Calcutta, India.

S.K. Chakraborty, Convenor, Management Centre for Human Values, Indian Institute of Management, Calcutta.

Samir R. Chatterjee, Professor of International Management, Curtin Business School, Australia.

David Crowther, Professor of Corporate Social Responsibility, London Metropolitan University, UK.

Tanmoy Dutta, Visiting Associate Professor, Management Center for Human Values, Indian Institute of Management, Calcutta, India.

Ananta Kumar Giri, Associate Professor, Madras Institute of Development Studies, Chennai, India.

Kenneth E. Goodpaster, Professor of Business Ethics, University of St. Thomas, Minneapolis, USA.

Miriam Green, London Metropolitan University, UK.

Bengt Gustavsson, Associate Professor, School of Business, Stockholm, University, Sweden.

David Kimber, Associate Professor, School of Management, RMIT Business, Melbourne, Australia.

T. Dean Maines, University of St. Thomas, Minneapolis, USA.

O.V. Nandimath, Convenor, CEERA, National Law School of India University, Bangalore, India.

Peter Pruzan, Professor, Department of Management, Politics and Philosophy, Copenhagen Business School, Denmark.

M.R.C. Ravi, Advocate, High Court, Karnataka, Bangalore, India.

Mitchelle D. Rovang, University of St. Thomas, Minneapolis, USA.

Swami Satyarupananda, Secretary, Ramakrishna Math, Raipur, Madhya Pradesh, India.

Subhash Sharma, Director, Indian Institute of Plantation Management, Bangalore, India.

Fran Siemensma, School of Management, Victoria University, Victoria, Australia.

Swami Someswarananda, Chairman, Vivekananda Center for Indian Management, Indore, India.

Damodar Suar, Associate Professor, Department of Humanities and Social Sciences, Indian Institute of Technology, Kharagpur, India.

N. Vittal, Formerly a member of the Indian Administrative Service, until recently Central Vigilance Commissioner of India.

Preface

Corporate responsibility is a vital issue in contemporary business climate. Much of its currency comes from the scale and influence of the present day corporate. Some business houses are bigger than many nation states. Their domain and economic imperialism is worldwide. Nevertheless, business houses are subject to constant and intense scrutiny and surveillance by the State and the society in which they function. It is well established that their freedom to operate is not a license to abuse.

Of course, profit has to be the primary concern of any business: without profit, it is impossible to carry out any other activity for the welfare of the society at large. However, there are two overriding criteria, which assume significance in this context. While profit may be the overall objective, the methods employed to achieve profit have to be above board, they must be ethical and moral. Secondly, having achieved profit, the company must look around for ways and means by which it can return to the society some endowments for the welfare of everyone. The *summum bonum* of any enterprise is the lofty and noble objectives it seeks to serve in and for the society, in which it subsists.

The emerging values of humanism and humanization coupled with the burgeoning focus on creativity, the autonomy, which people are acquiring progressively and the focus of supply and demand have forced CEOs to acknowledge 'people power'. Moreover, people's expectation is fast changing and they cannot be taken for granted. They have the motivation to work and are to be treated different from other resources. As such, the conventional approach of Personnel Management to people treating them as a resource, as unnecessary evils who can only be motivated through fear, punishment, money or comfort has undergone a sea change.

And that is the people. And there lies the significance of such king of forum as this volume, which looks forward to in the way of varied and diverse experiences as well as observations and reflections being put forward on a platform for underlying the importance of values in individual, group and organizational contexts.

While working on this project, I received enormous support from all sides, from the academicians, from the contributors, from my Institute and from some other personal and public quarters. I would like to thank specially, *Mr. Shaji Kurian*, Programme Associate of the Institute for helping the editor in a big way by providing the support plank. Lastly I am thankful to my wife *Aruna* and daughter *Debarati* (a.k.a. *Chinki*) for their encouragements shown towards bringing out this volume.

Finally, my sincere thanks are due to the Series Editor Professor David Crowther and the entire editorial and production members of Ashgate Publishing Limited, United Kingdom.

Ananda Das Gupta

List of Abbreviations

BPI	Bribe Payers Index
CER	Corporate Environmental Responsibility
CINE	Controllable Internal and Non-Controllable External
CPI	Corruption Perception Index
CRT	Caux Round Table
CSR	Corporate Social Responsiblity
CTS	Carpal Tunnel Syndrome
CVS	Computer Vision Syndrome
DVC	Damodar Valley Corporation [A big multipurpose Project in India]
GM	General Motors
HLL	Hindustan Lever Limited
IIM-C	Indian Institute of Management, Calcutta, India
KFC	Kentucky Fired Chicken
LIC	Life Insurance Corporation of India
MBA	Master of Business Administration
MCHV	Management Centre for Human Values
MNC	Multi National Company
NGO	Non Government Organization
NPMP	New Paradigm for Management with Positivism
NT	Nurturant Task Model of Leadership
OSHA	Oneness, Spiritualistic, Humanistic and Animalistic Model
PIL	Public Interest Litigation
QSC	Quality, Service and Cleanliness
SAIP	Self Assessment and Improvement Process
SME	Small and Medium Enterprises
SVM	Shareholder Value Management
TQOM	Total Quality Of Management
UNESCO	United Nations Educational, Scientific and Cultural Organization Organization
VBM	Value-Based Management
VEDA	Vision, Devotion, Enlightenment, Action Model
XLRI	Xavier Labour Relations Institute, India

Introduction

Ananda Das Gupta

I

There has been a long history of philosophical debate as to the complex nature of values/ethics as well as the validity of business or its purpose in society. Therefore it is often argued that one should find a way to lead one's business-life in harmony with one's inner life. Thus with this 'connectivity' between the subjective and objective perspectives, business is not to be regarded as something evil, unethical or tainted. Business should be considered to be sacred, depending upon the spirit in which it is set up and carried out. All is a matter of attitude and approach, which is based on three major attributes: (1) Formulating attitude of business (2) Humanization of and (3) Interiorization of management.

It becomes imperative, therefore that the fresh thinking is done so as to underline the role of Man in contrast to mere emphasis on the wage earner. Technology makes things possible but it is Man who makes it happen. Man is an integrated creature of the Divine Craftsman.

Understanding of the nature of human values may be so intimately associated with what might otherwise be considered to be distinct concepts that they cannot be effectively separated from some perspectives:

(a) Economic value: The concept of the value of a thing is central to traditional economic value theory for which value is the so-called exchange or market value of a commodity. Economists distinguish between value in this sense and the value of individuals or societies, which in welfare economics mean much the same as preferences or tastes. Such values may then be realized by the appropriate allocation of resources.

(b) Value assessments and imputations: Value assessments are assertions to the effect that something did, will or would favourably affect the life of someone. Value imputations are assertions to the effect that someone or some group has, holds, or subscribes to some value (e.g. achievement, work, altruism, comfort, equality, thrift, friendship), or that some such thing is one of his values. The word value then means different things in these two contexts. Assessed values then become measures of the capacities of various kinds of entities, including persons, to confer benefits, whereas imputed values are measures of tendencies of persons to promote certain ends, for certain reasons.

(c) Instrumental and intrinsic values: A distinction may also be made between instrumental values, which are the means to something else, and intrinsic values, which are those desired for themselves (such as goodness, truth, and beauty).

(d) Attitudes and opinions: Many surveys of the 'values' held by people do not find it useful to distinguish between attitudes or opinions held by people and the values that they hold. A survey of values then becomes a survey of attitudes and opinions. Presumably some attitudes may be considered as relating to values, but the distinction is then difficult to establish in that context. It is difficult to identify 'values' from such survey data.

Human Development and Values

Human development can be seen as the process of giving more effective expression to human values. Many of the advocated approaches to human development are quite explicit concerning the values in terms of which they are conceived or which they are desired to enhance. The more sophisticated approaches to policy-making and management are quite deliberate in their efforts to identify the values on which any action is to be grounded.

Through some processes of human development, providing access to more subtle modes of awareness, new value insights emerge. In such cases there may be a very intimate relationship between the state of awareness and comprehension of the value. Emerging awareness of certain states may even lead to the articulation of more subtle understanding of commonly identified values. Certain modes of awareness can be understood as the embodiment of specific values or configurations of values.

Perhaps of most importance is the manner in which certain processes of human development integrate together previously disparate insights. Values can easily decay into empty, 'bloodless' categories unless they are sustained by appropriate levels of awareness. Human development may thus build a subtle connecting pattern between values. Such integration provides a new foundation from which action may be undertaken in a sustainable manner.

Again it is ironic that there is less and less in modern society that people are prepared to die for, or to allow others to die for. Whole societies can now be held to ransom for a single known hostage. Millions can be spent to maintain a comatose, brain-damaged patient on life-support for decades. Euthanasia is illegal, no matter what the desire of the person concerned. Exposure to risk is progressively designed out of society, to be replaced by vicarious experiences of risk through videos or with the protection of required safety devices. The paradox is that unknown numbers are however sacrificed through carcinogenic products, abortion, structural violence, massacres, gang murders, cult rituals, 'snuff' movies and associated perversions, or a failure of food and medical supplies.

The attitude to life has become as immature as that to death. Millions of dollars are spent on efforts to maintain youthfulness, whether through cosmetics, cosmetic surgery or attempts to reverse the ageing process. Every other value is sacrificed to save lives in industrialized societies, whilst allowing others to die elsewhere. Individuals in industrialized societies are prosecuted for life-endangering neglect. But these same societies fail to apply the same standards in their policies towards other societies. Reproduction is tacitly encouraged without any provision for the resulting population growth or for the effects on the environment. Society evokes problems to provide solutions for its own irresponsibility – a control mechanism for the immature lacking the insight for a healthy relationship.

The challenge of the times would seem to involve a call for personal transformation through which social and conceptual frameworks can be viewed anew. Willingness to sacrifice inherited perspectives is an indication of the dimension of the challenge – most dramatically illustrated by willingness to risk death. However physical death is not the issue, and may easily be a simplistic, deluded impulse lending itself to manipulation. Destruction of frameworks valued by others is equally suspect. Such dramatics provide rewards within the very frameworks whose nature the individual needs to question, but by which he or she may need to choose to be constrained.

II

Values are deeply held beliefs, the fundamental building blocks of a workplace culture reflecting a view about 'what is good.' In a law firm, they can include integrity, superior performance, putting the client first, making a big profit, and so forth, but it is important to note that there is no real right or wrong in values.

There are two visions of the new approach of management: First is a new vision of business based on an evolutionary spiritual humanism. Second is the possibility of business becoming an experimental workshop for a creative synthesis of ethics and management? This second possibility, if it becomes a reality, can provide the insights, learning, experience and the capabilities for a creative synthesis of East and West in Business.

To succeed in today's competitive market requires a high professional competence as well as a continual improvement of that competence. Equally important is co-operation among professionals, often of a great variety. Success also requires communication and co-operation with customers and with the community. Communication and co-operation require social and cultural competence. Cultural competence is shared knowledge and hence communal knowledge. Cultural or communal knowledge bridge the gap between individuals and between professions.

The whole set of values needed for management can be summed up in the words of *dharma* is the code of right conduct. In these days when corporate governance is emerging as a significant factor, we find that Indian management can emerge successfully in the market place if it is able to draw on its route for good corporate governance, which is available in our culture and tradition. But then the question may arise, how many of us are aware of scriptures, Upanishads, culture and so on. Though one may not be consciously aware, one learns about basic principles from childhood, from parents and from religion.

Spiritual identity of the character is essential for the build up of a new paradigm characterizing integrity, truthfulness, caring, compassion, honesty and supportive attitude.

Ethics and Conflicts

First, there is a private or personal interest. Often this is a financial interest, but it could also be another sort of interest, say, to provide a special advantage to a spouse or child. Taken by themselves, there is nothing wrong with pursuing private or personal interests, for instance, changing jobs for more pay or helping your daughter improve her golf stroke.

The problem comes when this private interest comes into conflict with the second feature of the definition, an 'official duty' quite literally the duty you have because you have an office or act in an official capacity. As a professional you take on certain official responsibilities, by which you acquire obligations to clients, employers, or others. These obligations are supposed to trump private or personal interests.

Third, conflicts of interest interfere with professional responsibilities in a specific way, namely, by interfering with objective professional judgment. A major reason why clients and employers value professionals is that, they expect professionals to be objective and independent. Factors, like private and personal interests, that either interfere or appear likely to interfere with objectivity are then a matter of legitimate concern to those who rely on professionals – be they clients, employers, professional colleagues, or the general public. So it is also important to avoid apparent and potential as well as actual conflicts of interest. An apparent conflict of interest is one, which a reasonable person would think that the professional judgment is likely to be compromised. A potential conflict of interest involves a situation that may develop into an actual conflict of interest.

This book is a collection of contributions representing academicians and scholars from America, Europe, Australia, England and India for exploring topics of business ethics confronting individuals, groups, administration and society at large. Ethical issues are emerging as the most important challenge in all spheres of life. The competitive market-economy model has widened the scope for all players to violate the fundamental values and integrity to maintain and enrich a civil society. These violations stretch from personal lapses of bribery and corruption to the wider areas of moral questions related to an ethically grounded competitive business system.

III

In the first part of the volume, the first paper written by Peter Pruzan presents the hypothesis that a radical shift is taking place in the way that power is won and manifested by leaders in modern organizations. It is then argued that a new concept of power is evolving within an organizational setting – *power as the capability to serve others*. He refers to this form of power as *spiritual power* and argues that it is based on a personal and organizational existential search for self-knowledge, meaning and wholeness. Finally, it is suggested that the concept of spiritual power, though new in an organizational context, can best be understood by considering concepts of freedom, duty, equanimity, selflessness, non-attached action, unity and non-violence as they have developed over thousands of years in the moral-philosophical traditions of the 'West' and the spiritual traditions of the 'East', in particular those of Buddhism and Hinduism.

In the second paper Damodar Suar argued that institutionalization of ethics can prevent such adverse consequences, has inculcate morality in the organization and its constituents, do what is beneficial to the organization and lager society, and provide directions to decide right and wrong. Drawing evidence from the corporate world, various strategies are justified at individual, interpersonal and organizational levels for incorporating ethics into daily business life. Such strategies are ethical auto-suggestion, mind-stilling exercise, ethical awareness, ethics training, ethical leadership, group decision-making, whistle-blowing, managerial norms and practices, employment of ethical staff, establishing an ethical code, ethics committee, reward system, ethical audit, and ethical benchmarking.

In the third position, Swami Satyarupananda believes that the sole purpose of human life is to find out and realize this infinitely valuable jewel of 'Atman'. 'Life without' represents the grand total of the psycho-physical part of human personality dominated primarily, amongst others, by the desire to live, to know and the desire for happiness. Building 'life within' is fundamentally characterized by morality.

On the other hand, Subhash Sharma puts forwards that the Indian model of a balance between the spiritual and materialistic achievements, could provide a new foundational premise for a balance between excessive individualism and extreme altruism. With this, the new-age management models discussed here would find increasing acceptance in the corporate world. Perhaps it is time for the 'Asian *Dharma*' to provide the new social vision for the new millennium – a vision of sacro-civic society based on 'spiritualization' of modernity.

Samir R. Chatterjee strongly argues that in spite of a growing awareness in the importance of ethical centrality in an intensely competitive international business arena, very little empirical work has been conducted to strengthen the relevant management literatures. The purpose of the research reported in this paper was to examine the perceptions of ethical probity among managers in six Asian countries. The results of the study indicate interesting convergences and divergences across countries and organisational demographics. The findings lead to observations in respect of the apparent similarities of ethical conceptualisation in global, societal and often in the organisational arena while noticeable divergences characterise the domain of individual ethical perceptions.

IV

In the second part of the volume S.K. Chakraborty observes that Sci-tech must nurture enough humility to be able to absorb this message and modify and moderate its course. The eighteenth-century Enlightenment projects to achieve human perfectibility through secular science, accompanied by equating religion with magic, leads critics to avoid discussing the 'good or bad' of techno-science and choosing only to ask 'who is responsible for the production and distribution' of technology. The quality of this 'who' – by what standards to measure it – is not dealt with. That religion is spirituality, not magic, is a truth which only realizers can tell because they know what they are talking about. The philosopher who considers himself as a mere 'translator' of diverse discourses, not as a realizer, is apt to forget that the same tests for qualifying as a critique of techno-science also apply to one who wishes to be the critique of religion. With technology there is more diversion today, which strengthens separation rather than unity in society. Evolution towards involved Divinity for unity will be the correct direction to follow. This may entail a slowing down for sci-tech.

David Kimber's paper reflects on the author's experiences as a tourist in India as well as theoretical perspectives identified in the literature. Themes addressed include trust and relationship building, the awkward interaction between friendship and business practice in the tourist industry, the transcendental aspects of ecotourism in India, confusion and cultural difference – the values perspective. The paper also reviews the relationship between social responsibility and business and concludes by reflecting on how ecotourism in India could be an international influence, changing some of the apparently dominant paradigms of western management practices.

Tanmoy Dutta believes that to capture the deeper ethical issues of the Cyber Age, we need to be reminded of a few words about the status of science and scientific knowledge. The scientific approach is by no means the only mode by which people have attempted to understand their environment and themselves. Lest, our admiration for scientific knowledge may lead us to scientism, scientific fundamentalism, scientific egoism or scientific dogmatism.

The paper contributed by R.P. Banerjee discusses the scope of transformation in the values identification of the corporate sector. Whereas the Indian companies have an edge over many others, it has been observed that many global corporations and western enterprises have gone much ahead of the Indians. Issues fundamental to the human society and essential to its long-term sustainability require a definite transformation in the understanding and practice of values. One has to rise above the dichotomous mix of human values and be authentic in personality to reckon divine values in human existence. Further, the paper discusses various aspects, giving Indian corporate examples, global examples and global expectations. It has dwelt on the conceptual aspects of different human types for an individual and a corporation as well.

While discussing the Corporate Environmental Responsibility (CER), O.V. Namdimath and M.R.C. Ravi try to capture the changing ethos of policy makers and public towards 'development'. The general tendency is to view development as highly environmentally dangerous and business enterprises as profit minded; in this the image of many corporations are getting badly affected. The second half of the paper looks into the picture the judiciary, in its various decisions, painted of a business enterprise and how they have issued guidelines many times placing environment in a pivotal position. The paper finally tries to find out how today's management can take environmentally appropriate decisions so as to overcome the abovementioned difficulties. Here the paper also looks into various strategies the management may adopt to maintain its green profile.

The paper written by Fran Siemensma applies themes addressed by feminist theory to examine the normative concepts associated with the Master of Business Administration (MBA) program as taught in three Australian and two Indian institutions between 1995 to 1997. It explores the role of women in terms of Derrida's contention that 'the attribution of difference is never a benign act, but one in which 'difference' is always attributed by those with power to the characteristics of less powerful groups'.

Swami Someswarananda believes firmly that the core of human values in Business center round the basic principles of motive and concepts. The lack of holistic approach is the core problem. As the people of business are to serve the society, we must know the social objectives first. Through the methodology of Indian philosophy the author has strived to solve the ethical dilemma that is constantly haunting the business scenario in juxtaposition of wealth and prosperity. The author, through his experiment, has posed some fundamental questions to be asked by the practitioners of business:

- What is expected of me?
- What is my performance level?
- How can I be more focused in my job?
- How can I add value?

The author finally summed up: 'values, in essence, means working for a great cause'.

V

In the final part of the volume Bengt Gustavsson puts forward the argument of Samhita theory in the organizational perspective. His paper is based on the assumption that pure consciousness is the common basis for all of creation, including our mind. By developing our consciousness to fathom greater ranges of inner wholeness, the less alien will the 'outer' be and the more we will recognize in terms of ourselves. The inner and outer reality is nothing but the same.

N. Vittal, a seasoned bureaucrat himself, has a strong belief that the whole set of values needed for management can be summed up in the words of *dharma* is the code of right conduct. All religions have highlighted the need for being truthful and kind and helpful. Ultimately, perhaps the universal principle and human value is that honesty is the best policy.

Ananta Kumar Giri, while discussing the Habermasian concept, strives to make a critical assessment of the claim of discourse ethics to meet with the challenges of moral consciousness and communicative action today. The paper argues that in order to realize the lofty agenda of transformation that discourse ethics sets for itself, it must now make a dialogue with critical and practical spirituality. It gives a brief sketch of the agenda of spiritual transformation that can help discourse ethics, solve some of its own stated problems and act as a transformative agent in thinking through the theory and practice of moral consciousness and communicative action today.

C. Panduranga Bhatta's paper explores the ingredients of effective leadership such as character, based on human values, selflessness, self-effacement, leading by example etc. through classical and contemporary writings besides holding mirror to a few corporate examples for the sake of helping future leaders to develop their full potential for good and effective leadership.

In the first part of this paper, Kenneth E. Goodpaster, T. Dean Maines and Michelle D. Rovang seek to clarify the idea of 'stakeholder thinking, since it is seldom used clearly or consistently either by its proponents or its opponents. In the process of this clarification, they identify two conceptual barriers that seem to block the application of stakeholder thinking by business decision-makers: the Partiality Paradox and the Common Good Paradox. In the second part, they describe the Caux Round Table (CRT) Principles for Business as a stakeholder-based, trans-cultural statement of business values. Beyond their aspirational formulation, however, the CRT Principles are now associated with a managerial tool called the Self-Assessment and Improvement Process (SAIP). The SAIP is designed to assist executives in shaping the consciences of their firms by means of an organisational self-appraisal process. This process, even though it does not pretend to be a decision-making tool *per se*, lays the foundation for improvement initiatives that enable the corporation to clarify and fulfil its ethical responsibilities.

In the third part, they indicate a way in which the CRT-SAIP may help organizations avoid in practice the two barriers that are difficult to avoid in theory. An appendix contains the full text of the CRT Principles. During a crisis of confidence in corporations, this message may have special importance.

Lastly, David Crowther argues that many would argue that currently there is too great a concern with encouraging corporate self-interest at the expense of the public interest and that people are very much absent from the equation of concern regarding the effects of corporate activity. Indeed the continuing conversion of public service provision to market testing by many governments suggests a strengthening belief that the two interests are not in conflict. Self-interest and altruism (promoting the welfare of others over self) need not be in conflict. There is ample evidence that encouraging corporate self-interest (and risk taking) does benefit society (albeit unequally from a Marxist perspective). Some of that evidence is contested, as in the case of genetically modified foods. Nevertheless, during the last two decades most of the world's nations have set about creating anew, or refining, (capitalist) economic and political institutions that encourage corporate self-interest.

VI

Ethics should start from the top down in any organization. Being honest and open is the only way to succeed in business. As a Chief Executive Officer (CEO) or top manager, how can one avoid ethics problems within the business? The Better Business Bureau offers the following tips:

- Bringing highest sense of ethics to business and lead by example. Demonstrate high ethical standards of behaviour toward the customers, suppliers, shareholders, employees and communities in which one do business. Be honest in all the dealings.
- Developing an ethics policy. Make certain that the policy starts at the top level so that company management sets an important example for all employees. Set up training programs that will assist employees in carrying out established ethics policies. Although an ethics policy may not stop unethical behaviour, it may give people something to think about and provide a measurement against which to assess their behaviour.
- Establish an internal communication system that allows employees to express concerns directly to top management if they suspect wrongdoing or are uncomfortable with current practices. Consider appointing an ombudsman.
- Treating employees with respect and fairness.
- Rewarding employees for ethical decision-making and actions.
- Meeting with the accounting staff to reinforce the highest reporting and accounting standards and expectations. When the line between doing what is right and what is legal is not clear, move back to what one knows is right.
- Know what is going on in the company. Routinely walking around and talking to the employees directly. Getting a feel for what they are doing. Becoming accessible and interested.

We are almost bound to welcome the New Paradigm in Business because it opens the path for a decisive step forward in evolution from an authoritarian, mechanistic, Taylorian era to a freer and a more humanistic ethos in business. But even while the New Paradigm values are spreading fast and getting established in business, we have to think ahead and visualize the next stage in the evolution of business. The crucial question we have to ask is what is the highest potentiality of humanism or in other words what is the highest potential in man and how to manifest it in the individual and corporate life, especially in business? Some ideas can be put forward, we believe, as a New Paradigm for Management with Positivism (NPMP):

A Holistic Approach to Management

- Managing others
- Need to play one's role well
- Need to understand the importance and place of one's role
- Need to understand and function within a proper hierarchy
- Need for common and individual goals
- Need to 'give' and 'take'

Value Based Administration: To add value to administration an administrator should:

- Possess strategic thinking to integrate one's region with the nation

Human Values in Management

- Recognise the world beyond one's office and face its challenge
- Understand society's goals
- See people as potential and strategic resources and mentor them accordingly
- Nurture belief in value adding

The Real Need

- Hierarchy should be replaced by self managing structures such as (a) Networks; (b) multidisciplinary teams (c) Small action dyads
- Information dissemination should be a routine work
- Delivering service should be effective in terms of its cost, quality and quantity.

Working With Others

- Empathy
- Team Work

Modern business philosophy has a certain viewpoint or perspective on human potential based on the secular humanistic values of the west and the scientific theories on the nature of man and his evolution. We are presenting a complementing perspective based on the values of spiritual humanism and the spiritual vision of the Vedantic sciences of the East. In general most of the conceptions on spirituality emerging in business and management denote some form of moral, religious, social and psychological fulfilment, like creativity, self-expression, sharing, charity or community service.

VII

Business cannot be abstracted from the society in which it exists and functions; it is an integral part of the human society. This 'holistic' view of business is another perception emerging in modern business philosophy. And business happens to be the most dominant and representative organ of the modern society. So in an organic vision of business it has to be viewed as an integral part of the economic, technological, social, political and cultural environment in which it functions. And this environment, and the forces of the environment, at once influences and is influenced by the social organs which constitute it. But our focus will be not on the environment that belongs to the past, but of the new world of the future which is struggling to emerge from the ashes of the past and the facts of the present.

There are three major factors or forces, which, we believe, will shape the new world of the future. The first is the urge for a new synthesis in thought and action; the second, in the external world, is the development of Science and Technology; the third, in the inner-world, is mapping a new horizon for the development of consciousness.

PART I

THEORETICAL PERSPECTIVES

Chapter 1

Blending the Best of East and West in Management Education: A View from Northern Europe

Peter Pruzan

Introductory Remarks on Purpose, Scope and Delimitations

This paper is based on my personal experiences as a professor in Denmark who was born and educated in the United States, who has worked with the theory and practice of management in Europe for almost 40 years, and who has visited India 18 times and established a teamwork between the Copenhagen Business School and some of India's best reputed schools of management.

It would be audacious and misleading to say that the reflections provided here really cover 'the best of the East and West in management education'. For each of the terms 'best', 'East', 'West' and 'management education' invites considerable interpretation. Nevertheless, a series of observations are made and conclusions drawn which should provide food for thought when attempting to determine how eastern and western developments in management education can contribute to each other. Let us start then by some terminological considerations – and personal biases.

By '*best*' I will refer to those leading-edge developments in management education, which contribute to the development of a humanistic, democratic and sustainable frame of reference for the profession of management. By sustainable here, I refer to a holistic view of governance, which encompasses corporate economic, environmental, social and ethical responsibility.

This conception of 'best' leads to a particular perspective on '*management education*'. The term management traditionally has been conceived of as comprising such activities as strategy, planning, administration and control. In recent years, particularly in 'the West', the term 'management' has been supplemented with the term 'leadership'. This later term is being used today to relate to concepts and activities that had not until recently been central to the traditional themes of management. These include vision statements, codes of values, change management, coaching and facilitating. The term values-based leadership has become part of the vernacular. Parallel to this development in the West – and to some extent as a reaction to the hegemony of its materialistic focus – there has been a return to basics in the East. Here, at some leading-edge schools of management there has been a focus more on the leader than on leadership – on the qualities, values, virtues and integrity of the leader, on 'character' rather than on technologies, methods and processes. This focus is rooted not in new concepts, but in fundamental perspectives on the purpose and potentials of human life – and of human organizations. In other words, while developments at the leading-edge of management education in the West have tended to focus on the practice and processes of leadership, in the East, a major focus has been on the qualities and competencies of the leader.

By '*West*', I will primarily refer to a Scandinavian perspective on leadership education since, being a Dane, this is my home base. There are many differences in attitudes and behaviour between e.g. Danish developments in the theory and practice of leadership and those in e.g. Spain, Poland and the UK – or for that matter the United States. These differences, which will not be delineated here due to considerations of time and space, reflect the different historical, cultural and political traditions of such countries and differences in the roles and responsibilities of business and government in these countries in developing societal welfare. The Scandinavian countries, Denmark, Norway and Sweden are small, homogeneous countries. They all have a very high standard of living, highly educated populations, a high 'quality of life' and a narrow spread of incomes compared to the rest of Europe (for example, it has often been said of Denmark that it is 'a land where there are few who have too little and fewer yet who have too much').[1] In addition they are characterized by an absence of corruption, a high level of social order and welfare and a concomitant high level of taxation – and perhaps even more important with respect to the task at hand, a high level of trust in their business and political leaders compared to almost all other nations in the world.

In connection with these comments on the heterogeneity of 'the West', it is instructive to compare some of the above mentioned characteristics with those of another part of 'the West', the US, which has dominated much modern thought as to notions of corporate success and management education. While the US justifiably is regarded as a world leader in the generation of materialistic success, this has been achieved at considerable costs to broad segments of its society and the environment. For example, the spread of incomes in the US and the rate of incarceration are shocking to someone from Scandinavia and are indicative of and underlie the tensions, inequality, violence and lack of trust which appear to exist in the US society.[2] So the concept of 'the West' and even that of 'Europe' is not very precise. Therefore, in the sequel, the reflections on the 'best of management education' will be from a Scandinavian, and primarily, a Danish perspective.

The final distinction to be made before proceeding to my reflections on 'blending the best of the East and the West in management education' regards 'the *East*'. Following the arguments presented regarding the heterogeneity of 'the West', the reflections and generalizations to be provided would suffer in accuracy and relevance if one were to consider an 'East' that is a conglomerate of such different nation states as e.g. India, Australia, China, Pakistan, Japan, Bangladesh, Burma and Vietnam. Therefore, and given the setting of this conference, my reflections here will be delimited to India. Of course, India itself is a highly heterogeneous society (with 23 languages spoken by more than 1 million people, roughly as many alphabets, the world's third largest population of Muslims, a great and rapidly increasing spread between the incomes of 'those who have too little and those who have too much', and considerable barriers to societal mobility due to caste distinctions). Nevertheless, my experience indicates that it is not unreasonable or misleading to speak of 'Indian' management education.

In summary then, the exposition will consider developments in the education of mangers/leaders in Scandinavia and India, provide tentative explanations of these developments and their differences, and suggest areas where both societies could learn from each other and contribute to 'blending the best of East and West in management education'.

Developments in Management/Leadership Education in Scandinavia

I will now consider what appear to be rather striking developments in leadership education in my part of the world. To do so I will assume a rather simplified concept of cause and effect; that leadership education is reacting to observable developments in the world of business. Of course in reality the theory and teaching of leadership on the one hand and business practices on the other hand affect each other simultaneously; the causal relationships are systemic, not linear. Nevertheless, for the sake of our exposition the more simplified linear cause-and-effect relationship is assumed since it permits a more straightforward logic while not seriously weakening the arguments provided.

What then are these developments in the world of Scandinavian business, which lead to new developments in leadership education? Let me highlight a few. First the strong trend towards flatter, less hierarchical organizations. The 'distance' between the top management and the workers is significantly less than a generation ago. New forms of organization, technology and communication characterize these flatter organizations. There is far greater use of self-organizing project-teams, where employees from different offices and having different specializations and competencies come together to meet a specific challenge by a specific deadline. Communication in these more fluid organizational forms is far more dialogical than earlier, where it was dominated by top-down communication in bureaucratic hierarchies. These developments have inspired the development of educational programs in leadership emphasizing business ethics, organizational theory and a focus on the competencies required by both leaders and the led which will enable them to thrive in such organizational structures and social environments.

A second causal factor has to do with new types of production and production processes. While production of physical goods used to provide the major share of national revenues, the major sources of both wealth and employment are now service industries and, in particular, so-called knowledge-heavy sectors, e.g. IT. This has led to a greater reliance and dependence on the individual 'knowledge worker' and to far more flexible forms of employment. Considerable evidence indicates that in this so-called 'knowledge society' younger people strongly emphasize their own personal development in their choice of workplace, while such matters as title, income and opportunities for leadership roles are of lesser importance.[3] This is reflected in Scandinavian leadership education via an increased emphasis on the development of competencies (as opposed to professional and managerial skills). These competencies deal with such matters as the ability to develop meaningful visions and to generate enthusiasm and a strong sense of purpose among the employees, 'emotional intelligence' and other such talents and characteristics not traditionally dealt with in management education. But not only is there an emphasis on personal competencies. The developments as to more flexible forms of employment are also reflected in modern leadership education in the emphasis on organizational-existential concepts of corporate identity and reputation.[4] These deal with matters relating to corporate 'we'ness and 'branding' which are vital today if the corporation is to be able to attract and hold on to the creative, dynamic, talented, devoted employees who want to be proud of their place of work and the meaning they derive from their employment. They also appear to be of significance for the organization's ability to maintain the trust and respect of its customers, local societies and shareholders.

This leads up to consideration of a third factor, which can be said to underlie new developments in Scandinavian leadership education: demands from that rather new social creation, the 'stakeholder'. While the concept of shareholder is as old as the concept of a corporation, it is only since the late 1980s that serious explicit attention has been paid in the 'western' literature to the concept of the stakeholder. Stakeholders are those groups who affect and/or are affected by an organization's decisions. This attention has led to what could be called a 'stakeholder theory of the firm', where the organization is not simply conceived of as a judicial unit having employees, a management, assets and a corporate name – and where the corporation and its management is not solely responsible to the shareholders. Rather, the corporation is conceived of as an arena for interplay between its diverse stakeholders. This more inclusive depiction of an organization is reflected in a number of new phenomena and corresponding focuses in leadership education. Included here are, for example, the following concepts:[5]

- '*values-based leadership*', a perspective on leadership whereby the values of the organization are based on the values shared by the organization and its stakeholders and constitute a framework for corporate identity and self-reference;[6]
- '*social and ethical accounting*', which are alternative forms of reporting that report on how well the corporation lives up to these shared values and provide thereby multi-stakeholder, multi-value descriptions of corporate success that supplement traditional financial reporting;
- '*corporate social responsibility*', which extends the notion of managerial and corporate responsibility from that of maximizing return to owners to that of being a '*corporate citizen*' that is accountable to all its stakeholders, primary amongst these being employees (as well as those marginalized groups who have difficulty gaining access to the labor market) and local communities as well as to the 'environment';

- '*corporate reputation/corporate branding*', whereby corporations focus on their image and their identity. This enables them to be sensitive to the demands of '*critical consumers*' whose purchasing behaviour is not only determined by traditional notions of functionality and price but also by which company made the product, how it was made, and where. It also enables corporations to be sensitive to the expectations of potential and existing employees who seek meaningful work in a well functioning social environment in an enterprise they can feel proud of;
- '*ethical investing*', whereby traditional investment criteria are supplemented by considerations of which types of products and production methods are to be rejected and which are to be supported. Typically consideration is given to such matters as respect for human rights, pollution, the impact of both production processes and of products on health and welfare, the use of non-replenishable resources etc. etc. According to the Social Investment Forum, in 1999 in the US roughly one out of seven US$ that were invested in stocks by professional investment managers (e.g. by mutual funds and pension funds), were invested employing some kind of ethical evaluation.[7]

Summing up, I have focused on 'leadership education' as a supplement to more traditional management education in Scandinavia. The concepts and methods provided by this focus on leadership have been inspired by underlying shifts and trends in perceptions of the roles and responsibilities of corporations in a world characterized by the globalization of commerce and finance and by new information technologies. What has not been nearly as much in focus is the personal competencies and qualities which are required by leaders of the more flexible, dynamic and reflective organizations.

Developments in Management/Leadership Education in India

The reflections to be presented are based on the following: an interest in Indian society, culture and spiritual heritage; 18 visits to India starting in 1974 when I led a project for the World Bank in Bangladesh; visits to and interviews with leaders of a number of 'values-based' Indian corporations; the establishment of working agreements between the Copenhagen Business School and Indian Institutes of Management in Calcutta, Bangelore, Ahmadabad and Lucknow as regards exchange of students and faculty; lecturing at these institutions as well as at the Sri Sathya Sai Institute of Higher Learning; and finally, a close and inspiring teamwork with Professor S.K. Chakraborty, Management Centre for Human Values (MCHV) at IIMC.

While my reflections on teaching in Denmark/Scandinavia led me to focus primarily on what I referred to as 'leadership education', as opposed to 'management education', I will not emphasize this distinction here. This is due to the fact that my observations indicate that, with a few notable exceptions, the term 'management education' tends to characterize teaching at Indian schools of business, many of which have been inspired by traditional western, particularly American, management education. This focus on management rather than leadership reflects as well what is still the dominating organizational structure of Indian corporations: hierarchical, and in many cases patriarchal organizational structures with their reliance on planning and control systems – rather than on shared values, project-organizations, self-organizing teams, dialogue-cultures and a high degree of reliance on new communications technologies.

I should add, however, that the management education provided at leading Indian business schools appears to be of high quality and comparable to that provided by leading institutions of higher learning in the West.

Thus, I will not focus on Indian education in leadership (i.e. on the methods and tools of leadership) – but on developments at several major Indian institutions of higher learning as to education regarding the personal qualities and competencies of leaders. On leaders, rather than on leadership.

There are two factors which are challenging the existing Indian organizational structures and managerial mind-sets and, therefore, educational programs. The first of these is the competition arising from the more liberal trade and monetary policies in India that began about a decade ago. The most visible reaction to this new competition appears to be a belief among many educators and business leaders that the best way for Indian corporations to compete with foreign producers and with multinationals that establish themselves in India is by emulating their views and management methods. If not, so the argument goes, they will not be able to be as effective and innovative as these competitors. Nor will they be able to attract and keep top quality Indian employees who may find it more attractive to work for the multinationals or to leave India – leading to a 'brain drain' similar to that which previously characterized e.g. the medical and university teaching professions and, more recently, the IT branch.[8] The second, but far less obvious challenge to current Indian organizational structures, managerial mind-sets and educational programs is not directly precipitated by external competition. Rather, it appears to be an internal matter, although it can be said to be catalyzed by the external challenges arising from globalization and its concomitant deification of materialism. I am referring to the challenges to corporate governance in India arising from a perspective on corporate purpose, success and identity based on India's ethos.

Instead of attempting to meet the challenges arising from western materialism on their own terms, some leading educators and managers have sought guidance, concepts and methodologies from India's rich and deep-rooted cultural and spiritual heritage, a heritage which transcends the barriers arising from India's pluralistic diversity.

In the sequel I will mainly refer to this challenge to, and the potential rewards for, Indian business and management education of a focus on the qualities and competencies required by leaders in a more competitive, globalized world of business. Before proceeding, however, it must be noted that it would be naive and irresponsible to suggest that what I have referred to as a modern Scandinavian approach to management and a framework for Indian corporate governance based on its ethos are antithetical or mutually exclusive.[9] Just the opposite is true. As best

I can judge, a significant challenge facing Indian enterprises and schools of management is how best to build upon the rich Indian values and ethos while at the same time integrating the best of the approaches from the West. In other words, a question to be answered by management education in India is: how can Indian businesses maintain those aspects of their identity, integrity and strengths which are rooted in Indian culture, traditions and 'mind-sets' while competing with firms having a western materialistic focus where 'the business of business is business'?

The mirror image of this challenge to eastern/Indian business and management education is the challenge to western/Scandinavian business and management education as to how to supplement the dominating economic rationality with its focus on corporate leadership with an eastern/Indian focus on personal qualities, self-leadership and on the spiritual nature of man.

In my overview of a Scandinavian perspective on leadership I mentioned what could be called a 'stakeholder theory of the firm' where the corporation is conceived of as an arena for interplay between its diverse constituencies. I also introduced a number of new terms and concepts characterizing this more inclusive, multi-stakeholder, multi-value perspective on corporate identity and success. Included here were values-based leadership, social and ethical accounting, corporate social responsibility/corporate citizenship, corporate reputation and branding, and ethical investing. These were all concepts relating to how the modern, more inclusive organization can interact with its stakeholders.

Modern and Ancient Indian Perspectives on Management

A similar list can be developed to characterize 'a modern' and 'ancient' Indian perspective on management. Only this time the focus will not be on methods and tools of leadership – but on the qualities required by a 'good leader' good in both a moral and productive sense. With the reservation in mind that I am now writing about a heritage far removed from my own, let me present a brief list of concepts that could be central to such an Indian perspective on management.[10] As will be seen, these concepts are closely interrelated and it is impossible to consider any of them without involving one or more of the others.

Nishkamakarma   A perspective on action and decision making that emphasizes performing one's deeds without attachment to the fruits thereof – and where both the action and the fruits are offered to the divine.[11] A leader who behaves in accordance with this perspective is grounded in wisdom and in a state of equanimity. This perspective is in stark contrast to the current emphasis upon unbridled materialism and competition – and the resultant high levels of stress characterizing many so-called dynamic corporations and their leaders.[12] The performer of deeds who follows his conscience and is sensitive to the needs and values of those affected by his behaviour does not require courses in 'stress management'. He follows his conscience, acts in accord with basic concepts of ethics in organizations,[13] 'walks his talk' via values-based leadership and promotes corporate social responsibility via his respect and reverence for the organization's stakeholders. His motivation for such behaviour is however slightly different from that provided by a modern perspective on ethics; the underlying *raison d'être* for his behaviour is not business 'success' but his own spiritual progress as well as that of all those affected by his behaviour.

Selflessness and non-attachment Prominent terms in an eastern concept of spiritual growth and closely related to the concept of nishkamakarma. Although these concepts are very foreign to most Westerners, the Catholic concept of 'holy indifference' is similar.[14] A useful synonym is 'detached involvement'. The underlying idea is that instead of plying our egos and appraising our activities by the payoffs that result, and instead of being elated when our desires are fulfilled and disappointed when they are not, there is another way of performing action. This is by acting without attachment to the fruits of our efforts. From this perspective, all work can become transformed into selfless service.[15] This should not be confused with indifference to the work itself; rather the work is to be performed with detachment. Nor should this be confused with fatalism. We must follow our inner voice, our conscience, and do what we find to be important to do to the best of our ability. But such action is selfless in that it is performed with indifference to the outcomes, be they success or failure, praise or blame. Another way of looking at this is to say that past is past. Certainly we can learn from our experiences, but we cannot turn the clock back and undo what has been done. Work performed in accord with one's values and a sense of interconnectedness with others leads to the transcendence of the lower, ego-dominated self. Detached involvement frees one from the chains of personal desires and ambitions, the mind becomes 'free of and above the dualistic see-saw of daily experiences' (Chakraborty, 1991, p.163). A person who performs action in this spirit is not bound; his efforts become a sacrament of devotion to his duty. He manages his selfishness and gains access to his higher Self.

Servant leadership A concept, which although developed by the American Greenleaf[16] is clearly inspired by an eastern concept of duty and leadership. The leader who gains the trust and good will of his employees and his other stakeholders is the antithesis of the power-seeking manager who gives orders and controls their effectuation. He is sensitive to the needs of others and he leads by serving and serves by leading. In so doing he earns their trust as a person of deep integrity. And he gains their confidence in his ability to elicit and effectively promote corporate values which are in harmony with their individual values. He is thus able to coordinate and motivate employees who seek meaningful work that contributes to their personal and spiritual development. He performs his work as worship and he inspires others to follow his example and to serve.

Duty or right action (dharma in Sanskrit) A fundamental concept in an eastern approach to one's relationship with others. It complements the notion of 'servant leadership' with its focus on one's duty to others and is in stark contrast to the current western focus on rights. For example, a western understanding of the concept of freedom typically is based on having the right to do what one wants to do. A concept of freedom based on an eastern approach to human development might typically include searching for a clarification of one's duty in relation to one's position in life and behaving in accord with that duty. In the modern western organization, characterized earlier by such terms as 'flat', 'learning' and 'self-organizing', traditional power is becoming powerless – it is increasingly difficult and counter-productive to control creative and independent employees and expect them to be enthused, productive and loyal. Their commitment and sense of obligation is obtained in a work place that lends meaning to their lives, promotes those values they adhere to, and contributes to their personal development. In such environments a leader who selflessly performs his duty is a trustworthy source of inspiration. For an American concept of 'dharmic management', see (Hawley, 1992).

Santhi   The term that Hindus and Buddhists conclude their prayers with. It connotes being able to have such *equanimity* and *peace of mind* that one is able to be calm and discerning even in contexts characterized by turbulence and chaos. A person who, via his devotion and spiritual search, has obtained a state of perfect peace is no longer affected by this world's pairs of opposites. He experiences joy and sorrow, success and failure with the same spirit of detachment since he acts in perfect accord with his conscience and is one with his Higher Self. The leader who is able to perform his work in a state of equanimity is able to conserve energy, avoid destructive stress and act with concentration, discernment and effectiveness. In so doing he gains the respect and confidence of his employees.

Self-realization   The direct experience of the *Self* or the *Atma*, realizing the quintessence of one's being, the spark of the divine within each and every human being, our higher consciousness. According to the eastern perspective on life and reincarnation, there is a divine purpose to life and it is *not* simply the fulfillment of materialistic desires or a life of comfort and pleasure. Rather it is to develop the knowledge of one's true self, i.e. to obtain self-realization. This knowledge, experience or realization cannot be obtained via the study of learned books or holy texts, although these can help one on one's path. A paradox here is that although a goal in life is to seek this knowledge of the higher Self, the Self can only be realized by the person whose ego has been tamed and who is truly selfless and does not seek rewards for his deeds. The selfless leader who is not attached to the fruits of his actions does not only achieve spiritual growth, peace of mind and freedom from fear. He also becomes an exemplar for his employees and his surroundings in general. He is stable, strong, trustworthy and, based on a sensitivity to the aspirations of the organization's various stakeholders, clear in his visions as to what is in the best interests of the organization as a whole. He not only motivates, he inspires. Without seeking it directly, he is granted power.

Unity A term referring to the oneness or identity with creation and the source of creation. It is a notion that is extremely disturbing for a Westerner who has been brought up to focus on his individuality and his individual success in a dualistic world.[17] It expresses the belief that we are all interrelated at a deep existential level, that when we peal away the various physical and psychological factors that distinguish us from each other, we share an identical core. When we ask, 'who am

I?' the answer is not provided by either our name or physical form, but by our very essence, what we referred to above as the *Atma*, the higher consciousness and conscience, the true, divine Self. With a focus on the inter-relatedness of all life the empathetic leader's sincere sense of compassion for his employees inspires and empowers them.

Non-violence or ahimsa An ideal value in Hinduism, Buddhism and Christianity closely related to the concept of 'unity'. According to Chakraborty in (True and Datta, 1999, p.198), the 'feeling of oneness … eliminates separative egoism (and) is the ultimate emotional foundation of non-violence.' Non-violence here does not just mean physical violence. Rather it refers to non-violence in thought, word and deed. The leader who is guided by the value of non-violence performs his duties in peace, free from the demands of his lower self and its ego and in a deep awareness of his connectivity to all living creatures, to all of existence. His daily practices of e.g. meditation and prayer lead to his shedding his feelings of anger, hatred, jealousy and greed. He realizes that when he hurts others he is really hurting himself. Non-violence in thought, word and deed becomes a creed for him. He is acknowledged as a person of deep integrity and obtains the trust of not only his employees, but also of his customers and his local society. Four national leaders in modern times, each from their own continent and culture have exemplified this concept: Mahatma Gandhi in India, Martin Luther King in the United States, Nelson Mandela in South Africa and Vaclev Havel in the former Czechoslovakia. They achieved almost universal respect by 'fighting' their respective 'wars' in a non-violent way due to their belief in the brotherhood of man and the fatherhood of God.

Conclusions as to 'Blending the Best of East and West' in Management Education

We are now prepared to consider how both eastern and western approaches to management education can learn from and contribute to each other.

As regards the 'West', it is argued that this can be achieved by supplementing the current emphasis on leadership methods and processes with an eastern approach to the leader and leadership virtues. This eastern focus is on the leader and his/her character and derives nourishment from India's age-old spiritual traditions and beliefs.

It appears that such a more holistic approach, which includes a focus on both process and character, on leadership and the leader, is in fact in an embryonic phase in the 'West'. There is an increased awareness among younger leaders of a need for a greater educational focus on the personal character of business leaders.[18] In addition, there are an increasing number of western management educators who are trying to experiment with approaches to the teaching of leadership based upon or inspired by an eastern approach.[19]

Similarly, the opportunity available to 'the East' is to do more than supplement the teaching of traditional management subjects by building upon its own rich heritage and ethos with its focus on the character of the individual leader; this is of course a major challenge in itself. The challenge from the 'West', is to 'teach the teachers' to expand their perspectives on management by focusing upon leadership in more fluid organizational forms than hitherto have characterized Indian business (and management education). This includes developing concepts and attitudes dealing with notions of collective/corporate identity and responsibility where the leader is not simply a powerful decision maker, but is a visionary, inspiring, empowering and facilitating role model – as well as highly competent professional manager. Clearly, this challenge too is already being met at leading Indian schools of management, often via collaboration with leading western educational institutions. An example of this may be found in the collaboration between several of the Indian Institutes of Management with, in particular, American and Australian schools of management, in developing educational programs for middle and top-level managers. Another example is the increasing number of working agreements as to exchange of students and faculty with western institutions of higher learning; my own home institution, the Copenhagen Business School, is most pleased to be able to participate in such exchanges with a number of leading Indian schools of management. Of course such collaboration, if well conceived, fructifies the ambitions of all the participating institutions – and the recipients of the programs as well.

Before concluding, some comments are called for as to the question of 'how'. Attempting to integrate these complementary focuses can not simply be achieved via traditional courses and traditional pedagogies at business schools. They are related to both professional skills as well as to the mind-set, character and personal competencies of the leader – and the teacher. We are here speaking of such matters as the ability to generate trust and confidence, to embody work with a meaning which transcends traditional notions of success such as effectiveness and profitability, and to contribute to the personal, one might even say the spiritual development, of all those affected by the organization's decisions and actions. While at the same time promoting effective, competitive, sustainable and profitable enterprises. That notions of process as well as structure, and of character as well as skills, are at the forefront does not mean that such an expanded concept of management cannot be taught and learned. Rather it means that 'management education' must develop arenas for the development both of professional leadership skills and of personal leadership qualities – by teachers who embody such skills and virtues. Herein lies a huge challenge to our institutions of higher learning in both 'East' and 'West'.

Developing one without the other will not be efficacious or wise. Ethics, values and personal character are not simply 'management tools', such as computers or communication techniques. Traditional management tools are *used* by the manager – and can be replaced or renewed when economic rationality deems appropriate. Personal qualities and competencies on the other hand cannot be separated from the individual; they *are* the essence of his being. The 'tool' and the wielder of the 'tool' are one.

Attempts by educators to simply teach matters dealing with values, responsibility and sustainability without embodying these virtues and being a role model for the students will lead to cynicism and an instrumental approach to ethics in business. And attempts by managers to simply develop such qualities as if they were technical skills or tools will lead to cynicism amongst employees and other key stakeholders – rather than to a feeling of corporate 'we ness' and to a sense of obligation and pride in 'who we are' and what 'we stand for'. They will regard with distrust managers who do not really mean what they say, who are not people of deep integrity who demonstrate harmony between thought, word and deed – who turn ethics into cosmetics and values into shareholder-value.

Therefore, although the focuses from 'West' and 'East' are different, they are complementary and provide great challenges as well as fertile soil for positive cross-fertilization.

There is much to be received and much to be given by both 'the East' and 'the West'. May our educators and the leaders of our institutions of higher learning be blessed with the wisdom that will enable them to promote such sharing – for the benefit of us all.

Acknowledgement

For this paper, permission has been taken from Ms. Sangeeta Bhattacharya, the Co-editor of the Volume entitled: *Blending the Best of the East and the West*, the Conference Proceeding published by Excel Books, New Delhi, 2002.

Notes

1. According to a number of international surveys, Northern Europeans, and in particular, the Danes are the most happy, satisfied people in the world. For example, an article in the *Daily Telegraph* Dec. 15, 1999 (T. Utley, 'As happy as a Dane?') presents the results of a survey performed by the American market research company Roper Starch Worldwide that 'interviewed 22,500 adults in 22 countries and finds that the Danes are happier by a comfortable margin than the people of any other country. Some 49 per cent of them said that they are 'very happy' with the overall quality of their life'. They are reported to be 'happiest in the world about their jobs, their money, the amount of leisure time they had and the overall quality of their lives'. The *San Francisco Chronicle* Dec. 24, 2000 (K. Davidsen, 'Science Tracks the Good Life: It turns out the Bluebird of Happiness roosts in Denmark') presents an analysis of several decades of social surveys around the globe covering hundreds of thousands of people in more than 20 nations. The results are clear: 'The world's happiest nations are Denmark, the Netherlands, Norway and Luxembourg. … Denmark ranks far and away as the happiest nation on earth with a rating of 7.96 on a 10-point scale.' A press release by Associated Press Newswire on June 7, 1999 states that 'Northern Europeans (are) wealthier, happier with their jobs than southerners'. This is based on a survey carried out by the EU Statistics Office (Eurostat) amongst 60,000 households including almost 130,000 adults in 13 of the EU's 15 member states. The results indicate that 'Among those able to make ends meet very easily were Germany and Denmark', and 'Happiest with their jobs were Danes' (37 per cent totally satisfied). A final reference can be made to a report from the highly respected international opinion research company Ipsos-Reid that states that Danes are the world's most satisfied employees; 60 per cent are 'very satisfied' with their job. The analysis, presented in the Danish weekly *Ugebrevet*

Mandag Morgen (March 19, 2001) was based on responses from roughly 10,000 employed people in 39 countries.

It is also interesting to note that in spite of their apparent high quality of life, young leaders from Northern Europe still focus more on 'quality of life' than those from Southern Europe and the US; see the results of the survey (A.T. Kearny, 2001).

2　According to Gray (1998, 114-116), 'The average weekly earnings of 80 per cent of rank-and-file working Americans, adjusted for inflation, fell by 18 per cent between 1973 and 1995 from $315 a week to $258 per week'. The decline was most pronounced amongst the poor. The remaining 20 per cent of the population had increasing incomes, and the increases were larger the larger the income level. These discrepancies are even more pronounced when consideration is given to effective overall tax rates. The richest families paid lower tax rates primarily because of sharp reductions applicable to non-salary income (capital gains, interest, dividends and rents). According to Gray, 'Such policies have left the United States with a distribution of wealth that resembles the Philippines or Brazil more that it does any of the world's other major economies.' The information on a large and increasing variance in the distribution of income can be juxtaposed with the demographic analyses provided on pp.116-119: 28 million Americans live in privately guarded buildings or housing developments. In 1997 roughly one out of 50 adult males was incarcerated and one out of 20 were on bail or probation. This rate is 10 times that of European countries. California alone (population 32 million), with more than 150,000 prisoners, has more than Britain and Germany combined (population 140 million). In 1997 the male homicide rate was roughly 8 times that of the EU (and ¾ of all child murders in the industrialized world took place in the US) while for each robbery in Japan there were 147 in the US. More than 1 out of 3 lawyers in the world are in the US; for each lawyer in Japan and for each 8 lawyers in Germany and Britain there are 25 in the US. Tort liability payments in the US in 1987 represented 2.5 per cent of the US GDP! A baby born in Shanghai in 1995 was less likely to die in its first year of life, more likely to learn to read, and could expect to live 2 years longer than a baby born in New York City.

3　According to a recent extensive survey amongst Danish people in their 20s (reported on in *Ugebrevet Mandag Morgen*, January 8, 2001, p.15), this is 'a generation that without compromise seeks positions and working environments that stimulate their personal project and for whom every thing else is secondary. ... The project generation clearly places a higher priority on independence and personal development than on improved wages and job security. ... Almost 8 out of 10 young people say no to collective wage negotiations. Only 15 per cent have a clear wish to be a leader. Only one out of four want fixed working hours and a fixed number of hours to work.'

4　For a discussion of organizational-existential concepts of corporate identity and reputation see (Pruzan, 2001A) and (Pruzan, 2001B).

5　See for example (Pruzan, 1998A) for an overview of the manifestations of business ethics in a Danish context and how these have been integrated into the teaching of leadership at the Copenhagen Business School.

6　See for example (Pruzan, 1998B) which relates the concept of values-based leadership to those of corporate accountability and ethical accounting.

7　See the website: http://www.socialinvest.org.

8　These developments appear to be accompanied by a shift in traditional Indian values and behavioural patterns that will contribute to increased job mobility. There is evidence for example, that the extended family will be an 'endangered species'. The threats arise from a number of factors. One of these is the powerful influence of the media which are spreading glamorous pictures from the west of the materialistic (and egoistic) nuclear family which is not allowing traditions and cultural heritages to interfere with its search for wealth. Another factor is the increasing number of females who are receiving higher education and who will not accept their more traditional roles in an extended family.

9   Perhaps the only non-communistic nation today which has an expressed policy of keeping western influence at bay is India's neighbor, Bhutan, which for many years has attempted to protect its predominantly Buddhist society from outside influences, for example, until recently, by not permitting TV reception.

10   I have previously attempted to provide a brief presentation of several of these concepts within the context of an analysis of power within western and eastern contexts; see (Pruzan, 2001C)

11   Chapter two of what has been referred to as the Gospel of Hinduism, the *Bhagavad Gita*, describes in detail the qualities of the *sthitaprajna*, a man of steady wisdom, characterized by equanimity and peace of mind. Note that these qualities are closely related to those of selflessness and non-attachment to the fruits of one's actions. See for example the poetic translation of the *Bhagavad Gita* provided by (Prabhavananda and Isherwood, 1944).

12   According to a report *Research on Work-Related Stress* from the European Agency for Safety and Health at Work in Bilbao, Spain, more than 40 million Europeans, corresponding to 28 per cent of all employees, have health problems due to stressful working conditions. Only back pains are a more frequent work-related health problem. See http://europe.osha.eu.int for further information.

13   See for example (Pruzan, 2000) which develops the concept of 'ethical accounting' where an organization's ethics is based upon the values of its stakeholders.

14   This concept was central to the teachings of St. Francoise de Sales (1567-1672), Bishop of Geneva. According to Aldous Huxley in his introduction to (Prabhavananda and Isherwood, 1944), de Sales' follower Camus summarized his master's teaching on this point as follows: 'He who refers every action to God and has no aims save His glory, will find rest everywhere, even amidst the most violent commotions.' So long as we practice this holy indifference to the fruits of action, 'no lawful occupation will separate us from God; on the contrary, it can be made a means of closer union.' The concept of 'holy indifference' can be said to have had its roots in the writings of Plato and 'indifference' was a core value of the Roman Empire's ethics. In a more modern western setting the concept of indifference permeates many of the themes in the best selling book (Covey, 1989), *The 7 Habits of Highly Effective People* (over 10 million copies sold); see e.g. the discussion of peace of mind and integrity on page 298.

15   According to (Chakraborty, 1995, p.261) 'The real test of creativity, inner growth etc. should be: can I invest even a mundane, unexciting chore or assignment with the power of my inner richness?'

16   See for example (Greenleaf, 1977) and (Greenleaf, 1998). The Robert K. Greenleaf Center for Servant Leadership has been founded to develop and spread Greenleaf's approach to leadership.

17   Of course there are significant differences in the attitudes which characterize an American or even a British focus on individuality and 'getting ahead' with that say of a Scandinavian, who has been brought up in a social-welfare system.

18   At the Future Leaders Forum, 16-18 November, 2000 at Davos, Switzerland, 100 young leaders (average age around 35) from 16 European countries were surveyed as to the major issues of importance to them in their roles as 'high flyers'. A striking result was the response to the question as to 'which skills for future leaders are not properly addressed by education?'. Seventy-three per cent of these up-and-coming top leaders referred to 'interpersonal skills' and 66 per cent to 'ethics' – while only 7 per cent

referred to 'technical/technological skills' and a bare 2 per cent referred to 'financial skills'. See (Kearney, A.T., 2001).

19   The following are just a few of the many examples of this new focus in the West: In 1998 the 'Spirituality, Leadership and Management Network' (SlaM) had its origin at the University of Western Sydney in Australia; in 1999 the book (Mitroff and Denton, 1999): *A Spiritual Audit of Corporate America* was published in the US; in April, 2000 The University of Notre Dame held a conference on 'Business, Religion and Spirituality' and in the same month the conference 'Spirituality and Governance: Reigniting the Spirit of America was held in Washington D.C.; in the 1990s a series of international conferences on Business and Consciousness were held in Mexico; in April, 2001 the International Academy of Business Disciplines will for the first time have a track on 'Spirituality in Organizations' at its 13th annual meeting in Orlando, Florida; in July, 2001 an international workshop on 'Spirituality in Management' will be held in Szeged, Hungary; in August, 2001 the American Academy of Management will for the first time have a session on 'Management, Spirituality and Religion' organized by a new interest group of the same name; the website http://www.spiritatwork.com contains many links and a large and growing reference material on publications and research dealing with spirituality in the workplace.

References

Chakraborty, Sitangshu K. (1991) *Management by Values: Towards Cultural Congruence*, Oxford University Press, Delhi.

Chakraborty, Sitangshu K. (1995) *Ethics in Management: Vedantic Perspectives*, Oxford University Press, Delhi.

Covey, S.R. (1989) *The 7 Habits of Highly Effective People*, Simon & Schuster, London.

European Agency for Safety and Health at Work (2000) 'Research on Work-Related Stress', Available from the Internet at http://europe.osha.eu.int.

Gray, John (1998) *False Dawn – The Delusions of Global Capitalism*, Granta Books, London.

Greenleaf, Robert K. (1997) *Servant Leadership: A Journey into the Nature of Legitimate Power and Greatness*, Paulist Press, Mahwah, New Jersey.

Greenleaf, Robert K. (1998) *The Power of Servant Leadership*, (edited by L.C. Spears), Berrett-Kohler, San Francisco.

Hawley, J. (1992) *Reawakening The Spirit in Work: The Power of Dharmic Management*, Berrett-Kohler, San Francisco.

Kearney, A.T. (2001) Results of the live electronic voting held in Davos on 'Innovation and Leadership in International Organizations', http://www.futureleadersforum.com.

Mitroff, Ian I. and Elizabeth A. Denton (1999) *A Spiritual Audit of Corporate America*, Jossey-Bass.

Prabhavananda, Swami and Christopher Isherwood (translators) (1944) *Bhagavad Gita – The Song of God* with an introduction by Aldous Huxley, Mentor Books.

Pruzan, Peter (1998a) 'Theory and Practice of Business Ethics in Denmark' in (Zsolnai, L., ed.) *The European Difference: Business Ethics in the Community of European Management Schools*, Kluwer Academic Publishers, London, pp.1-15.

Pruzan, Peter (1998b) 'From Control to Values-based Management and Accountability', *Journal of Business Ethics*, 1379-1394.

Pruzan, Peter (2000) *Ethical Accounting: History, Theory and Practice*, Civilekonomerna, Stockholm.

Pruzan, Peter (2001a) 'The Question of Organizational Consciousness: Can Organizations have Values, Virtues and Visions?', *Journal of Business Ethics*, vol. 29, 271-284.

Pruzan, Peter, (2001b) 'Corporate Reputation: Image and Identity', *Corporate Reputation Review*, vol. 4, 1, 50-64.

Pruzan, Peter (2001C) 'The Trajectory of Power: From Control to Self-control', in Battacharya, P. and S.K. Chakraborty (eds), *Leadership and Power: Ethical Explorations*, Oxford University Press, Delhi, pp.166-181.

True, Michael and Amlam Datta, (1999) 'The Tradition of Non-violence: The American Experience and the Gandhian', *Journal of Human Values*, 4, 183-199.

Chapter 2

Institutionalization of Ethics in Business

Damodar Suar

Institutionalization of Ethics in Business

Newspapers, magazines, radio and prime-time television have devoted much time and space to scandal, scam, corruption and other ethical improprieties of the organizations in public, private, and nonprofit/voluntary sectors. In the last few years, the number of such incidences has increased. A day is not passed without hearing something. Transparency International had ranked 90 countries of the world in 2000 on the basis of annual 'corruption perception index'. Scores were allotted from '10' to '0', with 10 indicating 'very clean' and 0 'highly corrupt'. While Finland score was highest 10 and Nigeria score was lowest 1.2, India's corruption perception index was 2.8 (transparency.org) and it occupied 68th position close to corrupt category. Mega-scams such as bofors, fodder, bitumen, fertilizer, security and many more have already rocked the country. Unfortunately, ours is a country of moral prophets with ethical infants. We have not successfully inculcated ethics in our citizens. Private and public sector employees have succumbed to the pressures from insurgent groups, naxalites, mafia dons and crime lords. Dropsy, in August 1998, claimed over 50 lives due to contaminated mustard oil. Neither the producers surrendered nor the producers withdrew the product from the market. Examples abound, malpractices are well-known in some organizations and is little known in others where data are unavailable. That corruption is rampant is a hard fact. Given the intense public, media and legal scrutiny of business, such as Godrej, Infosys, Tata and others have tried to institutionalize ethics through a variety of structures, polices and procedures. Institutionalization of ethics means incorporating ethics in daily business decision making and work practices at all levels of employees. It grafts a branch in the corporate tree that decides right, just and fair as opposed to wrong, unjust and unfair respectively, and directs to do what is beneficial to the *vis-à-vis* society.

Business generates surplus or profit and also creates employment, and produces goods and services for the society. Thus, business has a commercial and a social objective. A business has the most to gain over the long-term from its activities that increase profits, reduce human sufferings, and sustain environmental, ethical and social reputations. A firm or its employees' unfair decisions and actions defame the company, cost hard cash, reduce share price, dampen business prospects and encourage lawsuits. Managers from America, Germany and France agree that sound ethics are good for business in the long run (Becker and Fritzche,

1987). Empirical evidence also suggests that managers find ethics to be good for the bottom line of the s (Jose and Thibodeaux, 1999). In liberalized, privatized and globalized economy, whether it is taxation, knowledge generation, working conditions, pollution or ecological crises, the short-term benefits can be gained by embracing lower ethical standards. For example, if a country has no standard with regard to pollution control, it is almost always in a company's best immediate interest to pollute freely. When the company does this without following any standard, the world knows, company's reputation along with business prospects slide down and last for decades. It is far easier to stay on the high ground than to climb back up. Short-term benefits produce disastrous long-term consequences. Suresh Krishna, the scion of the TVS group of companies in India, endorses ethical standards for export, industrial relations, networking, and for any other conceivable strategies to stay in business (Bhat, 1997). So also Aditya Narayan, President ICI India, has maintained higher standards on ethics, safety, health and environmental policies in India without cutting corners than the national standards to sustain local competitiveness and global reputation as a MNC subsidiary.

Business ethics is a fuzzy area. Ethical decision making models available so far justify that ethical decision making is a complex process and it is influenced by a variety of individual, organizational, situational and environmental factors (Jose and Thibodeaux, 1999). What is ethical depends on the (a) decision/act itself, (b) the circumstances in which the act is done, (c) motives or intentions of the actor, and (d) consequences of the act for the stakeholders. The growing realization of this has led to change in thinking about the effective approaches to getting firms and their employees to behave ethically. Initial approaches were based on compliance to rules and systems of the company. But rules are hard to draft, quickly become out dated, and employees can forge links with executives to break the rule. Rules deal with 'don'ts', and ethics with 'dos' and values – for example, 'ensure good after-sales service' that may not be covered by rules. Although compliance is necessary, what is necessary additionally to institutionalize ethics is to instill values into the corporate body and its constituents.

Strategies to Comply with Rules and Inculcate Values

Fortune 500 companies have institutionalized ethics through various forms (Center for Business Ethics, 1992). The explicit forms of ethics programme include codes of ethics, ethics training, ethics newsletter, ethics hotline, ethics officers, ethics committee, and employee orientation programme. The implicit aspects being important to formalize ethics include reward system, performance evaluation, promotion policies, corporate culture, top management support, ethical leadership, and open communication. (Brenner, 1992; Jose and Thibodeaux, 1999). These two forms undermine the scope to enhance employees' values by themselves but emphasize on the influence of others and control mechanisms. However, values or the inner desirable ideals that guide a person's outer activities – the object one makes or acquires, the decision one takes, the act one engages, etc. are the cornerstone of ethics and cannot be lost sight of. Accordingly, three strategies are outlined to inculcate ethics in daily business practices.

A strategy is the means by which the objective(s) is achieved. First, the individual level strategy deals with the individual's internalization of values through own efforts. It is like a non-directive therapy. The top management needs to critically aware the employees so that they can implement this strategy. Second, the interpersonal level strategy is the implicit ways to formalize ethics where corporate citizens can influence other constituents. Third, the organizational level strategy is the explicit ways where the top management can institute check-posts to halt unethical practices.

Individual Level Strategy

Ethical Autosuggestion

Autosuggestion or self-talks before or during behaviour can control the mind and accordingly regulate actions and reactions. Self-talks or self-instructions are found to reduce bizarre speaking patterns, improve performance, and creativity (Meichenbaum, 1977; Meyers, Mercatoris and Sirota, 1976).

For inculcation of values, individuals can appeal to their selves for practicing what is desirable. It comes down to develop a set of values or attitudes for self-instructions that one believes in and that one can apply to all areas of life. During the morning hours daily, in *padmasan* (lotus pose), the individual can appeal through silent self-talk: (a) Just for today, I will live the attitude of gratitude; (b) just for today, I will do my work sincerely; (b) just for today, I will be truthful; (c) just for today, I will be co-operative; (d) just for today, I will not fear or worry; (e) just for today, I will not harm others; (f) just for today, I will not speak ill of any one; (g) just for today, I will not yield to sensual temptation; (h) just for today, I will not be angry; (i) just for today, I will be righteous; be tolerant; peaceful; and so on (Suar, 2000). It cleanses and purifies mind from wretched and impious thoughts. Daily reiteration of these is likely to stamp in mentally and surface naturally in day-to-day business. Nothing is more powerful than persuading one's own self to practice the valued behaviour. This exercise hardly takes three minutes, involves no financial cost, and can be done with negligible effort. However, if any self-instruction and its corresponding action creates problem, remove that. If necessary, develop and substitute new ones to inculcate values.

Mind-stilling Exercise

Chakraborty (1993, pp.38-43) has developed a 'breathing control exercise' to fine-tune the mind for ethical behaviour. It is done at a time suited to the individual, on an empty stomach, eyes closed, loose clothes, and a relax position in a squatting posture. The individual recollects few good qualities or *sattwa gunas*, and bad qualities or wrong elements of *rajas and tamas*. By breathing slowly through one nostril while closing the other one with a finger, the individual also imagines breathing out the bad and breathing in the good qualities. When the rhythm is established, she/he slowly reverts to normal breathing and sits with eyes closed for five to ten minutes. Imagining that the top of the brain is open, she/he drains out the accumulated information, thoughts and images, and gets into total serenity. The person prays to the supreme consciousness to drip into the mind and seep down into the whole body. Then the person repeats five statements for five rounds with feelings and conviction: '(1) I possess the body, but I am not the body; (2) I possess the senses, but I am not the senses; (3) I possess the mind, but I am not the mind; (4) I possess an intellect, but I am not the intellect; (5) I am the self-luminous pure consciousness which is *'poorna'* (complete), in bliss, and perfect.'

Then the individual submits her/his body, mind, senses, and intellect to the Supreme Consciousness or to the chosen deity for chastening, purification, and guidance. The individual experiences purity and *ananda* (happiness) in the cave of heart-center and sends these thought-waves of goodwill, peace and tranquility to all competitors, enemies, work situations, and others. Furthermore, the individual visualizes and identifies mentally with the steady nature (such as with the deep core of an ocean) and disidentifies with its surface (such as with roaring waves of an ocean). Experiencing everlasting peace, the person comes back to normalcy and remains silent for 15 to 30 minutes. Its practice strengthens will power, develops introspective insight, brings inner serenity, detects wrong mental movements and fosters the will to tackle them, and nurtures an instinctive ethical rectitude in decision-making. Initially taught to Godrej employees, this exercise has been successful subsequently in achieving its objectives.

Cognitive Inconsistency

It is well-known that a prerequisite for cognitive change is the presence of a cognitive state of disequilibrium or inconsistency (Colby, Kohlberg, Gibbs and Lieberman, 1983; Festinger, 1957). This can be initiated by exposing employees to information about the values of top level managers who internalize and practice the al values – reputation of the firm, employee welfare, service to the general public, budget stability, growth, innovation, product quality, customer service, cost consideration, participative management, obedience to al rules, maintenance of working conditions, protection of surrounding environment, reward for worthy contribution, etc. If there is any discrepancy between their own values and those of top level managers, this will generate cognitive dissonance and dissatisfaction. This will lead to change in values of employees in the direction of the organization's demands. Let us cite an example, how this can be done through computer feedback of information. A computer programme needs to be developed for such a purpose. Sitting in front of the computer and pressing the defined keys, an employee is instructed to rate the pre-stored organizational values displayed on the screen. Then the stored rating of the same values by top management is displayed on the screen. The employee observes the discrepancy. Through instant calculation, the discrepancy between the two evaluations is displayed on the screen. A printout of the same is given to the employee with the instructions to reflect on it (Suar, 1993), and to chalk out strategies and adopt those strategies to change her/his values in the direction of the organization's demands.

Ethical Awareness

Sri Krishna convinced Yudhistir to tell a lie in the Kurukshetra to ensure that unethical behaviour did not cripple the society. In that great war of Kurukshetra, Arjun expressed and experienced despair and despondency to slay the noble-minded elders and his kinsmen. Sri Krishna with persuasive and fair logic made Arjun aware of his duties. Sri Krishna mentioned: either killed in battle, you will attain heaven or being victorious, you will enjoy the earth. In either case, you will only be a gainer. Performing one's duty in war field is the only way to salvation. Such dialogues changed perception of Arjun, sensitized and elevated him to a higher plane for performing action (Vireswarananda, 1948). Ethical awareness is the capacity to perceive and be sensitive to relevant moral issues that deserve consideration in making choices that will have significant impact on others. Whether an employee will see, recognize, and act ethically and give importance to ethics depend not only on early socialization in family, school and neighborhood but also on occupational socialization. Circulating ethical speeches of celebrities, ethical decisions of professionals, popular religious books and articles on ethics, and showing videocassettes on Indian ethos, ethical dilemmas and their decisions can raise ethical perception and sensitivity.

Awareness about Mission and Vision

When the mission accommodates the future state of affairs of relevance to the market forces, it depicts the vision. While many mangers are convinced about the vision and mission statements, they remain frustrated in their attempts to realize the full value of these concepts (Raynor, 1998). From the vision and mission flow the strategies, priorities, objectives, methods, staff motivation, and source of energy that bind the constituents together. Values are given concrete shape in vision. Corporate mission was resurrected at IBM by Gerstner, Jr., the CEO of IBM, and drafted in late 1993, when losses at Big Blue exceeded 8 billion US dollar. IBM statement of principles is slowly being disseminated through the company. Xavier Institute of Social service, Ranchi (Jharkhand, India) has the mission and vision in a single statement 'to put the last first' that directs its employees to serve the downtrodden through preparing professionals for rural management, disseminating information, conducting research and implementing field projects.

IBM's Principles

- The marketplace is the driving force behind everything that we do.
- At our core, we are a technology company with an overriding commitment to quality.

- Our primary measures of success are customer satisfaction and shareholder value.
- We operate with an entrepreneurial zeal with a minimum of bureaucracy and a never-ending focus on productivity.
- We never lose sight of our strategic vision.
- We think and act with a sense of urgency.
- Outstanding, dedicated people make it all happen, particularly when they work together as a team.
- We are sensitive to the needs of all employees and to the communities in which we operate.

Many private and public sector companies in India do not have a clearly defined vision that make their employees difficult to direct efforts and decide what is right and wrong for the company. Organizations and their stakeholders need to redefine their vision periodically in accordance with the changing socio-economic environment and global standards, and make their employees aware about it to channelize their efforts rightly.

Training Programme

Employees may think they know how to make an ethical decision. But they may not know how to evaluate the consequences of their action or understand what they would like them to do in difficult situations. Compelling evidence suggests that employees can develop values, advance in moral reasoning and incorporate philosophical rationality of utilitarianism, deontology, social justice and virtues through moral development training programmes (Trevino and McCabe, 1994). That is why Arthur Anderson, Hewlett-Packard, Citibank, IBM, General Electric, and Johnson & Johnson have formal programmes to teach ethics. These programmes teach employees not only the theories and what is right or wrong but also to think about the effects of their decisions on others. The contents and pedagogy in ethics training are as follows:

- Expose the employees to the moral reasoning and philosophical theories, clarify ethical values and enhance ethical awareness.
- Use case study method to analyze business dilemmas. Also, use open discussion in groups and skilled Socratic probing to understand how employees justify decisions. Then the facilitator can review and present the reasoning – drawing from trainees' justifications, linking to moral reasoning and philosophical theories, and values from scriptures – at a higher level that challenges employees' justifications. This would reinforce to move to the higher level of moral reasoning to resolve moral dilemmas. Discuss the context-specific criteria for ethical decision making because the organization may not embrace a too altruistic decision.

Ethical Algorithm

Algorithms solve problems. Ethical algorithm is a process to take ethical decisions. It consists of four major interactive elements (Henderson, 1992, pp.36-78). (a) Goals: what do we want to achieve? (b) Methods: How will we pursue our goals? (c) Motives: What needs drive us to achieve? (d) Consequences: What outcome can we anticipate? Let us cite an example. The goal of top-level management is to create wealth in a manufacturing sector. This can be achieved through the method of (a) increasing productivity or (b) using cheap and low quality raw materials. Motive is the inner needs or feelings, which fuel behaviour. The motive is known from the observation of outer behaviour. Is the motive shared by stakeholders or exclusively of the top management? Motive is also examined from ethical perspectives. Stakeholders can object to the use of low quality raw materials. It is unfair and can stall the future of business. Are the consequences short or long-term and beneficial? Use of low quality raw materials can boost the creation of wealth in the short-term but defame the business in the long-term. Use of such algorithm can help the management to reach sound, long-term decisions that are acceptable to a wide range of constituents including employees, customers, vendors, competitors, wider community, pressure groups, consumer advocates, and vocal agnostics.

Mentoring

A mentor is a senior and respected person who counsels protégés, listens to feelings as well as facts, and stimulates them through ideas and information as in the *guru-shishya* tradition of ancient India. The mentor can clarify and make aware to the protégé about al values over time. When personal values mismatch with al values, the job satisfaction of employees reduces sharply (Suar, Panda and Sharan, 1989). If a sizeable gap exists between what the person externally does and what she/he internally values to do, she/he experiences a series of distressful emotions – anxiety, insecurity, self-role incongruency, and dissatisfaction (Sharan, Prasad and Suar, 1989). When the protégé does not wish to expose such happenings within the formal process, the mentor can help to alleviate the protégé's mental disharmony.

Interpersonal Level Strategy

Ethical Leadership

An ethical leader sets examples for others to follow. As Lee Iacocca mentioned: ' I began by reducing my own salary to $1.00 a year. Leadership means setting an example. When you find yourself in a position of leadership, people follow your every move ... But when the leader talks, people listen. And when the leader acts, people watch. So you have to be careful about everything you say and everything you do ' (Iacocca and Novak, 1985, p.241).

Lee Iacocca, ex-chairman of Chrysler Corporation, saved the company from near bankruptcy to repayment of its $1.2 billion loan. Chrysler employees were susceptible to Iacocca's influence because of his exemplary behaviour. First, followers freely adhere to and trust the ethical leader because they realize that the vision of the company *vis-à-vis* satisfaction of their needs can be achieved through the activities of the leader. Second, the leader looks into followers' personal and professional development. Third, the moral virtues, personal traits and social skills of the leader are exemplary and worthy of emulation (Guillen and Gonzalez, 2001).

Kanungo and Mendonca (1996, 1998) have conceptualized three dimensions of ethical leadership – (a) leader's motive, (b) leader's influence strategies, and (c) leader's character. Each of the three motives of affiliation, power and achievement (McClelland and Burnham, 1995) is further categorized on the basis of intent to benefit others and intent to benefit self. Ethical leaders are primarily motivated by the criteria to benefit others even if it results in some personal cost to self. Need for affiliation has two manifestations: (a) 'affiliative assurance' and (b) 'affiliative interest'. Leaders, guided by affiliative assurance, experience personal insecurity, cultivate relationships to protect themselves, and do not provide negative feedback on performance of subordinates. This makes the subordinates dependent, discouraged, irresponsible and demoralized. On the other hand, ethical leaders' affiliative interest manifests itself in task-oriented interventions, providing information on efficacy, and recognizing subordinates' ability to solve problems. Similarly, there are two types of need for power: (a) 'personal power' and (b) 'institutional power'. Leaders high on personal power use power excessively, rely on their positions in office, exploit others, become insensitive to followers' needs, and expect followers' unquestioning compliance. Contrarily, ethical leaders governed by institutional power display self-discipline, emotional maturity, and arrange tasks so that followers accomplish al objectives. They reward followers impartially and are open to criticism and disagreement. Where need for achievement is concerned, ethical leaders motivated by 'social achievement' rather than 'personal achievement' engage in collective activities that benefit the organization and its members. It was well-known that Maximillan Kolbe, the Polish priest, gave up his life in the Auschwitz concentration camp to save a man who had a wife and children. This heroic act of courage and sacrifice reflected the affiliative interest of highest order to save the man. Mahatma Gandhi's truthfulness and nonviolence mesmerized thousands of Indians to follow him in achieving his altruistic social goal of India's independence.

The leader can influence the followers in two ways, through the (a) transactional, and (b) transformational mode. In transactional mode, leaders' rewards and sanctions ensure that the followers perform the required behaviour. By contrast, ethical leaders in transformational mode change the beliefs, values and behaviour of followers so that they are consistent with the vision of the organization. They influence the followers through empowerment rather than control strategies. In such strategies, the leader inculcates self-efficacy beliefs by seeking followers' participation in goal setting, problem solving and decision making, providing helpful feedback on task performance, and taking steps to remove deficiencies through coaching, counseling, training, guidance, and monitoring the assigned tasks. Gradually followers develop and function as autonomous persons. Mapping the characteristics of Indian employees –

dependency, preference for hierarchy, personalized relationship, familial ethos, leisure ethics, and show-off. Sinha (1980, 1995) has proved the nurturant-task (NT) style to be effective in Indian organizations. A leader's nurturance is expressed in terms of care, consideration, warmth, support and affection to the subordinates, and deep interest in their growth and well-being. Nurturance facilitates task achievement and the latter creates conditions for more nurturance. As the leader guides, monitors, and assigns responsibility to the subordinates, they gain experience, expertise and develop self-confidence. NT style, thus, parallels with the empowerment strategy of the ethical leader.

Ethical leaders transform themselves habitually, incorporating moral values in their behaviour which become worthy of emulation by followers. Their characters exhibit commitment to higher purpose, prudence, pride, patience, and persistence. Researchers mention other virtues of ethical leaders such as integrity, determination, fairness, honesty, humility, tolerance, enthusiasm, courage and responsibility (Guillen and Gonzalez, 2001; Solomon, 1999). Tony Wang, vice-president of the KFC for Southeast Asia in the late 1980s, faced tremendous pressure from his Chinese partners to lower corporate standards for quality, service and cleanliness (QSC). Chinese partners perceived that their customers placed less emphasis on QSC than did Americans. Yet Wang understood that KFC's worldwide profitability was based on its ability to attract new franchises around the world because of the company's high QSC worldwide. Lastly, Wang did not agree to lower the standard of QSC in China guided by the higher purpose of his character to best serve the and its vision.

Higher moral disposition of the leader increases group performance (Dukerich, Nichols, Elm and Vollrath, 1990). When Luthar took the chairmanship of Damodar Valley Corporation (DVC) in 1980, employees' discipline was at its lowest ebb. There were 20 militant unions. Overtime payment was not rationalized. Grievances were unsettled. The DVC office looked shabby with posters and slogans pasted all over. He himself set about the task of removing the posters and slogans first. He checked undue overtime payments and settled about 80 per cent of the grievances within 90 days. He told the employees that the corporation would take care of them as long as they observed rules and did their best. There were many incidents where he communicated his stand to workers, unions, and employees' families, and refused to negotiate under threat even suffering physical injuries. He provided dynamic welfare facilities, started centers for handicrafts and cottage industries, and introduced a scheme for rural development. His commitment to the 's' vision, self-discipline, integrity, exemplary behaviour, and concern for employees and surrounding communities, influenced all and ultimately transformed DVC from a losing concern to a profitable one (Luthar, 1987).

Dialogue and Discussion in Group

Dialogues and discussion in group bring higher levels of reasoning to bear on moral judgement problems than does individual decision making (Nichols and Day, 1982). Dialogues on a moral dilemma proceed with why, what, how and other questions. Information, creativity and expertise of group members are scrutinized through dialogues to arrive at a consensual decision. People feel proud to implement the decision that they have arrived at collectively. Here follows the ethical guidelines for an effective group decision through dialogues and discussion.

- The group can be composed of seven or eight members to avoid chaos. A high quality decision can be obtained from the group when members have different perspectives on the issue, and differences are evaluated and resolved in arriving at a final decision.

- Group members intimated for dialogues and discussion need to posses empathy, tolerance, and accommodative attitude or what Chakraborty (1998, pp.30-31) calls human values. Otherwise, dominance and non-participation will result.

- Group members make an effective decision when they suffer the consequences of their own decision. Accordingly, the group can incorporate the representatives of potential or actual sufferers of the problematic issue.

- Both sexes should be represented in such groups because they tend to process moral issues differently. Women think about moral dilemmas in terms of relationship, caring, and co-operation. Men judge moral issues in terms of justice, rules, and individual rights (Gilligan, 1982). Both considerations are needed to resolve ethical dilemmas. Moreover, when 47 studies published in *Journal of Business Ethics* on gender-based ethical sensitivities were reviewed, 15 studies found that men and women had similar ethical sensitivity whereas 32 studies concluded that women were more ethically sensitive than men (Collins, 2000). Hence, women in the dialogical group would induce better ethical decisions.

- The discussions of decision-making groups are often dominated by information that is widely shared before discussion and that supports the preferences of group members. Groups are unlikely to discuss information that is unique or known to only one or two members (Stewart and Stasser, 1995; Wittenbaum, 1998). Research findings suggest that if the facilitator at the onset of dialogues introduces the group members with their respective expertise for contributing to the discussion task, the unshared information would be recalled considered and accepted by group members (Stasser, Vaughan and Stewart, 2000). Group members can seek and accept the information from expert persons when the discussion on ethical problems centers on specific issues (such as doctor on health-related issues, and HRD manager on legal issues).

- Ethical guidelines are discovered that describe ways to be *consciously and intentionally* adopted among group members. Group members should express views straightforwardly with sufficient reasons on controversial positions. They should not intentionally present arguments that are incongruent with what they do or say; and should not claim or transfer responsibility to others (persons or institutions) without justification. They should not intentionally make assertions that are either false or merely subjective, nor repeat contributions and facts in such a way as to intentionally distort their original meaning. They should not demand compliance or reasons from others that others will not be able to do. They should not express hostility towards or discredit other participants (arguments based on emotion) nor interact with others so as to impede their participation (Schreier and Groeben, 1996).

- During dialogues and discussion, arguments may control others. To eliminate control, Maguire (1999) has pleaded for accountability in discourse. On one side, reciprocal accountability includes the asking of the right questions, seeking ideas from other participants, settling the differences, and agreeing on a common worthwhile choice and its implementation. On the other side, individual accountability includes autonomous reflection before voicing a choice, moral doubts, disagreement, and willingness to share the rationale with others rather than picking up the first feasible solution to the issue. To ensure accountability, dialogues and discussion need to be in an environment of fraternity, supported by openness among members and a willingness to learn from others.

The last two ethical imperatives can be implemented if prior to dialogues and discussion, each group member is given a write-up containing the instructions mentioned in the two points, asked to read and sign it, indicating her/his willingness to comply with it.

Whistle-blowing

Employees can check unethical practices by reporting such practices to the higher authorities. This is called whistle-blowing. It is common in India against sexual harassment, corruption and environmental issues. Whistle-blowers in the public sector are accorded better protection and they evoke public sympathy. Unfortunately, they meet a tragic fate in private and service sectors. Boisjoly, a Morton Thiokol engineer, blew the whistle on his employer regarding the design flaws in the O-rings that went into space shuttle Challenger. The problem was ignored. The result was the tragic loss of seven astronauts. Boisjoly was sacked because he had acted against the perceived interest of the company. He and other corporate members realized that blowing the whistle leads to punishment, not reward. When an MIT scientist exposed false research data in a scientific article co-authored by a Nobel Laureate, she was fired from her job (Robbins, 1994, p.191). Dr. Subramaniam Swamy, a nineteen-year-old, was not tolerated when he charged Professor Mahalanobis of plagiarism. The law provides little protection to whistle-blowers anywhere in the world. One can blow the whistle if, there are sufficient reasons to do so, the act has undesirable social consequences, and the employment contract specifies whistle-blowing or the employer provides protection to the whistle-blower. Many have installed hotlines and have ombudspersons. Employees can call the confidential hotline or can seek advice from an ombudsperson without fear of retaliation before blowing the whistle.

Whistle-blowers are encouraged in situations where incentives are so structured that the group shares the cost of consequences of one's misconduct. Some dock the pay of all workers for losses due to employee theft (Feinstein,

1990). The consequences are salient to all group members. Stealing may be viewed as stealing from the group rather than from the organization, and reporting of misconduct to higher authorities may be justified as protecting the group rather than harming the group. Conversely, when the consequences are not shared, group members reject the whistle-blower and judge him unlikable (Trevino and Victor, 1992). If the management focuses on gaining acceptance of a code of conduct initially that mandates the employees' responsibility to report misconduct, whistle-blowers will be supported and corporate criminality will be reduced.

Involvement in Community Development Activities

Rockefeller, Carnegie, Morgan, and Stanford were extraordinarily successful businessmen in USA who managed to strike a balance between self and society. They took personal risks and became rich. They have their critics, then and now. Nevertheless, each demonstrated a concern in some form or other for the lager community of which business is a part (Henderson, 1992, pp.109-134).

Community development activities of industries foster good relations with surrounding communities, develop localities socially and economically, and boost-up the long-term marketing strategies of companies. The expenditure on such activities sensitizes corporate members that a share of each employee's contribution is spared for developing the local people who bear the brunt of pollution and other consequences of industrial activity. These activities induce ethicality in the minds of employees. Local people and managers reciprocate with goodwill and co-operation in crises that amount to social morality. There was a well-known case in Cadbury India almost two decades ago. Cadbury operations were being stifled by massive import tariffs on cocoa. Cocoa was needed to produce the company's staple product-chocolate. At the same time, coconut farmers in certain regions of south India were financially frustrated by their once-a-year yield crops. When both farmers and company were facing a crisis, the company provided cocoa plants and technical back up. The farmers agreed to cultivate a second crop along with the traditional one and to sell the produce to Cadbury. These types of partnership along with community development activities are seen in sugar, oil, and other agro-based industries in India. These incidences induce ethicality in the minds of both managers and surrounding communities and foster mutual goodwill and cooperation.

Shared values, attitudes, and beliefs preached and practiced among employees over a period of time in an organization constitute the mainsprings of al culture. It is kept alive informally and symbolically through rituals, norms, stories, heroic acts and managerial practices.

Matsushita of Japan instills its norms in newly hired employees, providing training not only in basic skills but also in company values through a long apprenticeship. Each employee in the group is asked to give a 10-minute talk to her/his group at least once every month on the activity of the corporation and its relationship to society. Before joining duty on the dot, employees sing the company's song that sets forth its fundamental values – national service, harmony and co-operation, struggle for betterment of all, courtesy, humility, willingness to adjust, and gratitude. First, by giving a talk, the new employee reflects and becomes aware of her/his role in society. Second, through the song, the employee persuades herself/himself to practice the company's norms.

The heroic ethical decisions of executives influence employee behaviour. There is a case in Tata Steel. A crane operator dashed the crane into gantry and caused damage worth lakhs of rupees. The man was going to be dismissed. Russi Mody, the former managing director of the Tata Iron and Steel Company, came to know about the incident. Mody checked the past records of the operator. The operator was punctual, honest and had handled all kinds of cranes. Mody called him and assured him: 'Don't worry, you will not be dismissed but be careful in future' (cited in Sinha, 1995, p.71). Such a heroic decision sent a message to other members that an employee's punctuality, honesty and star performance during the service career were underscored, jacketing genuine mistakes despite heavy financial loss.

Stories and sagas drawn from the history influence employee behaviour. At IBM, a story has been told and retold. It describes how a lower level employee denied Tom Watson, the former IBM president, entry into a restricted area of the company because Watson was not wearing his IBM identification badge. Watson praised the employee, suggesting the importance of upholding company rules and applying them to everyone without fear or favour.

The ethical conduct of the firm in crises influences employees. In 1982, grisly reports of death hit the newsstand due to cyanide poisoning of Tylenol capsules in Chicago area. The disaster resulted from 'tampering' rather than manufacturing error. Within hours of hearing, McNeil Laboratories, a subsidiary of Johnson & Johnson, voluntarily withdrew this product from the market regardless of cost. The company offered opportunity to replace Tylenol capsules for tablets free of cost. Within ten weeks, Tylenol was reintroduced in tamper resistant packaging. With advertising and marketing efforts, Tylenol had regained most of its market share. The Tylenol plan for action sprang directly from the company's credo, which makes service to consumers as its uppermost goal and financial returns come last (Buchholz, Evans and Wagley, 1989). This incidence is reiterated and inspires the employees to adhere to values to avoid tempering.

Coca-Cola's June 1999 crisis in Belgium dampened business in Europe. Several dozen Belgian school children got nauseated drinking 'tainted' Coca-Cola. Belgian officials and later French officials pulled Coke products from grocery store shelves. Coke traced the problem to cans contaminated on the outside by chemicals found on wood-shipping pallets and on defective carbon dioxide used in making soft drinks. While the problem involved outside vendors, Coca-Cola was severely criticized for not quickly assuming public responsibility for the contaminated soft drinks. In contrast to Tylenol's prompt action, Coca-Cola was portrayed in the media as uncaring and exploitative of European consumers by acting slowly. Public perception of unethical behaviour can often seal the fate of business.

Ethical managers talk about honesty, integrity, transparency, sincerity and good character in carrying out decisions, functions and tasks. They inspire subordinates for periodic examination of conscience. The ways in which managers preach and practice the values influence the behaviour of their subordinates.

Level Strategy

Employing Ethical Staff

The first line of defence against unethical behaviour is the employment of ethical staff. First, all potential candidates are required to read and sign a statement obligating them to abide by the al values and ethical standards as a part of the employment process. Second, paper-pencil honesty tests can be administered on such candidates for ethical screening. Third, the interviewer can gauge the candidates by presenting ethical dilemmas, asking for decisions and justifications. Further, morality of candidates can be cross-checked from the comments of earlier supervisors, or from the information collected from their community, village, or town. Those candidates can be easily groomed with respect to ethical duties and responsibilities of the job.

Ethical Code

General Dynamics, the US government's largest defence contractor, developed an ethical code to remain eligible for its navy contracts after allegations about improper contracting procedures surfaced in 1985. An ethical code contains messages of corporate norms, values, policies and rules to regulate employee behaviour and to maintain public trust. A code addresses issues on extortion, gifts, kickbacks, conflict of interest, illegal political payments, violation of laws, use of insider information, misuse of corporate assets, leakage of confidential information, bribery, insider trading, etc. Recently, an international group of business executives spelt out seven principles for a responsive business code called 'caux principles'. These principles emphasize values of improving the lives of stakeholders, innovation, justice, trust, amity, peace, co-operation, environmental improvement and judicious liberalization of global commerce (Xavier Labour Relations Institute, 1994). The existence of an ethical policy significantly reduces unethical decisions (Hegarty and Sims, 1979).

A code is handed over to an employee through a separate booklet, an annual report, or as part of the personnel document. Out of the surveyed Fortune 100 corporations, three-fourths have codes but one-half of the companies only distribute codes beyond the level of officers and 'key employees' (White and Montgomery, 1980). If the code is incongruent with prevailing al practices, and is not evolved through the participation of stakeholders, it fails to guide enforcement authorities negotiating sticky wickets. A code either contains information on compliance or is enforced by top management, ethics committee, government agencies or judicial board. Non-compliance or violation of the code results in termination, suspension, demotion, appraisal comments and other penalties. Thus, the code institutionalizes moral norms and ethical behaviour.

Ethics Committee

An ethics committee is essential for (a) enforcement of ethical code and (b) formulation of ethics policy. The committee can hold regular meetings to discuss issues relating to 'grey areas', communicate the code to all members, check the possible violation of the code, and suggest punishment to the higher authorities for code violation. Motorola has successfully experimented with this concept.

The committee can evolve mechanisms where employees can appeal for others' unethical behaviour without fear. Membership of the committee can rotate among employees, so that each employee can get exposure to unethical issues submitted by others. The committee can issue bulletins on its decisions, and formulate policies based on its decisions with the approval of board of directors. It can report its activities to board of directors, monitor policy compliance, and recommend to the board to review and update the code.

Reward System

Conventional wisdom prevails that reward is better than punishment to encourage ethical behaviour. But, doing the right thing often goes unnoticed. An employee is seldom praised for not padding an expense account and a manager for not exploiting a secretary. Rewarding ethical behaviour in day-to-day business is impractical. Only the heroic ethical behaviour that goes beyond the call of duty is singled out for praise. Punishment of unethical behaviour is the most effective inhibitor of unethical behaviour and a booster of ethical behaviour (Trevino, Sutton and Woodman, 1985). Organizations interested in promoting ethical behaviour should punish the unethical behaviour. In accordance with the law of effect, a behaviour that is punished is stamped out, and which is not punished or rewarded is stamped in. Punishment creates precedence that consequences await those who indulge in unethical practices.

Changing some conventional procedures help employees to be ethical. Rather than giving an opportunity to employees to fiddle expenses using expenditure claim forms, some companies are allocating a fixed amount for weekly expenditure. The employee is free to spend that amount. By changing the conventional system, companies have eased the burden of moral responsibility on employees.

Ethical Climate Survey

An ethical climate refers to the perception of employees regarding ethical procedures and policies existing in the five dimensions of an ethical climate – law and code, caring, rules, independent, and instrumental – having been validated (Victor and Cullen, 1987, 1988). The predominance of an instrumental dimension and the deficiencies in all other dimensions of an ethical climate promote numerous unethical practices.

Administering the ethical climate questionnaire on executives and analyzing their responses, the management can decide: Does the firm's ethical climate misfit with the strategic goals and the values the company wants to espouse? If the answers are in the affirmative, the top management can formulate strategies for changing the climate through code revision, education, training, changing supervision, selection process, incentive structures, etc.

Ethical Audit

Ethical audit implicitly concerns with issues such as economic performance, work practices, training, human rights, environmental and animal protection, ethical trade, community development, and hence with the sustainability of a company's activities. It explicitly concerns with interests and expectations of stakeholders, pressure groups and NGOs, and with social norms and regulations. It is value-linked and centered. It enables a company to establish clear guidelines about the limits of acceptable behaviour that are consistent worldwide, while recognizing where appropriate local societal differences. By taking a picture of the value system of an organization through interviews, surveys, and listening to employees; and workshops and group discussions to build consensus on values – at a given point in time, it can: (a) clarify the actual values to which the company operate, (b) provide a baseline by which to measure future improvement, (c) learn how to meet any societal expectations which are not currently being met, (d) give stakeholders the opportunity to clarify their expectations of the company's behaviour, (e) identify specific problem areas within the company, (f) learn about the issues which motivate employees, and (g) identify general areas of vulnerability, particularly related to lack of openness. This is intended for accountability towards stakeholders such as product safety, environmental protection, employee relations, etc. and transparency towards stakeholders. The stakeholders knowing this and through focus group discussion can provide feedback about company's values. It provides opportunity to the company to track progress through the years and to find out moral gaps, if any, and prepare an action plan where there is still some work to do with regard to a company's values.

The Indian Constitution lays down 14 years as age below which children should not be employed in factory, mine, or any hazardous work. But children work in carpet weaving at Mirzapur (Uttar Pradesh in India), handicrafts and handlooms in Kashmir, and gem-cutting in Maharastra and Rajasthan. When such items are exported, European Union guided by ethical concern has the bills seeking the ban on Indian goods produced by child labours.

Benchmarking with Ethical Firms

Benchmarking embodies the idea that it is possible to examine best practices in similar types of companies and then implement changes based on those observations. Divulging the best practices in other companies involves questioning, research, and qualitative and quantitative data analysis. It also requires a good deal of internal analysis, observation and introspection to determine what improvements are desirable and possible within the firm. Xerox's benchmarking process includes 10 steps: (1) Identify what is to be benchmarked. (2) Identify comparative companies. (3) Determine data collection methods and collect data. (4) Determine current performance levels. (5) Project future performance levels. (6) Communicate benchmark finds and gain acceptance. (7) Establish functional goals. (8) Develop action plans. (9) Implement specific actions and monitor progress. (10) Recalibrate benchmarks. Similarly, a firm can compare its existing ethical practices and procedures with locally and globally reputed ethical firms in similar types of industry. Thereby, the gap in existing practices and procedures of a firm can be found out, providing scope for designing interventions with the participation of employees to reduce immoral corporate practices, whether it is related to quality, wage discrimination against women, work issues, environmental protection, etc.

Conclusion

There is evidence that business is facing up to ethical issues. Clearly, unethical behaviour of an organization and its employees can damage reputation and hit its bottom line and share price. It can often force a company out of business. Just one legal transgression can cost a company millions of dollars and s that have not institutionalized ethics run the risk of more stringent penalties than those who have. Furthermore, bad publicity can have a profound impact on brand value and an organization's ability to attract and retain best people, thus eroding its competitive edge. Some companies have institutionalized ethics even adopting stringent polices on gifts and gratuities. When allegations of abuses surfaced including General Motors (GM) involvement in kick-back scheme (Stern and Lublin, 1996), GM announced a policy in June 1996 that forbids GM employees from either giving or receiving gifts beyond the most nominal of trinkets. Wal-Mart Stores Inc. has even tougher policy that bars employees from accepting anything with a monetary value. Tata houses have decided not to give any donation to politicians. Reputation in business counts. Incorporating ethics in day-to-day business increase not only shareholder value but also other stakeholders gain too.

Different countries have adopted different approaches to institutionalize ethics. In recent years, many companies in United States have appointed a senior manager with (dedicated responsibility for promoting ethical behaviour throughout the company. In Europe, such appointments are the exception rather than a rule, but majority now have ethical code or code of conduct. India is yet to follow suit.

This discussed prescriptive paradigm cannot be applied everywhere. Indeed, this paradigm can provide food for thought and help designing alternative strategies wherever necessary. The three strategies can be broadly classified into two categories. The interpersonal and organizational level strategies entail to infuse ethics through influence and control-oriented mechanisms respectively. Contrarily, the individual level strategy focuses on ethical transformation of the self that can have enduring effects to cultivate values. Only human being is a self-conscious system because it can think rationally and apply ethical behaviour at the individual, group, organizational and societal levels. If the management can enable the employees through information dissemination, group discussion and training to introspect and exert effort mentally to change them, the influence and control-oriented strategies can only supplement that. Moreover, the individual level strategy is easy to execute with minimum effort for the employees. Also, institutionalization of ethics can be accomplished by making financial resources available in managers' budgets for providing training, conducting ethical climate survey, rewarding exceptional ethical behaviour, undertaking ethical audit and benchmarking.

India in the past had produced abundant literature on values and ethics. Though the knowledge base was introspective and experiential in nature, its credibility could not be doubted because people of high integrity and stature produced it. This knowledge is not extracted adequately through qualitative research. Extracting this knowledge from the *Arthashastra*, the *Bhagavat Gita*, the *Ramayan*, the *Mahabharat*, the *Upanishads*, the *Bible*, the *Manusmriti*, the *Yoga Sutras* and other scriptures and making it available in easy and practicable ways will provide guidance for inculcating values in individuals and institutionalizing ethics. Considering the current unethical practices globally, inculcation of values and institutionalization of ethics have already become an important agenda in the 21st century. India's rich knowledge on ethics from time memorial can make it the global leader on knowledge provision rather than the follower. Perhaps, this is the only potential area where ethical knowledge base will flow from eastern to western countries.

References

Becker, H. and D. Fritzche (1987) 'Business ethics: A cross-cultural comparison of managers' attitudes', *Journal of Business Ethics*, 6(3), 289-295.

Bhat, V.P. (1997) 'The focused manager', *Indian Management*, 36(12), 9-16.

Brenner, S.N. (1992) 'Ethics programs and their dimensions', *Journal of Business Ethics*, 11(4), 391-399.

Buchholz, R.A., W.D. Evans and R.A. Wagley (1989) *Management response to public issues*, Englewood Cliffs, NJ: Prentice-Hall.

Center for Business Ethics (1992) 'Are corporations institutionalizing ethics?', *Journal of Business Ethics*, 11(9), 863-867.

Chakraborty, S.K. (1993) *Managerial transformation by values: A corporate pilgrimage*. New Delhi: Sage.

Chakraborty, S.K. (1998) *Values and ethics for s: Theory and practice*, Delhi: Oxford University.

Colby, A., L. Kohlberg, J. Gibbs and M. Lieberman (1983) 'A longitudinal study of moral development', *Monographs of the Society for Research in Child Development*, 48(1 and 2, Series No. 200), 1-107.

Collins, D. (2000) 'The quest to improve the human condition: The first 1,500 articles published in Journal of Business Ethics', *Journal of Business Ethics*, 26(1), 1-73.

Dukerich, J.M., M.L Nichols, D.R. Elm and D.A. Vollrath (1990) 'Moral reasoning in groups: Leaders make a difference', *Human Relations*, 43(5), 473-493.

Feinstein, S. (1990) 'Worker theft imposes rising costs on retailers, customers', *Wall Street Journal*, 215(24), 1.

Festinger, L. (1957) *A theory of cognitive dissonance*, Stanford: Stanford University Press.

Gilligan, C. (1982) *In a different voice: Psychological theory and women's development*, Cambridge, MA: Harvard University.

Guillen, M. and T.F. Gonzalez (2001) 'The ethical dimension of managerial leadership: Two illustrative case studies in TQM', *Journal of Business Ethics*, 34(3-4), 175-189.

Hegarty, W.H. and H.P. Sims, Jr. (1979) 'Organizational philosophy, policies, and objectives related to unethical decision behavior: A laboratory experiment', *Journal of Applied Psychology*, 64(3), 331-338.

Henderson, V.E. (1992) *What's ethical in business?* New York: McGraw-Hill.

Jose, A. and M.S. Thibodeaux (1999) 'Institutionalization of ethics: The perspective of manager', *Journal of Business Ethics*, 22(2), 133-143.

Iacocca, L. and W. Novak (1985) *Iacocca: An autobiography*, New York: Bantam Books.

Kanungo, R.N. and M. Mendonca (1996) *Ethical dimensions of leadership*, Thousand Oaks: Sage.

Kanungo, R.N. and M. Mendonca (1998) 'Ethical leadership in three dimensions', *Journal of Human Values*, 4(2), 133-148.

Luthar, P.C. (1987) *Effective management: Lessons from experience*, Ahmedabad: Allied.

Maguire, S. (1999) 'The discourse of control', *Journal of Business Ethics*, 19(1), 109-114.

McClelland, D.C. and D. Burnham (1995) 'Power is the great motivation', *Harvard Business Review*, 73(1), 126-139.

Nichols, M.L. and V.E Day (1982) 'A comparison of moral reasoning of groups and individuals on the 'Defining Issues Test'', *Academy of Management Journal*, 25(1), 201-208.

Meichenbaum, D.H. (1977) *Cognitive behavior modification: An integrative approach*, New York: Plenum.

Meyers, A., M. Mercatoris and A. Sirota (1976) 'Use of covert self-instruction for the elimination of psychotic speech', *Journal of Consulting and Clinical Psychology*, 44(5), 480-483.

Raynor, M.E. (1998) 'That vision thing: Do we need it?', *Long Range Planning*, 31(3), 368-376.

Robbins, S.P. (1994) *Organizational behavior: Concepts, controversies, and applications*, New Delhi: Prentice-Hall.

Schreier, M. and N. Groeben (1996) 'Ethical guidelines for the conduct in argumentative discussions: An exploratory study', *Human Relations*, 49(1), 123-132.

Sharan, M.B., S. Prasad and D. Suar (1989) 'Factors influencing stability of the self-concept', *The Creative Psychologist*, 1(1), 9-17.

Sinha, J.B.P. (1980) *The nurturant task leader*, New Delhi: Concept.

Sinha, J.B.P. (1995) *The cultural context of leadership and power*, New Delhi: Sage

Solomon, R. (1999) *A better way to think about business: How personal integrity leads to corporate success*, Oxford: Oxford University Press.

Stasser, G., S.I. Vaughan and D.D. Stewart (2000) 'Pooling unshared information: The benefits of knowing how access to information is distributed among group members'. *Organizational Behavior and Human Decision Processes*, 2000, 82(1), 102-116.

Stern, G. and J. Lublin (1996) 'New GM rules curb wining and dining', *Wall Street Journal* (June 5), B1-B2.

Stewart, D.D. and G. Stasser (1995) 'Expert role assignment and information sampling during collective recall and decision-making', *Journal of Personality and Social Psychology*, 69(4), 619-628.

Suar, D. (1993) 'Work value formation and change among young managers', *Management and Labour Studies*, 18(2), 73-80.

Suar, D. (2000) 'A man can be made human: Understanding and enhancing morality, values, and ethical behaviour', *Indian Psychological Abstracts and Reviews*, 7(1), 1-41.

Suar, D., B. Panda and M.B Sharan (1989) 'Value comparison, organizational identification and job satisfaction among hospital employees', *The Creative Psychologist*, 1(2), 69-80.

Trevino, L.K. and D. McCabe (1994) 'Meta-learning about business ethics: Building honorable business school communities', *Journal of Business Ethics*, 13(6), 405-416.

Trevino, L.K. and B. Victor (1992) 'Peer reporting of unethical behavior: A social context perspective', *Academy of Management Journal*, 35(1), 38-64.

Trevino, L.K., C.D. Sutton and R.W. Woodman (1985) 'Effects of reinforcement contingencies and cognitive moral development on ethical decision-making behavior: An experiment', Paper presented at the 45th Annual Meeting of the Academy of Management, San Diego, CA.

Victor, B. and J.B. Cullen (1987) A theory and measure of ethical climate in s. In C. Frederick (ed.), *Research in corporate social performance and policy* (pp.51-71) Greenwich, CT: JAI Press.

Victor, B. and J.B. Cullen (1988) 'The Organizational bases of ethical work climates', *Administrative Science Quarterly*, 33(1), 101-125.

Vireswarananda, S. (1948) *Srimad Bhagavad Gita*, Madras: Sri Ramakrishna Math.

White, B.J. and R.B. Montgomery (1980) 'Corporate code of conduct' *California Management Review*, 23(3), 80-86.

Wittenbaum, G.M. (1998) Information sampling in decision-making groups: The impact of members' task-relevant status. *Small Group Research*, 1998, 29(1), 57-84.

Xavier Labour Relations Institute (1994) 'The caux principles: Business behaviour for a better world', *Management and Labour Studies*, 19(3), 148-151.

Chapter 3

Life Within and Life Without: A Managerial Approach to Living

Swami Satyarupananda

Introduction

Man is the highest among the living beings in this world. Except man all other living beings are controlled and guided by nature. They don't have their own choice. Sometimes it seems that the other living beings also have some choice. But if we probe deep we will see that their choice is very limited within the gamut of their nature. But when we study human nature we find that man has almost infinite choices to make or mar his life. Man is the only being who can control, conquer and mould the nature, external and internal. This capacity of man gives him a special place and status in the plan and program of the universe. Man has a unique capacity to look back into his past and to take lessons to correct his present and future. Man has a capacity to plan and realize his future as well. Man is the only being who can alter and improve his own life in this present life.

For all other living beings nature herself has fixed purposes for their lives. They have no choice in this respect. A dog has to live and die like a dog. It has no choice in this respect. But if man chooses to degrade himself then he can cultivate and imbibe canine qualities and live like a dog. On the other hand if he chooses to become a divine being and live like a living god he can do that also. This shows that man can give meaning and value to his own life. Once a man decides to give meaning and value to his life he can make use of the nature external and internal to help him achieve his sublime goal. This choice is absolutely with the man himself. He has to decide what he wants to make out of himself. Once decided he himself has to execute the plans and programs to achieve his desired goal. This puts the whole responsibility on the shoulders of man himself. The Gita beautifully puts it 'Let a man lift himself by himself, let him not degrade himself, for the self alone is the friend of the self and the self alone is the enemy of the self' (6.5 Gita).

Man the Conscious Being

What is that quality which makes man superior to all other living beings under the sky? It is his uniqueness in the knowledge of his own existence. An animal exists and a man exists but an animal does not have the knowledge that it exists; but man consciously knows that it exists.

There is one very good incidence in the life of Swami Vivekananda which explains the unique capacity of man which makes him superior amongst all living beings. Once in Calcutta Swamiji was travelling by horse carriage along a railway line with his disciple Sharat Chandra. They saw that a steam engine was coming from the opposite direction. Swamiji said to the disciple, 'Look how it goes majestically like a lion?' The disciple replied, 'But that is inert matter. Behind it there is the intelligence of man working, and hence it moves. In moving thus, what credit is there for it?'

Swamiji: Well say then, what is the sign of consciousness?
Disciple: Why, Sir, that indeed is conscious which acts through intelligence.
Swamiji: Everything is conscious which rebels against nature: there, consciousness is manifested. Just try to kill a little ant, even it will at once resist to save its life. Where there is struggle, where there is rebellion, there is the sign of life. There consciousness is manifested.

This is very important truth which Swamiji has revealed before us, that the sign of consciousness is struggle or rebellion against nature as Swamiji puts it. This struggle makes a Man out of the human being.

Being born as a human is something like a raw material dug out from a mine, may be from a gold mine. However good the quality of raw material may be to make it useful and valuable it has to be processed. It is through processes in various stages in a mill or a factory that the raw material becomes valuable and useful.

Likewise to make human life valuable and useful it has to go through various stages in this big factory known as our world.

First Step

The Goal/Aim

What is the end or purpose of this process? What is that finished product that we want to achieve through this process? Swami Vivekananda the great pathfinder of human destiny of modern times has told us unambiguously about this purpose. He says in his famous book Raja Yoga – 'Each soul is potentially divine. The goal is to manifest this divinity within by controlling nature external and internal. Do this either by work or worship or psychic control or philosophy by one or more or all of these and be free'.

The Human Personality

The human personality has two parts – without and within external and internal. Our external personality that we see when we stand before a mirror is not the alpha and omega of human personality. The external personality is just like a case in which a very valuable diamond has been kept which is a million times more valuable than the case itself. But suppose if any person is allured by the beauty of the case itself and does not try to find out its valuable content what will we call him? Shall we not call him a man without wisdom?

Likewise the human body is like a casket in which the jewel of supreme value – the Atman or the Soul of the man is residing. The aim of life is to penetrate this casket and find the jewel of Atman or Soul. The human soul is omnipotent, omniscient. The human soul is the eternal mine of existence, knowledge and bliss (*sat, chit, ananda*). Even if we get a glimpse of that soul it makes our life a blessing to ourselves and benediction to the society.

Thus we see that the sole purpose of human life is to find and realize the infinitely valuable jewel of Atman. Any lesser purpose in human life cannot give the full and real meaning to human life.

The Means

The law of *karma*. We have not come into this world from nothing or nowhere. Our experience in this world tells us beyond doubt that whatever exists is an effect of a cause which we might not know. Nothing can come into existence in this world without any cause. The causal law is infallible and inevitable. We are also the effect of a cause known as *karma* in Hindu scriptures. Swami Vivekananda puts it into his inimitable language 'you know it already that each one of us is the effect of the infinite past. The child is ushered into the world not as something flashing from the hands of nature as poets delight so much to depict, but he has the burden of an infinite past. For good or evil he comes to work out his own past deeds that makes the differentiation. This is the law of *karma*. Each one of us is the maker of one's own fate' (*lectures from Colombo to Almora, Page 27, 11th Impression, 1984*).

This shows clearly that if we want to give a valuable meaning to our life we must bring in operation the law of cause, which will produce the desired result in the form of effect. It is our past *karma* which has made our life what it is today. This naturally follows that what our life will be in future depends upon our present *karma*. Let us therefore be very much cautious and careful about our present *karma* and know it for certain what value we want to give to our life in future. We must know for certain what meaning we want to attribute to our life in future.

Livelihood is Not the Goal of Life

Unfortunately because of our present marketing and shop keeping culture almost all of our present generation wrongly thinks that livelihood or earning money is the goal of life. We had many occasions to share the views and thoughts of our young bright boys and girls regarding the aim of their life. Most of them are of the opinion that becoming an engineer, a doctor, a business executive, a lawyer or some high officer is their aim in life. But if we think deeply these vocations are means of earning money and livelihood, they can support life but cannot give meaning to it. Although they can become very useful if once we decide to live for a higher cause.

These vocations can make sufficient provision for improving our standard of living. But they can never improve and raise the standard of our life itself. Raising the standard of life does not come within the jurisdiction of the material means which raise the standard of living. There are other things which raise the standard of life and give meaning to it.

Identity Gives Meaning to Life

One of the major and perplexing problems of our age is the problem of identity. Man has lost his identity and therefore individuality. Our present system of education, the social interaction, modern civilization, impact of science and technology, invention and discoveries and the political chaos all the world over has totally confused the modern generation. Man has lost his individuality because in this state of chaos and confusion he is trying to identify himself with the things external which have no values in themselves e.g. man has identified himself with wealth and properties thinking that they will give him status in society and satisfaction to himself. But when we probe deeply into the values of wealth and property, we find that although it has utility in the human life, it can only make human living a little more comfortable. The value which has been attached to wealth and properties has been given to them by Man. It is man who has made them valuable because of their utility in life. Wealth and properties are not equally and justifiably distributed in the modern society. Therefore those of us who have more of it unwisely flatten our ego and feel that we are superior to them who have less wealth and property than us. This wrong identification with wealth and property has given us a false idea of personality and that too is a super personality. Wealth and property can never reach and touch the real being of man. It is not the fundamental and permanent base for building human personality. Whenever fluctuation comes in wealth and power for some reason and man loses wealth and mean is exposed, the whole personality of man shakes from the bottom. Man loses all the ground under his feet and finds no place to stand and ultimately lands on misery and sorrow.

There are people who identify themselves with power and position. Wealth may not matter to them as much as it matters to the person who identifies himself with wealth and property. These persons are ready to sacrifice any amount of wealth for achieving power and position in society either politically or otherwise. Power and position in politics or in other social institutions are not everlasting. As soon as power and position are lost the man who has identified himself with it and which has become the core of his personality, crumbles to the ground and lands into de-individuality.

There are persons who have identified themselves with learning and professional skills like scientists, technocrats, doctors, lawyers, etc. when they also reach the acme of their skill and find that they have nothing more to do and as time goes on their efficiency and skill are diminishing and then they also lose all ground under their feet and stand no-where, ultimately realizing that life is meaningless to them.

Person Without Personality

The present techno-scientific culture has made man also a cog in the machine, which is this present society. It considers man as one of the commodities in the world. It gives value to a person so long he is useful for the purpose of material gain.

Is man simply a cog in the machine or a thing among the infinite things? The experience of each one of us denies this fact vehemently from within. Man is not the grand total of the various minerals, chemicals and electrochemical functions found in his body. He is something more than the all psycho-physical grand total of his personality.

The Real Man

The crux of the whole problem is what is this something more which makes a person a real man. If this problem can be solved we shall reach to the very source of human personality and we shall be able to find it out and identify yourself with this original source, our life will be really valuable and meaningful.

If we probe deeply into our own mind we shall find among the thousands of desires in our mind, three desires are always dominantly persisting (i) The desire to live (ii) The desire to know (ii) The desire for happiness and bliss.

The Desire to Live

None of us wants to die. We have a natural desire to live eternally. We can think of other people dying but rarely we remember or think that we have to die. That day and night people are dying but those who are living are constantly desiring to live eternally. This shows that man has eternal desire to live eternally. One question may be asked here, how is it that many people commit suicide? To find out the answer we shall have to probe deeply into the causes and circumstances in which people commit suicide. Invariably we will find those people who want to commit suicide or have committed suicide did not like the situation or the circumstances in which they were forced to live. The conditions for their continuing life were hard and in most of the cases the difficulties were imaginary. Had they got the things they wanted or if circumstances altered in their favour, they would never have committed suicide. In fact they did not want to commit suicide but wanted to end an undesirable situation and could find no alternative other than to end their lives. The lust for life in them is as intense and deep as it is in any man.

The Desire for Knowledge

I am speaking before you. Had there been a dark black screen between you and me which would have hidden me completely from you sight everyone of you must have been anxious enough to see the face of the speaker. This desire to see the speaker would have very well disturbed your concentration in listening the speech. It is ingrained in human nature that it wants to uncover everything which is hiding from him. Man wants to know the mystery of everything which he know. He wants to know the cause of everything. Unless we know the thing we want to know our mind remains restless and we feel sad. As soon as the knowledge dawns in our mind and we know the things we feel very much satisfied.

If we look at the behaviour of a baby we will find that the baby puts everything into his mouth because at this age the tongue is the only means by which he understands things because the other senses are not fully developed. When the child grows a little more it wants to dissect its toys, tears off the paper, toy etc. and wants to know what is within and looks into it. When the same baby learns to speak he asks hundreds of questions to understand everything which it perceives. When the child grows into a mature man, reads and writes and acquires various other means of knowledge, then constantly he tries to use the means of knowledge to gain more and more knowledge about the world around him.

The wonders of science and technology which we see around us; the sweet and lofty literary works of the world; the mysterious writings of the great philosophers and the thinkers are all proof of this fact that man has an unquenchable thirst for knowledge. In fact this thirst has produced all the knowledge we have today and will produce in future which is yet to be achieved. This shows that the thirst for knowledge is ingrained in our very being.

Desire for Happiness or Bliss

Every one of us wants to be happy and blissful in our life. We want to enjoy the world, why? Because enjoyment gives us happiness. Many people under-take world tours or tour their own countries, why? Because this wandering gives them happiness. Many people practice various kinds of arts such as singing, painting, drawing, dancing, playing instruments, drama etc., why? Because they get pleasure out of their art. One may ask this question of people who voluntarily accept hardship or take on arduous activities for climbing high mountains or wander in the deep impenetrable forests of Africa or other parts of the world. How can we say that all these things are pleasurable? Friends, but if we can probe into their mind and try to understand we shall find that these heroes get intense pleasure in their adventures.

Even the sadist who inflicts pain on others, or the human being who murders a person or maims him gets joy from his cruel act, though these are perversions and wrong means of getting pleasures which ultimately lead to misery.

There are persons who sacrifice everything – hearth and home, wealth and comfort, name and fame for the sake of others. There are highly evolved persons who sacrifice their own lives to save the lives of others. There are innumerable examples of persons who have donated their most vital organs such as their kidney to save the life of another person without any expectation of any return. Were they not the persons who were happy in sacrificing all? In fact they are the persons who were the happiest of all.

Thus we see that the desire or happiness is also ingrained in our very being.

Our proposition in the beginning was this that there is something more than the GRAND TOTAL of psycho-physical part of our personality that makes a man a real man. The Vedanta says this something is *Atman* the SELF, the nature of the self is Sat-Chit-Anand. Our very being is existence, knowledge and bliss eternal. The Real Man is deathless and therefore birth less also. It eternally exists and shall continue to exist eternally. Because of our ignorance we have forgotten our real nature and therefore we are sunk in misery.

Life Within and Life Without

Our senses have been made to look without to perceive and sense the things other than the senses themselves. From birth to death, as long as we are healthy and our senses are in working order, we perceive the world without. Our senses give us the knowledge of the external world only. Lifelong we accumulate the knowledge from without. But the knowledge from without gives no information to us about ourself. Everyone of us feels that we have a world within as well. Even the most ignorant man of the world knows and feels that he has some feelings and experiences like love, friendship, sympathy and ill feelings like jealousy, anger, enmity, etc. These things have no external existence, they are within us. No sense organ can perceive them and yet we feel we have these feelings.

How do we feel it? It is through our mind that we know and feel them. Therefore the only instrument by which we can know and feel our world within is our mind. When we withdraw our senses from without and try to see the things within through our own mind we get acquainted with our world within. This world within is our real personality. This world within gives us the knowledge about ourselves. We know that there are innumerable greater things and possibilities within us. Then we come to realize that our personality without is not even half of our personality within. But the personality without is no less important. It is through the personality without that we know the world. This knowledge of the world helps us to know our personality within. This shows that he is the really integrated man who knows both sides of his personality, within and without. Half knowledge is ignorance, rather more dangerous than ignorance. To live a meaningful life worth the term itself we must know both sides of our personality within and without. Here we must remember a fact that personality without is nothing but a reflection of our personality within. What we are within expresses itself through our personality without, it thunders so loudly from within that people do not listen to what we say without, however hard we may try to hide or disguise it. Therefore we have to take the utmost care of our personality within. If everything within is systematic and well adjusted the personality without will also naturally be systematic and adjustable to the world without. We can say this is the secret of living a meaningful life.

Building the Life Within

Spirituality is the bedrock of meaningful life: but morality is the building block, which builds the edifice of meaningful life. Morality is applied spirituality. A man can never reach to the goal of spirituality unless he travels trough the path of morality. Thus we can say for all practical purposes, to give meaning to our life we must be moral first. If we study human nature we will find that morality is inseparable from human nature. There cannot be a meaningful life divorced from morality; therefore to build the life within we must be moral first and moral last. There is no substitute for morality. A man divorced from morality becomes an animal. It is the morality, which distinguishes a man from an animal. The instinct or animal forces are also found to some extent in human nature. By curbing and conquering the animal instinct a man becomes a moral person. Morality is a fundamental characteristic of a meaningful life. Those who do not care much for moral life soon lose the human dignity and fall into the realm of the animal world. Therefore to build the life within we must cultivate and practice moral virtues in our life.

Truth

The first moral virtue to build a worthy character is truth. In fact no moral character can be built without truth. Therefore we can say truth is the bedrock of moral life. Here we must remember a fundamental fact about truth. Truth has two dimensions:

- Absolute truth
- Relative truth

Absolute truth can be one and one alone. But relative truth has many dimensions. e.g. this wall, which is on my right side, is also on the left side of those friends who are sitting facing me. Therefore we shall have to say in relation to the speaker the wall is on the right side. But in relation to the listeners the wall is on the left side, both are equally true.

This shows that we should not and cannot insist in the relative world that only my views are right, only my angle of vision is true, rather we should be generous enough to consider the views and the angle of vision of others and try to find out the other dimensions of truth as well. This is very important to live peacefully and harmoniously in this world of confusion and chaos. Ultimately we have to reach to the absolute truth, which is non-dual and one. The path to absolute truth is through the steps of relative truth only, e.g. reaching from circumference to centre.

Non-Injury

Non-injury and love are two sides of the same coin. Unless we develop love in our heart we cannot practice non-injury. Why does a person want to injure another person or for that matter any other living being? Because the person does not love him. Hatred and selfishness are the characteristics of injury. So long as we cherish these two evil feelings in our heart we shall never be able to practice non-injury. Thus we shall never be a moral person and a man who is is not a moral person can never be a man of character and therefore can never give any worthwhile meaning to his life and benefit to society.

Why should we practice non-injury? Some times this vexing question comes to our mind. Two answers have been given by the great saints and sages of all times. Because we are all the children of the almighty, we are very closely related to each other like the blood relation in the world. This answer is from the point of view of devotion. The other answer which the rational saints and sages or jnana yogis have given to us is this that the soul of all is one and undivided. My own self is appearing before me in different forms and name, therefore hurting others will be hurting my own self. May be I am not realizing it now but in the long run I shall be forced to understand that injuring others was injuring myself.

This leads us to the conclusion that for our own sake we must practice non-injury. Practice of non-injury itself will nourish love in our heart and we know that LOVE is the thing we love most.

Greedlessness

One of the greatest enemies of moral character which ruins and completely destroys the human character is greed. A man consumed with greed shall succumb to the slightest temptation and compromises with truth unhesitatingly. A greedy man never hesitates to injure others to achieve his selfish end without caring for the lofty moral virtues of non-injury. Greed and selfishness are warp and woof of immorality. If one doesn't care to save himself from any of these enemies of moral life, he falls victim to immorality without fail. Therefore to build our character and practice morality in our life, we must very carefully guard ourselves against these two enemies, selfishness and greed. The history of the world is full of examples of notorious barons and robbers who've bathed the earth with human blood because greed and selfishness overpowered their inner self and killed their conscience. Greed knows no satisfaction. The greatest drawback of a greedy person is that his mind never allows him to see what he has. Greed makes him blind towards all his possessions and wealth and always goads towards the things the greedy man does not have. This makes him always restlessly active to achieve more and more useless things knowing not what for. Unfortunately in the last decade of the 20th century our country also exhibited the shameful, notorious examples of such persons who have been possessed and consumed by selfishness and greed.

Purity

The Vedanta says the real nature of man is divine, absolutely pure. Purity is our very nature that is why every one of us hates impurity. None wants to live in a dirty and impure place. Every one of us according to our evolution growth and capacity tries to clean or purify the places we live in, the clothes we put on, the things we use and handle. We like purity by nature. Sometimes we come across very dirty persons, doing filthy and dirty works. When they also return to their hearth and home they clean themselves and want to be more clean and pure than what they were at their jobs. Even the dirty person would not like to sit or live in a place, which is dirtier than himself. Although all these examples look like trifle and insignificant but they point out towards the fact that purity is inherent in man. Man likes purity and wants to be pure.

Though the word purity appears to be very simple, when we probe deep into its meaning and purport, we find that it has very deep meaning. Purity is a life-transforming element in the human personality.

Let us remember that purity is not only external cleanliness, it means internal cleanliness also. A man may be very clean outside but may be absolutely impure inside. A very neat and clean well dressed and well mannered man, suppose, is a liar and cheats everybody. Suppose he forges documents and illegally takes the money and property of innocent people. Because of his external cleanliness and neatness can we say that he is a pure person? Everybody, I think will agree with me that he is certainly not a pure person. Purity and honesty go together. Howsoever clean he may be externally, if not honest a person can never be pure. Chastity, honesty and truth are the essential characteristics of purity. Unless one practices purity in one's life, one can never become a man of character and a man without character can never give meaning to life.

Purity is power A pure man will always be fearless. Sincerity will be in his very blood. A pure man will never be insincere. Purity is the very base of spiritual life and we all know that it is spirituality, which gives worthwhile meaning to human life. All of us know about Swamiji Vivekananda. His premonastic name was Narendra Nath Data. Before becoming a monk when he was a college student his father suddenly died and great economic and family difficulties ensued. At this juncture of his life when he was in great difficulties a rich young woman offered her great wealth if Naren would accept her. But Narendra Nath rejected it like pinch of ashes. Similarly when he was in America after having become a monk, the daughter of a multi-milionaire offered herself to Swamiji with her wealth. Swamiji calmly said, 'You see I'm a monk and I have nothing to do with it'.

We all know about Tirthankar Mahavira, Bhagwan Buddha, Shankaracharya, Samarth Ramdas and saints and sages of our country who were shining examples of purity incarnate. No gold could purchase them, no flesh could tempt them, no power could frighten them. Because they were pure to the marrow of their bone.

Thus we see purity is real power.

Acknowledgement

For this paper, permission has been taken from the Editor, *Tatwa*, vol. 1, no. 2, Shegaon, Maharastra, India, April-June 2001.

Chapter 4

Indian Ethics and the Spirit of Development: The VEDA Model of Leadership and Management

Subhash Sharma

Many of our ancient books display a uniqueness of futuristic looks and timeless ideas. They are *sanatana* or eternal in their approach. They form a basis for articulating a vision for social and management theory as reflected by an emphasis on the eternal human values. Though the nature of political system, production system and al forms has undergone a change and innovations in technology have affected our life-styles, however, the human yearning for idealized values has not in any manner diminished. This is indicated by the emphasis on revival of human values. With the flow of time, many isms have come and gone. In future also new isms would arise and go, but the *sanatana* or the eternal aspect of human values would continue to inspire the humanity and its institutions. Indeed during each era of social upheaval, a great need has been felt for revival of human values. This upheaval-revival dynamic or the dialectic is captured by the famous *sloka* from Gita viz. *Yada yada hi dharmasya* ... which indicates that whenever there is erosion of human values or the *adharma* takes over, there is a need to re-establish the human values. It is in this context that a new model of development as well as leadership and management is required to guide us to take up the challenges of the new millennium.

Two Sides of Life: The Essence of the Indian Model

Indian thought favours a holistic view of life, a balanced approach to the material and spiritual development of individuals and society. In today's context, it implies combining the spiritual heritage with scientific advances. In the holistic model of development, the spiritual side of life is also represented by the yin and the material or the materialistic side by yang. The holistic model strives to achieve a balance between the two. Thus, it is based on the complementary principle or the harmony of opposites. The concept of the 'dialectical harmony' has its origin in Eastern thought and is best represented by the yin-yang concept of the Chinese and the *Ardhnareshwar / Shiva-Shakti* in the Indian thought. Hegel's thesis, anti-thesis and synthesis concept also bears interesting similarities with this idea. In the holistic model of development, the emphasis is on dialectical harmony of the spiritual and material side of life. Management concepts and theories as derivatives of this model imply that both sides of life should be combined in such a manner that it leads to holistic happiness while operating in a competitive situation. This is the essence of the Indian model of development.

The Indian model of holistic development has also been metaphorically described as the two wings of a bird – one representing the material side and the other the spiritual side. Both wings are needed to fly. Thus, development implies a balanced approach to life and progress. If there is only one – sided materialistic development, it leads to several social problems, as the Western experience indicates. Similarly if there is an emphasis only on spirituality there would be no material progress. Hence, the 'spirit of development' demands that for the progress of life in the 'material' and the 'spiritual' world, a balanced approach is needed.

Indian Ethics and the Spirit of Development: Foundations of the Indian Model

Indian Ethics also referred to as Indian ethos is at the heart of the Indian model of development. It is in sharp contrast to the Western model of 'Protestant Ethics and Spirit of Capitalism', that is rooted in extreme individualism and has resulted in the emergence of mal-developed societies. Hence, the need for correction. The Indian ethics model with its emphasis on holistic development provides us a new model for the future development of human society, in which 'spirit of capital' or the *artha* dimension of life is not negated but is driven by *dharma* or ethics. Thus, '*dharma* driven *artha*' or the 'spiritually guided materialism' represents a balanced approach to development. While Western ethos are rooted in individualism or the primacy of self-interest, Eastern ethos favour *loksangraha* or the primacy of collective interest and altruism. What is required is a balance between the two.

The intellectual foundations of the Indian model could be traced to three fundamental 'theories' from Indian scriptures viz. The *panchkoshas* theory, the *purushartha* theory and the theory of *gunas*. The essential aspects of the three are presented below. By combining the three theories we can arrive at the foundational basis of the Indian model.

The *panchkoshas* theory provides a framework for holistic self-development. It identifies five levels of self-development viz. the physical, psychological, mentological, intellectual and the spiritual consistent with the *annamaya, pranamaya, manomaya, vijanmaya* and *anandamaya koshas*. It provides foundations for the idea of '*Panchmukhi vikas*' or the fivefold holistic development 'Physical, Practical, Aesthetic, Moral and Intellectual' at the individual level.[1]

The theory of *purusharthas* takes a holistic perspective on balancing the four 'objects of life' viz., the *dharma, artha, kama* and *moksha* or the ethical, material, sensual and spiritual dimensions. This theory suggests a balanced approach for the holistic development at the individual level as well as that of society.

The theory of *gunas* identifies three *gunas* viz., the *tamasik, rajasik* and the *sattvik* as three aspects of nature. *Tamasik* is indicative of the selfish and self-interest, *rajasik* connotes the enlightened self-interest and *sattvik* connotes the enlightened collective interest. This theory is applicable at the individual and society levels and has also been applied at the corporate level. This theory also provides a framework for transformation of work culture in organizations from *tamasik* to *sattvik* with a view to improve the quality of work-life.

By combining the three theories we get a general theory of development, wherein individual, society and organizations are driven by eternal human values and a balanced approach is taken towards material and spiritual development of individuals and society.

Figure 4.1 provides the framework of the general theory of holistic development.

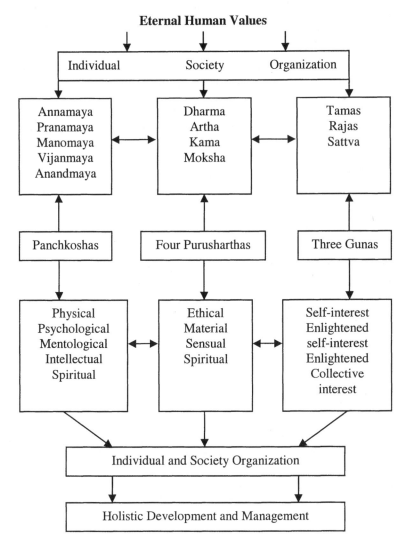

Figure 4.1 Foundations of an Indian Model

It may be indicated that there have been several scholarly efforts to formulate conceptual frameworks drawn from Indian ethics for application in management and administration particularly in the corporate context. In fact, need to move beyond American and Japanese models has been felt strongly (Gupta, 1991).[2] During the recent years these efforts have gathered momentum and it has been realized that Indian concepts though developed for the individual and social development are also useful for corporate management. Swami Ranganathananda (1982) provided a lead in showing the relevance of Indian thought to corporate management.[3] M.B. Athreya (1995) drawing upon *darsanas* provides us a conceptual model for National Human Resource Management.[4] S.K. Chakraborty's (1987, 1993, 1998) pioneering work in applying Indian ethos in corporate context through his frameworks of 'Managerial Effectiveness and Quality of Work-life' and 'Managerial Transformation by Values', is widely known.[5] Swami Someshwarananda (1996) provides many interesting insights from Indian Ethos Management and applies them in corporate context.[6] Subhash Sharma (1996, 1999) provides several workable models rooted in Indian ideas.[7]

A number of Indian models of leadership have also been developed during recent years. These include Nurturant Task Leadership Model (Sinha, 1980),[8] Maternalistic Model of Leadership (Rao, 1990),[9] Transcendental Leadership (Bodhananda, 1994),[10] Four Steps Model of Enlightened Leadership (Sharma, 1995),[11] Theory K Model of Enlightened Leadership (Sharma, 1998),[12] Mother Leadership (Banerjee, 1998),[13] and Wisdom Leadership (Chakraborty, 1999),[14] etc.

The VEDA Model: The Essence of Leadership and Management

For translating the idea of 'Indian Ethics and the Spirit of Development' in practical context, a supporting model is required. This model is presented here as the VEDA model of leadership and management. In this model we identify the following four aspects of leadership:

V : Vision
E : Enlightenment
D : Devotion
A : Action

It is interesting to note that the academic literature on Transformational Leadership is coming closer to the above – presented model of leadership.

Our model has many interesting insights to offer. VEDA is at the heart of the Indian model articulated through the expression, 'Indian ethics and the Spirit of Development'. Further, it also reveals the convergence of the four *margas* viz. *raj-yoga*, *gyan yoga*, *bhakti yoga* and *karma yoga*. The parallels are given in the box below:

The Veda Model	
V : Vision	*Raj-yoga*
E : Enlightenment	*Gyan yoga*
D : Devotion	*Bhakti yoga*
A : Action	*Karma yoga*

Thus, all the four *margas* viz. *raj-yoga, gyan yoga, bhakti yoga* and *karma yoga* are revealed through the individual letters V, E, D, A. In a way this de-coding or 'discovery' is interesting because essence of Vedas in the form of four *margas* to self-realization, is reflected in the very expression VEDA. While the four *margas* were evolved for traversing the path of self-realization, they also lead to the emergence of several spiritual centres rooted in one or the other path. Thus, '*bhakti-vedanta*' emerged as a strong movement because *vedanta* was articulated through the *bhakti* route, which has a popular appeal. One reason for the emergence and spread of 'American Hinduism' as a 'modern religion', is its rootedness in the *bhakti-vedanta. Bhakti vedanta* is in a way a new concept as it brings down the *Vedantic* ideas and ideals within the grasp of the common people in the Post-Modern, Post-Marxist societies. It may be indicated that *bhakti* concept has also found its expression in work ethos. 'Work is worship' is a well-known phrase and perhaps forms the core of the work ethos of many who have excelled in their profession and work. To capture the essence of this idea, Chatterjee (1998) suggests the concept of 'workship' as a key concept to infuse the proper work ethos in ours.[15] Das Gupta (1995) argues for 'Action by Objective'.[16] Enlightened leaders not only believe in karma-yoga but practice it as their 'work-religion' immaterial of whatever be their 'personal religion'. Biographies of many enlightened leaders provide testimony to this observation.

In view of this author, Vivekananda's 'Practical Vedanta' could be best summarized by the VEDA model discussed here because for the success of any enterprise, all the four elements viz. Vision, Enlightenment, Devotion and Action should find convergence.

A discussion on the different paths to self-realization is available in the well-known book, *The Call of the Vedas*, authored by A.C. Bose and published in 1954 by Bhartiya Vidya Bhavan, Bombay. In this work, Sanskrit slokas from Vedas have been classified in terms of path of mysticism and splendour, path of knowledge, path of devotion and path of action. English translations of the Sanskrit slokas are also available. This book is a good source for an understanding of the four paths to self-realization. Our interest is primarily in the managerial context and usefulness of these four paths in enhancing managerial effectiveness.

Managerial effectiveness is linked with the VEDA concept as defined in this paper. Managerial effectiveness is high when Vision, Enlightenment, Devotion and Action are integrated together. This implies that person should reach the level of '*sthithpragyan*', wherein he/she completely controls his/her mind. Whether mind controls the person or person controls the mind, represents the key to managerial effectiveness. A stressful and uncontrollable mind would often lead to wrong decision making. Hence, the need to master the mind. For this *Raj-yoga* is considered the ideal yoga. During the modern times, an organized effort in transmitting the knowledge about *Raj-yoga* has been undertaken by Brahma Kumari Spiritiual University, Mount Abu. Many managers in their individual capacity and many corporates have benefited from the teachings of Brahma Kumaris. Considerable literature exists with respect to tools, techniques and experiences of individuals undertaking a course in this school of *Raj-yoga*. We may call it as 'BK School of *Raj-yoga*'. The practitioners of this school of *Raj-yoga* should accept its fundamental assumptions to make an advancement towards self-realization through soul-consciousness. To accept or not to accept these assumptions is a matter of individual choice.

Models for Corporate Management

Having discussed the broad perspectives on the Indian model of holistic development, we need to evolve the specific frameworks and models that can help managers in improving the performance of their enterprises in a competitive environment. While the VEDA model discussed above is a model of enlightened leadership, there is a need for development of such new models rooted in the philosophy of 'Indian Ethics and the Spirit of Development' and relevant for corporate management.

The wheels of modern society are turned by four types of individuals viz. Leaders, Managers, Entrepreneurs and Workers. Leaders provide the vision, managers achieve results and translate vision into reality, entrepreneurs innovate and workers provide the support function. All the four complement each other in achieving the goals of a society or an organization. Thus, there are four roles a society demands from its citizens viz. Leadership, Managership, Entrepreneurship and Workership. This is now well recognized in HRD and OB literature. Indeed these phrases are now being used widely in the academic community and also by practitioners. They also provide a functional classification of the tasks/roles performed in a society. Balakrishnan *et.al.* (1999), provide a discussion on conceptual distinctions between leadership, managership and entrepreneurship in terms of task demands and personal dispositions.[17] An economic enterprise would run effectively if all the four roles viz. leadership, managership, entrepreneurship and workership move in rhythm leading to synergy. However, if the orchestra of the four roles is out of tune with each other, the music produced will have several flaws. Figure 4.2 provides a diagrammatic representation of the wheel model of modern society and corporates.

The above discussed framework provides an understanding about the forward movement of s which is dependent upon the proper synchronization in the four types of roles indicated above. This framework also provides us a foundational premise for developing models of corporate management and good governance.

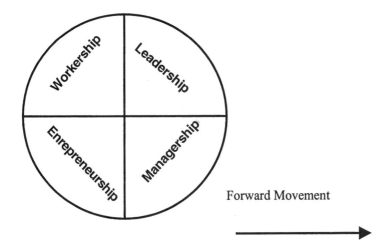

Figure 4.2   Four Pillars of Society and Organizations

New Age Management for Corporate Development

This author has taken a model-building approach to draw upon Indian intellectual heritage. From this approach, author has developed a number of management models that managers have found useful in their day-to-day work to improve the performance of their enterprises. Rooted in Indian ethos, these models blend the Indian and Western concepts in a holistic form. These models represent the conceptual frameworks that have relevance for corporate enterprises. Detailed discussion on these models is available in this author's two books, viz. *Management in New Age: Western Windows Eastern Doors* (1996)[18] and *Quantum Rope: Science, Mysticism and Management* (1999)[19] and other writings. These books attempt to provide systematic, analytical and structured approach to the Indian indigenous knowledge available in tacit form in a variety of sources. Thus, the tacit knowledge has been converted into structured knowledge in the form of management models and 'mantras' that are directly relevant for managing enterprises. Indeed, converting intuitional wisdom or tacit knowledge into structured knowledge in the form of workable models for improving the overall performance of enterprises is the essence of 'New Age Management'.

Examples of 'new age management models' include the OSHA model,[20] the negergy-synergy grid,[21] the 'MBA' (*Manas-Buddhi-Ahankar*) model,[22] a four steps model of enlightened leadership,[23] Total Quality Of Management (TQOM),[24] Omnijective OD,[25] Theory K of leadership and management,[26] CINE Matrix,[27] etc. These models have been tested in the al context and have been found to be useful for corporate development. These models in conjunction with other models developed on the basis of Indian ethos could provide a foundational premise for future development of 'Indian Management' based on the Vision, Enlightenment, Devotion and Action (VEDA) approaches to leadership and management.

With the advent of spirituality-at-work movement, the application of the Indian ethos in corporate context has acquired a new relevance (Kalburgi Srinivas, 1998).[28] It is perhaps because of the realization of the need for spirituality at work place, that Indian concept of 'Transcendental Meditation' and similar other techniques of stress reduction have become part of the 'received knowledge' on corporate management. Indeed, in the future development of management theory and practice, the Indian model of a balance between the spiritual and materialistic achievements, could provide a new foundational premise for a balance between excessive individualism and extreme altruism. With this, the new age management models discussed here would find increasing acceptance in the corporate world. Perhaps it is time for the 'Asian Dharma' to provide the new social vision for the new millennium – a vision of sacro-civic society (Sharma, 1999, 2001)[29&30] based on 'spiritualization of modernity (Pathak, 1998).[31] The four paths of VEDA viz. Vision, Enlightenment, Devotion and Action are at the heart of this new vision.

Notes

1   The concept of 'Panchmukhi Vikas' has been developed by Banasthali Vidyapith. For details, see Institutional Profile of WISDOM (Women's Institute for Studies in Development Oriented Management), Banasthali.

2   Rajen K. Gupta, (1991) 'Employees and in India: Need to move beyond American and Japanese models', *Economic and Political Weekly*, pp.M68-M76.

3   Swami Ranganathananda, (1982) *Human Values in Management*, Punjab National Bank, New Delhi.

4   M.B. Athreya, (1995) 'Ancient Wisdom for National Human Resource Management', in *Ancient Indian Wisdom for Self Development*, Ahmedabad: Ahmedabad Management Association, pp.55-75.

5   See books by S.K. Chakraborty, *Managerial Effectiveness and Quality of Work Life*, New Delhi: Tata McGraw Hill, 1987; *Managerial Transformation by Values: A Corporate Pilgrimage*, New Delhi: Sage Publications India Pvt. Ltd., 1993; *Values and Ethics for s*, New Delhi: Oxford University Press, 1998.

6   Swami Someswarananda, (1996) *Indian Wisdom for Management*, Ahmedabad Management Association, Ahmedabad.

7   See books by Subhash Sharma, *Management in New Age: Western Windows Eastern Doors*, New Age International Publishers, New Delhi, 1996; and *Quantum Rope: Science, Mysticism and Management*, New Age International Publishers, New Delhi, 1999.

8   Jai B.P. Sinha, (1980) *The Nurturant Task Leader*, Concept, New Delhi.

9   G.P. Rao, (1990) 'Work Ethics, Work-Ethic and Indian Psycho-Philosophy: Some Ideas on a Maternalistic Model' in S.K. Chakraborty (ed.) *Human Response Development: Exploring Transformational Values*, Wiley Eastern Limited, New Delhi, pp.110-118.

10   Swami Bodhananda, (1994) *Gita and Management*, Sambodh Foundation, New Delhi.

11   Subhash Sharma, (1995) 'Towards Enlightened Leadership: A Framework of Leadership and Management, in *Evolving Performing s Through People: A Global Agenda*, K.B. Akhilesh, et. al., New Age International Publishers, New Delhi, pp.209-214.

12   Subhash Sharma, (1998) 'Enlightened Leadership in Indian Ethos: The way of the Theory K', *Management and Change*, vol. 2(1), 93-104.

13   R.P. Banerjee, (1998) *Mother Leadership*, Wheeler Publishing, Allahabad.

14   S.K. Chakraborty, (1999) *Wisdom Leadership: Dialogues and Reflections*, Wheelers Publishing, New Delhi.

15   Debashish Chatterjee, (1998) *Leading Consciously: A Pilgrimage Towards Self Mastery*, Viva Books Pvt. Ltd., New Delhi.

16   Ananda Das Gupta, (1995) 'Economic Management and Ethics: The Vedantic Answer', *Indian Journal of Public Administration*, vol. 41(3), 1-9.

17   Suresh Balakrishnan, N. Gopakumar and Rabindra N Kanungo, (1999) Entrepreneurship Development: Concept and Context, in *Management and Cultural Values: The Indigenization of s in Asia*, (eds) Henry S.R. Kao, Durganand Sinha, Bernhard Wilpert, Sage Publications, New Delhi.

18   Subhash Sharma, *Management in New Age: Western Windows Eastern Doors* (No.7 above).

19   Subhash Sharma, *Quantum Rope: Science, Mysticism and Management* (No.7 above).

20   Subhash Sharma, (1995) 'OSHA Model for Relationship Management', *Abhigyan*, Spring, pp.29-40.

21   Subhash Sharma, *Management in New Age: Western Windows Eastern Doors* (No.7 above).

22   Ibid.

23   Subhash Sharma, 'Towards Enlightened Leadership: A Framework of Leadership and Management' (No.11 above).

24   Subhash Sharma, (1996) 'Total Quality Of Management (TQOM): An Endological Basis for Human Values in Corporate Management', *Abhigyan*, Summer, 35-39.

25   Subhash Sharma, (1997) 'Towards an Omnijective Theory for New Organizational Development', *Chinmaya Management Review*, 1(1), 12-18.

26   Subhash Sharma, 'Enlightened Leadership in Indian Ethos: The way of the Theory K' (No.12 above).

27   For discussion on CINE Matrix, see Subhash Sharma, *Quantum Rope: Science, Mysticism and Management* (No.7 above), pp.109-114.

28   Kalburgi Srinivas, (1998) 'Spirituality-at-Work in the Land of Dollar God', *Journal of Human Values*, Jan-June, 4(1), 45-64.

29   Subhash Sharma, (1999) 'Corporate Gita: Lessons for Management, Administration and Leadership', *Journal of Human Values*, vol. 5(2), 103-123.

30   Subhash Sharma, (2001) 'Routes to Reality: Scientific and Rishi Approaches', *Journal of Human Values*, vol. 7(1), 75-83.

31   Avijit Pathak, (1998) *Indian Modernity: Contradictions, Paradoxes and Possibilities*, Gyan Publishing House, New Delhi, pp.225-229.

Chapter 5

Ethical Perceptions of Managers in Six Asian Countries: Journey from Tradition to a Pan-Asian Managerial Frame

Samir R. Chatterjee

Introduction

The ethical frontiers of corporate functioning have been challenged significantly in recent years with the rise of international business, technological innovations and a global concern for protecting ecological sustainability. The basis of generally espoused ethical approaches underpin the moral responsibility of individuals within the context of social institutions like business organizations (Best, 1997; Donaldson and Dunphy, 1999; Hood, 1998; Sirgy 2002). Some of these moral understandings transcend the cultural boundaries while others are specific to the societal contexts. The emergence of Asia as a powerhouse of global dominance has introduced the subject of ethical performance as a major challenge in many countries. Interestingly, the emergence of the Asia-Pacific region as a significant economic force in the current decade has prompted interest in the Eastern roots of ethics and values (Jackson, 2000; Phatak and Habib, 1998). This exploration has primarily been focused around the ideas of Confucianism during the well-known East Asian miracle of the eighties. Confucianism is essentially a model of social order placing great emphasis on such values as duty, family orientation, thrift, and network loyalty. In addition to the Confucian values, Asia has been enriched by an osmosis of Hindu, Buddhist, Islamic and other sources of ethical guidelines (Enderle, 1997). A stronger contribution of scholars from India is needed in providing a boost to his pan-Asian development.

Ethical beliefs and behaviour in the Asian business arena have been primarily shaped by philosophical and religious roots, and they have nourished various social institutions and customs. But the contemporary societal transformation of values generated by this new imperative of globalism has presented unprecedented dilemmas. In fact, a number of leading publications profoundly illustrate wide regional variations in ethical standards. For example, the annual Corruption Perception Index, published by Transparency International 2002, highlights there is a wide variation in the ethical rankings across the Asian countries. Indeed, the Corruption Perception Index (CPI) for 102 countries surveyed in 2002, ranks Japan 20, Malaysia 33, China 59, Thailand 64 and India 71 which are relatively high scores in these countries indicating the degree of perceived corruption. Paradoxically, another survey measuring 'Countries using other unfair means to gain or retain business' places Asian countries in a much ethical strength compared to strong Western economies like USA and France. A third measure called Bribe Payers Index (BPI) shows Malaysia and Japan as countries with a strong bribe culture (*Transparency International, 2002*). These considerable variations in Asian countries, which are undergoing a diversity of economic and social achievements, invite examination for better understanding ethical cultures and moral sensitivities in the international business arena.

The study presented in this paper aims to go beyond the generally held ideas about business ethics in Asia by:

- Exploring the variations of ethical intensity along global, societal, organizational and individual levels.
- Identifying the divergent perceptions on ethics across demography and occupational levels.
- Suggesting reasons for ethical convergences and divergences across these countries.
- Recommending frameworks of global managers in dealing with ethical issues in Asia.

The longstanding traditional practices Asia are being challenged with the intensification of the global linkages. In spite of the unmistakable trend towards a converging market culture, the ethical culture will obviously remain considerably divergent. Conceptualization and research in the area of Asian business ethics therefore, will need to be polycentric in scope (Stajkovic and Luthans, 1997; Lasserre and Schutte, 1999).

Business Ethics in the Asian Context

An impressive economic growth and transformation during the 1990s in many East Asian countries attracted worldwide attention and many credited the region's success to the 'Asian values' (Lasserre and Schutte, 1999; Hampden-Turner and Trompennars, 1997). These values had a distinctive difference from the Western values. Indeed, they placed a higher priority on social order than individual freedom, as well as family and social networks being more emphasized than individual goal achievements. In fact, most Asian countries are high on power distance, collectivism, masculinity, long-term orientation, but low on uncertainty avoidance. In contrast, most Western countries are low on power distance, collectivism, masculinity, long-term orientation, but high on uncertainty avoidance. Consequently, '…Western values may place too much emphasis on freedom and the pursuit of individual material wealth, often at the expense of sustaining social principles. More importantly, Asian values are still relevant in today's societies, as they contain certain principles that are both positive and universal. However, Asian values do not contain all the necessary components required by the dynamic changes taking place today, especially the existence of a system that guarantees transparency and fairness (Kotler Kartajaya, Hooi and Liu , 2003, p.182).

Managerial efforts in understanding and responding to contemporary challenges in Asia goes beyond mastering cultures and practices. This requires not only investment in terms of comprehensive cultural and social knowledge, but also the trends and transitions that characterize the dynamics of this knowledge. One of the areas attracting considerable managerial attention in Asia is the development of ethics and trust as the central platform of managerial approaches. Historically, the Confucian, Islamic and Hindu religious traditions have inspired some of the key tenets of Asian ethical base in contrast to the Greco-Roman philosophical roots of contemporary Western ethical roots. Consequently, the personal, organizational and institutional values and priorities of Asian entities are deeply embedded to the national cultures. In recent years, ethical lapses have been the most significant area of concern for not only the managers in Asia, but also leading multinational corporations working in Asia. For instance, well-known corporations like Disney, Mattel, Nike, Levis, Adidas have all had major weaknesses in developing long-term philosophical understanding needed to operate in Asia.

The complexities of these misunderstandings are highlighted by the ethical lapses of various degrees from child labour, use of prison workers to corruption, environmental damage. For example, in spite of promoting a clean image, in 1995 the Singapore legal-technical and managerial cultural allowed one of the world's most spectacular ethical disasters. This was evidenced when a $21.6 billion fraud caused the collapse of Britain's oldest merchant bank, Barings. The examples of Nick Lesson of Barings and Hamanaka of Sumitomo Corporation demonstrate the transnational character of the seriousness of ethical depth of demands that can be created by technology. These high profile ethical distortions of large corporations are no different from many unreported violations of Small and Medium Enterprises (SME) or other such organizations. Without ethics being integrated as the key theme of Asian management, a deeper level of understanding is likely to evolve.

Indian ethos may be of relevance in the search for a pan-Asian model of ethics. The classical Indian message of 'basudeva kutumbakam', universal brotherhood and the Buddhist term 'Zhen shan mei' meaning the worthy goal in life is to seek truth, grace and justice can serve as the basis of ethical principles in the Asian region. The Confucian ethical ideals and the Indian ethos are not mutually exclusive rather hold complement each other in arriving at a moral foundation for Asian business and act as anchors for institution building. The proposed paper argues that many of the traditional indigenous values of India can effectively be utilized for secular purposes of a strong foundation to the contemporary Asian challenges of business ethics.

A leading Indian Scholar passionately argues: 'Besides the indigenous vedantic, Buddhist, Jain and Sikh traditions, Indian culture has absorbed numerous enriching strands from Islamic, Christian, and Parsi traditions ... it is more important to understand and accept that there is indeed one Indian ethos at the level of the vedantic "deep structure"' (Chakraborty, 1996, p.4). It is this deep structure that had defined the common set of ideals actively practiced and subscribed by a greater part of humanity; contained in the geographical landmass of India.

The distinctive strength of the Indian tradition has been the exploration of the inner world of human self called *atman* while the western focus has been on the external world of matter and energy. The *Upanishadic* mantra has been to enrich individual, organization and society with *poornatwa* or the fullness of holism. *'Tamosa ma jyotirgamaya'* and *'asato ma sat gamaya'* meaning let the inner-light be filled by truth, purity and morality and let it guide everyone to holism. This concept is much deeper than the western view of actualization. Poorna self is independent of externalities and relies entirely on the empowerment of the inner self. As Gupta observes 'India has seen always in man the individual a soul, a portion of the Divinity enwrapped in mind and body, a conscious manifestation in Nature of the Universal Self and spirit. Always She has distinguished and cultivated in him a mental, an intellectual, an ethical, dynamic and practical, aesthetic and hedonistic, a vital and physical being, but all these have been seen as powers of the soul that manifests through them and grows with their growth' (Gupta, 1996, p.10).

> Indian socio-economic and cultural tradition transmits its economic ideals into life with a message for the entire human race. The broad and generous outlook that it inherited from its birth time has enabled it to grow and flourish with rigour for centuries with age-old experiments and experiences of the ancient Sages and Seers. The inner thread that holds and connects one another, must remain in the garland of culture with all the essential qualities. The remarkable qualities that indicate one's culture are the compassion, the sympathy, the will for welfare, the forgiveness, and above all the sense of fraternity for others. Artha (wealth) is in the traditions of India. Artha, an economic value (material in nature) is only helpful as a means for satisfying one or other of the diverse needs and desires of life. Their satisfaction is Kama (pleasure) which is not only physical but also psychological in that it satisfies the natural impulses and cravings of a person. Economy or wealth which is called Artha in Indian terminology is considered as a preparatory need for attaining the ultimate goal of life as ascertained by the ancient Indian seers. Money is valuable only to the extent it serves as a means to acquire goods. It is not desired for its own sake except, perhaps, by a miser. Artha thus is an instrumental value as it acts only as a means to the realization of pleasure (Kama) which is an intrinsic value, for, it is desired for its own sake (Biswas 1998, p.1064).

Ethical Perceptions and Economic Transition: Dissonance Model

Global and local pressures associated with the economic transformation are challenging the levels of ethics in Asian societies in an unprecedented way. The degree of privatization and globalization have seen far-reaching attitudinal changes in these countries. While socio-economic nuances underpin the mindset patterns of managers, the global imperatives have also strongly influencing the work related values and belief systems. The ethical model espoused for this study is presented as Figure 5.1. The dual pressures creating the ethical dissonance are arranged in two dimensions, 1) *Acceptance of Global Values*, and 2) *Strength of Cultural Tradition*. These two axes create four typologies for clarifying the basis of the empirical investigation. The individual level 'A' of this dissonance model, the pressures of globality and locality are only present in an implicit way. At this level, individuals have a large scope of implementational responsibility. Level 'B' of the model shows societal values dominate, thereby creating significant dissonance where such values are parried against global pressures. Level 'C' elucidates the globality domain. This is very similar to the concept of 'hypernorm' espoused by Donaldson and Dunfee (1999). The most important area of the model, however, is level 'D' where the forces of context relevant traditional cultural values come in direct opposition to the forces of globality. The distinctly different parameters by which managers respond to the various levels of ethical intensity become more explicit as societies move away from traditional anchor and embark on large-scale reform or transition (Griffith and Maye, 1997; Chatterjee, 1998; Fulop, Hisrich and Szegedi, 2000).

The four domains of ethical dissonance highlighted in the model presented (e.g., global, societal, organizational and individual are particularly relevant in examining the changing perceptions of managers during economic reform and transition. An example of the global ethics (Level 'D' in the model) may be how an individual manager would view dumping the company's toxic waste products into another country where due to legislative and social weaknesses this may be allowed for a fraction of the cost. To illustrate the socially determined ethics (Level 'B'), the practice of guanxi in China may be a case in point. The dissonance created by this strong societal expectation has been widely discussed in literature (Loverr, Simmons and Kali, 1999). Cross-national alliance, for example, is an area where all four levels of ethical domains may be experienced (Chatterjee, 1999).

Figure 5.1   **Ethical Dissonance in the Asian Context**

Purpose of the Study

The purpose of this study is to understand the changing managerial perceptions of ethics in Asia. Three major Asian countries (India, China and Japan) and three smaller Asian countries (Malaysia, Thailand and Brunei) have been selected for study specially to provide a representative sample of the diversity characterizing Asia.

This study aims to explore the level of dissonance experienced by the managers in these countries as global linkages create multiple layers of ethical demand in their work roles. In the aftermath of the Asian financial crisis, brought about largely by the ethical lapses, it is relevant to explore the converging and diverging aspects of ethical perceptions of managers in these countries. Generalizations based on globally accepted norms or locally dominant values are fraught with danger. This paper aims to examine the demographic group differences in the ethical perceptions around four key segments. The theoretical model presented for this paper clarifies the rationale of the empirical investigation.

Empirical evidence over the past decade has indicated variations in ethical perceptions amongst organizational members (Gatewood and Carrol, 1991; Robertson, 1993). Organizational demography which is highlighted by institutional variables such as age, gender, educational level and position are obviously more relevant in explaining the impact of economic transformation in Asian countries. Recent research examining the demographic correlates of ethical perceptions among Indian managers led the authors to conclude, 'As the demographic composition of the workforce changes, such differences will command greater attention of human resource managers and consultants. On the other hand, such demographic differences seem to exist in other countries also. Programs designed to generate ethical climates in international contexts should be aware of, and take into account, these differences' (Viswesvaran and Deshpande, 1998, p.29). The salience of demographic variables in the Asian context cannot be over emphasized. This is because of the changing economic and social infrastructure for managers.

Methodology

Sample and Setting

Data were obtained from 1446 indigenous managers in six Asian countries. The number of respondents in each country is shown in Table 5.1. All managers completed a questionnaire which was administered by the authors to a relatively small number of the respondents, who in turn administered the questionnaire to a larger number of manager colleagues. This procedure attracted a meaningful array of respondents from Asian communities where a mail out system is unlikely to accommodate contextual challenges such as a low exposure to intricate questionnaires in Asian workplaces or the reluctance to complete forms to disclose information about others. Indeed, several of the managers of this study reported this was the first time they had completed a questionnaire of this type.

The managers were employed in a diversity of organizations. In addition to attracting responses from government and non-government organizations data were also obtained from institutions that varied in size from large corporations to small family firms. Moreover, data were drawn from a diversity of business sector types that included financial institutions, health and medical companies, science groups, education and engineering bodies, mining and technology corporations as well as a range of small service enterprises. As the profile of the organizations varied across countries it was considered less than meaningful to assess data across these organizational properties.

Procedure

The importance of networking in Asian contexts underpinned the study design strategy. Co-operative linkages proliferate in all societies (e.g., Japan, *keiretsus;* Korea, *chaebols*), and one of the most widely employed organizing frameworks in Asian communities is the Chinese *guanxi* (pronounced gwan-see). The guanxi (a deep rooted socio-cultural phenomenon), which enhances social harmony, maintains correct relationships and addresses the sensitive issue of face, is a reciprocal obligation to respond to requests for assistance. The authors employed their *guanxi*, which had been acquired during an extended period of conducting educational programs and academic based relationships in the region, to obtain data, and later, additional information to enrich the survey findings. Specifically, the authors held a lower hierarchical level in the relationship while the respondents (higher level) were, by feudal tradition, obliged to contribute more to the connection. Hence, to accommodate the issue of poor response rates a mail out method was not employed, but instead a number of inaugural respondent managers became administrators of the questionnaire to colleague managers.

In addition to optimizing data collection this personalized system also reconciled recognized impediments to cross-cultural management research. For instance, costs and time were reduced. A further reported methodological challenge is the reluctance by Asian citizens, and particularly the Chinese (who may have memory of the era of the Red Guards), to disclose information about others. Consequently, it is unusual for Asian workers to complete complex questionnaires, yet by employing a collaborative study design trust relationships were developed and substantial responses were obtained as demonstrated by the amount of data collected. Moreover, the issue of equivalency of meaning of questionnaire items was addressed. Involving committed managers to identify threats to interpretations was more comprehensive that the normal mechanical translation – back translation procedure. For example, certain English words have yet to become a common part of the developing Thai language, or the English nomenclature did not have a perfect correspondence in the very rich languages of the Chinese and Japanese extant societies. By involving interested members of these communities, suitable substitute symbols and characters were derived. Finally, and arguably, an enriched understanding of the findings was obtained by employing collaborative focus groups. This system embellishes the North American positivist approach which emphasizes rigorous quantitative methods that focus on precision of measurement, as well as reliability and validity. These traditional behavioural science guidelines were melded with relevant socio-cultural priorities with a plurist research methodology.

Measurement

Consensus or divergence in decision-making, in terms of ethical business perspectives, was assessed with an 18 item, seven point Likert scale. Each item was a mini vignette (of one or two lines) that was designed by the author in a three-stage process. First, the literature was examined to determine what scales were available to evaluated ethical decision making in the four dimensions (global, societal, organizational and individual) of interest. The second stage was in two parts when, after establishing a total number of 24 items they were reduced in number by a two step pilot study. The first step was undertaken when a small focus group of expatriate Indian managers were invited to examine the 24 items and provide feedback on their appropriateness. The second step of this endeavour was extended to another small group of academics at an Indian university, before administering these 24 items to a sample of Indian managers. Collaborative procedures were used to complete the third stage of scale determination. The collective responses provided by the focus groups, together with the data of the survey (Chatterjee and Pearson, 2001) led to the deletion of six items.

Data reported in this study are for 18 items. These items provide aggregated means for four levels of ethical decision making. A higher score represents a more ethical orientation in terms of moral principles or values that determine whether actions are more right than wrong, and outcomes are good rather than bad. This orientation is aligned with the Western conventions of utilitarianism, individual rights, and distributive justice. A total of four items contributed to the global dimension. An example of a global item was, *The national and cultural context influences the moral and ethical standards of managerial work*. Also, four items were used to assess an average score for the societal dimension. One of these items was, *It is easier for managers to operate in a social environment where legal codes and conventions are well entrenched in institutions and business practices*. A further four items were employed to obtain an average score of the organizational dimension of ethical decision making. Such an item was, *In times of strategic or technological change or downturn, organizational profitability is more important than maintaining psychological contracts of organizational loyalty*. Assessment of the mean score for the personal dimension was from six items. One of the items was, *Managerial ethical values are more likely to be bound with their religious and personal values rather than regulations and influences from their business environment*.

Analysis

Data were evaluated by quantitative and qualitative procedures. Questionnaire responses were assessed with traditional frequency distribution procedures, analysis of variance and comparison of means tests. To accommodate the contextual challenges of cross-cultural management research focus groups were employed in each country to better understand the findings. These focus groups consisted of small groups of managers who were invited to provide commentary about the meanings of the findings. Arguably, this idiographic design provides both rigor as well as addressing well-documented obstacles to comparative management research.

Results

Table 5.1 shows the profile of the study respondents. It is evident the sample of the six countries are not equivalent, particularly in terms of gender. Indeed, the low proportion of female respondents in both the Indian and Japanese samples were unexpected despite literature which reveals in the Asian workplace women have often been discriminated, strategically. A salient finding of Table 5.1 is the importance of education. In all samples, and particularly in the Indian and Thailand samples, an exceptionally high proportion of the study managers held higher education qualifications (degree, post graduate, and PhD). Although endeavours were made to obtain a balanced representation of managerial levels, a prominent detail of the Indian sample is the high proportion of executive managers, which contrasts with the large percentage of supervisory Thailand managers. The distinctiveness of the study population is also revealed across age categories where the Japanese sample was the oldest, while the Chinese and Thailand samples were among the youngest. A summary of the particulars of the key examined demographic variables is displayed as Table 5.1 which illustrates the emerging role of working managerial women in a cross section of Asian organizations.

Table 5.1   Demographics of Six Asian Countries

	India (N = 421)	China (N = 416)	Japan (N = 195)	Malaysia (N = 143)	Thailand (N = 156)	Brunei (N = 115)
GENDER						
Females	6.9	43.0	5.6	32.9	71.8	26.1
Males	93.1	57.0	94.4	67.1	28.2	73.9
EDUCATION						
High school	0	13.7	30.2	30.1	6.4	50.4
Trade/Vocational	6.2	18.8	6.7	14.7	12.2	19.2
University	93.8	67.5	63.1	55.2	81.4	30.4
POSITION						
Executive	70.1	18.8	26.1	37.0	14.7	19.1
Middle	25.4	44.7	34.9	35.7	26.3	39.1
Supervisory	4.5	36.5	39.0	27.3	59.0	41.8
AGE GROUPS						
30 years or less	21.9	59.9	9.7	30.0	50.0	13.9
31 to 40 years	33.7	28.6	33.9	44.8	26.3	30.4
41 years and above	44.4	11.5	56.4	25.2	23.7	55.7

Table 5.2 shows means and standard deviations as well as contrast results for the four levels of ethical decision-making across countries. As to be expected there were significant differences between the six study countries for each examined level of ethical decision-making. These results demonstrate a major challenge for conducting business in the global marketplace as moral intensity, ethical sensitivity and situational factors, which are central concepts of ethical behaviour, vary considerably between nations. Nevertheless, a close scrutiny of the date is revealing in terms of the degree of consensus for ethical decision-making. Frequently, the mean scores for the global dimension and the societal dimension are higher that the mean scores for the organizational and personal dimensions. This finding infers there is greater agreement for what is considered to be ethical decision making in the global and societal domains, but managers are less sure what actions to endorse to meet acceptable ethical decision-making and practices in their organizations. Also, the standard deviations of the means present an interesting feature. These data reveal the Japanese managers, whose standard deviations of the means have the lowest score for each assessed dimension, have expressed the most focussed responses.

Table 5.2   Means, Standard Deviations and Contrasts of Ethics Dimensions

Ethical Dimension	India (N = 421)	China (N = 416)	Japan (N = 195)	Malaysia (N = 143)	Thailand (N = 156)	Brunei (N = 115)	Mean contrasts TUKEY
Global	4.79 (0.86)	4.85 (0.90)	4.64 (0.69)	5.11 (0.81)	5.13 (0.80)	4.91 (0.82)	M>C*, J***, I***; T>C**, J**, I***
Societal	4.64 (0.79)	4.95 (0.88)	4.25 (0.64)	4.70 (0.92)	4.33 (0.75)	4.69 (0.76)	B,M<C*; C>J***, I***, T***; M>J***, T***; B>J***, T**; T<I**
Organiz-ational	4.56 (0.81)	4.29 (0.93)	3.92 (0.68)	4.54 (0.90)	3.72 (0.81)	4.47 (0.78)	B>J***; C>J***, I***, T***, T***; I>J***, T***; M>C*, J***, T***
Personal	4.07 (0.86)	4.41 (0.83)	4.06 (0.58)	4.77 (0.77)	4.61 (0.65)	4.52 (0.74)	B>J***, I***; J<C***, T***; M>C**, J***, I***; C>I***

Notes: a. B = Brunei, M = Malaysia, J = Japan, C = China, T = Thailand, and I = India.

b. The values in parentheses are the standard deviations of the means

c. *** $p < 0.001$, ** $p < 0.01$ and * $p < 0.05$

Table 5.3 presents ethical mean scores across the examined demographies. Overall, these data show the greatest consensus for ethical intensity was for the global and societal orientations. However, there were departures for some demographic variables. For instance, the data suggest female managers and more highly formally qualified respondents perceived they were more ethically oriented. The consensus across all managerial levels for the global and societal dimensions is remarkable, and is indeed the values substantially contrast with respondent perceptions for the organizational and personal dimensions. Partitioning of responses across age revealed divergences in ethical orientations were more likely for the organizational and personal dimensions. Table 5.3 reveals education appears to be factor that impinges on global and societal dimensions of ethical practices, but the greatest opportunity for ethical violations is likely to occur in organizational and personal frameworks.

Table 5.3   Means of Ethics Variables across Demographics for Six Countries (N = 1446)

	Global	Societal	Organizational	Personal
Gender				
Male (n = 1038)	4.82 (0.86)	4.62 (0.83)	4.34 (0.88)	4.26 (0.81)
Female (n = 408)	4.98 (0.81)	4.73 (0.85)	4.19 (0.90)	4.50 (0.80)
Education				
Non university (n = 406)	4.69 (0.83)	4.54 (0.89)	4.32 (0.92)	4.42 (0.82)
University (n = 1040)	4.93 (0.84)	4.70 (0.82)	4.29 (0.87)	4.30 (0.81)
Management				
Executive (n = 522)	4.86 (0.83)	4.65 (0.81)	4.43 (0.88)	4.22 (0.82)
Middle (n = 498)	4.86 (0.85)	4.64 (0.85)	4.30 (0.84)	4.35 (0.80)
Supervisory (n = 426)	4.87 (0.86)	4.66 (0.86)	4.13 (0.92)	4.43 (0.82)
Age (years)				
Less than 30 (n = 19)	4.81 (0.90)	4.72 (0.89)	4.15 (0.89)	4.43 (0.80)
31-40 (n = 66)	4.89 (0.83)	4.67 (0.82)	4.27 (0.89)	4.35 (0.80)
41 and above (n = 110)	4.88 (0.81)	4.59 (0.81)	4.42 (0.86)	4.25 (0.83)

Discussion

As Asian management emerges in a distinct area of intellectual and practical attention, no other managerial concern attains more significance than the values and competencies of operating global organizations in ethically divergent contexts. This is particularly relevant as the challenges are deeply rooted in the cultural, social, religious, political and managerial traditions in Asian countries. Navigating these perplexing manoeuvrings cannot be through the development of Asian ethical codes of behaviour. The managerial approaches developed in the West are based on the tenets of an individual's freedom; democratic nuances, universalism of rules and a key focus on strategy. In contrast, attachment to extended family, deference to social interest, thrift, respect for authority and fulfilling traditional obligations are some of the Asian characteristics. In developing a context-relevant perspective, the universalistic principles and practices of the mainstream management ideas need to be explicitly accommodative and responsive to the context relevant imperatives.

With the emergence of Asia as a significant driving force of global business, ethical challenges have become significant issues of concern. However, managerial literature in this area has tended to be more conceptual than empirical. Tensions between cultural traditions and emerging business imperatives have not been explored against changing demographic and occupational trends. The cross-national empirical research base in business ethics is relatively weak in spite of a wider acknowledgement for its need. As Hood has pointed out, 'Practitioners managing TNCs do not, therefore, have a large research database on which to draw from within the international business literature' (Hood, 1998, p.194).

The ethical challenges in Asian business are essentially of polycentric character. Normative decision-making even in respect to converging global issues like human values cannot be taken for granted. Human rights violations in Myanmar may provide an example. 'The hallmark of a polycentric problem are as follows. First, there is no clear single issue to which an affected stakeholder can direct proofs and arguments ... Second, it involves situation with interacting points of influence, so that any decision in favour of a given stakeholder will result in a complex set of repercussions affecting other stakeholders ... Third, Ploycentricity is a matter of degree ... Fourth a large number of stakeholders is not the dispositive element of polycentricity.' (Jackson 2000, pp.133/134).

The shift towards a global ethical benchmark is evident in the presented empirical evidence. The idea that the global and national business systems need clearly spelled out ethical frames were universally endorsed by respondents across countries, gender and other demographic segments. Perhaps this signals the first step towards a clear value frame for the organizational and individual domains. As a recent study by a group of eminent scholars have concluded, '... several Asian countries are now beginning to apply a system of governance and business practices that is cleaner, more transparent and more professional, following the Western model. Following the crisis, collusion and nepotism and seriously adopt principles of public accountability' (Kotler et al., 2003, p.184).

The idea of a managerial culture combining the Western efficiency model with concerns for ecology, equity and ethical integrity may be more compatible to the Asian context than elsewhere. The ideas of 'yin-yang' demonstrate how such divergent concerns can be accommodated to create holistic managerial world view (Snell and Tsang, 2001). A number of Asian management scholars have been emphasizing the limitations of contemporary managerial concepts and practices in not being able to balance and synthesize ethical, environmental and efficiency concerns and develop an economic system that enriches social harmony and sustainability (Sharma, 1996, Hampden-Turner and Trompennars, 1997).

Conclusion

The study presented in this paper does not suggest a set of formulations determining acceptable ethical behaviour across these six countries. Instead, it accepts a much more modest objective of exploring the trends and transitions in Asia in the dualities of global-local interfaces. As Donaldson and Dunfee had suggested, 'International business ethics seldom come in black and white. On the one hand, managers must respect moral free space and cultural diversity. On the other hand, they must reject any form of relativism. Common humanity and market efficiency are part of the equation, but so too is certain amount of moral tension.' (1999, p.62)

A decade has passed since the World Bank coined the phrase, 'The Asian Miracle' that had seen an unprecedented scholarly interest in Asian economies. This euphoria ended with the Asian financial crisis of 1997. As the World Bank again signals the re-emergence of Asia's competitiveness (Yusuf and Evenett, 2002), reverse knowledge based on the tradition roots need to be integrated with the emerging knowledge of the economic transformations and globalism.

Acknowledgement

This paper is based on an international research project in collaboration with Dr. Cecil Pearson, Murdoch University.

References

Best, B. (1997) 'International Business and Ethics: The Role for Ethical Displacement', *Business and the Contemporary World*, IX (1), 209-227.

Biswas, N.B. (1998) 'Economics and Ethics in an Indian Society: A Reflective Analysis', *International Journal of Social Economics*, 25(678), 1064-1072.

Chakraborty, S.K. (1996) *Ethics in Management: Vedantic Perspectives*, Oxford Univ. Press, Delhi.

Chatterjee, S.R. (1998) Convergence and Divergence of Ethical Values across Nations: A Framework for Managerial Action, *Journal of Human Values*, 4 (1), 5-23.

Chatterjee, S. (1999) 'Role of Ethics in International Alliances' in S. Chakraborty and S. Chatterjee (eds) *Applied Ethics in Management: Towards a New Perspective*, Springer-Verlag Publications, Berlin.

Chatterjee, S.R. and Pearson, C.A.L. (2000) 'Indian Managers in Transition: Orientations, Work Goals, Values and Ethics', *Management International Review*, 40(1), 81-95.

Donaldson, T. and Dunfee, T. (1999) 'When Ethics Travel: The Promise and Perils of Global Business Ethics', *California Management Review*, 41(4), 44-63.

Enderle, G. (1997) 'A Worldwide Survey of Business Ethics in the 1990s', *Journal of Business Ethics*, 16, 1475-1485.

Fulop, G., Hisrich, R. and Szegedi, K. (2000) 'Business Ethics and Social Responsibility in Transition Economies', *Journal of Management Development*, 19(1), 5-31.

Gatewood, R.D. and Carrol, A.B. (1991) 'Assessment of Ethical Performance of Organization Members: A Conceptual Framework', *Academy of Management Review*, 16, 667-690.

Griffith, D. and Maye, M. (1997) 'Integrating Ethics into International Marketing Strategy: An Extension of Robin and Reidenbach's Framework', *The International Executive*, 39(6), 745-764.

Gupta, G.P. (1996) *Management by Consciousness: A Spirituo-Technical Approach*, Pondicherry, Sri Aurobindo Society.

Hampden-Turner, C. and Trompennars, F. (1997) *Mastering the Infinite Game: How East Asian Values are Transforming Business Practices*, Capston, Oxford.

Hood, N. (1998) 'Business Ethics and Transnational Companies' in Jones, I. And Pollitt, M. (eds) *The Role of Business Ethics in Economic Performance*, Macmillan Press, London, pp.193-210.

Jackson, K. (2000) 'The Polycentric Character of Business Ethics Decision Making in International Contexts' *Journal of Business Ethics*, 23, 123-143.

Kotler, P., Kartajaya, H., Hooi, D. and Liu, S. (2003) *Rethinking Marketing: Sustainable Marketing Enterprise in Asia*. Prentice Hall, Singapore.

Lasserre, P. and Schutte, H. (1999) *Strategies for Asia Pacific: Beyond the Crisis*. Macmillan Business, London.

Loverr, S., Simmons, L. and Kali, R. (1999) 'Guanxi Versus the Market: Ethics and Efficiency', *Journal of International Business Scholars*, 30(2), 231-247.

Phatak, A. and Habib, M. (1998) 'How Should Managers Treat Ethics in International Business?', *Thunderbird International Business Review*, 40(2), 101-117.

Robertson, D.C. (1993) 'Empiricism in Business Ethics: Suggested Research Directions', *Journal of Business Ethics*, 12, 585-599.

Sharma, S. (1996) *Management in New Age: Western Windows, Eastern Doors*, New Age Publishers, New Delhi.

Sirgy, M.J. (2002) 'Measuring Corporate Performance by Building on the Stakeholders Model of Business Ethics', *Journal of Business Ethics*, 35, 143-162.

Snell, R.S. and Tseng, C.S. (2001) 'Ethical Dilemmas of Relationship Building in China', *Thunderbird International Business Review*, 43(2), 171-200.

Stajkovic, A. and Luthans, F. (1997) 'Business Ethics Across Culture: A Social and Cognitive Model', *Journal of World Business*, 32(1), 17-34.

Transparency International (2002) [Online] http://www.transparency.org/pressreleases_archive /2002/dnld/cpi2002.pressrelease.en.pdf.

Visweswaran, C. and Deshpande, S.P. (1998) 'Do Demographic Correlates of Ethical Perceptions Generalise to Non-American Samples: A Study of Managers in India', *Cross Cultural Management*, 5(1), 23-33.

Yusuf, S. and Evenett, S.J. (2002) *Can East Asia Compete: Innovation for Global Markets*. World Bank and Oxford University Press, Washington D.C.

PART II

TOPICAL PERSPECTIVES

Chapter 6

Ethical and Moral Implications of New Technologies including Genetic Engineering

S.K. Chakraborty

Invention as the Mother of Necessity

At the outset I would join many others in congratulating technology for its wide-ranging, often spectacular, contributions to human existence. It therefore involves the dilemma whether I am being ungrateful to a benefactor while critical of it. Yet I cannot help taking a holistic look at technology in both dimensions: its apparent glories and its real worries. In the process I will adopt a primarily subjective stance regarding objective technology – reflecting on some of the impacts of the advances in the realm of the measurable on the fate of the immeasurable of existence. The Indian psycho-philosophical theory of *gunas* (primordial elements constituting everything in Nature) will be used as a framework to open up the subject. The perspective will be that of the *Gita.* The other theoretical foundation of our analysis will be built around the concept of self v. self (the empirical v. the transcendental, or the *vyavaharika* v. the *paramarthika vyaktitwa*). The plight of the third world getting caught in the technology whirl will also be briefly tackled. The role of greed, fear, aggression and similar values in stimulating technology will also be touched upon. The conversion of the human being into a compulsive wanting machine, playing a puppet to innovation/invention, is the deep subjective concern I would like to address.

Marrying in Haste and Repenting at Leisure

Let me offer a few snapshots of technology-based life-style, which is becoming more and more common.

Personal Computers

Some years ago it used to be a status symbol. Now it is nearly ubiquitous. Its glories have been sung in terms of unlimited information processing powers in a trice. This would leave the user free to think, to escape drudgery, to explore numerous alternatives and thus reach excellent solutions or decisions and so on.

A recent report, however, exposes the worries from PC with the smart phrase 'cyber sickness'. The writer mentions about new ailments like Computer Vision Syndrome (CVS) and Carpal Tunnel Syndrome (CTS), and quotes the finding of a pharmaceutical company that 60 per cent of all eye complaints come from computer users. He also states that seven out of ten people with computer-concerned jobs have CVS in the west.[1]

Cheating Calculators and Websites

An Australian newspaper has recently reported about the latest examination-cheating weapon – a line of Japanese calculators which allow pairs of students to invisibly beam answers to each other during examinations. Proliferating sale of 'electronic essays' and 'term papers' through rogue websites like the Evil House of Cheat or School Sucks (in the US) is a growing menace in academic institutions.[2]

Compulsions of Technology Investment

Dow Corning had developed and begun marketing a silicon gel product. A number of individuals within the firm were apprehensive about the ambiguous but potentially harmful effects of the product. But their dissent was submerged in the corporate consensus, which wanted the product to be marketed to secure a reasonable return on the investment in R&D and production of the item. However, later on, due to accumulating unfavourable evidence, government intervened, a lot of adverse publicity occurred, the old management was replaced and the new management had to withdraw the product.[3]

Technology Response to Technology Problems

Engineers are being exhorted to reduce the weight and increase the fuel efficiency of cars, while conceding that the number of car users will go on increasing. Such technological breakthroughs are expected to solve both traffic congestion and air pollution problems. Similarly, in the field of information technology the enticing picture of being able to have a pocket telephone with cable and radio inputs with one personal number is being projected.[4]

It is difficult to grasp how increased car use will not complicate and aggravate our problems, whereas the increase in human population is readily treated as amongst the greatest concerns. Similarly, pocket telephones and such other adult toys will constitute nagging threats to the mental equilibrium and health of the possessor. How is it that such serious, soon-to-follow dangers to the individual are glibly ignored? That such an on-the-move, 24-hour society is bringing mankind to the brink of insanity has been sensed in these words by non-technical authors.[5]

Americans are fired by work, frazzled by lack of time. Technology hasn't made their lives better. No wonder one-quarter of them say they're exhausted. They need to chill out before they hit breaking point.

Internet Networking

It has been reported that one of the cutting edges of cyberspace technology is to permit Internet users to have the same surfing facility by remote controllers as TV viewers are at present enjoying. To have this project on by 2002 would mean launching 840 satellites in two or three years. But already the earth's orbit is full of dangerous space debris. Besides, the project will also involve the complex problem of passing signals from one satellite to another.[6] The question is will this technological marvel contribute in any way to the alleviation of poverty, ill health, and joblessness? Is it not likely to be a breeding ground for unimagined problems for future generations?

Bio-technology or Genetic Engineering

The journey in this sphere had begun with hybrid seeds and hybrid cows for greater output. It is now culminating in animal and human cloning. At some point such laboratory breakthroughs will be commercialized or militarized – because these are the two dominant impulses in the world today. Recently two women authors had observed thus: 'When Dolly, the cloned sheep, preened for her first photographs last week, the public learned that all sorts of genetic mischief, including mammal cloning, is now possible'.[7] It is a fact commonly forgotten that most of the technological feats the common man encounters today have had their origin in times of wars. In 1985, when the world was politico-militarily bipolar, a Nobel Laureate, bio-physicist Maurice Wilkins, had admitted that about 'half the world's scientists and engineers are now engaged in war programs, that the whole American space program was very largely based on military needs, and that the true extent to which the whole of science throughout the world is being driven along by military needs is not fully realized yet'.[8]

So what we see now is: innocent children dying in hidden minefields, hotels being planned on the moon, brisk marketing of human organ transplants etc. Whatever may therefore be the promises of genetic engineering today, going by historical trends of earlier technological developments of science, the future springing from this new thrust area is unlikely to be benign as a whole whatever may be the promises of genetic engineering today.

TV Entertainment

Within three decades of its mass use, the TV has come to be called an 'idiot box'. It has become a menace, causing degrading homogenization amongst children and youngsters across the world in terms of violence, promiscuity, conspicuous unsustainable consumption and so on. These harmful effects outweigh the much-proclaimed benefits of TV like information, entertainment, education etc. In fact, the present generation (our children) has forgotten the habit of reading for self-education or even enjoyment because everything comes cooked and dressed up on the TV screen. Shallow restlessness is a natural outcome of this trend.

Human Health

Instead of being one of the most sacred callings of the human race, health care has become a high-tech commercial profession. So much has technology invaded this field that we have to-day only narrow specialists with no ability to understand the patient as a whole. It often turns out be a dreadful experience for a patient to be subjected to countless costly and complicated tests, often ending up in a whimper. Recently a cardiac patient was taken to the USA from a very reputable Calcutta nursing home. The Calcutta doctors, based on their experience with the patient, advised their American counterparts to go slow and steady with their hi-tech processes. The latter did not heed, and the patient died very soon due to the rush of hi-tech tests inflicted upon him. His system gave way even before any treatment could start.

Fertilized Infertility

Scientists from the Centre for Earth Science Studies have recently reported that the 'rice-bowl' of Kerala (Kuttanad) has been nearly ruined. For over a period of 30 years, following the construction of a *bund*, ostensibly to prevent seawater salinity, the unanticipated side effect has been the steady deposition and accumulation of residues from chemical fertilizers in stagnant waters. This has harmed the ecology of the area to an extent that not only has the annual paddy output not increased at all, but fish in lakes and palm trees (used for toddy tapping) along with fields have begun to die. Local people are being forced to migrate out of the area due to the erosion of their sources of living.[9]

The few cursory examples provided above should prompt us to think seriously about the wisdom contained in the witty saying quoted in the sub-title of this section.

Nectar to Start With, Poison to End With

The first line of verse 37, and the second line of verse 38 in Chapter 18 of the *Bhagavad Gita*, read as follows:[10]

> *yat tad agre vishamiva, parinamey-amritopaman*
> *parinamey vishamiva, yad tad agre amritopaman*

The first quote refers to that pleasure which initially is poison-like but finally nectar-like, while the second one speaks about that pleasure which initially is nectar-like but ends up by being poison-like. We have people who could be dominated by the propensity to seek well-being or happiness by adopting either of these two characteristic motives. Of course, by far the majority amongst us lean towards the second option. Whether divinely-ordained or genetically-conditioned, contemporary humanity reveals, more than ever before, the common tendency to choose short-term gain, and incur long-term pain. What is the psychological explanation of this phenomenon?

The Indian theory of triune, elemental psychological energy-forces (called *gunas*) seems eminently fitted to interpret this predicament. Qualitatively the most refined and excellent of the three is *sattwa guna* which constitutes illumined understanding. This is how verse 14.11 of the *Gita* on this mode of Nature (*guna*) is interpreted by Sri Aurobindo:[11]

> The intelligence is alert and illumined, the senses quickened, the whole mentality satisfied and full of brightness, and the nervous being calmed and filled with an illumined ease and clarity, *prasada*. Knowledge and a harmonious ease and pleasure and happiness are the characteristic results of *sattwa*.

The second, *rajo guna* or *rajas*, combines an essential positive ingredient with several associated dangerous features. Verse 14.2 on this *guna* is thus explained by Sri Aurobindo:[12]

> *Rajas* is the kinetic force in the modes of Nature. Its fruit is the lust of action, but also grief, pain, all kinds of suffering; for it has no right possession of its object, and even its pleasure of acquired possession is troubled and unstable because it has not clear knowledge. All the ignorant and passionate seekings of life belong to the rajasic mode of Nature.

The third, *tamo guna* or *tamas* is the poorest of three, being opposed to both *sattwa* and *rajas*. As Sri Aurobindo puts it:[13] '*Tamas* is inertia of nescience and inertia of inaction, a double negative'.

This *guna* theory is the result of long experiment and sustained experience of the ancient seer-psychologists of India. All manifestation in Nature, including that of human personality, is some combination of these three *gunas*. It is the preponderance of one over the other two which explains variations in behaviour, attitudes and dispositions. If *sattwa* is the most dominant *guna* then a leader, for example, will act with illumined dynamism, will guide himself and others towards long-term gain (or nectar) by resisting short-term gain (which truly is poison in the long run). If, on the other hand, the leader, or for that matter anyone in any role, is dominated by *rajas*, he acts with blind dynamism lured by short-term gain (with long-term pain). The preponderance of *tamas* of course leads to the inertia of inactivity.

My view of the galloping speed of technological innovation (I prefer not to use the term progress) is this then: it symbolizes the vehement dominance of the blinding *rajo guna*. *Rajas* is narcissistic, fascinated by its own dazzling charm. It lacks objective detachment, which flows from *sattwa*. In our epoch, in this age of calculative commercialism (not of noble chivalry, not of sagacious serenity), the world seems to be ruled and managed by the predominantly 'rajasic temper' of nations, leaders, institutions, and so on. Commercialization of any aspect of our existence, springing from this *rajasic* drive, seems to have always led to a qualitative decline in human values – be it in sports, music or art, education or health care. Science and technology too have become the tools of the *rajasic* commercial spirit. Hence, brilliant and laudable though their achievements may in themselves be, their cumulative impact on man and earth has repeatedly substantiated the truth contained in the warning: 'Marry in haste and repent at leisure'.

Cooper has recently written about the 'relative chaos' created by technology which 'disrupts the possibility of life-as-a-whole', and also about the 'threats to intimacy offered by technology'.[14] Of course what is poison to many could be nectar for a few. Thus we have avid takers of *rajas*-inspired chaos who write dictionary-sized books about how to thrive in chaos.[15] We also have ardent votaries of 'virtual worlds', created on computer screens, where 'houses are lived in, roses are smelled, and hugs can hold together friendships'.[16] *Rajasic* arcissism seems to make these writings blind to the fact that such virtual realities merely prove the withering of the cherished realities of human society. Little is it realized that virtual realities are vacuous and unsustainable. Mechanical or electronic mediation cannot replace direct human relationships. Virtual environments for the individual will tend to become sterile and lifeless as soon as the initial excitement about them ebbs.

I Need Your Greed For My Greed

The *Hitopadesa* (Counsel For Well-being) narrates the story of a wily and hungry tiger, grown old and rather immobile, enticing a gullible man with a golden chain in its paw. It feigns having completely abandoned its violent habits and is only waiting to really do good to that person by handing over the chain for which it has no use. The man hesitates for a while. But his greed overcomes his sense of prudence. So he goes near the tiger and stretches his hand to get the chain. The tiger clutches at his hand, drags him into its jaws and finishes him off.[17] This parable is profoundly suggestive of the real nature of the techno-commercial age in which we now live.

It is true that human desires and greed have always been there with us. But to have brazenly legitimized it and to have turned it into the principal engine for managing human society seems to have been a post-Enlightenment phenomenon. This period has yielded much to be proud of and to cherish by the human race. Yet, and this is not recognized by the rationalistic protagonists of the Enlightenment, this very period has witnessed episodes like the spread of colonialism world-wide, slavery in the New World, and the decimation of helpless indigenous peoples, apartheid, two disastrous World Wars, the holocaust, the dropping of atomic bombs in Japan, imperialism, a burgeoning arms-trade that foments local wars, spiraling violence and social disruption, ecological destruction, and so on. Given such a record of the post-Enlightenment period, reinforced by new technologies, is it not clear that it is greed, which has acted as the key motive force behind all such disasters?

The historian-thinker, Arnold Toynbee, has leveled the charge that modern scientific-technological civilization has given virtually free rein to material greed. The root of this phenomenon is traced by him to the original Judaic monotheism, amplified later by Christians and Muslims, which implied that nothing else but the one Creator-God was divine, and that the whole of non-human creation was placed by Him in the hands of human beings to do as they wished.[18] This world-view has eliminated all awe and reverence for Nature. As a result, alongside the ascending curve of technology, the technology-ethics gap has been widening, and human dignity and happiness have suffered.[19] Clearly, Toynbee's insights challenge the often-facile glorification of enlightenment rationality by its votaries (to the extent that some of them deny the word greed itself).

What theoretical insight did the ancient *Upanishadic* sage have to offer in this regard? Let us take, for example, the first verse of the *Isha Upanishad*:[20]

Isha vasyam idam sarva,
Yat kincha, jagatyam jagat;
Tena tyaktena bhunjitha,
Ma gridha, kasya svid dhanam.

[All this – whatever exists on the earth – should be seen as covered by the Lord. Enjoy with detachment. Do not covet anybody's riches.]

The type of educational philosophy, the kind of moulding of consciousness for human development implied in this verse is:

Everything on earth, as much as one's own self, is a manifestation of Supreme Divinity – cultivate and nurture this awareness by constant effort. There is no reason therefore to dominate over or be aggressive or acquisitive about anything. The truth being oneness and identity of all, what to possess or to grab? Only take that much which serves your reasonable needs. The earth has enough to meet that for all. Beyond this learn not to be covetous or greedy.

Evidently the ashram-dwelling releasers of a few thousand years ago had precisely formulated the preventive recipe for the human predicament which thinkers like Toynbee have started articulating today. Significantly, two of the latest writers on genetic engineering have also voiced concerns similar to Toynbee's about a strong strand in Judaism, Christianity and Islam which treats creation to be meant for humans to exploit. Again, like Toynbee, they look hopefully towards Hindu and Buddhist philosophy for a corrective approach.[21]

It should therefore be clear from the above that Vedantic *monism*, instead of Judaeo-Christian monotheism, provides a more holistic and therefore sustainable philosophy for educating the human mind in the next millennium. The monistic orientation may alone help science and technology to recoup its sense of balance and proportion. At first sight this might seem impossible or irrelevant. But since no better alternative is available, in theory and principle, efforts are called for widespread determined arousal of monistic consciousness. If the divisive, dualistic consciousness, underpinned by monotheism, has taken a few centuries to penetrate into our cells and tissues, we need to be patiently farsighted to gradually replace it with the unitive, monistic consciousness. Abatement of sci-tech fuelled greed could be achieved by such efforts only.

We have in India a psychology of the self, which corresponds with and matches the philosophy of monism. Briefly, this psychological theory tells us that it is necessary to interpret the human personality in terms of two levels: the lower or unripe or empirical self, and the higher or ripe or transcendental Self. The *Swetaswatara Upanishad* conveys this two-level concept through the metaphor of a tree on which two exactly identical golden birds are seen. One of them is restlessly hopping from branch to branch, continually nibbling at fruits bitter and sweet. The other sits contentedly on the top calmly gazing as a witness at the restless companion jumping between transient pleasure and pain.[22] At some point in time however, the lower bird looks upward, glimpses the bird atop which is exactly like itself, yet so composed and steady. Then it recovers its sense of identity with the higher bird, flies up to it and merges with it in perfect consummation. Hierarchy after all is not so abominable as it is made out to be in certain intellectual quarters.

Psychologically speaking, the bird perched on the lower branch symbolizes our deficit-driven, perpetually hungry self. The bird on the higher branch, on the other hand, is the self-contained, *poorna* Self. It represents the non-contingent, bliss-in-itself substratum of the human personality. This Self is verily the fountainhead of dignity of which Toynbee speaks. The lower bird, greedy and hungry forever, is prone to meanness and pettiness. The Biblical pronouncement that 'The Kingdom of Heaven is within', or the *Gita* declaration: '*atmany eva atmana tusta*'[23] (the *atman* or higher Self is contentment in itself) – these are the calls which can save us from the clutches of the inveterately greedy *rajasic* lower self. Modern technology reveals the relentless sway of this self. The lower self in fact feeds on the *rajo guna*, much like an effect-cause relationship. The restless, externally-driven temper of *rajas* is the key psychological factor behind the exploding technology cloud. It is the self-contented, *sattwa-nourished* higher Self which can protect science from degeneration at the hands of technology. Let us remember these beautiful lines from Shelley's *Stanzas Written in Dejection, Near Naples*:

> that content surpassing wealth
> the sage in meditation found,
> And walked with inward glory crowned.

Science can be treated as humanity's quest of 'knowledge for the sake of knowledge' in the outer realm. But technology is suspect because it almost always uses 'knowledge for the sake of greed'.

Cooper is right in saying that attempts to immunize 'reflective moral judgments' against contamination by sentiment are incoherent.[24] I fully agree with him when he comments further on that the felt horrors about bio-engineering of animals, and that 'objective' judgements about them can arise only from 'proper feelings' in people with 'whom there is nothing wrong'.[25] Elsewhere I have discussed at length the psychological theory and process of *chittashuddhi* or *antarshuddhi* (purification of heart, feelings and emotions) as the ground for wholesome, holistic and objective decision-making.[26] This is so because each human being is subjective at the core, struggling to be objective but ending up in failure to be so. Unless we face this fact, the contaminated (and greed constitutes a psychological pollution) lower self will continue to manifest a subjective element which is degenerate, and we shall miss the goal of creating an objective outer environment which can be uplifting for the individual – despite all the claims of technology. The nettle has to be grasped right at the heart: the issue of self v. self.

The rousing reception accorded today to the marketplace, globalization, privatization, liberalization and all that is a direct sequel to the deification of self-interest – an euphemism for greed. Saul is correct to argue that 'Everything, from school education to public services, is being restructured on the self-destructive basis of self-interest'.[27] The marketplace is the new all-powerful clockmaker God, aided solidly by his archangel, technology.[28] Later in his book, Saul goes on to say that invoking the 'marketplace' as the Holy Spirit serves only to restrict ourselves 'to the narrow and short-term interests of exclusion';[29] the often loud and misleading talk about the powers and benefits conferred by technology amount to little more than 'minor technical manipulations'[30] and that when 'globalization' (and trade) is proclaimed as 'pure Destiny', its protagonists care little about its effects on jobs and living standards.[31]

Having pushed the purely 'economic model of man' to the pinnacle, it became inevitable that technology would serve single-mindedly the bidding of governments and institutions for turning every aspect of the social environment as a-human as possible. From the viewpoint of Vedantic spiritual psychology this implies building our society exclusively on the foundation of the lower or empirical self which is constitutionally deficit-driven.

Mainstream modern psychology seems to have helped considerably the economic (or lower or deficit-driven) model of self to attain supremacy by resolutely denying the trans-empirical, higher Self. This spiritual Self is self-fulfilled, whole and complete in itself. This is the psychological meaning of the declaration: 'The Kingdom of Heaven is within'. The furious pace of technology-driven commerce is turning humans into thoroughly exteriorized beings. The crowding of our lives with exponentially-burgeoning technology is creating a debilitating, exhausting centrifugality of consciousness. Such an exteriorized, centrifugalized existence tends to lose its charm very soon, driving us to seek forever fresh inputs of technology that invade a daily life. This chaotic, anchor-less environment is the real psychological fallout of technology for the lay individual.

The *Isha Upanishad* caveat about not coveting others' wealth can be heeded only if the individual is not wholly engrossed in the *rajasic*, deficit-driven lower self. At least some part of his/her consciousness should be imbedded in the awareness of the autonomously whole (*poorna*) higher Self within. If technology is dragging the individual farther and away from this higher Self, then it should begin to quietly retract its fatal dash. A bit of Shelly's sage must occupy every individual's inner space.

Early in this century Rabindranath Tagore, India's mystic Nobel Laureate in literature, had spoken about Simplicity as the source of truth, power and beauty.

Simplicity removes the obstructions that block inner vision and fosters transparence. Both are essential for the sake of Truth, which though intangible, 'is more real than the gross and the numerous'.[32] Explaining the 'philosophy of poverty' underlying his school at Shantiniketan, Tagore had told his American audience that 'Poverty brings us into complete touch with life and the world, for living richly is living mostly by proxy, and thus living in a world of lesser reality. This may be good for one's pleasure and pride, but not for one's education'.[33] Hence his audacious advice that everyone should have some limited period of his/her life reserved to be spent like that of primitive man – in direct touch with Nature and the natural.[34]

During a lecture in China in 1924, Tagore had emphasized that 'simplicity is the product of centuries of culture; that simplicity takes no account of its own value, claims no wages, and therefore those who are enamoured of power do not realize that simplicity of spiritual expression is the highest product of civilization'.[35] *Sattwa guna*, higher Self and Simplicity are complementary in creating the only sustainable environment for humanity – a spiritual one. The highest humanism, the loftiest dignity has been attainable only through spiritual simplicity.

Technoxication? Beware

In 1989 the United States launched the Human Genome Project which is going to cost more than three billion dollars and take perhaps fifteen years to complete. Its purpose is to identify the entire human genetic code.[36]

This is a spectacular sci-tech research project by any standards. The highest quality of scientific dedication inherent in such an effort is unquestionable. Yet an outstanding feature of this endeavour is that it is entirely focused on the material, physical existence of humans. It talks of 'human enhancement' by planned alteration of genetic codes. Of course, new diseases and ailments of the affluent sci-tech era may also be more effectively tackled by the findings of such research and their application. Yet, the entire range of such hopes and aims appears to totally ignore the role of human will to transcend his/her physio-sensual boundaries, and step into the realms of non-egoistic, non-body centered-levels of psychological perfection. Objective genetic manipulation, not subjective consciousness elevation, seems to be regarded as constituting the next round of human evolution. The greatest modern Indian philosopher-sage, Sri Aurobindo, had said this:[37]

To be shut up for ever in his ego is not his ultimate perfection; he can become a universal soul, one with the Supreme Unity, one with others, one with all beings. This is the high sense and power concealed in his humanity.

This statement is of capital importance because it conveys a view of evolution altogether different from what the human genome project is driven by. The Aurobindovian framework tells us that dynamic Nature has been manifesting herself successively through this sequence: 'matter - to life - to mind - to spirit' (above mind). Increasingly refined and perfect unfoldment of consciousness is the keynote of this evolutionary journey. To the extent that the human body is a better mould than that of the plant or the animal to allow mental consciousness to flourish, Nature's progressive intent is unmistakable. But the present confused, stumbling, problem-creating mind-set of humanity cannot be the final or supreme intent of evolving Nature. Until the arrival of the human form on earth, Nature has been profusely creative in putting forth millions of physical forms. However, once the human form emerged, it appears that Nature ceased to create further new forms. The human form seems to be the culmination of the physical aspect of evolution. Henceforth evolution is intended to take place in the subjective realm of higher and higher consciousness in the direction of the Spirit.[38] This consciousness is termed by Sri Aurobindo as 'yogic consciousness'. He explains that it is:

> not only to be aware of things, but of forces, and not only of forces, but of the conscious being behind the forces. One is aware of all this not only in oneself but in the Universe.[39]

Granting that the therapeutic aspect of human genetic engineering is of some positive relevance to the physical life of humans, does the thrust of human advances in genetic technology show any sign of incorporating the line of the Aurobindovian theory of evolution? What is the meaning of 'human advancement'? – that indeed is the supreme issue. Some authors like Singer and Wells do warn that:[40]

    'When we try to improve upon evolution, we may find that for some quite unexpected reason we have only made matters worse. But they do not go beyond pointing out the danger of such sci-tech endeavours. No positive view of the evolutionary trend in Nature-in-itself can be gathered from what they say. This difficulty arises because evolution for them seems to carry no sacredness, no wisdom, no amelioration'. Evolution, for this school of thought, is 'utterly indifferent to the well-being or ultimate fate of our species'.[41] Anderson is more categorical in his views than Singer and Wells, and unlike them also mentions spirituality:[42]

    Our disagreements about what constitutes 'humanhood' are notorious. And our insight(s) into what, and to what extent, genetic components might play a role in what we comprehend as our 'spiritual' side are almost non-existent. We simply should not meddle in areas where we are so ignorant.

    This is a counsel of prudence beneath a coating of apparent conservatism. Cooper, taking technology as a whole, complains of 'technological society's lack of a centre', its substitution of 'relative chaos' for the 'gradually evolving norms of earlier societies', and the resultant danger it poses to 'life-as-a-whole'.[43] Kwame Gyekye, while pleading the case for social transformation with the aid of technology, rightly cautions that this will be unattainable 'unless technology moves along under the aegis of basic human values', unless it 'be guided by other – perhaps intrinsic and ultimate – human values'.[44] If, without heeding such human values, technology tends to trigger a social transformation which is primarily chaotic and anchorless, making for perpetual uncertainty, insecurity and emotional alienation, then what kind of evolutionary stage is it building up for humanity?

Between them, then, Singer and Wells, Anderson, Cooper and Gyekye – all represent voices of sanity in an era when large segments of world population are tipsy with the effects of technoxication. And yet one looks in vain to them for a bright horizon of hope and light for the individual in search of a profound life – a life of powerful self-endeavour to propel the lower self towards the higher Self, and not one of impotent genetic engineering which knows not what Self is.

If human advancement were to be defined in terms of the growth of his/her capacity for alignment with the Universal or Cosmic and Transcendental Forces, beyond the egoistic-empirical ones, and be thus truly empowered to both become and do good, then genetic technology would have the correct benchmark to be measured against. My own view is that genetic engineering is inherently incapable of passing this test for it simply cannot lay its hold on something that is higher and beyond mere reason and measure – Spirit or Consciousness. The table cannot show the light, light shows the table. The fragmented intellect cannot realize holistic Consciousness. The moment this attempt is made, it results in splits and splinters. That is why when asked about God (who is nothing but Pure Consciousness), Buddha response was silence. This I believe, is the nature of the psycho-philosophical principle behind Anderson's skepticism about the role of genetic engineering in human advancement. The chances are strong that this line of technology will breed made-to-order, tailor-made robots in a robotized environment.

The simple, yet basic question is: can genetic engineering ever reduce greed, cruelty, envy, lust and increase contentment, gratitude, humility, compassion and the like? What then will be left for character-making education by and for each individual? Adams voices his worry on this score, although he speaks in relation to technology as a whole. He is concerned with the sustainability of 'demand economics' (an euphemism for greed?) fostered by new technologies. He speaks about explicit direction of economic activity 'by and towards positive human values'. For once he does mention 'greed'.[45] But his argument is not forthright enough as we are suggesting here: should human advancement, supported by self-education, dissociate itself from the list of negative-values like greed etc., and embrace the list of positive human values mentioned above? How does technology visualize its position in this values matrix?

Bhagwan feels that in regard to developing countries 'The dark side of the picture is currently more in evidence than the bright side'. He cites the examples of the ruination of the peasantry of the Philippines, Caribbean and Madagascar, whose export crops like rice, sugar, vanilla etc. have been displaced by bio-technologically engineered industrial substitutes in the advanced economies. Possibly in future highly populated developing countries may end up by being net importers of technology-intensive food from the rich economies.[46] Bhagwan also points out that while the 'green revolution' has been lauded for its short-run positive results through laboratory-bred high-yielding cereal crops, it has also severely endangered the existence of hundreds of natural, indigenous, low-yielding varieties of those crops. The dangers of the 'bio-revolution' in the wider plant and animal kingdoms, causing manifold greater man-made loss in bio-diversity, are serious enough. So, Bhagwan doubts the wisdom of the establishment in developing countries which are lured by the immediate hopes of dramatic productivity increases through the bio-revolution.[47] Another instance of 'marrying in haste and repenting at leisure' indeed!

We have a growing body of such critical literature regarding bio-technology, genetic engineering and scientific research in general.[48] All of them however seem to confine their focus to the diverse social implications of sci-tech. An implicit acceptance of the awesome march of sci-tech, a kind of resignation to its inevitability, seems to ring through this body of literature. The psychological impact of sci-tech invasion into the daily life of the citizen is not addressed. Nor are the still deeper philosophical issues like the meaning of human birth, the meaning of true humanness, the ultimate human destiny being given any attention in these writings. It is to some such neglected issues that this paper has attempted to draw attention.

Conclusion: Globalizing Spiritual Ambitions

Sci-tech has done a marvellous job of globalizing material ambitions and in penetrating the remotest places on earth. A greedy global village seems to be our crowning achievement at the close of the second millennium. Let us hope and pray that we can go beyond half-hearted sociological critiques of this state of society, and begin to devote our energies towards globalizing spiritual ambitions from the very beginning of the 3rd millennium. To prepare for this paradigm shift we should be ready to take our lessons from the Tagores, Gandhis and Aurobindos – who had made it the business of their lives to progress within rather than progress without. And in this they were no less systematic, rational and meticulous than any scientist in his laboratory. Only that their laboratory was first within and next only without. They never shunned the without, but proceeded towards it after, or at least alongside, achieving elevation within. And they were God-centered, not in the sterile theological sense, but with abiding being-level consciousness. So let us listen to them.

First we glean a few utterances from Gandhi:

> 'Who can deny that much that passes for science (and art) to-day destroys the soul instead of uplifting it, and instead of evoking the best in us, panders to our basest passions'.[49]
> 'If the circulation of blood theory could not have been discovered without vivisection, humankind could well have done without it'.[50]
> 'I quite understand that your 'mass production' is a technical term for production by the fewest possible number through the aid of highly complicated machinery. I have said to myself that this is wrong. My machinery must be of the most elementary type which I can put in the homes of millions'.[51]

To the technoxicated mind all this might seem simply bizarre and utterly gullible. Harmful as they are, such reactions are not unnatural. Mad people are not known to accept that they have gone mad. Many nationalistically minded citizens of India feel inferior about India's lack of innovative capability and the apparent technological backwardness of the common man's daily life. This defensive mentality had perhaps been anticipated by Gandhi, and therefore he had responded to a reader as follows:[52] 'It was not that we did not know how to invent machinery, but our forefathers knew that, if we set our hearts after such things, we would become slaves and lose our moral fiber.'

Accordingly, a few days later he had emphasized to another reader: 'We therefore, say that the non-beginning of a thing is supreme wisdom'.[53] Why? Because each link in the sci-tech chain makes the next step almost inevitable. But since the universe is a highly complex and subtle system, sci-tech tampering with it tends to breed problems beyond man's normal rational reckoning. Eluded of any final solution sci-tech rushes along a spiral of ever complex problems and calls this progress.

Let us now turn to Tagore once more. In one of his early morning discourses at the Shantiniketan Ashram in 1908 he had spoken thus:[54]

> No matter how many railway trains we run and telegraph lines we lay, in the field of power we remain infinitely far from God.

If we dare to compete with Him, then our endeavour, transgressing its limits, becomes cursed and faces annihilation. No scientist, no technologist has the ability to plumb completely even a grain of dust within which He resides. Therefore the person who would compete with God in the sphere of power is like Arjuna shooting arrows at the disguised Mahadeva – arrows that do not touch him. Defeat there is inevitable.

These warnings had issued from a sage-level consciousness, which could gaze across the fragmentary and transient towards the whole and the eternal. For over-confident sci-tech to continue to brush them aside as poetic prattle would be an unpardonable act of irreversible recklessness. Ninety years after Tagore had uttered these words at a winter dawn in a small, quiet, simple corner of the earth, we realize to-day their prophetic accuracy in so many facets of our existence.

True, human beings cannot live without ambitions, desires and aspirations. The question is: what is the quality and direction of such propulsions? If they are exclusively material, and therefore outer-directed, the individual will continue to live in a chaotic, unintelligible, exteriorized environment. This has been the long-term psychological trend underlying the development of sci-tech. His/her whole life is now spent in a furious race simply to cope with the torrent of sci-tech objects invading from without. On the other hand, if the primary human ambitions and aspirations could be re-directed, beginning with those who already have more than enough for material sustenance, towards becoming aware of the stable interior core of being, then should commence the revival of the individual's lost mastery of his/her outer environment. The loss of paradise without has been caused by the loss of paradise within. Here we turn once more to Sri Aurobindo for a precise formulation.[55]

Man is a spirit veiled in the works of energy, moving to self-discovery, capable of Godhead. He is a soul that is growing through Nature to conscious self-hood; he is a divinity and an eternal existence. The natural half-animal creature that for a while he seems to be is not at all his whole being, and is not in any way his real being.

Bio-technology, genetic engineering, cyber communication and all that must be judged, therefore, against the above definition of the human being – a definition which is the only true hope for a sustainable world. Discovery of, stabilizing in, and working from one's spiritual identity has to become the top universal agenda of all human beings – not confined just to a few specialist seekers as has been the case in human history so far. Globalization of this kind only is truly worthy of human labour.

A contemporary physicist, Goran Wall, strongly perceives the need for such a shift because 'From the ecological point of view, the present resource use in society faces a dead-end technology leading to nothing but annihilation in the long run'. Why has our civilization reached such a dead end? Wall answers, sensitively and sensibly, that this calamity has been caused by 'its lack of spirit and soul'. Though massive propaganda deployment of intellectual and other varieties of capital 'Gradually the soul of society is reduced to greed, competition and entertainment. A sick soul in a healthy body can never work, it will also make the body sick'.[56] Such failure of the currently fashionable 'intellectual capital' mantra lies in what Sri Aurobindo discerns about man: 'a particular intelligence limited by his reason' which is 'incapable of largeness'.[57] As a result, his absorption in what he takes up for the time being prevents his seeing where it will hurt him or will go against cosmic purpose.

Arnold Toynbee had asserted without mincing words that 'Karma, not scientific and technological progress, is the factor in human life that produces welfare and happiness, or alternatively, misery and sorrow'.[58] And *karma* is a keyword in all schools of Indian thought dealing with the ethico-moral development of the individual. For one's own true welfare, as well as for that of society, each individual must improve his/her own *karma* by increasing one's self-mastery. Does sci-tech contribute to or detract from self-mastery, dignity, humility and ethicality in the individual? Pointing out the increasing disparity between technology and ethics, Toynbee answers this question by declaring that 'Human dignity cannot be achieved in the field of technology in which human beings are so expert. It can be achieved only in the field of ethics'.[59]

Unfortunately the *rajasic*, lower-self, deficit-driven dominant leadership around the world today has been turning a deaf ear to such wise insights from both realizers of past and present, as well as thinkers of past and present. Consequently, civilization continues to remain a 'disease'[60] with the slow virus of misdirected *karma* eating into its vitals. There is not much hope then right now for an individual to fulfil the promise of Nature's evolution latent in the human form.

Yet, long-term trust and faith in Nature's irresistible ascending evolutionary force is something we must go on cherishing through all our interim despondencies. Let us listen to Sri Aurobindo for voicing this assurance:[61]

Every state of existence has some force in it, which drives to transcend itself. Matter moves towards becoming Life. Life travails towards becoming Mind. Mind aspires towards becoming ideal Truth. Truth rises towards becoming divine and infinite Spirit.

Sci-tech must nurture enough humility to be able to absorb this message and modify and moderate its course. The eighteenth-century Enlightenment Projects to achieve human perfectibility through secular science, accompanied by equating religion with magic,[62] leads well meaning critics to avoid discussing the 'good or bad' of techno-science and choosing only to ask 'who is responsible for the production and distribution' of technology.[63] The quality of this 'who' – by what standards to measure it – is not dealt with. That religion is spirituality, not magic, is a truth which only realizers can tell because they know what they are talking about. The philosopher who considers himself as a mere 'translator' of diverse discourses,[64] not as a realizer, is apt to forget that the same tests for qualifying as a critique of techno-science also apply to one who wishes to critique religion.[65] The Goswamis are right to say that 'with technology there is more diversion' today, which strengthens separation rather than unity in society.[66] Evolution towards involved Divinity for unity will be the correct direction to follow. This may entail a slowing down for sci-tech.

Notes

1 B. Kumar (1988) 'Brave New World of Cybernetics', *The Economic Times*, March 13.
2 G. Healy (1988) 'Exam Scammers Gain High-Tech Edge on Universities', *The Weekend Australian*, February 28.
3 D.D. Singer and R. Smith (1997) 'The Ethical Significance of Corporate Teleology', *Journal of Human Values*, January-June, pp.86-7.
4 W. Barlow (1977) 'Engineering and The Future of Planet Earth', *RSA Journal*, August-September, pp.52-3.
5 *Newsweek*, (1995) March 6.
6 The *Financial Express* (1996) August 17.
7 J.O.C. Hamilton and J. Flynn (1977) 'When Science Fiction Becomes Social Reality', *Business Week*, March 10, p.84.
8 Interviews with Nobel Laureates (1986) The Bhaktivedanta Institute, Bombay, p.36, p.42.
9 *Times of India* (1998), May 12.
10 Sri Aurobindo (1977) *The Message of the Gita*, Sri Aurobindo Ashram, Pondicherry, pp.253-4.
11 Ibid., p.205.
12 Ibid., p.206.
13 Ibid., p.206.
14 D.E. Cooper (1995) 'Technology: Liberation or Enslavement?' in *Philosophy and Technology* (ed.) R. Fellows, Cambridge University Press, Cambridge, p.18.
15 T. Peters (1989) *Thriving on Chaos*, Tata McGraw-Hill, New Delhi.
16 E. Reid (1995) 'Virtual World, Culture and Imagination' in *Cyber Society* (ed.) S.G. Jones, Sage, Thousand Oaks, p.182.

17 *The Hitopadesa*, trans. V. Balasubramanyan (1989) The M.P. Birla Foundation, Calcutta, p.54.

18 A.J. Toynbee and D. Ikeda (1987) *Choose Life*, Oxford University Press, New Delhi, pp.38-9.

19 Ibid., p.342.

20 *Shankara's Commentary on Isha Upanishad*, trans. Swami Gambhirananda (1983), Advaita Ashrama Calcutta, p.4.

21 M.J. Reiss and R. Straughan (1996) *Improving Nature?*, Cambridge University Press, Cambridge, pp.80-1.

22 *Shankara's Commentary on Svetasvatara Upanishad*, trans. Swami Gambhirananda (1986) Advaita Ashrama, Calcutta, hymns 4.6, p.145.

23 *The Message of the Gita*, op. cit., II.55.

24 D.E. Cooper (1988) 'Intervention, Humility and Animal Integrity' in *Animal Bio-Technology and Ethics* (eds) A. Holland and A. Johnson: Chapman and Hall, London, p.148.

25 Ibid., p.149.

26 S.K. Chakraborty; (1991) *Management By Values*, Oxford University Press, New Delhi, pp.62-4, pp.142-3.

27 J.R. Saul; (1997) *The Unconscious Civilization*, Penguin, Australia, p.36.

28 Ibid., p.19.

29 Ibid., p.140.

30 Ibid., p.142.

31 Ibid., p.146.

32 Rabindranath Tagore (1985) *Personality*, Macmillan, New Delhi, p.25.

33 Ibid., p.121.

34 Ibid., p.122.

35 R. Tagore; (1998) *Lectures and Addresses*, Macmillan, New Delhi, p.50.

36 *Ethical Issues in Scientific Research*, (eds) E. Erwin, S. Gindin and L. Kleiman (1994), Garland Publishing, New York, p.303.

37 Sri Aurobindo; (1972) *Collected Works: Sri Aurobindo Ashram*, Pondicherry, vol.14, pp.98-9.

38 Sri Aurobindo; (1982) *The Hour of God: Sri Aurobindo Ashrama*, Pondicherry, pp.35-37.

39 Sri Aurobindo; *Collected Works*, op. cit., vol.24, pp.1149-50.

40 P. Singer and D. Wells; 'Genetic Engineering' in *Ethical Issues in Scientific Research*, op. cit., p.313.

41 Ibid., p.312.

42 W.F. Anderson; 'Human Gene Therapy', in *Ethical Issues in Scientific Research*, op. cit., p.347.

43 D.E. Cooper; 'Technology: Liberation or Enslavement?', op. cit., p.18.

44 K. Gyekye; 'Technology and Culture in a Developing Country' in *Philosophy and Technology*, op. cit., p.141.

45 R. Adams; (1977) 'Functional Markets and Indigenous Capability For Sustainable Development' in *New Generic Technologies in Developing Countries* (ed.) M.R. Bhagwan, Macmillan Press, Great Britain, pp.210-1.

46 M.R. Bhagwan; 'The Major Issues Under Debate' in ibid., pp.300-1.

47 Ibid., p.303.

48 For example, A. Davison, I Barns and R. Schibeci, 'Problematic Publics: A Critical Review of Surveys of Public Attitudes to Bio-technology' in *Science, Technology and Human Values*, vol.22, no.3, Summer 1997, 317-348; H.P. Sagal, *Future Imperfect*, Amherst: University of Massachusetts Press, 1994, 33; O. Renn, T. Webler and P. Wiedemenn (eds), *Fairness and Competence in Citizen participation*, Dordrecht:

Kluwer Academic Publishers, 1995; L.J. Frewer, C. Howard and R. Shepherd, 'Public Concerns in the U.K. about General and Specific Applications of Genetic Engineering', *Science, Technology and Human Values*, vol.22, no.1, Winter 1977, 98-124; D. Vaughan, *The Challenger Launch Decision*, Chicago: University of Chicago Press, 1996; S. Jasanoff, *Science at the Bar*, Cambridge MA: Harvard University Press, 1995.

49   Mahatma Gandhi; (1994) *Collected Works*, Government of India Publication Division, New Delhi, vol.34, p.319.

50   Op. cit., vol.29, p.325.

51   Op. cit., vol.48, p.166.

52   *Selected Works*, (ed.) S. Narayan (1969), Navjivan Trust, Ahmedabad, vol.4, p.151.

53   Ibid., p.190.

54   *Human Values: The Tagorean Panorama*, trans. S.K. Chakraborty and P. Bhattacharya, (1996), New Age International, New Delhi, pp.85-6.

55   Sri Aurobindo; Collected Works, op. cit., vol.14, p.98.

56   G. Wall; (1997) 'Energy, Society and Morals'; *Journal of Human Values*, July-December, p.202, p.204.

57   Sri Aurobindo; *The Hour of God*, op. cit., p.54.

58   *Choose Life*, op. cit., p.54.

59   Ibid., p.342.

60   Mahatma Gandhi; *Selected Works*, op. cit., pp.118-22.

61   *The Hour of God*, op. cit., pp.34-5.

62   R. Sassower; (1997) *Technoscientific Angst*, University of Minnesota Press, Minneapolis, p.10.

63   Ibid., p.129.

64   Ibid., p.128.

65   Ibid., p.16.

66   A. Goswami and M. Goswami; (1977) 'Scientific and Spirituality: Project of History of Indian Science', *Philosophy and Culture*, New Delhi, p.38.

Chapter 7

Values and Ethics in Eco-cultural Tourism: Reflections from a Spiritual Voyager in India

David Kimber

Introduction

How does one begin a paper in an area where personal experiences flood in to overwhelm academic reflections? As a traveller to India on an annual basis since 1995 I confess to a state of seduction. I cannot be a dispassionate chronicler, an unbiased observer in the area of cultural tourism in India. The enigmatic quotes of Raine's book *India Seen Afar*, which are noted as a forward, give some sense of eco-cultural tourism I have encountered in India. It is these aspects, the ephemeral, the rich fleeting glimpses, the moments of insight recaptured later, which suggest to me India has so much to offer in this area. It is what brings me back, an annual pilgrim, to discover more. I live with some dread that, without care, thought and planning, mine will be the last generation to discover this Orient, the one India so vibrantly unveils. Hence eco-cultural tourism is perhaps India's most important 'export' industry, the world's last point of connectedness with a former world of natural and spiritual richness rapidly being lost in the flurry of modernity.

So I intend to intertwine aspects of academic work previously developed here, through the kind support from Professor Chakraborty at the Management Centre for Human Values at the IIM in Calcutta and friends from Mt Abu and in Bangalore, with personal reflection, guided by many teachers throughout India and recorded during the various journeys Fran and I have taken in India.

I will adopt the common philosopher approach of raising questions rather than answering them. An approach to business ethics which I am attracted to suggests it is to do with getting people to think about 'what ought I or we to do?' rather than to propose ethical solutions. Those solutions inevitably are best determined by those who have to live with them.

Hence the aim of the paper is to cover a number of arenas. International, individual and environmental ethics will be considered, taking account of international and local writers views. Also human values, social responsibility and the impact of the spiritual dimension will also be addressed. I will conclude by optimistically suggesting that India can be one of the founts of wisdom in a new emerging age of consciousness especially.

International Ethics Issues

So what are the issues effecting eco-cultural tourism which can be identified in the literature on international business ethics? The works of recent American business ethics writers are amongst the most dominant influences reflecting on the moral dimension of globalism. However, that is not to suggest their orientations are necessarily the most relevant. One of the debates emerging in this field is the need to recognize the moral frameworks which come from non Judeo-Christian or Western business philosophies. The paper will attempt to develop these themes as well as recognize the impact of Western business perspectives.

Ethical Universalism versus Relativism

Perhaps the most significant issue which emerges from international business ethics is the discussion around the notion of universal versus relative ethics. Are certain principles and moral norms universally applicable or do they always have to reflect the culture or society being considered? Bowie[1] and Frederick[2] suggest the argument for universal principles has become well established in the last fifty years. United Nations declarations, international trade and labour agreements and documents such as the Caux Round Table principles of Business[3] are clear indicators that some universal doctrines of ethical practice are understood. These are also well evidenced in much basic theological literature of the world religions. Principles such as respect and care for others, co-operation, honesty, responsibility and duty, fairness and equity, are notions which are generally accepted as universal.

The Caux statement[4] makes direct reference to the environment indicating businesses 'should protect and, where possible, improve the environment, promote sustainable development, and prevent wasteful use of resources'.[5] It also indicates that 'communities', as key business stakeholders, must be supported. Business has a responsibility to 'play a leading role in preserving and enhancing the physical environment and conserving the earth's resources' as well as 'respecting the integrity of local cultures'.

However Bowie and De George[6] recognize that there is a case for relativism. Both writers use utilitarian arguments to justify the need to recognize the moral norms which underpin a specific society or culture, when considering what is likely to 'work' in those countries. When discussing this issue at a seminar in Calcutta a couple of years ago, it became evident that, whilst one might agree on a base line of universal principles, how they are prioritized is likely to vary in different countries. Some would go further to suggest that the differences in political, economic and social circumstances can be so great that the application of universal principles is not feasible. Population pressures and resource availability have a clear impact when comparing different countries.

One can conclude that there is justification for both ethical perspectives. Universalism can be valuable in terms of providing aspirational directions. Relativism may become a necessary factor when the practicalities of application are considered.

Rights, Duties and Eco-Cultural Tourism

The libertarian stream of philosophy argues that individual rights should be recognized and protected. It has been an area extensively reviewed in the last fifty years, and is reflected in the writings about individualism so evident in Western philosophy. Donaldson[7] proposed ten fundamental international rights, which business should respect. Those which directly relate to eco-cultural tourism are; the right to freedom of physical movement, the right to physical security, the right to freedom of speech and association, and the right to subsistence.

However such rights relate to humans. Eco-cultural tourism immediately raises the rights of other species, nature and the 'unknown'. How far one goes in recognizing such rights is a constant dilemma. It brings into focus the other theme which is becoming better understood – the duties of humans towards other creatures, nature and the environment. It is an arena more deeply understood 'in the East' which is evidenced in much of the myths and legends of India. It was touchingly revealed to us by a old Indian who had voluntarily helped us, as helpless tourists negotiating our way around Calcutta. In response to our effusive thanks he simply said 'But it is my duty'. He was clearly talking of a higher duty of care than many from the West are even aware of. It was an incident that stays with us as one of the great 'memory-moments' of India, an element not unrelated to the theme of this paper.

Ethics and Culture

The 'spiritual quest' is a theme which is inherent in the relationships between values, culture and tourism in India. India, as Raine so aptly, or (to use the favourite Indian 'play on words' game) so 'raptly', notes, is seen by many 'from the outside' as the place to pursue, and to observe the search for, personal enlightenment. How these two 'touristic' yearnings can be achieved, whilst respecting the rights of Indians and the sanctity of their sacred places, is a constant concern. Our experiences vary significantly. Some temple areas clearly are in need of a wrathful prophet 'to cast out the philistines and traders' – something we observed in action a couple of years ago as a lathi-wielding official chased away would be spruikers at Sravanabelagola near Mysore. Others are very well managed quiet places which enable all to pursue their interests. A journey to Mt Abu, courtesy of the Brahma Kumaris community, gave me appreciation of this aspect of cultural tourism. It was an enlightening experience which provided considerable insight into the way an Indian philosophy can been embedded into daily life.

Personal Ethics – Ego and Eco-Cultural Tourism

Personal ethics and how it can affect the development of tourism is an important issue. The conflict between personal and communal needs provides a rich arena for debate.

Chakraborty[8] in his writings about values and ethics in Indian organizations draws on vedantic philosophy to consider the connection between ego and ethics. He suggest the constant urge for 'self extension to Infinity' leads to 'perpetual proliferation of external desires, wants (and) artefacts' and 'a craving for physical possession'. He believes Indian philosophy can provide the way for the 'transformation of the exteriorized, deficit-driven, hungering ego-self' (the lower self) to the non-contingent, self-existent fulfilment of the (higher) Self.

This point of view raises some dilemmas for the ethical development of eco-cultural tourism. Can the purity of this mission be preserved in a world which 'lets in' those seeking to achieve this awareness. Can the lower self, 'disvalues'[9] of pride, arrogance, deceit, vanity, hypocrisy and greed be held back if the spiritual world of India is 'opened up' to more 'secular' tourism. It is an issue that relates to both the 'spiro-cultural' as well as the purely ecological. Tourist-driven tainting of ashrams is a well-known phenomenon. The potential for 'lower self' forces driving environment movements is less regularly discussed but may be a cause for concern.[10]

Environmental Ethics

Power Over Nature

One of the most pertinent ego/ethics issues directly related to eco-cultural tourism is the relationship between humans and the natural environment. Again it poses a dilemma. Should forests be altered, paths laid, signs created to make nature more accessible? Recently we enjoyed a delightful holiday at a beautiful national park in Victoria. It is one of the state's favourite bushwalking areas and has been managed by the Victorian government for over 50 years. The impact of human interaction with this unique area has unavoidably altered it. How to allow thousands of people to walk around the park, enjoying the beautiful scenery without destroying the forest areas is a constant problem. Currently it is government managed and access is controlled. Three years ago attempts were made to 'privatize' the accommodation in the area, a move which created much protest and resulted in a 'win' for the anti-commercial 'protectionists'. It highlighted a constant issue relating to eco-cultural tourism, evident in India. How can management systems be set up, controlled and maintained to protect nature from the apparent 'natural' urge humans have to alter, use or take control over the environment? Different situations require different solutions, with 'balance' being an ideal to be preserved.

Conflict Between Different Groups' Needs

Sekhar[11] identifies a number of issues relating to environmental ethics which he summarizes under the heading 'Power Equity and Spirituality'. One of the major concerns he identifies is the difficulty of meeting different group needs, local, regional, state, national, and global. In the area of eco-cultural tourism this covers a wide spectrum; local villagers may want to preserve traditional customs and practices of agriculture, regional/state interests may be oriented towards maximizing resource utilization, national interests may be to develop a national culture whilst being part of a global community, global interests are increasingly to preserve natural environments. Many projects can meet one groups needs but may deny the rights of others. Sekhar notes the impact of the Narmada Dam project on tribal communities and suggests 'dams and deforestation' have led to 80 per cent of the '80 million tribals' being 'below the poverty line' and 'millions' being displaced.[12] Ideally eco-cultural tourism may help reverse the impact of such regional/state projects. However what is supportive for one group may have negative impacts on another. The economic well being of the broader state community being forfeited to the needs of a local community is an obvious concern.

Another dimension of this area is the potential conflict between culture and ecology. This is especially evident at Varanasi. Whilst there, we had conversations with people involved with river pollution monitoring and could not help but be aware of the paradoxes emerging from the maintenance of the burning ghats, spiritual tourism and the concern for the purity of 'Mother Ganges'. With smaller populations this could be managed, but given the increasing numbers of pilgrims, the 'poor devoted Hindu', as we were told by an eminent Professor in environmental sustainability at the Hindu University (who is also a priest and bathes daily in the Ganges), 'is likely to become 'an endangered species''.[13] Again, being aware and recognizing the need to assess the effect is an essential issue in eco-cultural tourism planning.

Inter-Generational Rights to the Environment

Rawls (1971) has argued that 'distributive justice requires that one should pass onto posterity what one wants or inherits from the previous generation'.[14] Thus the environment should be preserved intact and be an intergenerational asset. If this ethical theme becomes more accepted, eco-cultural protection will become a important public policy. Much of the concern for sustainability is directed by this logic. Sustainable eco-cultural tourism is then the practical process which ensures access is made available to all, both now and in the future. However it is not so simple. The poor management of large numbers of people who want to see eco-cultural treasures inevitably leads to their degradation. Seeing 3rd/4th century wall paintings in deep caves, surrounded by large numbers of school children running around in an underground temple near Chitradurga, made us well aware that equity of access and long term preservation can be mutually exclusive objectives.

Relationship Between Nature and Spirituality

The connection between the natural environment and spirituality is a recurring theme in much theological and philosophical literature. Chakraborty notes 'in classical India in the tapovans (forest hermitages) the young people's primary education used to begin with the cultivation of (the) learning and feeling ... of unity and infinity'.[15] Sekhar likewise notes the spiritual significance of the 'deep forests or mighty mountains'.[16]

The growing recognition of the sense of spirit/soul in the environment is also occurring in Australia. Today more and more Australians are accepting the connections between land, nature and spirituality. Aboriginal land rights, ecology/environment movements, and national parks management are three areas which reflect this trend.[17]

Human Values and Eco-Cultural Tourism

Trust and Relationship Building

Eco-cultural tourism can play a role in the development of the relationships between communities both regional and global. The tourist can be both a friend and an economic opportunity, as is evidenced by many experiences of travellers in all countries throughout the world. An extensive information industry has been built up around helping people manage this relationship effectively. India was the early arena of eco-cultural discovery for one of the most successful publishing companies in this field, 'The Lonely Planet', incidentally an Australian based organization. An important element of sustainable tourist development is ensuring trust and good relationships can be established. It is an integral ethical element which needs to be considered in terms of eco-cultural project development. The room for confusion in terms of relationship building is not insignificant as evidenced by the following incident.

One impression about truth came from experiences in a small country village visited whilst on a tour to a well-known temple region in India. It had become a tourist stopping off place and consequently its inhabitants, especially the young boys had developed the skills of tour guide as an alternative to employment in the fields. On arrival we were greeted by a gathering of such young men who clamoured either openly, 'Can I be your guide?' or more surreptitiously, declaring, 'I will be your friend' as we alighted from the bus. We fended off the more effusive of these would-be assistants. Later we were charmed into accepting the offer of a quieter, seemingly more innocent, youth who was working in the hotel where we stayed. He helped us with our luggage and offered to help us find our way around the village and to the temples.

It was his innocent guile – his naive, yet open, deception which intrigued us as we got to know him better. He would openly declare, with absolute certainty, apparent fact after fact. It became evident to us that these were made up on the spur of the moment to suit whatever interpretation he felt was needed. Hence, when we were hungry he declared he knew a special place which served the best food in the town. It just happened to belong to a friend of his. Our interest in old jewellery, indicated by a brief discussion near a shop window, immediately sparked a response. He knew a collector in a nearby village who specialized in the very pieces we had mentioned. It turned out to be his brother who had a shop with everything but jewellery in it. Later his explanations about the temples became more contradictory as his rudimentary knowledge, reinforced by thoughts made up on the spur of the moment, unravelled with more questioning. The more he spoke, the more his deceptions became apparent. But throughout our interrogations he never once faltered. A phrase which he used regularly with wide eyed incredulity, nodding his head vigorously, in response to our growing suspicions was, 'But it is TRUE!!'

Depending on our reaction, this declaration was often then accompanied by a disarming smile and an ambivalent headshake and shrug, which altered meaning, 'But if it's not, it doesn't matter'. And to him it didn't. Truth was a continuing moveable feast. Words uttered for the sake of connection – to maintain a conversation, to keep contact. He was proud of his skills in English and was happily developing ingenuity which no doubt would hold him in good stead as a trader at a later stage – how to converse with strangers, to deal and negotiate. Perhaps he would learn that falsehood sours relationships and even the most transient of tourist contacts can be unhappy ones, if truth is so carelessly treated. But perhaps not. He seemed to be innately aware that deception can be easily forgiven as long as it is offered without too much seriousness and with good humour.

It was indeed his warmth and apparent friendship which overcame much of our concerns about truth. He showed us his family home, insisting that we meet his parents, and showed us letters from a Japanese girl who he had befriended. She had stayed with his family for a couple of months apparently revelling in the chance to become acculturated into Indian village life. However eventually we became tired of his insistent friendship, especially as it appeared that commercial gain was a driving motive. We became less forgiving of his lapses into falsehood. Was this cultural insensitivity or simply us playing out the dance of destruction between the perceived wealthy and the apparently avaricious in another country? Had all parties got it wrong? I still wonder about such connections and the importance about truth and connectedness in different communities.

What is the importance of connectedness? In this case the boy was keen to be connected in all sorts of ways. He was very much part of his family, openly proud of their achievements and way of life. He was part of a village but also keen to be part of a bigger world. He had been going to college in a nearby town but had decided that dealing with English speaking tourists was a much more practical way of broadening his horizons and gaining practical insights into other domains. On a personal level he saw the value of friendship. It opened up all sorts of opportunities.

The interesting question is how far do we go to make sure we are connected. Do we forsake our integrity, our true feelings, our honesty to keep up connections. Do we maintain pretences, believing that the facade is necessary – if it drops we will be 'disconnected', abandoned by the people to whom such overtures are being made.

Clearly there are no simple answers. We all see different paths and pursue them with different motivations and levels of zeal. But eventually we all confront our behaviours. In some cases we gain wisdom, understanding and are able to see when we have chosen paths 'untruthfully'. In other cases we are permanently blind, fervently justifying our dubious actions, unable to see our weaknesses.

The role of cultural difference is worth acknowledging. The need to be part of a group is more significant in some communities than others. How far we go and what we will do or say to keep up such connections clearly varies. We departed from this village maybe a little wiser, certainly with new experiences to think about. But one point of nostalgic reflection stays with us. Today still we use our guide's regularly repeated statement as an indicator of suspicion. We raise our eyebrows after hearing a suspect explanation, look with open eyed innocence and mouth the silent mantra, 'But it is TRUE'.

This anecdote is not presented to judge the appropriate behaviour or otherwise of the young cultural informant. Rather to highlight the impact with different understandings about truth, trust, responsibility on relationship building. It is an issue which needs to be openly discussed and managed if eco-cultural tourism projects are to be effectively managed.

Friendship and Business Practise in the Tourist Industry

Going alongside the theme noted above is the thorny question about the appropriateness of building friendship, warmth and connection for purely economic purposes. Is it appropriate or even societally dangerous to offer hospitality with this in mind? It is one of the great dilemmas of tourism when wealth disparities are significant. How friendship and business are combined is a regularly discussed theme in cross-cultural management literature. A 'giving' orientation towards customers, and friendship based business relationships are factors which acknowledge innate human values, often more evident and openly practised in traditional cultures. How these aspects can be managed in a globally influenced, modern tourism setting requires significant consideration.[18] How they are managed depends very much on the circumstances. The prime concern this paper seeks to highlight is the need to consider the potential impact on the 'social capital' which all societies have developed. Changing the focus from a local base to a wider one creates tensions. Eco-cultural tourism projects need to be aware of these and ensure they are sensitively and affectively managed.

Transcendental Aspects of Inter-Cultural Tourism

The fear that the spiritual base of communities can become tainted by tourism, is not an insignificant concern. The section above on ego alluded to the potential problems when spiritual sites become tourist sites. Another question is, 'Can a spiritual community be preserved if it is being 'used' as a source for economic gain?' How a recent conference[19] on spirituality, leadership and management in Australia grappled with this problem, illustrates the issue. The planning group, which I convened, wanted to maintained a policy of limited advertising and tried to ensure that commercialization would not intrude on the spirituality aspect of the program. However it was not a black and white situation. Clearly without some form of advertising and networking the event would not take place. As an event run by volunteers which requires considerable financial input, commercial matters could not be entirely forgotten. We could only hope that the feelings of connectedness and community building – a prime focus for the conference, would not be interfered with by the need to ensure the event was financial viable. It is a problem for any community which wants to 'freely' share its ideas but to also be economically sustainable. Some spiritual groups in India seem very able to do this with peace, tolerance and equanimity. The principles and processes which ensure this can happen are well worth considering, developing and promulgating.

Social Responsibility and Eco-Cultural Tourism

One of the great opportunities open to this industry is to be at the forefront of social responsibility. In Australia we are becoming aware of the need to confront our responsibility to all sections of society, especially the indigenous communities who have been significantly disadvantaged by migration to Australia. It is currently a major national agenda item. Movements to help reconciliation and to recognize Aboriginal people's rights are growing. We are slowly becoming aware that one of the ways of returning their dignity is to enable them to take control of land care and to foster and support their arts and culture. Melbourne has a number of galleries and cultural centres run by Aboriginal communities. Inclusion and harmonization rather than exclusion and differentiation are becoming understood as factors we have to grapple with. Eco-cultural tourism represents a way forward in this movement. It can be a significant element in ensuring a more stable peaceful society is established if it fosters the recognition and valuing of different cultures and customs. It enables diversity to be preserved, a factor which we are recognizing adds to environmental and social sustainability.

Conclusion

One can see that the consideration of ethical issues raises a significant number of conundrums for the eco-cultural tourism industry. The themes of globalization, fragmentation, universalism and relativism, values, culture and spirituality addressed above identify a complex set of issues. Eco-cultural tourism must openly respond to the challenges identified, if it is to be more than a passing, or unsustainable, fad in the tourism market.

However the difficulties are not insurmountable and India may be the country which leads the way in solving them. Its spiritual and cultural base undeniably goes back thousands of years. Its capacity to preserve this is unusual if not unique. Consequently, India presents the world with a wonderful opportunity to help build a new set of values which one hopes will replace the excessive devotion to 'economic rationality' so evident in the last three decades. Eco-cultural tourism provides a key to enabling the valuable insights to be made available to a much wider audience.

It is evident that there are many predicaments. This paper offers some questions and reflections coming from ethics and values which highlights some of the challenges. If they are handled effectively and appropriately, eco-cultural tourism in India may forge a new movement which brings social, environmental and spiritual values into account in the world.

Notes

1 Bowie, N: 'The Moral Obligations of Multinational Corporations', in *Ethical Theory and Business*, T.L. Beauchamp and N.E. Bowie (eds), 5th Edition, New Jersey (Prentice Hall) 1997, pp.529- 30.
2 Frederick, (1991), pp.576-587.
3 Caux, Round Table (1994), pp.588-592.
4 Ibid., Principle 6.
5 Bowie, op. cit., pp.530-31.
6 De George, (1993), pp.545-555.
7 Donaldson, T.J., 'Fundamental rights and Multinational duties', in T.L. Beauchamp and N.E. Bowie (eds) *Ethical Theory and Business*, 5th Edition, New Jersey (Prentice Hall) 1997, pp.535-545.
8 Chakraborty, (1998), pp.89-104.
9 Ibid., p.30.
10 For further details of how this 'lower self' disvalues can effect international environmental project work refer to Kimber, D., 'Ethics in International Technology Transfers' in S.K. Chakraborty and S. Chatterjee (eds) *Applied Ethics in Management*, Springer-Verlag Berlin 1999a.
11 Sekhar, (1997), pp.223-35.
12 Ibid., p.226.
13 For further discussion regarding the ethical problems relating to technology transfer and the environment see Kimber (Note 10 above pp.14-15).
14 Sekhar, op. cit., p.229.
15 Charkaborty, op. cit., p.88.
16 Sekhar, op. cit., p.229.
17 For further discussion on the topic of emerging spirituality in Australia refer to Tacey, D., *Reenchantment*, McMillan Publishing, Melbourne 2000 and Kimber, D.: 'Sharing Giving and Friendship – The Forgotten Factors of Business Relationships', *Journal of Human Values*, Sage Publications, New Delhi/Thousand Oaks/London, 2000, Vol 6. No. 2.
18 For further discussion on this issue refer to Kimber, D. 'Sharing Giving and Friendship – The Forgotten Factors of Business Relationships', *Journal of Human Values*, Sage Publications, New Delhi/Thousand Oaks/London, 1997, Vol 3. No. 1.
19 The 3rd Spirituality Leadership and Management Conference at the University of Ballarat, Dec 2000. Refer website http://www.slaM.NET.AU/Conferences/ conferences.html for details.

References

Bowie, N. (1997) 'The Moral Obligations of Multinational Corporations', in T.L. Beauchamp and N.E. Bowie (eds) *Ethical Theory and Business*, 5th Edition, Prentice Hall, New Jersey, pp.522-534.
De George, R.T. (1995) 'Ethical Dilemmas for Multinational Enterprise: A philosophical View in Business Ethics', in W.M. Hoffman and R. Frederick (eds) *Readings and Cases in Corporate Morality*, 3rd Edition, McGraw Hill, New York, pp.487-491.
De George, R.T. (1995) 'International Business Ethics: Russia and Eastern Europe', in W.M. Hoffman and R. Frederick (eds) *Readings and Cases in Corporate Morality*, 3rd Edition, McGraw Hill, New York, pp.514-523.

Donaldson, T.J. (1997) 'Fundamental rights and Multinational duties', in T.L. Beauchamp and N.E. Bowie (eds) *Ethical Theory and Business*, 5th Edition, Prentice Hall, New Jersey, pp.535-545.

Donaldson, T.J. (1995) 'Moral Minimums for Multinationals', in W.M. Hoffman and R. Frederick (eds) *Readings and Cases in Corporate Morality*, 3rd Edition, McGraw Hill, New York, pp.491-503.

Donaldson, T.J. (1996) 'Rights in a Global Market', in J.R. Desjardins and J.J. McCall (eds): *Contemporary Issues in Business Ethics*, Belmont, Wadsorth Publishing Company, California.

Dyson, F. (1992) 'Cautionary Tales for Scientists', in *From Eros to Gaia*, Pantheon Books, New York, pp.11-19.

Kimber, D. 'Sharing Giving and Friendship – The Forgotten Factors of Business Relationships', *Journal of Human Values*, Sage Publications, New Delhi/Thousand Oaks/London.

Kimber, D. (1999a) 'Ethics in International Technology Transfers' in S.K Chakraborty and S. Chatterjee (eds) *Applied Ethics in Management*, Springer-Verlag Berlin.

Kimber, D. 'Spirituality in a Changing World – Issues for Education' in *Journal for Human Values*, Sage publications New Delhi/Thousand Oak/London.

Tacey, D. (2000) *Reenchantment*, McMillan Publishing, Melbourne.

Chapter 8

The Cyber Age: Appealing Now, Apocalyptic Later?

Tanmoy Dutta

The triumphant march of modern science and technology derived from it (Sci-tech) has brought us to the Cyber Age. We have witnessed the Industrial Revolution with standardized mass production, the Green Revolution with high-yielding variety seeds and chemical fertilizers, the White Revolution with milk from crossbred cows and the like. Now we are witnessing the Knowledge Revolution: the revolution of biotechnology, space research, computers, robotics, communications and networks. Enormous benefits we have already derived and have earned a potential for deriving more and more. Modern Sci-tech has brought huge comforts and pleasures in our living. But at the same time it has made our living more complex, more in secured and above all more dehumanized. And possibly many of us have derived from our own tormented experiences that the burgeoning knowledge of Sci-tech cannot provide a full answer to how we should lead our lives. After all life is larger than living. By now, with our secular improvement of rationality, we have already realized that 'quality of life' is more important than 'quantities of life'; 'happiness index is more significant than 'standard of living index'; and a deeper thought reveals that life of purpose' is more meaningful than 'life of desire'. And we are tempted to add that 'quality of human life' is more appropriate than 'quality of life' to emphasize that there is a difference between a man and a human. Maybe we all are instinctively aware of that.

Understandably arise the ethical issues of the Cyber Age: Are we for Sci-tech or Sci-tech for us? The burgeoning knowledge of Sci-tech is about what and to what end? Will massive investments in super-technologies make human beings truly human and happy? Finally, what rights do we have to tamper with the Nature at will? (Chakraborty, June 1997)

One point should be clarified at this stage. Theoretically it can be said that while science is more germane to the acquiring of knowledge, technology is to the using of that knowledge. But how far the distinction between science and technology is proper and useful depends on the very purpose of the cultivation of science. We have learnt that men everywhere have cultivated science from two principal urges: wonder and the pursuit of power. Thus, at one level science is concerned simply with a detached understanding of the Universe. In this lies the intrinsic value of science. At another level, the value of science is essentially instrumental. There it is important for the work it does. On the ethical issue, it should be recognized that even where science as technology has chiefly an instrumental value we should help make science an instrument of higher objectives than what the dominant interest groups of society would like to prescribe or promote (Datta, September 1987).

From an ethical viewpoint, therefore, we are more concerned with the application of science; where science as technology works for instrumental value. It can be said that a very characteristic phenomenon of modern science is science-technology spiral: where scientific work inspires new technology, which is used for even more profound scientific research. In our discussions, therefore, we have taken the terms 'science as technology', 'scientific technology', 'science-technology spiral', 'sci-tech', or bare 'technology' almost in the same meaning. Because, to our knowledge, huge worldwide investments in scientific researches are necessarily not for acquiring knowledge for the sake of knowledge but for their widespread applications.

In the present context, our ethical guideline is very simple: non-selfish motivation, just the opposite of corruption, which promotes the interests of the few over the many. S. Chandrasekhar once told: 'You know the worst thing one could do to science'? Use it for self promotion' (Valluri, June 2000). Keeping in mind this ethical guideline, let us now see what higher objectives are being served by the progress of modern Sci-tech.

It is our knowledge that every human endeavor in the material world has advantages or functions as well as unintended consequences or dysfunctions. Sci-tech endeavors are no exceptions. The functions of Sci-tech often have been gained only at the cost of a number of dysfunctions. Of course, a dysfunction presents a paradox in that some individuals or groups as advantageous may perceive it. Therefore, without going to their functional and dysfunctional aspects categorically, let us take a few cases of technological applications as 'technological paradoxes'.

Technological Paradoxes

It can be said that technology has touched almost every aspect of our living. The application of technology is not only widespread. it is often taken for granted. We do not even stop to think that the modern technological progress is not an unmixed blessing. It is evident from our technology crowded society that many technological applications were initially considered highly beneficial but subsequently proved more harmful. Take three examples:

(i) Our scientific knowledge once gave nuclear power a low cost tag without speaking of its safety and environment friendliness. And now after the Chernobyl disaster of 1986 most of the Western countries have stopped taking new initiatives in nuclear power. And it is heartening news that recently the Chernobyl nuclear power station has been declared to be shut down. In fact, while the generation cost of nuclear power is comparable to thermal and hydro power, the nuclear power plant costs are almost 50 per cent higher (Joardar, February 2000).

(ii) Once we considered petroleum as the harbinger of modern civilization. But it has been found to cause large scale pollution threatening the very survival of life on this planet. And now we are going to tap solar energy as an alternative and safer source of inexhaustible supply of radiant energy which illuminates the earth. The advanced nations hope that solar energy would meet 80 per cent of the world demand in the next five decades (Gupta, September 2000).

(iii) Once we propagated using tractors and chemical fertilizers in agriculture. Now agricultural scientists are in favour of using organic manures over chemical fertilizers for plant nutrition and animal power over tractor for preserving the health of the soil. It is said that the use of the tractor causes vibration, which damages the health of the soil. It is realized that the *food* produced under organic system are pollution free, delicious and nutritious: They have longer storage life. Regular application of organic manure improves soil fertility. The environment does not get polluted under this system (Maity, September 2000).

Another interesting point: Many technological paradoxes happen unnoticed in our lives. For example, the refrigerator that is supposed to *feed* us *fresh food*, is actually serving us more and more stale leftovers. Filter-tipped cigarettes originally intended to keep nicotine intake down, actually causing more nicotine intake because it induces more smoking. Edward Tenner, science writer, cans it 'Revenge Effects'; the hidden sting in technology, unforeseen and unanswerable. According to Tenner, revenge effects are the effects of a solution that breeds more problems. E-mail is a glaring example. It is expected that e-mail will soon be as common as making or receiving a phone call. But e-mailers do not worry much about spelling, grammar, sequence of thought etc. The fingers have to talk and typing speeds are far slower than the tongue in keeping pace with the mind. Moreover, a frequent computer user takes the risk of serious injury to hands, wrists or other joints. Besides, e-mail does not guarantee privacy. Thus, e-mail that is supposed to make communication easier, in reality makes communication more complex (Raja, July 1998). Similarly, take the case of internet. 'There is a growing problem as the amount of information on diverse subjects increases. It is becoming difficult to filter the useful *from* the useless; the accurate from the inaccurate and the reliable from the unreliable' (Balaram, March 2000). Besides, there are some inherent limitations of using even the useful, accurate and reliable information. For example, Steven Weinberg Writes: 'By now it is impossible for a theoretical physicist to read all the papers even in some narrow subspecialty, so most articles on theoretical physics have little impact and are soon forgotten'. (Weinberg, April 2000).

From the foregoing brief account of the technological paradoxes *one* ethical issue certainly emerges: how far technological progress is welcome. Our information and knowledge dictate us to state that technological progress should not be allowed to continue unchecked. In the words of Steven Weinberg: 'Individual technologies reach plateaus beyond which further improvement is not worthwhile. Computer technology clearly has not yet reached its plateau, but it will. Successful technologies also tend to be self-limiting once they become available to the general population' (Weinberg, ibid.) Besides, technological progress contributes to many social and environmental problems. Therefore, it is unethical if we give undue importance to technological progress disregarding its far-reaching effects on human society and physical environment.

Technological Progress and Society

We firmly believe that technological progress has an ethical obligation of ensuring social progress. And we subscribe to the view of Fredrico Mayor, Director General of UNESCO that there is a realization today that science possesses a huge force for change and a new awareness that this unprecedented power for change does not necessarily signify for progress (Mayor, June 1999). Of course, progress is always a matter of controversy. As a convenient starting point, therefore, we can take the very first sentence of the Foreword to the Human Development Report 1995: 'History is likely to judge the progress in the 21st century by one major yardstick: is there a growing equality of opportunity between people and among nations?' (Speth, 1995).

It is evident from the World Development Report 1999/2000 of the World Bank that the incomes of rich and poor countries continue to diverge. The Report contains

> rich countries have been growing faster than poor countries since the Industrial Revolution in the mid-19th century. A recent estimate suggests that the ratio of per capita income between the richest and the poorest countries increased six fold between 1870 and 1985. Such findings are of great concern because they show how difficult it is for poor countries to close the gap with their wealthier counterparts.

The Report also shows that 'the number of poor people has risen worldwide and in some regions the proportion of poor has also increased'. (Report 1999-2000). The same feeling has been expressed by J.D. Wolfenshon, President, The World Bank:

> Without equity we will not have global stability. Without a better sense of social justice our cities will not be safe and our societies will not be stable. Without inclusion, too many of us will be condemned to live separate, armed and frightened lives. Whether you broach it from the social or the economic or moral perspective, this is a challenge we cannot afford to ignore. There are not two worlds, there is only one world. We breathe the same air. We degrade the same environment. We share the same financial system. We have the same health problems. AIDS is not a problem that stops at borders. Crime does not stop at borders. Drugs do not stop at borders. Terrorism, war and famine do not stop at borders. (Wolfenshon, January 1998).

Therefore, as expected by Fredrico Mayor, we will have to take up the ethical challenge of ensuring that the change triggered by the science of 21st century can indeed be equated with social progress.

Technological Process and Physical Environment

New technologies have brought great changes in our living. Some of these changes are very frightening too. In the words of Steven Weinberg: 'Technology certainly gives us the power to wreck the environment in which we live'. We are now facing many dangerous environmental problems. It is evident from the World Development Report 1999/2000 (pp.7-8)

> Industrial Countries are responsible for most of the existing global environmental problems - especially man-made greenhouse gases - but developing countries are catching up rapidly. Their capacity to contribute to future environmental damage increases as they grow. The world faces a number of other pressing environmental problems that threaten the global commons. Perhaps the best known is climate change which is associated with increasing emissions of carbon dioxide into the atmosphere. Others include biodiversity loss which is occurring at an alarming rate; desertification; the depletion of fish stocks; the spread of persistent organic pollutants; and threats to the ecology of Antarctica.

It is therefore an ethical obligation of the 21st century scientific technology that its triumphant march does not contribute to' further environmental degradation and take up the challenge of repairing the already done damage as far as possible.

It is good to see from the World Development Report 1999/2000 that in 1980s scientists realized that allowing chlorofluorocarbon emissions to continue unchecked would dangerously increase ultraviolet radiation in the higher latitudes, raising rates *of* skin cancer and cataracts and damaging the environment. This realization gave birth to the Montreal Protocol of 1987. Thanks to Montreal Protocol and follow-on agreements, global production of chlorofluorocarbons has fallen steeply.

The Cyber Age and Some Deeper Ethical Issues

In the discussions so far we have followed an intellectual-analytical approach while dealing with the deeper ethical issues. We will have to go to the world of emotions or feelings. We will have to follow an emotional-holistic approach. Although many *of* us believe that everything can be understood and explained with the help *of* intellect, we do not think so. Rather we believe in the caution of Albert Einstein: 'And certainly we should take care not to make intellect our God. The intellect has a sharp eye for methods and tools, but is blind to ends and values.' (Chakraborty, 1991). To our knowledge, ethicality belongs to the world *of* emotions and feelings. Therefore, intellectual treatment *of* what belongs essentially to the domain of emotions *or* feelings incurs dilution and often obfuscation. It is emotional assimilation and not intellectual grasping, that we consider essential for awakening us to the truth of ethicality (Chakraborty, 1995). We are afraid; our modern Sci-tech orientation is robbing us of our feelings.

Many of us naively believe that digital technology and internet will free us from many social evils. Why? Does technology orientation make people more ethical? History is full of examples to show that technology was always used or committed to heinous crimes against humanity. We know of many cyber crimes. An unofficial estimate shows that banks and financial institutions in the USA lose nearly a billion dollars per year owing to credit card frauds. We have heard of hi-tech examination cheating on hi-tech terrorism. We knew of atom bomb, hydrogen bomb etc. and military warfare. And now we are hearing about computer logic bomb and cyber warfare. It is said that in cyber wars the aim will be to dislocate, paralyze and incapacitate the opposing commanders' minds to force the enemy to capitulate without fighting (Kanwal, February 2001).

Similarly, there are plenty of instances of unethical commercialization of Sci-tech. Take the case of Y2K problem, a short sighted money saving trick turned into a very expensive logistic nightmare. Approximately 33 per cent storage space would have been required to store the 4 number year field. The decision to use two digits was for cost saving, but it created what is today known as Y2K bug. It was a policy of saving now and paying later. Industry experts have estimated that the global cost of Y2K rectification might have involved trillions of dollars (Maity, December 1999).

In this connection it can be said that technological progress has facilitated developing free trade amongst nations and thus global understanding and cooperation. At the same time, it has helped to promote global competition. It is often propagated that competition develops cooperation. Because the competitors have to abide by the rules of the competitions for mutual interests. But a deeper thought reveals that any competition finally leads to conflict and not to cooperation.

Thus, on the whole, we have reasons to believe that information technology can analyze the causes of social evils in a nice and reliable way. But that analysis may contribute to increase or decrease of social evils.

With regard to the question of human happiness, although technological progress of the cyber age has given us huge physical comforts and mental pleasure, it has at the same time increased our greed for material prosperity. We know that our physical needs are limited but what is unlimited is our psychological greed. Technological progress has incited our psychological greed. What we talk of globalization today is in a Sense consumerist globalization. In the process, we are possibly forgetting that true happiness does not lie in material prosperity. The richest country is not the happiest country in the world. We believe that only the cultivation of universal humanity can make us truly happy. The cultivation of science can only be an executive aid. We believe that any technological progress without simultaneous, if not prior, progress of humanity can rob us of our true happiness. Thanks to modern information technology, we have got global information networks to facilitate global exchange of information and knowledge, and thus global understanding and agreements on many social, political, economic, environmental and other issues. But there is no guarantee that all this will lead to global meeting of minds to awaken the global consciousness of humanity – the condition of being a human being.

On environmental issue, We believe that when the cultivation of science is devoid of consciousness, science becomes blind and arrogant. We are afraid; our modern Sci-tech orientation is contributing to scientific arrogance too. It is often heard that the goal of science is to win against Nature. But the question is: how to win and for what purpose? Categorically speaking, should we increase our scientific knowledge about the Nature for better attuning to it and thus to make the planet Earth more habitable, or for using our scientific knowledge at will without paying heed to its dreadful consequences? We know that a bigger power should be own only by love and reverence. It is harder as well as dangerous to try to win a bigger power by force. The question thus remains and will possibly ever remain: should we know the Nature with love and reverence for better attuning to it or with arrogance for making it servile? It is our ethical proposition that we should continue all of our scientific inquiries with a sense of the profound complexity of understanding the Nature; with a humility to admit that the entropy of the Nature is ever increasing, as Steven Wainberg says: 'the more the universe seems comprehensible, the more it also seems pointless'.

Moreover, understanding the Nature is one thing and tampering with the Nature is another. The former is in the domain of pure science while the latter is of technology. We feel that tampering with the Nature at will is a corrupt practice. Because it promotes the temporal interests of the rich countries and distributes the burden of unintended consequences amongst all the countries. Natural catastrophes do not know national boundaries. Thus, tampering with the Nature is a corrupt practice to nationalize gain and globalize loss. Above all, it is a corrupt practice because it tends to promote the interest of the present inhabitants over their future generations.

Finally, to capture the deeper ethical issues of the Cyber Age we like to remind a few words about the status of science and scientific knowledge. It can be said that science is united not by its subject matter but by its methodology. Thus, in simple terms, scientific knowledge refers to the knowledge acquired through the scientific methodology which is a system of explicit rules and procedures against which claims for knowledge are evaluated; and this system is neither closed nor infallible. As 'truth' in science is relative to evidence, the methods and the theories employed, scientific knowledge is tentative and changing. Understandably, scientific 'truths' are not always enduring contributions (Nachmias, 1982). Since certainty is the real test of knowledge, how far scientific knowledge is qualitatively superior to the knowledge acquired through any other mode is subject to critical assessment. Modern science is only about four hundred years' old, if counted from Sir Isaac Newton (1642-1727). Our civilized world has passed several centuries even before that. We should have sufficient humility to acknowledge that throughout history knowledge has been acquired by various modes. The scientific approach is by no means the only mode by which people have attempted to understand their environment and themselves. Our admiration for scientific knowledge may lead us to scientism, scientific fundamentalism, scientific egoism, or scientific dogmatism, which attempt to hegemonize other ways of knowing and acting upon the world.

References

Chakraborty, S.K. (June 1997) 'Rising Technology and Falling Ethics?' *Journal of Human Values*, vol.3, no.1, 103-117.

Datta, Amlan (September 8, 1987) 'Tradition and Science', *The Statesman*.

Valluri, S.R. (June 10, 2000) 'Scientific Misconduct-Role of Academies', *Current Science*, vol.78, no.78, no. II, 1279.

Joardar, M. (February 2, 2000) 'N-Power risks won't go away', *The Statesman*. Gupta. Y.P. (September 4, 2000) 'Solar Power: Tapping And Inexhaustible Source of Energy', *The Statesman*.

Maity, R.G. (September 9, 2000) 'Farming Trends: Need to Reduce Chemical Inputs', *The Statesman*.

Raja, M. (July 23, 1998) 'The Demon in the machine', *The Statesman*.

Balaralm, P. (March 10, 2000) 'Information Overload', Editorial, *Current Science*, vol.78, no.5.

Weinberg, Steven (March/April 2000) 'Five and a half utopias', *SPAN*, p.7.

Mayor, Fredrico (June 26, 1999) 'A new commitment needed', *The Statesman*.

Speth, James Gustave (1995) 'Foreword', Human Development Report 1995, published by Oxford University Press for the United Nations Development Programme.

The World Development Report 1999/2000, published by Oxford University Press for the World Bank, pp.14/25.

Wolfensohn, (January 1998) 'The Challenge of Inclusion'. *State Bank of India Monthly Review*, p.8.

Chakraborty, S.K. (1991) *Management by Values: Towards Cultural Congruence*, Delhi, Oxford University Press, p.47.

Chakraborty, S.K. (1995) *Ethics in Management: Vedantic Perspectives*, Delhi, Oxford University Press, pp.81-82.

Kanwal, Gurmeet (February 10, 2001) 'Cyber Warfare: New Threats in the Information Age', *The Statesman*.

Maity, Damodar (December 13, 1999) 'Apocalypse Now?', *The Statesman*.

Nachmias, Chava and Nachmias, David (1982) *Research Methods in the Social Sciences*, London, Edward Arnold Publishers Ltd. pp.4-15.

Chapter 9

Beyond Human Values: Divine Values for New Era Corporations

R.P. Banerjee

Conceptual Background

Human dominance and human values in world affairs are increasingly becoming matters under question. Imperatives having been experienced as non-rewarding or partially rewarding, a new wave of thought is emerging from the present civilization to give new shape to the entities, interactions and existential imperatives. Human limit has been reached long ago in the pursuit of human society's fulfilment of cherished needs and objectives. Like other organizations in society, industrial and commercial organizations have also fallen prey to the 'purgatory habits' of the human entity. Driven by the desire of a lower order or, as has been consistently described by people of position in various fields, the 'human needs' societies, markets and economies have proved conspicuous by their consistent urge to create and procreate their own breed bestowed with the selfish objectives.

Human affairs have been dominated by values that some may consider lower than human values. Ethics has taken a root in them. While orchestrating corporate objectives they are leading top management, and professional management as well, into the collective awareness of the concerns for selfish fulfilment, as a tool to scale desired height and achieve desired goal. 'Profit maximization', 'shareholder value optimization', 'stakeholder delight', 'sustainable competitive advantage', 'liberation through values-judgment' are a few among many other buzz words prevailing in corporate circles these days. In their pursuit to deliver things as per declared mission statements corporate leaders soil their hands with the dirty linen of selfish considerations often going beyond the declared norms of the corporations they are leading. In the context of multinational decision-making, it has been observed by Thomas Donaldson (Malachowski, 2001) that boundaries of jurisprudence fail quite often to accommodate the issues of unfair policies and discrimination in the world. Some questions raised by Donaldson are worth discussing in the context of corporate ethics. He asks

> Is a factory worker in Mexico justified in complaining about being paid three dollars an hour for the same work for which a US factory worker, employed by the same company, is paid eight dollars? Is he justified when in Mexico the practice of paying workers three dollars an hour-and even much less-is widely accepted?

Studies investigating cross-country discrimination in certain aspects of the workers' conditions of work find similarities among different industry groups and companies. The issue is not the specific cases of discriminations, but the general nature and trend of business and commercial practices that prevail among organizations. Some of the collaborating communities working as vehicles of discrimination are as follows:

- Worker-management common interest affecting consumer integrity
- Business associations and groups combined on common parameters hitting customers in the back
- Trade union power dominating over and curving power of the masses
- Powerful misusing of the wheels of power for selfish gains
- Rhetoric and dazzling exterior made to provide noble appearances to ugly motives.

Whether it is the case of small shareholders in India eventually facing the onslaught of the market movers with ugly motives or the fund managers in America facing a similar kind of situation from the fraudulent depiction of the bottom line by massive companies, ethics is the first casualty and a matter of concern. The human initiatives retained at the human scale compare to similar types of fiasco time and again. Corrections become transient in their effects and scopes. The time has come for us to look beyond the human limits of thoughts and operations. The question that arises obviously is how? It is a deeper search within the individual and the collective that might give the answer.

So far, human efforts to make changes in the systems have been primarily aesthetic and intellectual. Rhetoric and jargon have spoiled the true spirit of transformation and the intrinsic potentials of it. The new search needs to be spiritual or else it will face the same fate of becoming polluted by the 'noble' forms of the corrupt forces. A search for the spiritual identity through the character of the individual as also the collective has been essential for the long-term sustainability of enterprises. Quite different from the tenets of behaviour, the character of the individual similar to the organization, establishes the sustainable dimension of the entity. Spiritual identity of the character is essential for the build up of a new paradigm characterizing integrity, truthfulness, caring, compassion, honesty and support. Spiritual in nature and content this character shall symbolize the 'divine in man'. Prevalent among three different types: the animal type, the human type and the divine type, the free choice to embody whichever has been with the individual, so to the collective as to which category it would prefer to become and exist. Basically an individual's choice in the context of a company can be exercised at the collective level through cultivation of collective consciousness. The issue of discrimination, described earlier as the issues of collaborating communities, becomes a 'non issue' with the cultivation of character at the individual and collective levels. Analysis of the features of different character types would explicitly explain the point. Obviously in the collective context an organizational character would entail the thing. Before discussing the issues of organizational character we shall discuss the saga of Indian organizations in the backdrop of the global eventualities and trends.

The Saga of Indian Enterprises

Awareness beyond the scope of the science and art of organizational behaviour are seldom found in circles. Behavioural interventions involving motivational needs and the urge to unfold hidden potentials in human beings have been practiced to achieve results. Indian organizations compete with global corporations in the same manner. There is no denying that certain contextual advantages favour Indian corporations. At least the awareness for the play of a superior consciousness is expected of them.

Let us examine the declared core values of three Indian companies who are honoured for their successes and/or legacy.

Core Values of ITC Ltd

The corporate website of ITC Ltd. holds the following as its core values: trusteeship, customer focus, respect for people, excellence, innovation and ethical corporate citizenship. ITC's Core Values are aimed at developing a customer-focused, high-performance organization which creates value for all its stakeholders.

Trusteeship As professional managers, we are conscious that ITC has been given to us in 'trust' by all our stakeholders. We will redeem the trust reposed in us by continuously adding value to ITC.

Customer Focus We will always be customer focused. We will deliver what the customer needs in terms of value, quality and satisfaction.

Respect For People We will respect and value people and uphold humanness and human dignity. We will value differences in individual perspectives. We want individuals to dream, create and experiment in pursuit of opportunities and achieve leadership through teamwork.

Excellence We will strive for excellence in whatever we do. We will do what is right, do it well and win.

Innovation We will constantly innovate and strive to better our processes, products, services and management practices.

Ethical Corporate Citizenship We will pursue exemplary standards of ethical behaviour. We will at all times comply with the laws of the land.

What if the ethical corporate citizenship is asked questions beyond the legal boundaries of corporate practices concerning its role *vis-à-vis* the society and the world. The company is satisfied with the ethical behaviour that conforms to the legal norms. Trusteeship obviously refers to individuals and customer focus to the company as a collective entity. Trusteeship has been considered as representing the core values of the company. However, what is the method or the way for the people in the company to achieve and maintain trustworthiness? Is it assumed to be automatic with ITC employment? Possibly this issue refers to the attributes of individual character. Human values cultivated by the individual or practiced at the corporate level can make the person or company utter words or communicate in terms of ethics, but that does not necessarily make them trustworthy. Divine values might be essential for a person or company to achieve the height of trustworthiness.

Tata Steel's ethics policy shows two unique features: transparency in its functions, especially when dealing with stakeholders, and maintaining an 'ethics office' as a mark of distinct emphasis on business ethics at the corporate level.

Ethics Policy of Tata Steel

Tata Steel's belief in business ethics is as intense as its passion for steel. Whether it be corporate governance or dealing with customers and employees, Tata Steel takes utmost care to be scrupulously transparent.

Tata Steel was one of the first companies in India to institute the position of an ethics officer reporting to the Board of Directors. Every executive of the Company is committed to the Tata Code of Conduct through a written contract.

'Tata Steel is of the firm belief that transparency in stakeholder relations and fair business practices are fundamental to the long-term success of an organization.'

There are ethics offices in many multinational corporations and western enterprises. To give an example, Texas Instruments had an ethics office in the 1980s with an ethics director offering the opportunity to every employee to speak out on corporate policies and practices. The ethics policy of Texas Instruments reads as follows (Aguilar, 1995)

> We will not let the pursuit of sales, billings; profits – distort our ethical principles. We always have and we always will place integrity before shipping, before billings, before profits, before anything. If it comes down to a choice between making a desired profit and doing it right, you don't have a choice. You will do it right. We must do it right, in every detail. Expedient compromises or shortcuts for near-term gains are not acceptable.

Texas Instruments wants to make senior management's intentions and concerns clear particularly with respect to ethical policies and practices. The company wants to uphold the core values of 'honesty, fairness, candour and respect in all business dealings' for all situations. The company thinks that the 'ethical character' of the corporation would be enhanced with the cultivation of the core values identified by it. This is again an imperative of the individual character of the persons in the company. Mr. Carl Skooglund, Ethics Director of the company in 1994, recollects his first interactions with the company chairman. Skooglund (Aguilar, 1994) says

> When I joined TI in 1962, the whole company had about 18,000 people. I now have 6,500 people reporting to me. The day after I was hired, I spent several hours with the top person, and the one thing I remember was being told, 'you do not have to make deals with anybody requiring you to lie, cheat, or steal. You just walk out.'

The ethics office itself gives direction to the people in the company towards an ethical attitude and rectitude. Again the question of dominant values arises. Is the cultivation of human values enough or does the company need to address the issue of cultivating a superior set of values called divine values?

Ethics Policy of Reliance Industry Ltd.

Reliance believes in the nine core values of honesty, integrity, respect, fairness, purposefulness, trust, responsibility, citizenship and caring. The company is seemingly committed to all the stakeholders and upholds respect for other person's interests as well as their own. The relevant part of the corporate website reads

> Reliance believes that any business conduct can be ethical only when it rests on the nine core values of Honesty, Integrity, Respect, Fairness, Purposefulness, Trust, Responsibility, Citizenship and Caring.
>
> We are committed to an ethical treatment of all our stakeholders – our employees, our customers, our environment, our shareholders, our lenders and other investors, our suppliers and the Government. A firm belief that every Reliance team member holds is that the other person's interests count as much as their own.
>
> The essence of these commitments is that each employee conducts the company's business with integrity, in compliance with applicable laws, and in a manner that excludes considerations of personal advantage.
>
> We do not lose sight of these values under any circumstances, regardless of the goals we have to achieve. To us, the means are as important as the ends.

The values of Texas Instruments and of top rated Indian companies lead us to some deeper issues. Now that we have some idea about a few trusted Indian companies in terms of their ethics policies and core values as compared to the global example, we can initiate a comparative analysis of their declared policies in the context of some observations by The World Bank and its president.

The World Bank's Observation

An estimation of the extent of poverty prevailing in the world as given by 'The World Development Report 2002' published by the World Bank, states that

> Of the 4.7 billion people who live in the 100 countries that are World Bank clients:
>
> - 3 billion live on less than $2 a day and 1.2 billion on less than $1 a day
> - Nearly 3 million children in developing countries die each year from vaccine-preventable diseases
> - 113 million children are not in school
> - 1.5 billion do not have clean water to drink

Effective poverty reduction strategies and poverty-focused lending are central to achieving the Bank's objectives. Bank programs give high priority to sustainable, social, and human development and strengthened economic management, with a growing emphasis on inclusion, governance and institution-building.

The World Bank's observation depicts an emerging dimension of the world situation particularly with respect to the prospects of growth and sustainability. Socio-economic factors like income, infant mortality, illiteracy, non-availability of clean drinking water and similar restrictive factors make the prospects of corporations quite bleak in the future. With many markets saturated in terms of continuous consumption of goods and services and many other markets not having the adequate purchasing power to buy goods and services at rates above their affordable limits the urge to expand the scope of the markets has grown considerably. But how can it be achieved? Can the corporate organizations consider this aspect of the present world as a part of their corporate responsibility? Should they? An answer is difficult to obtain. Policy statements made by the corporations do not touch upon the issue of customer affordability as a matter to reckon with. They are, to great extent, linked to the markets and policy formulations are usually limited to that.

In a recent speech made before the board of governors of the World Bank, Mr. James Wolfensohn (September 2000), the president made the following observations

> This new world, our greater understanding, a wiser development community, and a changing international institutional environment mean that through working together, doing development differently, and giving voice to the voiceless, we now have a chance to make the next decade one of real delivery in the fight against poverty. The opportunities and promise of a global economy, the information age, and life-saving and productivity-enhancing technologies are all ours to seize. We must work together to harness the benefits of globalization to deliver prosperity to the many, not just the few. This is not just a new economic program. It is an obligation, an obligation based on shared moral and social values. It is an obligation that is also based on enlightened self-interest. It is an obligation to the next generation to leave them a better world: a world of equity, a world of peace, a world of security.

In his keynote address delivered at the Institute of Internal Auditors' international conference in June 2002, Mr. James D. Wolfensohn furnished in a different manner the data on poverty and inadequacies in the world. According to him

> We have a planet today of 6 billion people, and 5 billion of them live in developing and transition economies – 5 out of 6 billion. They have 20 per cent of the world's GDP, and the 1 billion has 80 per cent of the world's GDP. There are 3 billion people in the world that live under \$2 a day. There are 1.2 billion that live under \$1 a day, and this number is growing. There are 125 million kids not in school. There are many other statistics I can give you about lack of clean water, and access to power, and sewerage, and so on, which will frighten you, but the basic element, in terms of being able to get aid to flow, being able to get investment to flow is essentially the construction of a set of reliable principles of accounting and ethics, which allow people to make cross-border transactions.

Mr. Wolfensohn quite reasonably gives a high degree of emphasis on the construction of a 'set of reliable principles of accounting and ethics' for corporations. By doing this the corporation goes beyond its own boundary to take care of the society at large and thereby enhances the potentials of corporate activities across the globe. The principle of 'distributive justice' was put forward by Swami Vivekananda (Banerjee 1998, 2002). So far construed as a matter of concern for philanthropic and social organizations the issues of global poverty and inadequacies must be addressed by business and industry in the long-term.

An attitude of distributive justice requires a particular spirit in the human character at the individual level and the group character at the collective level. Human aspirations at the individual and the collective level are blind to the selfish interests of the individual and group. Transformation in the intrinsic aspects of the character is essential for realizing the effects of perpetuating global imbalances and the emerging needs of global sustainability. We have highlighted some companies who may be regarded as superior in terms of policies and practices concerning ethics and values. Limited by the pettiness, meanness and smallness intrinsic in human values even the best lack in the spirit of transformation from what they are now and what they ought to be. A process of transformation should begin an elevation from the meanness, pettiness and smallness intrinsic in human beings. Transformation should change from grabbing to giving in the global context.

Transformation from 'Grabbing to Giving' Habits

As long as the grabbing habit persists no amount of warning or mentioning of the disastrous global scenario would bring in the urge to hear about. Corporations do not consider things beyond the corporate boundaries – directly or indirectly. Corporate social responsibility is limited to the 'teleological' aspects of ethics (Banerjee 2002) where a company may take ethical actions and view society in terms of certain responsibilities where the company's distant interest is involved. Stakeholders, customers and other people related to the company are the focus for the company to build its own values and ethical policies. Faith in human values can at best lead to this position. It is no denying that the culture of human values in these corporations has yielded good results and softened the ruptures created by heartless, careless, non-compassionate corporate or business forces. The limits have been reached by most of us. The best intentions among these companies can not take society to the heights of a true global concern for humanity at large. Poverty and inadequacy are not only the problems of those who are suffering. These are but problems of the global society and business and industry have their own stakes in that. It is not only in their interest of expansion and survival but in the interest of a decent existence in the current period that corporations have to transform as the dominant view. Transformation needs to be pursued at both the individual and collective levels. It is a case for transformation from the 'human' state to the 'divine' state.

The question arises as to how global concern will help the organization without a global scale of operation. Even multinational corporations would question their involvement into something, which they think is not their cup of tea.

Evolving into long-term things, sometimes at the cost of more short-term ventures could prove fatal to things such as: shareholder value, profit maximization etc. Risking the current profitability and immediate sustainability, companies invest in initiatives for a relatively longer term. This involves a trade off between and among different possibilities keeping an eye on the best achievable options for the corporations. There was a time when companies did not have to think about factors of sustainability the way they do now. Market development was not in the kitty of most of the companies who were used to skimming profit from the immediate current period. The concept of 'stakeholder responsibility' is relatively new. Even today, a large number of organizations neither believe in nor work towards the stakeholder well-being. Most companies want to make the most of opportunities for reasons obvious to their stakeholders. The selfish interest of the employee union meets those of the management; that of a single company meets that of a business association etc. It is the commonality of interest that binds them into one fold. Common identity is created with a view to establish homogeneity of existence as a part of an existential need.

Human aspirations will always seek a kind of fulfilment through creating and maintaining a balance between and among various parameters that are apparently in conflict with each other. 'Grabbing the opportunity' or 'grab in the garb of giving' is the scenario. Corporate social responsibility has usually come second in most cases. The World Bank's observation and the philosophical view of 'distributive justice' suggest a paradigm shift in approach. Divine values are essential for the understanding of the global human concerns. Essentially dichotomous, human values can not reach the realm of 'giving' which is the key to understanding the spirit of global concern. Limited to the human scale, one's scope of understanding is always bound by the expressed or hidden considerations of nourishing the 'ego'. Be it for a person or a company 'ego' shadows the vision and limits it to the span of understanding in the 'human' sense of the term (which could be essentially sensual, instinctive or selfish in nature). Transformation shall prove effective when society embraces it with its dominant organization honouring the concept and process of transformation from 'human' to 'divine' values.

Character – Individual and Organizational

In a joint paper published in the Harvard Business Review, Kegan and Lehey (November, 2001) made a statement as follows

> As organizational psychologists we have seen this dynamic literally hundreds of times, and our research and analysis have recently led us to a surprising yet deceptively simple conclusion. Resistance to change does not reflect opposition, nor is it merely a result of inertia. Instead, even as they hold a sincere commitment to change, many people are unwittingly applying productive energy towards a hidden competing commitment. The resulting dynamic equilibrium stalls the effort in what looks like resistance but is in fact a kind of personal immunity to change.

Intrinsic to the personality, a hidden competing commitment may be the product of the individual's personal ambition, and the organizational and social imperatives. It appears at times that the person is defeating himself through his own behaviour in the organization. Kegan and Lahey (ibid., 2001) have correctly mentioned this as the responsibility of management. According to them, 'Helping overcome their limitations to become more successful at work is at the very heart of effective management'.

What is really the root of a self-defeating behaviour? Is the hidden competing commitment a factor or an element of behaviour or does it come from a deeper realm of the personality, called '*character*'? Such a possession could be through inheritance, learning, experience and augmentation or through combinations to different degrees. Let us hear a small narrative case as explained by Kegan and Lahey (2001). They narrated the case of a manager whom they call Helen who was a rising star at a large manufacturing company. The description goes on to say that

> Helen had been assigned responsibility for speeding up production of the company's most popular product, yet she was spinning her wheels. When her boss, Andrew, realized that an important deadline was only two months away and she hadn't filed a single progress report, he called her into a meeting to discuss the project. Helen agreed that she was far behind schedule, acknowledging that she had been stalling in pulling together the team. But at the same time she showed a genuine commitment to making the project a success. The two developed a detailed plan for changing direction, and Andrew assumed the problem was resolved. But three weeks after the meeting, Helen still had not launched the team.

The story attempts to explore Helen's mind to get some exploratory answer to the question, 'why was Helen unable to change her behaviour? Helen had developed the hidden expectation to gain promotion and become Andrew's peer. She believed she could only offer her best to the organization as Andrew's peer and not as his subordinate. This shake up of the relative position in the corporate hierarchy was the hidden agenda that had made Helen immune to any kind of change within the organization. Helen believed that if a favourable change had occurred while she was the subordinate, the success would flow to Andrew, the boss as a mark of business gains through a team and Helen would have lost her achievements in the process.

What is Helen's motive? Is it behavioural? Helen's mind has to be explored to know the answers. How would one know the patterns of responses of individuals in different contexts and in different boundary conditions? The answer could come from a deeper domain, called conscience, which is fundamental to character.

We need to keep minds open to the problems of unfulfilled desires and basic needs – possibly drawing lines of distinction between them. Let us examine the case of Mexican girls brought to the United States through human trafficking to serve in factories, the sex industry, or on farms forcefully for the trafficker's profit. These people perform their work not from a sense of duty coming from within, but as a result of threat, coercion, compulsions and direct exploitation. A report published by the *Economist* (June 1st, 2002) says

One group, impoverished young girls from Mexico, was found earlier this year in a suburban house in New Jersey. They had been lured from their hometowns by an international trafficking ring, smuggled to the United States and forced into prostitution. The victims who were beaten if they resisted, sold their bodies to customers for as little as $35.

These groups of people are not prostitutes by virtue of their character traits. Rather, they are forced into jobs that they resist.

What happens, if there is a sudden call from the deeper realm of the individual? A wake up call? Richard Boyatzis, Annie McKee, and Daniel Goleman (2002) argue that the 'wake-up-call' is difficult to ignore. According to them

> A wake-up call can come from a mission: an irresistible force that compels people to step out, step up, and take on a challenge. It is as if they suddenly recognize what they are meant to do and can not ignore it any longer.

The wake-up call hits at the inner psyche of the individual and dormant attributes of the individual got back to the original characteristic tone of the person. The call is at times spiritual. This takes cognizance of the person's inner domain that remains unperturbed by the movements and atrocities of the external. Character is fundamental to the person, defining his traits and behavioural pattern in the long-term. The problem remains as to how to identify the character traits.

Organizational character emerges out of characteristic pattern of people holding different stakes in the organization and values, mission, vision set for it. It is essentially a composite of different traits and attributes of people manning the organization or somewhat linked to it. Its collective identity creates multiple tones and tenets of character in the organization. Whereas the dominant tone and set of basic attributes create fundamental identity of the organization potentially equipped with all possible means to develop a collective orchestra of multiple tones to take care of the different contextual and eventual possibilities.

Understanding Organizational Character

Organizational character has been defined as the collective attributes nurtured by individuals in the organization, which the power matrix links to the power map of the organization. The way she/he drives the wheel and uses the engine of the organization becomes the most important aspect for establishing the character of the organization. In this regard Peter Drucker (2002) has made the following observations

> The reader may wonder, how can a manager function who is not in charge of hiring, promoting, or firing the people in her department? I posed this question to a senior executive at BP Amoco whose workers, including senior scientists, are now managed by Exult. His answer: 'Exult knows, it has to satisfy me if it wants to keep the contract. Sure, they make the decision to fire someone or move them. But normally only because I suggested it or after they consulted with me.'

The situation narrated by Peter F. Drucker of BP Amoco draws attention to the power system of the organization and particularly the power dynamics. To a large extent, this system resembles the case of the Mexican. The senior executive at BP Amoco may or may not always take a decision on rational parameters. A personal disliking of the top boss may simply lead to being fired from a job. BP Amoco style of functioning would make the process of decision making more individual than collective. Organizational character becomes essentially a replica of individual character of the person having the most effective power in the organization.

Human attributes follow a pattern but may appear random or chaotic because of the error in observation and understanding. Field and Golubsky (ibid.) talks about the characteristics of a chaotic system saying

> They are deterministic but behave as though they are not. A tiny inaccuracy in our knowledge of the current position can be magnified to produce completely inaccurate predictions of the future position. Even the tiniest error in our data can be magnified over time to produce an outcome far different from what we would have gotten using the true data.

Attributes forming human character seem to be in random sequence with the behavioural parameters. An apparent view at this would reveal a chaotic field of attributes making it difficult to really identify and judge a character. Human behaviour is more truly a factor of the human mind than the character. The human mind is, in general, highly flexible and full of abstractions. The higher the flexibility of mind, the higher is the level of unpredictability of things done by the person. A person may interpret the chaos and abstraction in terms of extreme flexibility to read a concrete fact. A.N. Whitehead (1954) has emphasized this idea abstraction for a concrete fact. According to him

> The paradox is now firmly established that the utmost abstractions are the true weapons with which to control our thought of concrete fact.

It is possible to go beyond the abstraction only when we discover the pattern underlying the system. Apparently a complex field can yield a definite pattern when observed over a larger field or longer period of time.

It appears that apparent randomness can even reveal a definite pattern when explored. Apparent differences in the composition of the groups do not make any substantial difference to the pattern that emerges out of a system.

Observations of these patterns might involve problems of misrepresentation. One has to be cautious about this problem. Pierre Jacob (1997) has talked about this problem asserting the importance of the need for the right kind of observations. According to Pierre Jacob

> We may view this as a kind of cafeteria model of the acquisition of social attitudes. The individual does not inherit his ideas about fluoridation, royalty, women judges and nudist camps; he learns them from his culture. But his genes may influence which ones he elects to put on his tray. Different cultural institutions – family, church, school,

books, television – like different cafeteria, serves up somewhat different menus, and the choices a person makes will reflect those offered him as well as his own biases.

Fundamental tenets of personality, as observed by others or as expressed by the person through interactions with others, are the genotypes or the intrinsic characteristics of a person. The behaviour of a person may or may not be reflective of character in the short run. The long-term pattern comes out of the basic personality type, also known as individual character. Dobzhansky (1964) has confirmed the view discussed above through his observations. He maintains

> The nature-nature problem is nevertheless far from meaningless. Asking the right question is in science, often a large step toward obtaining right answers. The questions about the roles of genotype and the environment in human development must be posed thus: To what extent are the differences observed among people conditioned by the differences between the environments in which people were born, grew and were brought up?

This issue concerns the inheritability of traits or elements contributing to the building of a character. This connectivity makes the character a more reliable factor than behaviour. This could be seen as an important contributory factor towards the shaping of a personality that is revealed through character. Plomin, DeFries, McClearn and McGuffin (2001) think that the genetic influence is no less than the environmental and other influences on the behaviour of a person. According to them

> Genetic influence on behaviour is just that – an influence or contributing factor, not pre-programmed and deterministic. Environmental influences are usually as important as genetic influences.

Several authors have confirmed the fact of differences in the characteristic pattern of individuals as a result of the genetic differences. McCartney, Harris, and Berneiri (1990) have argued the importance of genetic factor as a fundamental trait. Views upheld by them can be summarized as

> General cognitive ability or 'g' factor grows in importance with the experiences an individual accumulates during the course of life. Genetic factors or fundamental traits become increasingly important throughout an individual's life.

Views as expressed above support the point that fundamental traits of a personality play a dominant role in shaping the pattern of interactions or the behaviour of a person. As has been mentioned already, this fundamental trait of a personality is her/his character.

In Search of a Divine Character

Various approaches are available to delineate and classify human character. This section will suggest the method adopted by the author. Banerjee (2002, 1998) has suggested that individuals could be classified into three broad categories as

- Animal type
- Human type
- Divine type

Some of the dominant attributes forming these types are:

Animal type Greed, lust, covetousness, indolence, gluttony, anger, etc.
Human type Dichotomy, selfishness, jealousy, envy, backbiting, dynamism, opulence, etc.
Divine type Selflessness, honesty, sincerity, transparency, co-operation, etc.

The attributes mentioned form the characteristic type of a person. A person with dominant attributes of the animal type reveals the animal-type character; similarly with the other two types. Characteristic identification defines the limits of conformity and performance of different persons.

For example, a divine type person can hardly be made to do things along the lines of the animal or human type. Bending the person beyond the logical limit of the attribute-category is not possible. Each type has its own pattern of action. The animal type, for example, is timid in its approach, can do anything it likes, does not think at all of others. Basically restless, it constructs things for personal delight and usage only. This type of person does not bother to reach the personal end through creating distrust among groups or poisoning the mind of people in the group or community through filthy things. They are said to possess a 'punctuate mind'. Fodor (1987) explains the 'punctuate mind' as

A punctuate mind is a device with no logical (or, inferential) abilities.

The animal type, having a 'punctuate mind' lacks in rational judgment. Take, for example, one of the attributes, say, 'anger'. Anger spoils an individual through a gradual process of destruction. The *Bhagawad Gita* (Banerjee, 1998), the Holy Scripture that communicates the words of divine to humanity, describes anger saying,

Anger leads to obsession
Obsession to loss of memory
Loss of memory to delusion
And finally, delusion leads to destruction.

Animal attributes engineer self-destruction through a certain range of attributes that not only kill the individual from within but also spoil the group or the community.

This indicates the fact that animal attributes are dangerous for the existence and long-term sustainability of an organization.

Concluding Remarks

Human attributes are basically dichotomous. They pull in the dualities of existence. At times this category of person is in the domain of the divine and at other times it is characterized by animal attributes. Oscillating between these two sets of attributes, the human category loses credential for long-term sustainability. This is the result and achievement oriented type of personality that presumably focuses on the outer domain of the individual and keeps on dragging towards the domain of animal attributes. In the collective, or group, this category lacks the spirit to be sustainable in the long term.

The divine character could be enthused in individuals and linked to the organizations to make the organization a divine type. Issues of global concern that have been raised can be visualized as something within the scope of human realization and within the emerging realities. Indian organizations can think of taking a lead in this direction.

References

Aguilar, Francis J. (1994), *Managing Corporate Ethics*, Oxford University Press: Oxford.

Banerjee, R.P. (1998), *Mother Leadership*, A.H. Wheeler and Co.: New Delhi.

Banerjee, R.P. (2002), *Stress Management Through Mind Engineering*, Wisdom House: England.

Bartlett, A. Christopher and Ghosal Sumantra (1998), *Managing Across Borders*, Harvard Business School Press: Boston, p.320.

Boyatzis, Richard, Anne McKee and Daniel Goleman (2002), 'Reawakening your passion for work', *Harvard Business Review*, Boston, April, p.89.

Dobzhansky, Theodosius (1964), *Heredity and the Nature of Man*, Harcourt Brace and World: New York, p.55.

Drucker, Peter F. (2002), 'They're not employees, They're people', *Harvard Business Review*, Boston, February, p.72.

Field, Michael and Martin Golubitsky (1995), *Symmetry in Chaos*, Oxford University Press: Oxford, p.13.

Field, Michael and Martin Golubitsky, ibid., p.12.

Field, Michael and Martin Golubitsky, ibid., p.148.

Fodor, J.A. (1987), *Psychosemantics: the problem of meaning in the Philosophy of mind*, MIT Press: Cambridge, Massachusetts, p.88.

Fodor, J.A. (1991), 'A model argument for narrow content' *The Journal of Philosophy*, 88, 1, pp.5-26.

Jacob, Pierre (1997), *What minds can do*, Cambridge University Press: Cambridge, p.93.

Kegan, Robert and Lisa Laskow Lahey (2001), 'The real reason people won't change', *Harvard Business Review*, Boston, November, p.85.

Kegan, Robert and Lisa Laskow Lahey, ibid., (2001), p.86.

Kim, J.J. (1982), 'Psychological Supervenience' in Kim (1994), *Supervenience and Mind, selected philosophical essays*, Cambridge University Press: Cambridge.

Lohelin, J.C. (1997), 'Genes and environment', in D. Magnusson (ed.), *The lifespan development of individuals: Behavioural, new biological and psychosocial perspectives: a synthesis* (pp.38-51), Cambridge University Press: New York, p.48.

McCartney, K., M.J. Harris and F. Berneiri, (1990), 'Growing up and growing apart: a developmental meta-analysis of twin studies', *Psychological Bulletin*, 107, pp.226-237.

McGue, M. (1993), 'From proteins to cognitions: The behavioural genetics of alcoholism.' In R. Plomin and G.E. McClearn (eds), *Nature, Nurture and Psychology* (pp.245-268). American Psychological Association: Washington DC.

Plomin, Robert, John C. DeFries, Gerald E. McClearn and Peter McGuffin, (2001), *Behavioural Genetics*, Worth Publishers: New York, p.92.

The Economist (2002), 'Human trafficking – a case of exploitable souls', Chicago, 1 June, p.36.

Whitehead, Alfred North (1954), *Science and the Modern World*, Macmillan: New York.

Wolfensohn, James D. (September 2000), 'Building a sustainable world', http://www.worldbank.org.

Wolfensohn, James D. (June 2002), 'Keynote speech at the institute of internal auditor's international conference', http://www.worldbank.org.

World Bank (2002), *World Development Report*, Oxford University Press: Oxford.

Chapter 10

Corporate Environmental Responsibility and Management Decision Making in the Flexible Scenario

O.V. Nandimath and M.R.C. Ravi

Introduction

There is no doubt that corporate decision making is proving to be more of a challenge than ever before, especially bearing in mind externalities. On one hand globalization, mechanization and computerization are the buzzwords, but on the other hand, values, social responsibility and community accountability are influencing the decisions of enterprises.[1] The information revolution has made geographical barriers meaningless – this has influenced the governance process tremendously. Owing to various pressure groups the policies at macro level are becoming much more fluid than ever – making governance of any enterprise a complicated task.

The present paper intends, to first account for the fluid external world at a macro level and focusing in particular on the growing awareness about environment and ecological preservation as 'value'. Especially in India after the Bhopal disaster[2] we have seen tremendous change in the attitude of government, judiciary and other civil groups and even individuals for that matter, towards corporations (and not only Multi-National Corporations). Much legislation to protect the environment, regulate business enterprises, policy changes, judicial activism, judicial administration, non government organization's protests etc., are some of the prime developments in the aftermath of the Bhopal disaster. The judiciary in India has taken a very pro-active stance almost dwelling on every aspect of policy making. There are experts who even to this day recognize (and rightly also) that as a country, we have failed to learn from the Bhopal incident and whatever policy change initiatives brought in, are highly insufficient. That is true. But on the other hand, this fluidness in externalities has placed corporate decision making in the hot seat. Today's corporate manager has to take all such aspects into consideration before taking decisions. This is challenge number one.[3]

Moving from here the situation is growing more complex than ever. There are some important initiatives both at local and global levels to control the activities of Multi-National Corporations. Civil society especially is up in arms. So we may expect some more stringent policy interventions in the name of environmental protection and conservation etc. This is challenge number two. How can a business enterprise take into its ambit all such policy interventions to thrust it self forward? The present paper also dwells into this sphere of future initiatives, which are on at global level. Finally, the paper looks into various positive strategies to take into account the environment as 'value' while the corporate manager takes such decisions.

What is Corporate Environmental Responsibility?

Corporate Environment Responsibility can better be described than defined. This concept refers to the corporation's role as protector of environment. At the very outset, this may appear as absurd, but it is the reality. It is generally accepted that we cannot go on using the resources of the world at the present rate. At the same time the economic development in any economy should continue. Unless this happens goods, services, employment and other such things all suffer. How to balance these two competing interests? how to have sustainable development? are the questions before us. How does a corporation stimulate its activities in such a fashion that it reduces the gap between two competing interests to achieve 'sustainable development'? How does the corporate realize its role as protector of the environment? When it amasses huge amounts of profits and reserves at the cost of society – it should repay its obligations.

People understand that all corporations work for the maximization of profits. This is a very simple and straightforward statement to make. Many corporations work beyond this parameter of earning and maximization of profits. In reality they are also like any other institutions that work to get recognition and powers in the political sense of the term. If it were to be maximization of profit at the outset then bending corporations to law and other regulations would have been very easy. But their desire to acquire prominence and political power make them difficult players to control. This regulation of corporations and diverting them towards the social cause has emerged as the single largest issue over a period of years for every one. Traditionally, the Contracterian Model of governance identified a small group of communities as enterprises' stake-holders (like Shareholders, Creditors, suppliers, Dealers and other types of investors etc.). Soon we realized that it is an entire community or society, which is the stakeholder and a corporation has to necessarily operate within this paradigm of society. Otherwise it is not possible for a corporation to operate successfully anywhere in this globe. The quote below clearly shows the mood of civic society, and advocates for some international initiative to regulate corporations towards environment, human rights, development and labour

> Corporations benefit from a global market for the development of their business but are not held globally accountable. Therefore, current moves to ensure sustainability require an international instrument of corporate responsibility, accountability and liability. Now is the time for an international instrument that ensures rights and duties, reporting, monitoring, and verification of consistent responsible corporate behavior. Such an

instrument should encompass *inter alia* compensation for damages, remediation, right to know and respect for human and community rights.[4]

There are nearly 48 reported and recorded cases from the industrial sectors, including chemical, forest, mining, genetic engineering, nuclear energy and oil industries in different parts of the world. Through this very bad experience the perception of the society is that corporations downplay damage and focus attention and liability on the local company in order to elude criminal and/or civil liability. Further to curb these abuses, governments must act globally to ensure that both transnational and national corporations are held liable for their actions, particularly in developing countries and countries with economies in transition where companies operate in less regulated environments. This further worsens the scenario for corporate management to act and take decisions. The aftermath of Bhopal and such other disasters called for implementation of what are popularly known as 'Ten Bhopal Principles on Corporate Accountability'.[5]

The Contractarian theory of management is just not implement-able. The corporation has to take the entire society as its stakeholder and operate. Hence there is a new concept emerging – industrialists and environmentalists have realized that in order to craft reasonable solutions to environmental problems, both environmental and profit concerns must be taken into account. This theory attempts to promote a simultaneous coexistence of economic growth and social concerns. The concept of corporate citizenship is fast becoming the *mantra* of the day.[6]

Decision Making and Uncertain Environment

Because of the unpleasant events of certain corporations, and unplanned and unregulated development the external environment is fast changing. Concerns over the result of this poorly planned development have resulted in public protests. International human rights and environmental pressures have increasingly been brought to bear against many developmental projects/enterprises. Enhanced public awareness and sensitivity to the environment and the social impact of development has led to the public playing an increasingly active and vigilant role in society in opposing development projects. Interestingly, one manner in which this increasing role has been played out is in the use of Public Interest Litigation or Social Action Litigation.[7] The dilution of *locus standi*, reduced evidentiary burden, the power of the courts to appoint special commissions and experts committees, the judicial notice of the 'facts' etc., increase the level of uncertainty to dizzy heights. There is no doubt, as pointed earlier in the first part of this paper, an inevitable development to save mother earth. But on the other hand this has led to litigation costs, project delays, the disruption or stoppage of day-to-day operations, expensive remedial measures (like compensation and clean-up costs, diversion of management time and attention, and adverse corporate publicity (greater vulnerability of public perception). These in turn lead to cost overruns, and the weakening of financials risk, closure risk, adverse impacts on society, poor enforcement, and the use of interim directions. It is no secret that many times the Public Interest Litigations are misused and used for meeting political ends. Hence in the beginning of economic activity if the establishment or management takes the environmental factor into consideration, to a great extent these hurdles can be overcome, if not completely eliminated. Environmentally proactive and anticipating regulation reaps gains financially by reducing costs and liabilities, increases efficiency, enhances customer loyalty and accelerates revenue growth for development projects in particular.

The history of development projects and multi-national corporations in India since independence is not that encouraging in terms of environment and human rights. This is perhaps the single largest factor, which our managers have overlooked including the macro level policy makers in government. Developmental projects such as, dams, thermal power stations, ports and railway lines, have often in the past been carried into effect without proper impact assessments and have become tombs of doom instead of the temples of progress envisaged. Large scale displacement without adequate attention paid to rehabilitation of the project ousters, destruction of flora fauna, besides escalation of costs owing to inordinate delay in the execution of projects, have been the outcome of such improper and short-sighted development. The following is an example of this. The Government decided that the north Chennai area and Ennore of Tamil Nadu, India, was a prime industrial site for industries and other infrastructure development. The area already had numerous state-owned power plants and a new satellite port. In a recent public hearing conducted for building a new industrial estate, the local communities were clear that they would oppose the project. They were severely concerned about

- The poor environmental record of the prior developments in the area including adverse impacts on fishermen's livelihoods;
- The poor track record in compensations received for lands acquired;
- The presence of a site of significant ecological importance within eight kilometers of the development area and the inadequacy of the impact assessment study.

It is interesting to note not only the local communities, but also academic institutions, Non Governmental Organizations, and other interested citizens were opposed to the project. A statement from the leader of a local village brought out the problem and mentioned 'we had accepted the earlier developments in the interest of the state and even sacrificed our land for the same. But we are not willing to do this anymore. We will oppose the project at any cost unless there is guarantee that our interests will be protected'. This protest delayed the proposed industries and projects. But this has also adversely affected the existing industries to a great extent.

Other reasons for the increasing interest and involvement of civil society and non-governmental organizations in this process include

- Post-modernist thinking and the value of individual rights and those concerning the environment have increased.
- In the light of above, the frustration associated with development that has adversely affected communities and populations, is growing, given a history of development in India that has generally adversely affected the environment.
- Improved communication and information available with local communities and the increasing role of NGOs and voluntary organizations those are keen to take up environmental issues. One possible reason for the confrontationist approach is because the people and NGOs inevitably struggle to obtain information about the impending project.

In 1987 the Factories Act, 1948 was amended with a new chapter regulating hazardous industrial processes (largely as a result of the Shriram Gas Leak Case of 1985), and amendments were made to the Air Act, 1987, and the Water Act in 1988, which further empowered environmental agencies and strengthened penal provisions. Effluent and emission standards were specified for over 20 industries and general standards for effluent discharge were prescribed for the others under Environment (Protection) Act, 1986. In addition to this citizens' suit provisions, measures were introduced concerning the statutory 'right to information' to enable a citizen to directly prosecute a polluter after examining government records and data; technology forcing deadlines, issued under the Central Motor Vehicles Rules of 1989, to compel the manufactures of petrol and diesel vehicles to upgrade their technologies to meet the prescribed emission standards by a particular date; and mandatory worker's participation in plant safety and stringent penalties on high level management for the breach of factory safety regulations, were expected to reduce industrial accidents. It provides a big canvas for understanding the legal changes that have taken place in India following the Bhopal disaster. This no doubt brought tremendous pressure for the enterprises to include the environment as one of the big considerations in their process of decision making.[8]

These many changes do reflect much more than the government's concern for the environment. These policy changes are due to the increasing public pressure. There are many experts who even to this day feel that all these policy/legal responses were highly insufficient for a state to control the activity of the corporate enterprises (especially multi-national corporations). We now clearly witness people taking it upon themselves to act as stewards of environmental causes. There are many protests (many of them are ongoing) against state sponsored developmental projects. Inevitably these instances have altered the complexion of environmental politics. NGOs active in lobbying and environmental litigation have benefited form the changes in environmental legislation.[9] With this growing environmental activism, the frequency of Public Interest Litigation (PIL) has also risen considerably. The combination of evolving legislation, growing public awareness, rapid industrialization, and an increasing threat to the maintenance of the ecological balance laid the ground for PIL in India to be the vehicle of public outcry against perceived environmental threats posed by industry and the government.

The dilution of *locus standi* reduces the burden of appointing special commissions and judicial notice of facts, the onus of proof being on the developer or industry – further, it makes the whole scenario unpredictable from the point of view of risks involved and *vis-à-vis* decision making. This uncertainty risks incurring litigation costs, project delays, the disruption or stoppage of day-to-day operations, expensive remedial measures (compensation and clean-up costs), diversion of management time and attention, and adverse corporate publicity (greater vulnerability to public perception). These in turn lead to cost overruns, and the weakening of financials and business management.

The ultimate lesson therefore, is that one cannot ignore the environment and environmental liability while taking decisions. Instead of ignoring it the best practice is to take the environment as one of the important component of decision-making. Developing environment as value will certainly help the management to acclaim public appreciation and reduce its liability in future. There are many proven stories around the world wherein many enterprises have won many hearts and done wonders with development of the environment as value. Many US corporations have successfully woven the element of environment with its Business Ethics Programmes since 1980s. However, there is very little documentation which clearly shows what the impact of these Business Ethics Programme has yielded in terms of profit or social capital to these corporations. The huge amount of budgetary allocations clearly show that the business enterprises have realized the utility of these Ethics Programmes, needless to say involving the environment as one of the important elements in it.[10] Further, the US are not the only country where corporations are adopting a programmatic approach to business ethics. Recent studies highlight the increasing number of European companies adopting codes and instituting training.

The Way Out

In this fluid scenario, the management of an enterprise should proceed cautiously, before embarking upon any decisions. There are plenty of strategies suggested by many to overcome this uncertainty. The first thing we can say about these strategies is that environment is an important criterion in the decision making process. There are plenty of means through which concern for environment and ecology can be mainstreamed.

Building Environment as 'Value'

This is the single most important element that can change the entire perception of the business enterprise, and make the venture (and of course the enterprise itself) overcome most of the difficulties arising out of uncertainties. It is no more a debatable issue that, the local communities look down upon these business enterprises as almost the sole contributors to pollution and environmental degradation; although in many cases the same may not be true. This brings down not only the public ratings of the corporation but also several potential conflicts with surrounding civil community and NGO organizations.

Training members of enterprises to treat the environment as their own, *suo moto* adoption of various abetment programmes etc., will change the public perception to a great extent. Many times it is seen that various conflicts and tensions between the business community and immediate surrounding civil society is due to lack of 'space' for mutual interaction between them. A proactive role on the behalf of the members of the enterprise in this regard can give tremendous results. Common programmes of entertainment, public entry on a limited basis to various enterprise run facilities, building of pubic parks etc., will bridge the gap between the enterprise and its surrounding community. The sole point perhaps is manifestly showing to the society that the enterprise is genuinely interested in the cause of preserving the environment. There are millions of ways if thought carefully, by the enterprise to prove to the society. The annual reports of the enterprise may contain a feature showing some new and innovative initiatives to protect and preserve the environment. This will make the community aware of the concern of the enterprise. In addition to providing mere employment opportunities, the fact that the corporation cares for the entire surrounding community should be brought out clearly. This strategy will certainly assist the corporation to enhance its rating and public perception in the long run.

Community as Stake-holder

As stated earlier its lack of common 'space' for interaction between enterprise and its surrounding community, is a major factor of tension and an obstacle for our enterprise decision makers. An ideal status would be to treat all the members of the community as its stake-holders. This is what the authors of this chapter mean when referring to a 'communitarian model of corporate governance'. Most corporations treat shareholders, debenture holders, creditors, directors and its employees as its stake-holders. In fact treating the enterprise as an indivisible element of the community and including each and every member of the community as its stake-holders will eliminate the 'mutual hatred' between them and the society. There are many legal requirements and regulatory provisions, which compel the corporations to develop these kinds of models to gain the confidence of the public at large. But one should note that there is no harm if the enterprise goes beyond all these mandatory requirements. This will pay the enterprise in long run.

Community stake-holder-ship can be developed with carefully drawn and executed participatory action plan by the enterprise. In India the Environmental Clearance will be accorded only after conducting a public hearing, and taking into account the perception of the public towards the economic/developmental activity.[11] But many experts note this as the single obstacle in seeking environmental clearance and try to manipulate the process of the public hearing. This is in fact very dangerous and from the beginning sows the seeds of suspicion among the members of a local community and makes them sometimes develop contempt towards the corporation. This tension will take the shape of litigation and hamper the whole project. If implemented in spirit, this process of public consultation gives a very rich and first hand perception of the local community. If addressed properly – it will no doubt, pay rich dividends to the enterprise itself in the long run. It may not be completely out of place to refer to those mandatory provisions of the Environment (Protection) Act in India which says that such public consultation is mandatory before seeking environmental clearance. But there is no harm if the enterprise continues this process of consultation further on a regular basis.

Many times most of the conflicts arise due to some misconceptions and miscommunications between the enterprise and the community. The dialogue or consultation process can be used as mediating ground to sort out their mutual doubts and misunderstandings to a great extent. The need to invoke the jurisdiction of the court etc. will certainly be eliminated, and naturally the cost of litigation (which is constantly rising nowadays) would be saved for the enterprise. More than anything else its management time and focus can be solely concerned with dealing with their thrust areas.

Transparency of Dealing

After the transformation of the industrial world into the information world this element of 'transparency' has become the buzzword of governance. Not only at the level of state, but almost all levels of our life. After a constant and consistent struggle in India we have freedom of information as one of the important rights. There are an endless number of decisions previous to this legislative intervention stressing the need for transparency and the right to information etc. After the statute ensuring this freedom of information – many feel that the right conferred upon the public is highly insufficient. The process of globalization had shrunk the public domain and government is rolling back giving way to private enterprises. So the claim is that there shall be right to information available against multi national corporations as well. One of the serious contentions in the aftermath of Bhopal tragedy was this right to information itself. Many opine that, had there been some transparency, the Bhopal disaster would have been prevented.

Here, if enterprises voluntarily enhance transparency through efficient and prompt reporting, it will help the enterprise itself to a great extent. Their annual reports, which generally carry some feature about their attempts at conservation and environmental protection, may be highlighted. Periodical newsletters from the enterprise to all the members of the community will add to the cause. Especially the amount of investment into treatment plants and adopting better technology to abate pollution etc., will make the enterprise gain public confidence. It is also highly advisable to have some sort of strategy to allow people to see the various aspects of the corporation activity that will erase many doubts the public carry in their minds with regard to the corporation. Every time when consent-permission of the enterprise is renewed by the environment protection boards – a communication to the community to this effect will make community realize that the corporation is taking the environment seriously.

Community Development

Popular analysis and belief is that, business enterprises owe their existence to profit earning. Their sole aim is profit maximization, at any cost. To add to this, experts note that these corporations, after a certain stage of amassing wealth, would try to gain political power. They work to attain political popularity and influence political decisions. These activities make the public perceive business enterprises as a selfish group of people. To change this perception, community development programmes come in handy.

Some portion of the profit gained by the corporation may be set aside to community development and building. Some percentage of funds may be invested in building new mechanisms of public amenities. Ideal is the situation where the corporation will develop a fund to be used for the purpose of environmental protection. There is substantial literature concerning community development by the corporations, hence this issue is not discussed in depth here.

Public Education

Education plays a key role in almost everything. Corporations can also use public education and awareness programmes to advertise their proactive role in the protection of the environment and community development to make the public realize their contribution. The public can also be sensitized to the vital role played by the enterprise to develop the community and as a contributor to the economic growth. They may be introduced to the notion that, both conservation and development are to be addressed together and that in reality, the focus on development or environment alone will not create the balance from which to move forward.

These kinds of educational initiatives will certainly help the members of the community to understand the important and inevitable role of the enterprises in shaping the whole economy. This will go a long way in helping them develop a positive attitude towards the corporations rather than merely suspecting them and considering them as culprits.

Strengthening Enforcement Agencies

This may at the very outset sound strange, but is very helpful to the corporations themselves. If watched carefully many of the projects are plagued with problems and acquire public wrath because of weak enforcement agencies and a weak framework. There are many instances where, the project proponent had invested millions of rupees after taking all licenses, consents and clearances from the state agencies. After intervention of the courts the whole project is stalled and the investment becomes dead, because courts feel that the enforcement agencies have not acted diligently. This poses formidable challenges to an entrepreneur who struggles between these uncertain stay orders and courts interventions.

On the other hand if the enforcement agency is very efficient in its working, takes its work seriously enough and acts professionally there is little scope for the courts to intervene and grant stay to the project. But there is no clear strategy as to how the state agencies will be strengthened because the state agencies will hesitate to take any assistance from the corporate houses for fear of some aspersions being cast upon them with regard to these kinds of programmes. The corporations can jointly organize many programmes along with state agencies to build mutual relationship to the common cause of environmental protection. Transparency of common agenda, no doubt, is very essential here. Otherwise the whole strategy may back fire.

Conclusion

It is evident that the 'environment' has acquired unprecedented prominence our contemporary society. So our corporate management can't be ignorant or silent about the environment when they make decisions. There are also no reservations when said that, much of uncertainty in externalities is owing to the conflicts over natural resources, or misconceptions about how the environment is to utilized/preserved. There are many environmental conflicts, which have made the corporations suffer losses. To over come these difficulties the only method is to take the environment as one of the important elements in decision-making by the corporate enterprise and its management.

But this concern towards the environment must be genuine and not tokenistic. Otherwise the corporations will one day or the other have to face public wrath. Given the fact that there are many reservations to these suggestions made in the article by the business entrepreneurs, a modest and honest beginning must be made to see that corporations attain meaningful objectives in the long run.

Notes

1   Multinational Corporations, Transnational Corporations, Business enterprises, etc., are interchangeably used in this article. Hence no technical/special meaning may be assigned to them by the readers.
2   On 3/4 December, 1984 the world witnessed the worst chemical disaster ever when there was a gas leak into the environment from the Union Carbide plant in Bhopal, India, which killed nearly 8,000 injuring 150,000 plus, in the first three days after the disaster and caused many problems to even the third generation even to this date. Eighteen years after this tragic disaster, the legacy of poisoning continues. Even today chronically ill survivors remain in desperate need of medical attention. Thousands of survivors and the children born since the disaster continue to suffer debilitating health problems. Many are unable to work. By deflecting responsibility for the disaster to the Indian government, Union Carbide managed to escape its obligations. By constantly downplaying the damage to limits its liability, Union Carbide has shown its ethical and moral bankruptcy.
3   Or low challenge indeed. This paper focuses upon this challenge alone. But nevertheless, other challenges are never undermined.
4   Corporate Crimes, Greenpeace publication, August 2002, p.1.

5   The Ten Bhopal Principles on Corporate Accountability are:
   1.   Adoption of international instrument to regulate multinational corporations (ie., implementation of Rio Principle 13)
   2.   Extend Corporate Liability
   3.   Ensure Corporate Liability for Damage beyond National Jurisdictions
   4.   Protect Human Rights
   5.   Provide for Public Participation and the Right to Know
   6.   Adhere to the Highest Standards
   7.   Avoid Excessive Corporate Influence over Governance.
   8.   Protect Food Sovereignty over Corporations
   9.   Implement the Precautionary Principle and Require Environmental Impact Assessments Promote Clean and Sustainable Development.

6   The term 'corporate citizenship' refers to the responsibility of a corporate house in promoting social, economic and environmental factors, which affect the functioning of the industry as also those that are affected by the industry.

7   In the early 1980s a new and radically different kind of case altered the litigation landscape; instead of being asked to resolve private disputes, the Supreme Court and High Courts were asked to deal with public grievances over violations by the state or to vindicate the public policies embodied in statutes or constitutional provisions. This new type of judicial business is collectively called 'public interest litigation'. Most environmental actions in India fall within this class.

8   In February 1992, the Union Government brought out the Policy Statement for Abatement of Pollution. This statement heavily leaned upon the integrating environmental considerations at all level of decision-making; and furthers peoples participation in decision-making as an important strategy:
      'the public must be aware in order to be able to make informed choices. A high government priority will be to educate citizens about environmental risks, the economic and health dangers of resource degradation and the real cost of natural resources. Information about the environment will be published periodically. Affected citizens and NGOs play a role in environmental monitoring and recognizing their expertise where such exists and their commitment and vigilance will also be cost-effective. Access to information to enable public monitoring of environmental concerns, will provide for. Public Interest Litigation has successfully demonstrated that responsible NGOs and public-spirited individuals can bring about significant pressure on polluting units for adopting abatement measures. The commitment and expertise will be encouraged and their practical work supported.'

9   There are, according to estimation, over ten thousand environmental and developmental oriented NGOs, citizen groups and pressure groups in India, which is roughly twenty times the figure in 1985.

10   Further evidence of the institutionalization of corporate ethics programs is demonstrated by the growing number of 'ethics officers' in corporate America. Ethics officers are typically tasked with overseeing the company's ethics program and providing an alternate reporting and advice channel for employees with questions and concerns on ethics related issues. According to one estimate the Ethics Officer Association, established in 1991 with less than 10 members, has grown to well over 200 members by 1996 and is still growing strong.

11   Through notification added to the Environment (Protection) Act, 1986.

Chapter 11

A Gendered MBA?
Australian and Indian Experiences

Fran Siemensma

Introduction

The question of whether the MBA was seen to promote doubt or certainty was central to this research. This paper discusses aspects of a larger research project into the values which students and staff experienced within the context of the MBA. Students and staff within three Australian and two Indian MBA programs provided varying and sometimes conflicting perspectives on gender. The analysis is based on individual and group interviews with staff and both local and international students involved in the program in Australia, as well as perceptions from MBA students in India.[1] Gender concerns expressed by local and international MBA students in Australia are contrasted with those of students in India. Drawing on techniques used in ethnography (Denzin, 1996) the individual 'voices' of those interviewed in this study are conveyed using hypothetical names and direct quotes (Johnson, 1990). The quotes are sourced from both group and individual interviews which were recorded and transcribed between 1995 and 1997. The initial Australian student material was collected within MBA classes which had a values' focus, such as courses on business ethics or business and society. These group interviews were followed up with individuals who demonstrated an ability to discuss values' based issues. This paper extends earlier work on aspects of MBA students' use of values' based concepts (Siemensma, 1999, 2000).

Sinclair distinguishes between 'sex' as physiology, and 'gender' as 'a social and cultural construction' (1995a, p.296). Those involved in this research perceived the influence of gender in both of these ways, namely women as women, and secondly as an approach to management and social theory described as either 'masculine' or 'feminine'. This paper explores both of these perspectives within the context of the MBA. Marta Calas and Linda Smircich, two American academics involved in MBA teaching, argue for applying 'feminist theory ... as a form of cultural critique to an analysis of the *epistemological* (FS italics) and ethical grounds of organizational science' (in Larson and Freeman (eds) 1997, p.51). They criticize the notion that 'organizational science literature focuses on the values, mostly implicit, of rationality, efficiency, and effectiveness of organizational performance' (op. cit., p.50). Feminist theory, according to their argument, allows the consideration of 'difficult questions' because it values those 'areas of social concern' which are typically ignored in the teaching of management. Sinclair similarly critiques 'the prevalent economic discourse [which renders a] discussion of managerial ethics as a non-business, frequently feminine one' (1999, p.12).

Perspectives taken from feminist theory promote the examination of normative concepts associated with the MBA program. Such concepts are often implicit. This paper also explores Sinclair's claim that Australian culture constructs business 'leaders [as] heroes' which privileges men of Anglo-Celtic origin (Sinclair, 1998, p.320); such men are 'invisible' so that only women and non-conforming men are seen to be gendered (op. cit., p.16, pp.24-33). Sinclair cites Derrida in noting that 'the attribution of difference is never a benign act, but one in which 'difference' is always attributed by those with power to the characteristics of less powerful groups' (op. cit., p.133). The following discussion and analysis also investigates, within the context of the MBA, the biological aspect of 'being male or female' typically described as 'sex' (Sinclair, 1995a, p.296) which is often equated with access to power and status.

Gender provides a focus to explore concepts central to the program, as well as how students and staff interpreted the MBA in terms of their personal and academic perspectives on politics, policies and classroom experiences. In common with this focus, writers including Clegg (1995, 1997), Handy (1998), Covey (1992) and Hofstede (1980, 1991, 1998) have proposed softer or more 'feminine' frameworks of management. One of the four dimensions formulated in Geert Hofstede's (1980) study, namely, masculinity/femininity,[2] influenced much cross-cultural management research. These theorists recognize the need to include women as women, but also the to adopt new metaphors of management. They promote a more 'feminized' management style, involving flexibility and interconnectedness, as desirable in knowledge based industries including education.

Did Sinclair's claim that powerful males fail to recognize the problems of women or minorities provide insight into the MBA (Sinclair, 1998, p.24)?[3] She reported that American women had by-passed the MBA, not only because of 'child-bearing and -rearing', and high tuition costs, but also because 'women appear to be rejecting the male model of management education' (Sinclair, 1995a, p.298). This latter aspect of her critique reflects the perspective raised by Calas and Smircich (1997).

How women and men saw themselves as MBA students, teachers and as leaders and how systems of organizational management – affecting both personal identity and society – were promoted through the MBA programs are central themes of this research. The paper also explores Sinclair's claim that women found the MBA to be 'an excluding culture' which needed to be remedied by 'the articulat[ion] and validat[ion of] alternative experience, and values' (1995a, p.301).

Gender, like religion, has both conscious and unconscious associations. Some interviewees equated gender issues with the pursuit of radical change and an increase in the power-base of women. Many men perceived affirmative action as a threat, others stated that these battles had been won and did not need to be repeated. The constraints associated with addressing gender resulted in this paper largely reflecting those who expressed clear opinions about it. The use of hypothetical names enables their comments and individual voices to be expressed.

Comments about gender, drawn from group and individual interviews, were compared and contrasted using Sinclair's (1995a, 1995b, 1998) research into the MBA, gender and leadership, as a foundation for discussing issues including family relations, power, and management style.

The Gendered University

In the context of the Australian MBA, women academics were the group most likely to raise gender as a major issue, while within the Indian MBA it was primarily female students who did so. Yet, both *Jeremy* and *Julia* demonstrate the risk associated with such generalizations. *Jeremy*, a male Australian academic, expressed gender-related issues through his MBA teaching. In contrast, *Julia*, a senior female academic, would not raise her concerns about gender in relation to MBA administration, planning and teaching because she felt that male colleagues did not share her perceptions. She feared being stigmatized as a 'feminist'.

Catherine reflected that 'economic rationalism had taken over' university management, which was no longer 'about ... how to motivate and get the best out of the people', but had involved a new style of manager – namely 'a hit person' who organized 'voluntary departure packages with no apologies'. She characterized the university as increasingly unsympathetic to women, anyone with family responsibilities and those who prized cooperation.

Her criticism can be interpreted on two levels. The social message was that economic indicators had taken priority over human or emotional concerns; at an individual level, she was angry that her own job was threatened by changes to MBA management and funding.

The Australian Experience as viewed by Academics

Helen, like many Australian women academics, stated that gender related concerns were wide-ranging and important. She stated that the constraints of gender also affected men because there was only 'one form of masculinity that gets you to the top' noting that it 'can be termed gender, but it is also about style'.

She conceptualized style as 'a good example of the public and private divide'. Although improvements in gender equity were mere 'lip service', *Helen* did not promote a gender-based critique within the university because she feared 'being out in the wilderness again'. For *Helen*, the 'level playing notion' was 'another way of restructuring society to benefit those who already had power'. Universities were 'only reflections of society' and 'mirrored society in different ways'. However, the slow recognition of the need for more inclusive attitudes to women would alter organizational cultures. This tardy progress meant *Helen* still experienced gender as a 'conflict between public and private' and consequently, would have 'to tip toe quietly on those sorts of things'.

Helen portrayed the privatization of the public sector as moving those problems which were 'too big to solve in the public arena' into the private sector.

Privatization – justified on financial grounds – was an attempt to disguise the 'worsening conflict' and 'increasing gap' between public and private. *Helen* felt that society had increasingly ignored difficult issues including sadness, loneliness and conflict by relegating them to the private sphere. Australia had become a society where 'we won't talk about them in the workplace and we won't talk about them in the MBA either'. *Catherine* shared this opinion and described sexist language which 'embodies so many values and keeps them unconscious, normalizing inequities'.

Jeremy espoused Sinclair's (1998) belief that 'feminine' values provide the basis for a more sensitive, inclusive and socially concerned world. He stated that the tensions of modern society were exacerbated by rigid gender-based roles which effectively excluded the majority of women from political and business life. He wanted MBA teaching to promote social models which recognized differences of gender, culture and power.

His attitude to society and his own teaching role involved 'accommodating fifty per cent of the population' – to discount women was akin to 'making sandwiches without butter or filling'. *Jeremy* also promoted a feminine management style because:

> I think that if we could have a society that was equal, where women and men could feed into the society in equal proportions, the worst excesses ... would be moderated ... So we need gender concerns in the workforce to be of paramount concern, because when there is gender bias, you'll end up with real conflict. You end up with structures in which the males create a working environment that's intolerable for the females to work in.. And it produces a fairly sick society.

Jeremy decried the 'philosophy of individualism' which prioritized competition and 'the profit margin'. His comments implicitly shared Sinclair's criticism of the 'heroic male'; his teaching aimed to promote more consensual models. In common with Sinclair, he advocated new ways to understand and resolve problems. He used the paradigm of 'female values' as a shorthand for a framework which would benefit all. Perhaps he expected students to criticize his stance; his teaching aimed to gently confront both ideas and behaviour.

These comments encompass a breadth of gender concerns. The women quoted above demonstrated concerns about both the role of women as women, and the consideration of role and organizational culture in ethical terms, as raised by Calas and Smircich. The latter perspective was demonstrated by those who epitomized the MBA as 'masculine' on the grounds that it was dispassionate, objective and public. In contrast, a predominantly female group of academics wanted intuition and emotion to play an explicit role in business.

Student Attitudes to Gender in Australia

Students enrolled in Australian MBA programs expressed various attitudes to gender. Some, such as *Bernadette*, a successful manager in her late twenties, stated that gender issues were 'hyped up' and that women were 'smart enough ... to get around it'. Describing her 'limited experience' in a largely male group of medical-technology managers, *Bernadette* attributed the lack of senior women to careers interrupted by parent-hood. Having criticized the absence of females, she then stated that if she had a child she would also become less career-focused. Her divorce soon after commencing the MBA had caused her to delay 'seriously considering' this option for herself. *Bernadette's* work gave her the chance to be 'a good example of something constructive and successful'. She described how she often treated her subordinates like a 'mother' despite being only slightly older than they were.

Linton, a male student in his mid thirties, responded to another male who had sympathized with women's experience of the 'glass ceiling' in the workplace, with the comment that it was both 'very advantageous' and 'handy to be a female these days'. His company was actively seeking the 'spread of females up at a higher level' but he did not question why these female managers had 'not been staying that long'.

To generalize, in several discussions within the Australian MBA programs, male students were prepared to discuss women being managers. In some groups dominated by Anglo-Saxon Australians, men raised arguments both for and against the role of women. However, in a group (A9-A15) which included Indian and Australian students, the strongest emotion was conveyed by a young Indian woman (A11) who derided her countrymen as sexist. Several Indian males responded that their sisters would not be 'allowed' to study overseas, because a woman's role was with her family and did not require her to be highly educated. These Indian males indicated that only men should be educated to become managers. However, in contrast, an older Indian student, *Parveen*, who was married and a father, supported women's rights to professional life.

Reflection on Gender by MBAs in India

Family, and the responsibilities of sons and daughters, was felt to be of primary importance in interviews undertaken in India with students from two different MBA programs. Many of them expressed the need to balance personal and parental wishes, such as the expectation that an elder son would provide financial, housing and emotional support to parents.

However, the MBA students interviewed in India typically came straight from undergraduate degrees, most were in their early twenties, were single and had little professional experience. As a result, their discussion of gender tended to combine theoretical knowledge with beliefs espoused by their families.

Female MBA candidates in India expressed more interest in changing social norms than their male counterparts. Some of these women stated that they appreciated the needs of minorities because they too were 'oppressed'. Several (In 11, In 17) sought an improved workplace for others more than personal power; they wanted to apply 'feminine' values to society, perhaps through harnessing the Indian esteem for the 'mother'[4] to professional life. However, *Pushpa's* description of how she had 'to fight' for the place she had 'earned' and 'deserved', dismissed any claims for pure altruism. She acknowledged the pressure on urban girls, while she ignored the documented hardships of rural or uneducated women. She was middle class, educated in a well-regarded Christian school, and highly competitive. In contrast, *Radha*, whose mother was a doctor, expressed a concern for social justice which might have been prompted by the social exclusion caused by her parents' divorce. She felt that male dominated Indian society oppressed even well-borne Indian women, such as herself, with engineering degrees and 'excellent' postgraduate qualifications. Her 'difficult' choice was to 'advocate [industrial relations] change' such as equal career opportunities for women and the poor.

Another female engineer in the MBA (In 9) was frustrated that women were disregarded as fellow students and potential managers. She stated that male students, and indeed society, denigrated women's professional potential. The MBA should 'educate males to recognize female students as equals', not 'as women' who were inferior. But she conceded that women might need to demonstrate flexibility, by, for example, eschewing personal preference and accepting a token drink at professional and corporate events. However, professional opportunities for women had improved, as borne out by her claim that the Indian Institute of Engineers had addressed professional issues involving women over the previous two years.

Some male MBAs in India were more sympathetic to the situation of women than the female students seemed able to recognize. However, many males expected women to shoulder domestic responsibility in deference first to their fathers and then to their mothers-in-law, and to a lesser extent, all the males in the family. A minority of men wanted to restrict women's behaviour, especially after they had children. Religion, family experience and social beliefs were used to justify traditional roles and practices.

At the same time, many recognized that multi-national corporations created employment opportunities for women. One MBA student in India conveyed the difficulty of blending modernity with tradition:

Moving towards more ... participation of women in organizations, but still in households, the lady is seen as the one who takes care of the household and the children. Women have been going more and more to work, ... but still do all the household work. The man comes, goes, rests.

[In] my year, [there were] 246 students, and 25 women. Marriage for them will be important, more than to become a CEO, [or] top management. [We] need to have more recognition of women. Women have a much tougher time.

Multi-national corporations coming into India, they try to implant their own successful methods of operating. Recruiting women for sales is difficult, especially with a predominantly male sales force. And yet Seagrams recruited a female last year in sales. She did well and they are looking for more – maybe no Indian company would have thought of doing that. ITC [Indian Tobacco Co] would not take a lady for marketing cigarettes. I am more traditional, I am not a typical member of my group. Most of the others would not mind, neither themselves nor women working for these companies [liquor, tobacco]. Indian tradition is 'no to meat, no to tobacco, no to liquor'. That means these things have a certain stigma, I shouldn't do it; women shouldn't do it (In8).

This MBA student's perception of gender moulded his understanding of marriage, domestic responsibility and career opportunities. His beliefs reflected a culture where women formed a minority of MBA students, a culture that was being changed by foreign transnational companies. For example, these companies had increased the social acceptability of industries such as alcohol or tobacco and had recruited women into roles previously considered inappropriate, namely marketing such products. This comment also reflected the generational divide. Most MBAs, in contrast to this particular student, indicated that they were less traditional than their parents.

Was it possible to predict whether an individual MBA student in India would pursue the 'modern' or the 'traditional' attitude to gender concerns? *Pushpa*, for example, displayed a nostalgic longing for the past, combined with a pragmatic pursuit of non-traditional career options. She deserved to be 'successful', yet worried about the consequences of that success. Gender provoked complex and sometimes self-contradictory opinions.

Family Considerations in Australia

Within the context of the Australian MBA, students variously recognized the influence of gender on their family roles. Males were inclined to identify themselves as partners and fathers; however, Australians, unlike Indian students, did not define themselves as sons or daughters with roles which entailed future responsibilities or conflicts.

In contrast to the younger MBA students in India, *Parveen*, whose wife and child had accompanied him to Australia, spoke about the diminishing role of family business. In his experience, younger urban Indians wanted to be independent, not tied to the bottom tier of a family dynasty. Most hoped to escape the emotional ties and its tight-knit paternalistic management of Indian family business. He had rejected the older styles of Indian business, which relied on a family model in favour of ' professionally managed companies'. However, he was saddened by the loss of the traditional Indian style of management because he believed the new professionalism diminished care, friendship and enjoyment at work. New professionally run companies relied on competition and financial rewards, which undermined their employees' commitment and loyalty. So, while he criticized the constraints associated with paternalistic management and family business, he appreciated the trust and emotional connectedness, which they engendered.

Gender Related Concerns in the Australian MBA Classroom

Female MBA students were more likely to conceptualize gender in personal terms. This claim is borne out by the comments made by *Di*, an Australian, *Willow*, from mainland China and *Paraswati*, an Indian studying in Australia. They addressed work related issues often ignored by men within the MBA. *Di* believed that females were not 'considered equal to males in terms of getting higher jobs' or equivalent 'salary packages'. She described how she 'lived to work' because she was 'at the bottom' and 'trying to break in ... at work', which combined with study, meant that she did not have time for 'family or friends'. Two males, with whom she had studied for three years, prompted her to balance career ambition against personal needs. They encouraged *Di* to prioritize so as to make time for her partner.[5]

Willow related how she and her husband had decided that she should pursue an MBA degree. When they came to Australia to study, their one year old child was looked after by grandparents in China because it was difficult and expensive to both work and study in a foreign country. Her experiences demonstrate the tensions between stated beliefs and action. While *Willow* criticized gender inequity in China, she described being the first of her university class to change jobs for a higher salary and subsequently, her proficiency in English meant that she, rather than her husband, should study the expensive MBA. *Willow* stated that this was for the whole family's future security, including the future private education of their child. Her perception that women were disadvantaged in China appeared to conflict with the independent way in which she pursued her career and education, as well as Australian expectations of the responsibility involved with being the mother of a young child.[6]

Paraswati, a young Indian MBA student in Australia, criticized those Indian sexual mores which precluded women from careers. Her comments could have reflected the period when she attended an American school. However, she was not unlike *Pushpa*, the MBA student who had become a self proclaimed 'rebel' within India, who refused to conform to gender stereotypes.

Most male MBA students interviewed in Australia ignored the disparities between the recruitment and promotion of men and women to senior levels of organizations. An increased role for women in management seemed to be based on the assumption that such women would be childless, as most of these males expected their partners to support them.[7] Any expressed concerns did not address how companies could become more equitable. The major images of males supporting partners in Australia came from international students such as *Parveen* from India, and *Yun-wei*, a Chinese engineer who acknowledged a couple's mutual need to make concessions in order for women to succeed in a career.

A discussion of the role of women in the workplace raised tensions between how individuals expressed beliefs and put them into action. Students from the one country, such as India or China, often differed among themselves about issues concerning gender. It is significant that no students raised values associated with the various management subjects, including law and organizational theory, which would deal with gender issues. MBA students lacked awareness of equal opportunity frameworks to a degree which questioned whether gender equity has been accepted throughout society. They gave no substance to Anna Yeatman's (1995) hope that equity would be advanced by a revolutionary re-conceptualization of gender issues within the university sector. The comments generally confirmed Sinclair's findings (1995b) that management education largely ignored equity issues. The expectation that more women would participate in management was not reflected in discussions of how to improve conditions in the workplace, and only rarely in the home.

MBA students adopted a personal and corporate attitude to equity. They did not discuss the role of under-privileged women with regard to accessing credit as promoted by SEWA in India (Bhatt, 1998) or recognize problems such as those associated with dowries (Jain, 1996). Social justice and equity have worldwide implications, especially with regard to the needs of dependent children. Despite the major changes in business and society, students rarely considered the need for strategies and structures to accommodate families, including the care of children and ageing parents. The concept of a 'family friendly' employer was dismissed as an oxymoron. Even companies, such as those for which several students worked, which claimed to hold such policies, were described as not practising them.

In contrast with Indian students interviewed in both India and Australia, few Australian female MBAs discussed their potential for having children. And similarly, Australian women academics tended to ignore the family aspects of identity associated with study and career.[8] *Julia*, for example, responded 'quite badly' to the 'metaphor that 'we're all one big family' because for her it recalled power based on 'patriarchy' and as she said 'we've probably experienced enough of that'. *Emma* was the only academic who discussed her own need to balance teaching and family responsibilities. Domestic and personal concerns were typically excluded from the subject of values. Female academics tended to describe their relationships with partners, parents and children as irrelevant to a discussion about academic roles and responsibilities.

Helen, a lecturer, felt that the predominant cultures were masculine and that women constantly experienced changes in the criteria for measuring performance which she described as moving 'the goal posts'. Her encounters caused her to believe that women were 'ever so subtly' treated as sexual objects. She recalled Pringle's (1988) research which characterized female administrators as a bimbo, a child, or a wife; these conceptions were still 'quite prevalent in the [university]'. As she said, 'you're not related to as a teacher, ... [but] as a woman first ' by many, especially older men.

She had started to address these issues in her teaching, because gender concerns were 'one of the big tensions' for a female academic in a business faculty. As she described this tension 'I am speaking about gender when I'm of the gender that generally speaks about it. And so the pressure's on me to always prove what I'm saying'. Which exposed her to the risk of 'sounding like sour grapes' and also being viewed as an obsessive and blinkered individual. She judged that individuals who were seen as difficult, non-conformist or critical would limit their own career options. This would be counter-productive, so as her confidence and awareness developed, she addressed such topics only within her classes.

In contrast, *Emma* highlighted gender difficulties she had experienced within the cross-cultural context. She stated that some international students perceived that women held lower academic and professional positions despite the claims that Australia provided equal opportunity to both men and women. And, consequently, she was not surprised when international students, who were used to a hierarchical and patriarchal structures, tested whether they could pass subjects in which women had assessed them as failing through an appeal to more senior (male) course managers.

Some female academics, such as *Julia*, focused their gender concerns primarily on career opportunities. She was concerned that society only paid 'lip service to giving credit' to women and that 'merit differences' favoured male professionals in the university environment. She felt that society, including management schools, chose inappropriate and unfair criteria to select and promote staff. She described academic administration as jobs done by women which were only notable when problems arose as much essential and arduous work was invisible to the university. Her ambivalence became more evident when she went on to criticize Australian industry, where women who wanted 'to reach the top' were 'forced out, into running our own businesses'. Not only did this discrimination, which she had experienced, personally upset her, she also regretted the overall loss of professional expertise.

Her professional persona appeared almost anti-feminist, but she felt denigrated because she was a woman. Despite the domestic metaphors which enlivened her language, in contrast to many male academics, she did not discuss family relationships. *Julia*'s ambivalence about gender was further confirmed in a comment about the classes that she took, where she tried 'to emphasize that we're all professionals, and gender isn't an issue'[9] because individuals had to contribute according to what they had to offer, rather than who they were. This was 'an ideal' approach which had to be 'battled through'. She addressed issues as they emerged through topics. Gender bias was 'just a fact of life' which *Julia* did not have 'to point out'.

Within her Australian MBA classroom, *Julia* aimed to demonstrate a style which dealt equally with males and females. She stated that she expected the students to model themselves on that experience and to detect injustice involving unfair treatment of women for themselves. Her classroom behaviour aimed to implicitly model how gender equity should be addressed.

In contrast with *Julia*, *Catherine* aimed to explicitly address issues of gender through her teaching. And for her, this included an emotional awareness of the implications of certain management activities. She criticized most MBA students for their impersonal acceptance of 'downsizing' which she blamed on the 'euphemistic language of management' which disguised workforce losses. Her alternative explanation was that the students were unable to empathize with a situation which they hoped never to experience. Perhaps these two interpretations together convey the complex reality. But *Catherine*'s reflections recognized business as a tough world, unlike her students whom she felt used professional language to obscure unpleasant realities. She described her approach as holistic and feminine, their approach as male, irrespective of their gender.[10]

Female academics addressed issues of gender in the classroom more frequently than males. They stated that women, both academics and students, experienced difficulties in the academic context and potentially in future management careers, as well as gender perceived in political terms. The political perspective ranged from the larger context of overall career prospects for themselves and their students, to more specific issues such as conflict management within the classroom.

However, women academics were not alone in recognizing and juggling the complexities raised by gender. *Lawrence,* an experienced management educator, described the business environment as tough and mean spirited. He expressed satisfaction that every year, four or five students would claim that their MBA studies had assisted them to leave the very corporate world normally associated with the degree. *Lawrence* stated he preferred not to make value judgments in the classroom, but acknowledged that his values matched those of students who decided to leave the competitive world of business. If an individual discovered a 'person job misfit', then this realization was a 'legitimate and desirable' outcome of the MBA. He believed that each student should be 'free to choose' so as to 'take responsibility for one-self' and also that a male-dominated management style was inappropriate for a significant group of men. While *Lawrence* recognized that only a minority held these beliefs, he also felt that students should be 'exposed to alternative world views ... [in line with] literature which indicated that the future of business [lay in] abandoning profit maximization'. He stated that the 'role of business' was 'really to serve the community', which, together with his belief that higher education should provoke students to consider alternatives, prompted him to promote a critical perspective.

Lawrence believed that the teaching of 'profit maximization' created a 'dog-eat-dog attitude' as well as a 'games-theory' approach to business which 'caused a lot of pain and suffering in organizations'. He prescribed readings which contended that business was not about 'winner takes all', or based on 'a win/lose situation'. He was keen to promote a more 'feminine' style of interaction within his class and to encourage his students to consider more cooperative ways of doing business. Yet curiously, even when he was interviewed by a woman, he did not mention female students. He accepted that gender was a major concern, but he addressed it in terms of men's needs.[11]

Through his teaching of management, he encouraged his students to verbalize and honour their own values. He did not believe that management education should promote uncritical compliance with business goals. He and *Robert* argued that students should be encouraged to criticize a system which encouraged them to adopt a tough 'macho' style of management.

Gender evoked a range of understandings and experiences. Many students and staff conveyed that it coloured their reactions and prompted their behaviour in ways which were outside the scope of beliefs associated with the MBA.

Several women academics commented on conflict provoked by expectations about the role of gender when it emerged as a topic within management. This difficulty was experienced in classes with Australian students and also international students. Such difficulties could be exacerbated when different groups in a class held diverse views on the role of women. *Helen* described how she had used humour to push her viewpoint:

> in teaching MBA international students ... I can't count how many times this semester, I've said 'she' and made a point of saying humorously, or seriously, that they have to change. It's unacceptable at all sorts of levels, but we still continue to use 'he'.

Other examples of the influence of gender in the classroom included *Emma*'s perception that a 'relatively unsophisticated' Indian male had disregarded the greater business experience of a Thai woman and consequently provoked 'a battle of the sexes'. In contrast, *Julia* related how a male student's cultural and religious beliefs had caused him to judge female managers as unacceptable. Over the semester she had seen him 'shift quite radically from being totally unable to accommodate having female managers', to giving 'some weight' to what females had to say in class. Whereas *Emma* was diffident about dealing with such gender issues, *Julia* stated that it was an important 'part of their education'.

Within the Australian MBA, local female students seemed more supportive of female academics than either male or overseas students. Women academics judged that both male and female international students did not respect their role and authority. Some female academics attributed this lack of respect not only to gender, but also to nationality, social status or wealth. In other words, they felt that they may be have been disregarded because they were perceived to lack appropriate family background or social status. A female academic saw tensions emerge when the teaching role, which had high status, was undertaken by a woman, who was seen to have lower status than a man. This perception was often linked with students from countries in which few women held senior positions.

Few male students introduced the topic of gender. Many Indian students in Australia indicated that gender was a provocative topic. *Paraswati*'s views on gender equity provoked strong disagreement by the five older Indian men in her group. Some male Indian MBA students in Australia (A9, A14, A15, A19) stated that a family would be criticized if daughters were allowed to study overseas or to take on jobs that involved travelling within India. The ensuing debate considered whether such constraints hinged on tradition, religion or safety. The younger Indian men seemed torn between being 'modern' and the expectations of their families. This discussion of gender-related issues caused the non-Indian students in the group (A12, A13) to recognize the complex and varied beliefs expressed by these Indian students.

Parveen, in another group, indicated how the world trend to employ more women had influenced India. He noted that foreign companies were using their female employees to attract further female recruits, including MBA graduates. At the same time, he characterized that women in certain roles for example, in marketing, would be subordinate to male staff members because of the risks faced by women who worked alone; he implicitly denied that women could be supported by subordinate-males. Perhaps his opinion reflected a traditional conservatism, or a pragmatic recognition of the difficulties associated with travel throughout the country and the use of public transport.

As the majority of Australian MBA students worked full-time and studied part-time and the MBA required students to have business experience prior to their studies, personal experiences were used to substantiate the claim that organizations' equal opportunity policies disadvantaged male managers. *Linton* claimed that affirmative action policies of the company he worked for advantaged females, at the same time as he acknowledged their low retention in certain 'macho' industries. This discussion raised questions about how, for example, the laws and practice of equal opportunity were addressed in various subjects and interpreted within an MBA class. *Linton*'s disparaging remarks about such policies could also reflect that personal career progress was the primary motivation for most students to undertake the MBA.

Gender and Personal Identity

For *Emma*, the essentially masculine style of the university contrasted with that adopted by female academic colleagues, who generally were 'more interested in taking the group with them'. Several of these women had demonstrated a 'more collective approach', such as promoting staff development programs, in contrast to the male academics 'who seemed to be out for themselves'. She described the culture of the MBA classroom and the management structure of the university as masculine, namely dominated by competition. Although keenly interested, *Emma* judged family and social concerns as equally important to her work.

Her identity reflected a gendered conception of the world, expressed through a style which was at once sensitive, assertive and diffident. She experienced tensions within herself. Within the classroom, she seemed as protective of the students' sensibilities, as she was of her own. Outside the classroom, she placed her trust in women and used gender as a lens which helped her to interpret the world. While she recognized the norms around leadership, she was prepared to test those which she confronted. But she was reluctant to verbalize her dissent.

Gender was described by *Lawrence* as a major issue for many of his male students that involved their 'self doubt of where they fitted in the overall scheme of things' and included how to connect with female staff, 'especially those who were demanding, who didn't show feelings', and 'female bosses, especially women with balls'. As he said, 'a lot of male managers were seeking to find a place for themselves in the 90s'. There was a search for 'societal roles' at a 'difficult time' when a lot of men were experiencing 'uncertainty'.

Some Australian students with children, such as *Peter*, recognized the conflict between family and business responsibilities. This was essentially an issue 'about self' because he needed to achieve 'the right balance'. He found it difficult to separate the 'family man' from the 'business man'. If individuals 'changed [their values] between business and family life' then they were 'not being true to themselves'. He left his wife to manage the family links with their local community 'in order to gain time for both family and business'.

This linkage of family and personal identity was shared by *Stewart* who rang his wife daily to recognize and support her 'full-time mothering' role. His 'very successful marriage' was focused on their children's interests. There was an apparent ambivalence between his reported admiration for his manager's decisive, yet 'sexist style', and concern voiced over his 'family friendly employer' which had sacked women because of work tensions associated with child-rearing. Yet, overall he seemed uncertain whether women with children should be in the workforce.

Di found that combining her full-time job, weekend work and MBA commitments, left no time for her partner. These constraints, plus the migraine headaches provoked by lack of sleep, were portrayed as the costs of 'climb[ing] the management ladder'. The Australian males in her group warned against sacrificing her personal life for a 'career'. She seemed uncertain about how to claim her female identity.

Willow, despite her personal circumstances, criticized China's gender norms. She stated that employers in China generally portrayed women as burdens because of security issues and the prospect of child-rearing. In contrast, another Chinese student, *Yun-wei*, whose wife was studying on a research scholarship in another Australian city, described Australia as 'more conservative' and less attuned to women's needs than China. He stated that the Chinese held more equitable attitudes to gender, claiming, for example, that his Beijing university class mates shared his beliefs about women and equality.

Some female MBAs stated that they were compensating for their mothers' thwarted ambitions. *Paraswati*'s mother wanted her daughter to continue her studies because of her own curtailed career as an engineer. This debate resonated with Indian males. Some accepted expanded-employment opportunities for women as long as 'family values' were given top priority.

In the group and individual discussions which included students from Australia, China and India, men discussed relationships with partners and children more frequently and positively than women did, especially in connection with a personal career. In contrast, women largely felt they had to compete in a world which preferred male employees. The Australian students indicated that having children would limit women's careers; men were able to compete and engage in MBA study, because their partners looked after children. Only *Willow* indicated that women with children could pursue a management career path, as distinct from the Australian[12] MBA students. They appeared more closely aligned with the Indian students in their acceptance of traditional 'family values'. Indian tradition implies the need to 'protect' women whereas Australian cultural norms reflect both 'mateship' and a physicality which marginalizes women and largely denigrates motherhood. The identity of 'mother' creates interesting points of comparison between the two countries. For example, Kakar's Freudian analysis of Indian women as either 'mothers or whores' (1989, pp.14-17) shares similarities with Summers' portrayal of Australian women as 'damned whores or God's police' (1975).

Management Style

The concept of gender was intricately interwoven with the individual perception of a suitable management style. However, this implicit awareness was best evoked by comparing how MBA students in Australia, including those from Australia, India and China, perceived what a manager should be.

Wendy anticipated risks in going back to China. She explained her doubts:

I am not sure whether I will be well accepted by companies that [conform to] Chinese culture. As I get to know more about Western company culture, I am gradually losing the other end. Somehow I can be in the middle, if I am in the middle it means that I am not at either end.

Wendy feared that her management style could cause her future problems in China. She demonstrated similarities with Hall's concept of domains (1996a, 1996b, 1996c) when she likened her personal style to positions on a continuum. She indicated that if her work style became 'too Western' she would lose her Chinese insights and capacities and risk her sense of belonging. However, as she toyed with situating herself on a continuum of cultural style, she recognized that various situations would influence her sense of self. Her sense of cultural 'fit' made her realize that she would be changed by the experience of work, for example, Chinese employees of Western companies would find it hard to relate to Chinese workers who had different experiences and expectations:

... as a newcomer, when I enter a new organization, I will have to be very careful not to be isolated. And also it depends on the situation. ... I am a Chinese national but sometimes in order to get things done, I put a lot of pressure on my Chinese counterparts. ... probably some of them would mind, but they would never tell, unless they became very close friends of mine.

This comment indicates how management style reflects personal style, and how personal style reflects the individual's psychological make-up as much as culture. Her comments provide insight into how she saw herself within the context of the MBA. *Wendy* recognized both psychological and cultural aspects of her identity; she felt that these, together with her organizational experiences, influenced how she sought to achieve organizational goals and her relationships with her fellow nationals. She acknowledged the tensions associated with these different aspects of her identity.

In contrast, *Julia* believed that management style was increasingly influenced by both East and West, because within 'twenty years time.. a global society' would promote 'a lot more common managerial staff across the world'. Management style was portrayed as a neutral artefact of the work environment rather than an individual or corporate expression of gender and cultural concerns.

This perspective contrasts with Sinclair's (1998) analysis of leadership, where the concept of the 'heroic male' underpins the ideal professional business image. Yet *Julia*, despite her stoic acceptance of tough business practice, was saddened by the harsh reality of business practice. She combined academic theory with flashes of concern for others. Despite her confidence, she was wary of being type-caste as a feminist. There were tensions between her stated desire to nurture others, her assertive language and her lack of self-revelation.

The ways in which many academics taught MBA subjects in Australia seemed to assume the existence of a just and open society. This provided the background against which to promote objectivity, merit and profit. However, as few academics contextualized their teaching in this way, *Helen* feared that culture and society would suffer if MBA students were not encouraged to relate social norms to management theory. Her major concern was that those Australians who had never experienced threats to democracy and civil society, recognized only those principles which were enunciated within the MBA.

Academic Perception of Management Style in India

In contrast, the Indian post-colonial use of secularism can be understood to embrace ethnic and religious differences. The concept of management style, as discussed within the MBA in India, was more nuanced[13] than in Australia. The complexity associated with renewed nationalism and the tension between Hinduism and other religions have influenced India's aspiring managers. For many Indian MBA students, the objectivity promoted by Western management represented a calm, mediating and equitable influence. Both male and female students admired the clarity promoted by objective and unemotional criteria. They were seen to provide a 'cooling' influence.

Concerns about management style became apparent at a workshop run by Indian MBA teachers in India which involved academics who have promoted indigenous Indian models[14] based on traditional writings. Several advocated values such as respect for age and status associated with a male-dominated management style which has largely ignored the role of women in business. Some link this perspective with a renewed sense of Indian nationalism. Within India, there are those academics who criticize this philosophical movement as a threat to the objectivity and secularism promoted by Western management theory. For them, management style not only related to the role of women but also to the inclusion of men from the lower classes and castes. Many critics of 'traditional' indigenous management styles stated that Western management theory promoted a more just and open system of recruitment, promotion and overall business practice. They associated Western styles of objectivity with social justice, fair competition, cooperation and more inclusive practices. The traditional world was portrayed as more patriarchal and non-consensual. In some ways these critics of Indian traditionalism appeared to attribute 'feminine' characteristics to Western management principles.

Student Attitudes to Gender in India

The MBA students interviewed in India indicated that perhaps the rules around gender were changing, but few males indicated that India should pursue a more equitable gender balance. *Pushpa* evoked themes and tensions raised by several Indian students, for example, whether to accept arranged marriages.

Pushpa indicated the complexity and regional diversity of Indian norms which affected women, for example she contrasted 'Calcutta which is more female oriented' where it was 'easier to move away from the traditional female role' with Delhi, 'where society is not so accepting'. She related not telling her parents that she smoked and drank as an example of the complex relationship between parents and children. She described a world where subterfuge allowed incongruent beliefs and practices to coexist. But there was insecurity, as the rejected rules were not replaced by new principles of action. *Pushpa* recognized the difficulties of achieving her personal expectations; her newfound freedom seemed cumbersome. In common with many young professional women, she recognized the dilemma of reconciling her needs with those of a future partner.

These MBA students typically aspired to be managers in large multi-national companies which paid high salaries and provided good training. However, a significant group of students hoped to work for specific local companies because of cultural and life style reasons. As one MBA student said:

> [In] international firms you get the sense that you will be in a constant state of flux …
> [with] appraisal every year and you are either up or out. [Rather than] that kind of
> environment, where I have to prove myself time and again, I would be attuned to
> Indian organizations which talk of a long-term relationship (In14).

Paternalistic management was valued; a good manager considered family situations, including diverse regional aspects such as religion, food, and festivals. MBAs wanted to work for managers who would nurture their early careers, and many, in turn, aspired to care for their own staff. Students saw the importance of combining this understanding with formal MBA study. While some feared aspects of Western management theory, such as constant performance reviews, others believed such practices helped managers to address India's disparate cultures and regional differences. The promotion of objective behavioural criteria would improve management of diversity such as was required in rural India:

> ... if this were implemented here [in this program] and instituted all over the country [it]
> would reduce the sense of tribalism [in the sense of urban/professional elitism] which is
> happening throughout India (In15).

These students recognized that managers needed to be malleable; many believed that paternalism helped to balance staff-development needs with the pursuit of profitability based on efficiency. Many students recognized that efficient work practices should be promoted, while several raised ethical issues associated with subjecting workers to undue pressure to achieve results.

For MBA students in India, management style provoked dilemmas. The espoused ethical values of a 'good manager' would be tested by the need to make company profit. These students often portrayed efficiency as more compelling than individual conscience, in a way which seemed to reflect their understanding of local business practice. Theoretical studies were often characterized as remote from the 'nitty gritty' of the 'real world'. Students stated that workers were alienated by corruption in society and in their work environments. Several students equated a successful management style with being 'manly ... aggressive and successful at work'; many accepted that 'being a successful manager' would conflict with personally held values, but this was part of the 'macho' reality of business practice.

In Conclusion

Gender was perceived to affect women's capacity to access fair treatment within both the business and university worlds. But for many there was also a realization that dominant masculinist models precluded the discussion of important social and business issues, such as equity. And there were also varying demonstrations of a gendered perception of management. For example, competition was constantly raised as an aspect of management style; gender stereotypes described males as competitive and females as cooperative. Some took these assumptions for granted, while others, largely women, were more critical.

Many academics and MBA students interviewed in Australia appeared to accept a style of leadership compatible with the 'heroic male' convention as described by Sinclair. A minority of staff and students questioned the tradition of male dominance and were committed to gender equity; of these, some chose to publicly flag their ideas, while others felt too uncomfortable or vulnerable to voice such comments, even within an MBA classroom. Those students who accepted gender equity rarely proposed how to make it happen. Their failure to re-conceptualize gender issues matched Sinclair's (1995a) findings about management education. These students did not confirm Yeatman's (1990b, 1995) hopes that universities would produce revolutionary ideas which would invigorate the pursuit of equity. An overview of gender conveys an implicit sense of women's marginalization which reflects Sinclair's (1993, 1994, 1995a, 1995b, 1998) findings.

But, of equal importance, a consideration of the feminist critique of organizational theory (Calas and Smircich, 1997, p.51) demonstrated that much of the MBA did not encourage students to address 'difficult questions', nor to critique a narrow business focus on 'efficiency and effectiveness'. Discussions of social justice were often prompted by experiences gained outside the formal program. Many students, both Australian and international, recognized 'areas of social concern', but, only a minority of MBA subjects prompted students to consider ways in which they could engage with such problems. In terms of gender, the MBA reflected the claims made by Calas and Smircich, that management theory was preoccupied with organizational performance (1997, p.50). In line with their analysis, only a minority of those interviewed raised, let alone addressed, 'difficult questions' which involved social concerns. Management educators were more likely than MBA students to critically reflect on management style and consider values other than business efficiency and effectiveness. Many considered these concerns to be outside the scope of their teaching. The perspective of gender confirmed that the experience of the MBA was complex and textured, and marked by self-censorship, especially by those who questioned the dominant ethos.

Given the MBA's brief to produce effective managers, it is appropriate to examine the style which such people are expected to acquire. Sinclair, in particular, has researched the culture of Australian leadership (1994, 1998) and specifically related the education of managers to the MBA (Sinclair, 1995a, and Sinclair and Hintz, 1991). Her writings consistently argue that a strongly gendered management culture within Australia, celebrates the 'heroic male'. MBA students, to a greater extent than staff, expressed their beliefs that business was a male domain. A significant minority of academics personally challenged this assumption; they varied in how they translated their convictions about gender into their professional roles. The sense of marginalization associated with both the process and content of the MBA expressed by many women reflected Sinclair's MBA research (1995a, 1995b).

Staff, more than students, demonstrated the influence of those management theorists such as Clegg (1997), Handy (1998), Covey (1992), Hofstede (1980, 1991, 1998), Solomon (1997) and Xavier and Ramachander (2000) who recognize the importance of a 'softer' or more 'feminized' style of management in line with Sinclair's desire to 'do leadership differently'. Discussion in Australia about career development, balance between work and family, management style and competition tended to confirm Sinclair's depiction of a leadership style (1998) which attributed 'gender' only to females and those males who did not conform to a heterosexual stereotype. As Sinclair states in relation to the Australian context:

> ... masculinity remains invisible and unnoticed ... [because of] unconsciously held attributions and assumptions ... because leadership as masculinity resonates so deeply with wider cultural mythology: our experience of history, religion and politics; our upbringing and experience of families, schools and workplaces (Sinclair, 1998, p.27).

This quote helps to explain the tension and ambivalence of women who attempted to confront the system within the MBA. Those men who raised these issues did not feel as personally endangered as women did. But for many male MBA students, the topic of gender highlighted the interaction of theory, organizational practice and personal ambition at a time when opportunities for middle managers had declined. Some male students felt personally threatened by equal opportunity and affirmative action policies. Thus, it was not surprising that this issue was initially avoided by many men, or that subsequent discussions were felt to be provocative. Sinclair highlights the challenge of changing business and society. However, before more inclusive models can be adopted management theorists must recognize the power of an 'invisible' masculinity.

Considering the MBA from a feminist theory perspective raised issues of power and fear. These concerns are consistent with Sinclair's 'heroic leaders' (1998) hypothesis. Many female Australian academics, and some of their male colleagues, doubted the certainty associated with the persona of the 'heroic male', but few were prepared to openly express their doubts. Such findings confirm Calas and Smircich's recognition (in Larson and Freeman (eds) 1997, p.51) of the need to address those 'difficult questions' which are typically ignored in management education. In both India and Australia, men were typically seen as the natural holders of power and authority. Potential critics censored themselves, so that problems were not voiced in the public or administrative sphere.

Gender raised the aspect of personal identity associated with child rearing. Older Australian males in this study, in common with many Indian males interviewed in both Australia and India, indicated that wives should deal with parental duties. In contrast, several Chinese MBAs demonstrated a more sexually inclusive attitude to parenting. Business educators generally advocated that merit rather than gender should influence whether women were promoted, but none acknowledged the problems caused by couples who were separated by work in different cities. Sinclair is one of the few educators to recognize such conflicts within the MBA and professional life (1995a, 1998). For most others this remains a 'black hole' of management education.

Sinclair raised the possibility of incorporating the role of motherhood into a paradigm of leadership.[15] Her claim (1998) that there were organizational taboos against combining a career with motherhood was confirmed by how Australian female MBA students implied that child rearing was an impediment to business success. In India, the maternal role is associated with power and prestige. For example, since her death Mother Theresa, although a religious rather than a biological mother, has assumed almost the status of a deity.[16] The Indian archetype of the mother adds complexity to the roles of its professional women. There were tensions for young women who sought to pursue non-traditional arenas; higher-level education created greater possibilities and also pressures. Even Indian men who expressed support for women argued that females, including MBA graduates, could be compromised by working late hours or business travel. Families had to protect their wives and single daughters; workplace responsibilities had to be weighed against the honour of the household.

Indian students, interviewed in both Australia and India, interpreted the role of the Indian woman in many ways.[17] They recognized a range of career choices, for a range of reasons, from social justice, in line with the feminist perspective of Calas and Smircich and extending to the female face of personal career success as discussed by Sinclair. In terms of personal identity, sexual identity would not be destiny, a pressure experienced by many female Indian MBAs, but neither would it be denied, as indicated by Australian women within the MBA. Australian male academics, more often than students, anticipated that a new model of leadership would encourage men to enjoy a range of roles, emotions and experiences within the workplace and beyond. However, such opinions did not conform to expected MBA norms. Consequently, male staff and students were often reluctant to comment on gender, role and management style.

Those who experienced doubts about their own career, business or social practices often recognized the risks of questioning dominant paradigms. This caused them to be frustrated, but also denied others access to their ideas. Sharing only part of personal identity and values could create feelings of inauthenticity. Many recognized the 'macho' style of the workplace environment; while some aspired to it, many, perhaps in their attempt to escape it, kept public silence. Several of the passive dissenters stated that their personal, including family, responsibilities stopped them from being openly critical. However, both male and female staff disparaged a male-dominated ethos within their organizations far more than did their students.

The MBA was seen to be gendered. This belief was founded on both attitudes and expectations of women as women, and men as men. But, perhaps more importantly, the models which guided course content and organizational culture were often perceived as both competitive and 'macho'. Analysis of these various perspectives indicates that new approaches to leadership are both possible and desirable. New paradigms of management and education which recognize the influence of gender can assist business and society to become more flexible and more cooperative. There are pragmatic business reasons for considering new models which match the needs of emerging knowledge-based industries. But more importantly, current political and global pressures make it essential to rediscover perspectives which promote justice, equity and inclusiveness.

Notes

1   NB (A1...) = interviewed in Australia, (In1...) MBA students in India.
2   Hofstede's dimensions are used in cross-cultural management studies. Later masculinity/femininity became a hardness/assertiveness – softness/nurturance metaphor.
3   Sinclair demonstrates how the absence of women influences concepts of leadership.
4   Kakar (1990, 131-32) 'certain forms of the maternal-feminine' (are) more central in India ... than in the West; Bumiller's (1991) study conveys a more Western understanding.
5   Female students in this study, in contrast to Sinclair's (1995a, pp.295-317), did not report the support of male mentors in relation to their studies or career.
6   Several Thai and ethnic Chinese students reported leaving children with extended families.
7   This finding reflects Sinclair's findings (1995a, pp.308-9).
8   These also confirm Sinclair's findings (1998, pp.64, 65, 97, 136-7).
9   See Sinclair's claim that career focused women avoid such matters because 'masculinity is interwoven into ... presumptions of organization and managerial leadership' (1998, p.63).
10   This comment reflects the gender perspective presented by writers including Sinclair (1998), Clegg (1997) and Hofstede (1991).
11   He confirmed Sinclair's findings that male MBAs were reluctant to discuss concerns about 'being male' (1998, p.73). His subject used personal diaries to promote self-reflection.
12   Most Australians had attended university after the implementation of equal opportunity legislation. They indicated that the spirit of these changes was not widely embraced.
13   Tension was apparent at a conference on values in management where Indian academics criticized an indigenous management style on the basis that traditional Hindu ideas could be divisive. The fiftieth anniversary of independence saw religious divisions being reignited (see D'Mello, 1999).
14   I attended this workshop in Calcutta, in February, 1998. Prof. S.K. Chakraborty promotes a traditionally based indigenous management style.
15   Interviewed by Faulkner (1999), Sinclair indicated that 'woman as a mother in public life' was seen as positive in India, and insulting in Australia.
16   Such as that demonstrated by the Mothers of the Pondicherry and Ramkrishna missions.

17 Kerala and West Bengal were described as giving women more freedom and independence than the northern states. Education, supported by elite schooling, and the extended household, allowed middle-class married women to pursue higher studies.

References

Bhatt, E. (1998) 'Empowering the Poor through Micro-Finance: The SEWA Bank', in *Social Change Through Voluntary Action*, Dantwala, M.L., Sethi, H. and Visaria, P. (eds) Sage, New Delhi, pp.146-161.

Bumiller, E. (1991) *May You Be the Mother of a Hundred Sons: A Journey Among the Women of India*, Penguin, New Delhi.

Calas, M. and Smircich, L. (1997) 'Predicando la Moral en Calzoncillos?' in Larson A and Freeman R.E. (eds) *Women's Studies and Business Ethics*, Oxford University Press, Oxford, NY, pp.50-79.

Chakraborty, S.K. (1995) *Human Values For Managers*, Wheeler, New Delhi.

Chakraborty, S.K. (1998) *Values and Ethics for Organizations: Theory and Practice*, Oxford University Press, New Delhi.

Clegg, S. (1995) 'Business Values and Embryonic Industry: Lessons from Australia' in Stewart, S. and Donleavy, G. (eds) *Whose Business Values: Some Asian and Cross-Cultural Perspectives*, Hong Kong University Press, Hong Kong, pp.247-266.

Clegg, S. (1997) 'Management for the 21st Century', in Stone R.J. (ed.) (1998) *Readings in Human Resource Management*, Jacaranda Wiley, Milton, Qld pp.147-151.

Covey, S. (1992) Principle Centered Leadership, Simon and Schuster, New York, London.

D'Mello, B. (1999) 'Management Education: A Critical Appraisal' in *Economic and Political Weekly*, (India) November 27, pp.169-176.

Denzin, N.K. (1996) *Interpretive Ethnography: Ethnographic Practices for the 21st Century*, Sage, Thousand Oaks, CA.

Faulkner (1999) 'No More Iron Butterflies' *The Age* February 26, p.A16.

Hall, S. (1996a) 'Cultural studies and its theoretical legacies' in Morley, D. and Chen, K-H. (eds) *Stuart Hall: Critical Dialogues in Cultural Studies*, Routledge, London, pp.262-275.

Hall, S. (1996b) 'Gramsci's Relevance for the Study of Race and Ethnicity' in Morley, D. and Chen, K-H. (eds) *Stuart Hall: Critical Dialogues in Cultural Studies*, Routledge, New York, pp.411-40.

Hall, S. (1996c) 'New Ethnicities' in Morley, D. and Chen, K-H. (eds) Stuart Hall: *Critical Dialogues in Cultural Studies*, Routledge, New York, pp.441-49.

Handy, C. (1998) *The Hungry Spirit: Beyond Capitalism – A Quest for Purpose in the Modern World*, Arrow Books, London.

Hofstede, G. (1980) *'Culture's Consequences: International Differences' in Work-Related Values*, Sage, Newbury Park.

Hofstede, G. (1991) *Cultures and Organizations: Software of the Mind*, McGraw Hill, London.

Hofstede, G. (1994) *Cultures and Organizations: International Cooperation and its Importance for Survival*, Harper Collins, Hammersmith.

Hofstede, G. (1998) *Masculinity and Femininity: The Taboo Dimensions of National Cultures*, Sage, California.

Jain, P. (1996) 'Ghandi on Women: Imaging a New Identity' in Jain, P. and Mahan, R. (eds) *Women Images*, Rawat Publications, Jaipur, pp.238-255.

Johnson, J.C. (1990) *Selecting Ethnographic Informants*, Sage, Newbury Park, CA.

Kakar, S. (1990) *Intimate Relations: Exploring Indian Sexuality*, Penguin, New Delhi.

Pringle, R. (1988) *Secretaries Talk: Sexuality, Power and Work*, Allen and Unwin, Sydney.

Siemensma, F. (1999) 'Hopes, Tensions and Complexity: Indian Students' Reflections on the Relationship of Values to Management Education' in *Journal of Human Values*, Vol 5, No 1.

Siemensma, F. (2000) 'The Feminine Leader' in *Management Review*, IIMB, Bangalore, pp.107-12.

Sinclair, A. (1994) *Trials at the Top: Chief Executives Talk about Men, Women and the Australian Executive Culture*, University of Melbourne, Australian Centre, Parkville.

Sinclair, A. (1995a) 'Sex and the MBA' in *Organization*, Vol 2, No 2, 295-317.

Sinclair, A. (1995b) 'Gender in the Management Curriculum', Equal Opportunity Unit, University of Melbourne, Parkville.

Sinclair, A. (1998) *Doing Leadership Differently*, Melbourne University Press, Carlton South.

Sinclair, A. (1999) 'The Ethics of Managers; Cause for Despair?' in *Res Publica*, Vol 8, No 1, pp.12-17.

Sinclair, A. and Hintz, P. (1991) 'Developing Managers: Re-examining Ten Myths about MBAs and Managers', University of Melbourne, Graduate School of Management Working Paper, No 2, January.

Solomon, R.C. (1997) 'Competition, Care and Compassion: Toward a Non-Chauvinistic View of the Corporation' in Larson, A. and Freeman, R.E. (eds) *Women's Studies and Business Ethics*, Oxford University Press, Oxford, New York, pp.162-73.

Summers, A. (1975) *Damned Whores and God's Police*, Penguin, Ringwood.

Xavier, M. and Ramachander (2000) Beyond Competition: Business Strategies for the 21st Century, Vikas.

Yeatman, A. (1990) A Feminist Theory of Social Differentiation, in Nicholson, L. (ed.) *Feminism/Postmodernism*, Routledge, New York.

Yeatman, A. (1995) 'The Gendered Management of Equity-Oriented Change in Higher Education' in Smyth, J. (ed.) *Academic Work: The Changing Labour Process in Higher Education*, SRHE/Open University Press, Buckingham, pp.194-205.

Chapter 12

Business Growth through Values: Concepts and Experiments

Swami Someswarananda

myai ek vyapari
vyapar mera dharam
dukan mera mandir
grahak mera bhagawan
grahak ki seva meri pooja
grahak ki samadhan mera prasad

(I am a businessman. Business is my sacred duty. Shop is my temple. Customers are my God. Servicing customers is my worship. Customers' satisfaction is the gift from God to me.)

Go to a retailer. You will find these sayings written on a board hanging on the wall of his shop. This is the mantra they try to follow. Call it human values or spiritual values. And Indian businessmen triy to teach their children the same truth.

A thousand years ago India's share in world-trade was 34 per cent. Even in 1700 India's share in world income was 22.5 per cent, but today it is around 5 per cent. And the share in world-trade came down to 3 per cent in 1947, and now it is 0.6 per cent. While Hieun Sang, a Chinese traveller, praised ancient Indians for their honesty, and in 1800 a French scholar highly spoke of Indian character, today India's image is quite pitiable in the corruption list.

Trend Setters

Human values can make one a market leader. This has been demonstrated by Tata, Narayan Murthy, Azim Premji, Subroto Ray, Varghese Kurien, Kantibhai Shroff, Sunil Mittal and others. And, of course, you will find the Dabba business (Mumbai), the only Indian organization to achieve the six-sigma quality standard according to the *Forbes* journal, and this is run by 'illiterate' people. Or, take the case of Udupi Hotels, spreading all over the country, even Europe and America, which offer excellent service at a price which even low-income-group people can afford. Then there is Mahila Griha-Udyog (famous for Lijjat papad) where all the employees are its share-holders.

These are just a few Indian organizations. Along with Infosys-Wipro-Excel-Unique Metamed, they stick to human or spiritual values as a corporate policy. Yet they could show their excellence. They are neither scared of globalization nor do they complain about recession and cheap imported goods.

They are not an exception. There are many more though the media ignores them. Go to Yash Paper (Faizabad) where there is not a single manager; with one paper technologist, the workmen and supervisors are running the plant. Human resource potential is being tapped to the maximum extent. And hear, hear. When a sales person, after a tour, submits bills (travelling expenses), the accounts officer or finance manager has the right to raise any questions. People are trusted. Or, take Kiran Industries (Vatva). Here the workmen are involved in R&D (research and development). In Harsh Lab (Indore), where the sales people have the final say in sales-planning, the company grew by 20 per cent last year in a so-called recession market. At Ubique Metamed (Durgapur) the workmen decide how much bonus is to be given to the employees. And this organization, which started as a small foundry, now has plants in 4 states, and all have the capabilibty to export alloy steel. Steel Builders (Tamluk) is run by the employees as the owner Mr. Sarkar has fully empowered them. Samanvaya (Chennai) involves local people in its business strategy. In Japan Lines (Pune) sales people are not allowed to sell its products till they themselves have used them and are satisfied with the quality.

These are just a few examples. Human values can make an organization a trend-setter.

Core of Values

What are these values? According to Indian heritage these are spiritual values. The two most important factors here are the Motive and the Concept.

Motive

According to Hindu scriptures, the duty of a *vaishya* (businessman) is to generate wealth for society and to enrich it. If one concentrates on this, profit and other fortunes will automatically follow. The *Mahabharat* speaks about four *purusharthas*: *dharma* (sacred duty), *artha* (wealth), *kama* (fulfilment of desires) *moksha* (salvation). If one starts with '*dharma*' the others will automatically come to him. Profit-maximization was never the prime goal, it is incidental. You can make your shareholders and employees happy when your customers are happy. This is the only way to increase shareholders' value.

Jamsetji Tata set up a steel plant in the jungles of Bihar. He did not complain about infrastructure. Cowasji set up the first power loom in India; Hirachand Lalchand started making aeroplanes. They did not ask for protection or a level playing field. What made them so bold and successful? They used to think themselves as freedom fighters in their respective fields, they wanted to make India self-reliant. Jamnalal Bajaj worked for the independence of India. They worked for the country. Their motive was spiritual. So the core issue is: Am I working for myself or for society?

Concept

In India you might have noticed that when people start something new, say constructing a house, launching a film, starting a business, or even purchasing a car, at first *puja* (worship) is performed. Why? Because they believe that God is everywhere, and he should be invoked before one starts anything. We may call it an energy-system. Indians believe that everything is God, i.e. energy-oriented. On the other hand Law-Commerce-Business management, influenced by the Western approach, stresses materialism. These consider an organization as a capital-system. All the regulatory controls of a business organization revolve round capital. The assets, setting up a business, managing, growth, loss and profit, everything is capital-oriented, considered in terms of money. This is materialism. This is the difference between Indian and Western approaches.

Let us explain

Say, your company has made a profit of Rs. 10 lakhs this year. Last year it was 7 lakhs, and year before 5 lakhs. Now the balance sheet shows steady growth in profit. But does it mean that you are doing well? Not necessarily. There may be various reasons for this profit. May be the government allowed some relief in the budget. Or, by hiking the price you can make more profit even if you lose market share. Or, by showing other income you can make the balance sheet brighter. Thus, the balance sheet does not give us the real picture. Why? Because it is based on capital-system, i.e. a capital-oriented, materialistic approach.

Consider this. The Fortune journal every year publishes the list of leading companies Fortune-500. It stresses net sales of these companies. And thus is capital-centric. But this concept is misleading because a Company, by virtue of its monopoly position, can be a large selling organization. (Indian Oil is included in this list. But can we give credit to this organization for this?) So today many experts are making lists based on market capitalization. Notice how they unconsciously are moving towards the energy-system. Earlier economists considered GDP and per capita income as the criterion of development. But Amartya Sen concentrated more on the condition of the people. He spoke about longevity, child mortality, literacy rate, and urged for empowering people.

Materialistic capital-system is not working. Remember Nirma? Capital-wise Hindustan Lever Limited (HLL) was much stronger. But Nirma could challenge it. Shivaji, with a handful of Maoli soldiers, could defeat mighty Aurengzeb. Tiny Vietnam could defeat America, a super power. What do these mean? It is how you use your energy, not your capital (materials) that is the decisive factor. Another point. Capital, land, machine, materials are fast losing their importance. Today it is knowledge (or, creative thoughts) which dictates. Why are the small industries at a loss? They do not explore their strength in the value chain, available opportunities, network etc. They are bogged down by material things – infrastructure, technology, money, etc.

Or, take the case of unemployment, especially in West Bengal. Although there is a lack of infrastructure or capital there the main problem is that the local people have a risk-aversion mindset. Banks are willing to sanction loans, the government is encouraging them to set up new business, and land is available. But the bottleneck is their mentality. The problem is with their energy-system, not the capital-system. But see, our friends Herbochem Remedies, Ubique Metamed in Kolkata, are growing fast even in a recession market though they have problems with technology. And the owners, in all these cases, are first generation Bengali businessmen coming from middle class families (and none of them is an MBA).

Now consider the Trade Union movement. This movement is failing all over the country. Bank employees were facing the same problem. Why? Until the 1970s this trade union movement was helpful as it took care of the workers. But after that it became reactionary. In the name of labour welfare these Unions concentrated on raising salaries and mundane facilities. They did not try to increase the awareness of the workers. Thus the Unions ignored the *Shakti* (energy) aspect, and stressed the material dimension (salary). With automation and emerging robotization, the workmen and office staff will be the worst affected as most of their jobs will be done by machines. You will need fewer people. And this will give rise to social unrest. Now, how can you help your Union members? Make them multi-skilled, teach them to go for value-addition. In short, help them to increase their energy-level, tap their hidden energy. The rest will take care of itself.

The Problems

There are two main industrial problems.

1. There is no philosophy as such. What is the purpose of business? This is not clear. (If profit is the ultimate goal, why do you blame the workmen when they ask for more overtime?) Though many organizations use words like 'strengthening the country' or 'welfare of the people' or 'creating wealth', they actually do not mean it. For example, many managers say that they share the same vision as that of the workers. Funny! They are not ready to share cost information and they speak about vision-sharing! If the directors have faith in the people, why are some parts of the ERP locked? According to Indian wisdom, as is said earlier, the purpose of business is to generate wealth for the society to enrich it. As the employees cannot grow at the cost of their Company, so a Company cannot grow at the cost of e society. This is a holistic approach. Before setting the corporate objective, understand the social objectives. And align yourself accordingly.

2. It seems, we are more inclined to ad-hocism and thus ignore long-term planning. The Companies say that they have long-term goals, they have a

vision, they do SWOT-analysis. If so, why are they repeatedly failing to anticipate recession? If I can't foresee two years hence, what sort of vision do I have?

Only with a holistic approach these problems can be tackled. If I am the owner of a company, let me answer the following questions.

- Does my product/service solve any basic problem of society?
- In what am I specializing – product/service or solving problems of the people?
- Does society need my product/service badly? Why?
- How can I diversify my role by playing complementary roles in other areas? How?
- Which new problems have emerged or are emerging in the customer segment I am presently serving?
- What is the global demand for this type of product/service? In which region? How much? How can I make an entry to serve people there?

The lack of a holistic approach (*Advaita* in *Vedantic* term) is the core problem. A hand-to-mouth policy or self-centred principle does not help. As the purpose is to serve the society, I must know the social objectives first. In Indore and Bhopal you can hire an MBA for Rs. 3000 a month. The picture is not much different in other parts of the country. Why? The B-schools are producing managers while the country needs more entrepreneurs and consultants (specially for the SSIs). Mr. Bimal Jalan, Governor of Reserve Bank, is bringing down interest rates every year. Businessmen are asking for tax cuts, interest cut, and all such things. This is ad-hocism. Recession can be tackled, on a long-term basis, when the purchasing power of the low-income group people will be increased. 'What can I get from the society' is a wrong approach. The right approach is 'What can I do for society?' If I can serve more and more people, profit will automatically follow.

The Three Mantras

The *Upanisads* suggest three mantras as the basic laws.

1. *Tatwamasi* (You are That): Each and everyone has immense potential.
2. *Advaita* (not many, but ONE): We can call this the Holistic approach.
3. *Sukshma* (intangibles, subtle, subjective elements) are more powerful than the *sthula* (tangibles, gross, quantifiable elements). Inner resources are more important than the external resources. In the 16th chapter of the *Gita*, Sri Krishna mentioned courage and clarity of mind (with pure motive) as the two most important qualities. In the name of waste-management and resource-utilization, most companies take care of capital, materials, and technology. Tapping the potential of people is generally ignored. (When there is a drive for cost-cutting, the first victim is the HRD department.)

How can these be applied a changing scenario?

1. The potential of the people (employees) should be tapped to the maximum extent. In the changing scenario automation and robotization will affect the bottom-line people i.e. workers, supervisors, staff, and junior management. Downsizing will affect the middle management; merger and acquisition will hurt the senior and top management. Side by side job opportunities will diminish though population is increasing. To solve these problems organizations have to take steps, they cannot leave everything to the government. Each company has to increase its business through setting up new units to absorb people. Otherwise there will be social unrest because of unemployment. Present employees should be made ready for any eventuality. This can be done in three ways. One, the contribution ability of the people should be increased through value-addition and product innovation. Two, they are to be taught how skills can be applied to other areas. Third, entrepreneurship is to be developed in them.

    VCIM had developed three modules, based on Indian ethos, to help an organization in this direction.

    (a) Ekalavya-approach in developing self-managing teams.
    (b) Arjun-technique in value-addition and product innovation.
    (c) Rajarshi-model of Leadership.

    Though *kaizen* and *Quality Circle* involve workmen, they are not allowed to change the system or structure. But our modules help them to go beyond the horizon. And this is what we see at Yash Paper, Ubique Metamed, Kiran Industries, Harsh Lab etc. Focusing on the emerging problems, business organizations have to face, special projects are designed to help people tap their hidden potential to concentrate on 'How much business am I giving to my organization?'

    Thus the interests of the employees, organization and society are integrated. The Upanisads say: *saha na bhunaktu, saha veerayam karababahai* let us all share together, let all of us become strong together.

2. Conventional 'market leader' concept will not help much any more. Say, you are the leader in the transistor market having a 90 per cent share. Then someone comes with IC (integrated circuit). Where do you stand now? After 5 years a new player comes with a chip. He drives away the product and the old players. Mark it, this is not the question of product innovation only, this is something deeper. Krishna, in the *Mahabharat*, was the king of a tiny land, *Dwarka*. Yet he was approached by both *Pandavas* and *Kauravas* to join them. Why? Krishna did not have the largest share of land but he could make himself a key player. Similarly, if you as an industrialist can make yourself a social key player, this will make you stronger. The secret is to make other players feel that they need you. How can one go about this? Instead of concentrating on any particular product, one is to address a particular problem

(social problem) and give a new direction in solving that. Financial, technological, material and other problems are mere symptoms; at the core there is a social problem always. Try to identify this social problem first. Instead of finishing off all other players, can you help them grow? For an example, a teacher generally thinks that his duty is to teach and take exams. But actually, the duty of teachers or education institutions is to make the students socially useful. If as a teacher or principal you focus on this social problem and can come out with a better solution, other education institutions will seek your help. Even with 100 students your organization can become a key player. Let me repeat: Make other players feel that they need you badly.

The basic question is: 'Am I to grow at the cost of others?' Or, 'Can I grow along with others?' 'Which values should we follow in business?' Of course, some western pundits speak about co-option. But this is just playing with words as ultimately it tries to finish off the partners. That is why, according to the Business Today, the average life of the joint ventures is 7 years in India. The *advaita* concept says that we all can grow together.

3.   Peerless Group started with only Rs. 2000, Reliance with Rs. 17000, and Minerva with no capital as such. The first two are market leaders in their respective fields. And the third organization, which publishes English books and exports, is literally a virtual organization with only two employees. All these organizations initially focused on the *sukhma* aspects (enterprising spirit, available opportunities, social awareness, etc.)

In product innovation this *sukshma* aspect should be of maximum importance. Generally the organizations, in their R&D work, concentrate on an objective problem. Ad agencies focus on the subjective problems. But there are two more problems – acute and emerging. If one explores these two and offers solutions, one can sweep the market. Many times we do not notice the side problems. For example, motorcycles make so much noise, but no automobile company notices this. If a revolver can be attached with a silencer, why not the two-wheelers?

An Experiment

Presently, at Indore, in India we are offering consultancy to three organizations – Malwa Feeds and Fertilisers, Harsh Lab., and Ultra Home Products. The focus is Ire-engineering the organization, and the method is the same everywhere – empower the people to the maximum extent. How did we start? First, we tried to convince the top management that they should become 'Business-Yogi' instead of remaining businessmen and professionals As the country needs their help, they are to concentrate on social welfare: how to help the society in some other fields. We tried to change their philosophy of life from business-man to business-yogi. A parent is the best example of leader as he/she keeps on empowering the child to make him self-reliant (Theory 'P').

Second, we started classes for the office staff and sales people with a simple question – If ants and bees do not need any leader (their society is so systematic, they show such a high standard of team spirit, communication, caring for the weak, self-managing teams. Though a queen is there, she only lays eggs, never leads or dictates.) Why do intelligent human beings need a leader? Gradually they framed self-managing teams, took up small projects focusing on some problems and developed working methods. The same process was followed with the workmen and supervisors at the plants. Each one was allowed to identify the problem he was facing and taught how he himself could solve that. And then they went through an example exercise:

- What is expected of me?
- What is my performance level?
- How can I be more focused in my job?
- How can I add value?

First they did it individually, then with their respective boss, and finally with other team members. Their mindset shifted from *nokri*-mentality to business-mentality. They started concentrating on how much business am I giving?

Then they (the sales/staff/workmen) were asked to identify the growth-opportunities available in their work place. We tried to help them develop positive approach. They are to treat their workplace as a laboratory where they come daily for self-development.

Gradually the senior and top management people were entrusted with starting new businesses, with the help of middle management people, to help the society (specially the deprived section).

The experiments are still on, and workmen and staff are busy developing the right system and structure for their organizations.

Back to Values

Management is always value-based. Otherwise it is manipulation. And only values (human or spiritual) can help one to grow in long-term business. Let me explain.

Industries try to develop their brand name. What is the significance of brand name? You are trustworthy; customers can rely on the quality of your product/service. Right? Trustworthiness is a value.

As regards leadership, Indian workers like to see a role-model, a father figure in their leaders, managers, bosses. This is possible only when as a leader your actions are value-based.

Decision-making. You may know decision-tree or quantitative analysis, or may have all the reports available. But have you noticed one thing? Your data may be objective, but decision is mostly subjective. One can draw different conclusions from the same set of data. So, you need something more. You can make a better decision when you transcend your petty ego, when you are neutral. That is why in the World Cup cricket the umpire is always from a third country. Only a quality mind can take a quality decision. A manager must develop a detached mind. This is again a value-based technique.

Some people argue: If I am honest, others will take me for granted; if I am truthful, I will be cornered; if I am transparent, others will take advantage. Unfortunately they make a mistake. The *Mahabharat* clearly differentiate a good man from a goody-goody man. Sri Krishna taught the *Gita* to *Arjun*, and not to *Yudhisthira*. What does this mean? The same *Mahabharat* suggests four techniques – *saam*, *daan*, *bhed*, and *danda*. If necessary one has to stand up for fighting. You should not allow anybody to take you for granted. But mind, the same scripture says that the fight should be for justice, not for your small ego. Values, in essence, means 'working for a great cause'.

PART III

AGENDA FOR HUMANIZATION OF ORGANIZATIONS

Chapter 13

The Nature and Understanding of Organization from a 'Samhita' Perspective

Bengt Gustavsson

What is an Organization?

Instrumental?

I believe it is difficult to exclude a teleological perspective of an organization. It is difficult to understand how an organization could exist without having an aim of some kind. The very word 'organization' has a teleological flavour: the word has its roots in the Greek word 'organon', which means 'to implement' (Webster's). That an organization has and must have a purpose seems pretty obvious for students of business administration. It would be difficult to find a company, a government agency, or a non-profit organization not having some kind of task to accomplish in order to achieve some kind of goal, purpose, or objective. The purpose-less organization would be hard to find – I cannot conceive of an agency or company which is 'just being there'. It is perfectly understandable if some or many or even all members of the organization don't see any purpose in the organization. But that does not mean that the organization *per se* does not have a purpose, seen from the perspective of the environment (e.g. the citizens in a society relying on the services provided by the governmental agency), the founder(s) (e.g. the entrepreneur), the owners, the management, etc.

The question becomes fuzzier, however, when we think of more loosely coupled organizations. I'm thinking of informal groups of people (and why not animals and plants) that does not have a formal founder, charter (or other sets of rules that guides the activities of the organization) etc. We could think of the society in general as being such an organization. 'Oh, the society', somebody would object, 'it certainly is a formal organization: we have the government, we have the governmental agencies, and we have all the football clubs'. Yes, all of these are examples of organizations within the loosely coupled organization 'society', having the purpose of organizing the society. But that's not the aspect I was thinking of. I was thinking of the phenomenon society where people are born, live their lives, die, love, hate, work, play, just exist, reproduce themselves – we do this together on the micro as well as the macro level. What is the purpose of the society (from Latin 'socius', 'companion') seen in this way as an organization? What does the society want to 'implement'? Are we all companions towards a common goal? Sure, would some say, the goal is to survive (a Darwinist version); to go towards an ideal state where everyone lives in unity and shares pleasures and pains as the cells in a body (a Platonist version); to further evolution (an undefined version). So even in this fuzzier version of organization it might be possible to attribute a purpose, though it might be more abstract and difficult to conceive.

One interesting approach to conceptualize the teleological problem is found in Abravanel (1983). Drawing on principles from Hegel and Lenin he concludes that an organization is a bridging medium between a desired state and the present, or real, state. The *raison d'être* of an organization is thus found in the process of fulfilment of desires. A thought experiment may reveal an image of a state where all desires have been fulfilled (some would call this state enlightenment, others utopian). In this state there would be no need for an organization: all the desires and objectives have been fulfilled – there is no room for teleology, we are 'there'. In other words, following Abravanel, an organization exists because of our unfulfilled desires. Unless unsatisfied desires, organizations are non-existent.

My conclusion from this brief contemplation on teleology is that I have to include that perspective on my journey for understanding 'organization'. Even though the *raison d'être* for an organization is teleology, it does not mean that an organization is teleology. Teleology is not the terminal station on the journey; it is just a station passing by.

When I ask students of business and management 'what is an organization', I usually get an answer with a teleological (an entity with a goal) or instrumental (the entity serves as a tool to reach a goal). Most students, though, find it difficult to answer my question. Those students probably agree that an organization has an instrumental flavour to it, but is that enough? There must be something more to it in order for us to define or explain what an organization is.

A Machine?

In the early days of our 'science' the definition of organization was probably not especially problematic. Even though the reality was as ambiguous and complex then as it is now, the dominant world-view made people perceive the reality in a pretty simple manner. In those days the so-called mechanistic, or functionalistic, paradigm is said to have been dominant in society. This 'collective perception' regarded the world as a mechanistic entity which could be explained in a material, precise, and causal manner. It was a way to categorize the chaotic, immanent, complex, and ambiguous reality in order to make it manageable. Even though most pundits within organization theory today consider the mechanistic categorization of organizations clumsy and crude, we still have put new categories into reality. The difference might be that there is no general agreement on the categorizations today as there was earlier in the century. We are said to be in a paradigmatic crisis and revolution (Kuhn, 1970) or in a state of 'metamorphosis' between different epochs (Kostopoulos, 1987).

The mechanistic perception of organization approaches its subject matter from an objectivist point of view (Burrell and Morgan, 1979). An objectivist focuses on concrete and rational values. When categorizing a complex matter such as an organization, a typical definition for an objectivist would be: ''Organizational theory' is the study of the structure and functioning of organizations and behaviour of groups and individuals within them' (Pugh, 1972, p.76). Such an approach studies the tangible aspects of an organization. It often assumes that the organization has an absolute and identifiable status of its own. In its most tangible and absolute form, theorists tended to view organizations as closed systems: Taylor's scientific management, Fayol's administrative principles of management, or Weber's bureaucracy (Thompson, 1967). Less concrete, but still with a fairly tangible form, was the open systems approach: the organization was categorized as a natural, homeostatic, system with a constant interchange with the environment (e.g. Katz and Kahn, 1966). Categorized in this way, the concept of organization was pretty uncomplicated and given, and most of the efforts was put on how to chose the appropriate structure of the organization to suit the operations and the environment (e.g. Wieland and Ulrich, 1976; Miller and Friesen, 1984).

Even though the concept of organization seemed uncomplicated, many problems aroused following the mechanistic perception *in practice*. For example, the bureaucratic mode of organizing, which has existed in effect, but not by name, for thousands of years in a rather fully developed form in ancient Egypt, China and in the Roman Empire (Gerth and Mills, 1958, p.204), is cramping to the creativity and initiatives of the employees in the organization. The dysfunctions of the bureaucracies are considered to be so great that they 'have a built-in tendency towards ineffectiveness or disorganization' (Argyris, 1968, p.315). One early reaction to this was the Human Relations Movement, which developed during the 1910s and 1920s. They emphasized the feelings and adjustment of the individual, his social acceptance in his work group, and his participation in decision-making (Hicks and Gullet, 1975).

The theoretical dysfunctions of the mechanistic categorization of organization have also been considerable. The criticism is well summarized by Burrell and Morgan (1979)

> The notion of the mechanical analogy is well suited for the study of organizations. if they are *assumed* to be rational, purposive, goal-seeking, adaptive enterprises coping with the demands of the environment. The conservatism or ideological and managerial bias, which many theorists have suggested, is built into the models, which are used as a basis of analysis. For this reason many theorists are not conscious of being biased one way or the other (ibid., p.220).

This 'paradigmatical blindness' of theorists and researchers has mainly been demonstrated by and within the mechanical approach to categorize an organization (or the 'functional paradigm' according to Burrell and Morgan), but it is certainly not limited to that approach. By Kuhn's (1970) definition, a paradigm is closely related to 'normal science' in which the adherent scientist's practice

... will seldom evoke overt disagreement over fundamentals. Men whose research is based on shared paradigms are committed to the same rules and standards for scientific practice. That commitment and the apparent consensus it produces are prerequisites for normal science, i.e., for the genesis and continuation of a particular research tradition (ibid., p.11).

In this way, the very nature of a paradigm suggests a fundamental blindness of the underlying assumptions the paradigm rests upon. As we shall soon see, this blindness is true for other, rivalling, paradigms also.

Or Just an Image?

Nevertheless, the uncomplicated blindness of the mechanical paradigm has given way for other ways of categorizing the phenomenon organization. Instead of seeing the organization as an objective entity with an absolute status of its own, one can see it from a subjective perspective. From this perspective the organization does not exist as an object in the outer, 'objective', world, but does so in the awareness of the observer. Burrell and Morgan (1979) identifies this way of perceiving the organization as the interpretive paradigm. They argue that the paradigm has its roots in the 18th century German idealism, where for example Kant claimed that all sensory data was a product of the inherent principles of man's consciousness and independent of the external reality. The interpretive paradigm

> ... would reject the utility of constructing a social science which focuses on the analysis of 'structures'. It rejects any view which attributes to the social world a reality which is independent of the minds of men. It emphasizes that the social world is no more than the subjective construction of individual human beings who, through the development and use of common language and the interactions of everyday life, may create and sustain a social world of intersubjectively shared meaning. The social world is thus of an essentially intangible nature and is in a continuous process of reaffirmation or change (ibid., p.260).

The interpretive, or subjective, approach to studying organizations has gained increased popularity among scholars in organization theory over the last decades. It has opened up many alternative ways of looking at organizations, including language and symbols. In this way many new avenues of thinking about organizations have emerged. It is legitimate (in some cases almost required) at many universities and business schools today to present an interpretive case study of an organization (e.g. Åredal 1989, Johansson-Lindfors, 1989).

Maybe foremost (but not first) in this area is Gareth Morgan. In several works he has identified and formulated an alternative, more subjective, approach to categorize organizations according to the spectacles of the observer. Morgan uses the analogy from an old Indian tale where six blind men are to describe an elephant: one describes it in terms of the trunk, another in terms of the ears etc. Thus, organizations can be seen as machines, organisms, brains, cultures, political systems, instruments of domination, and even as psychic prisons (Morgan, 1986).

Being able to view the phenomenon organization from almost any perspective, as the idea is in the interpretive paradigm, gives the researcher more freedom in his work and can bring out new and interesting aspects and understanding. But it is also the problem: the approach can easily lead to relativism, the notion that there is no fixed point of reference in knowledge and therefore every statement could be claimed to be true. What would be the need for that thing we call 'science' in that case? Morgan himself has obviously been working with the question of relativism, as it is a problem he always must face. The solution to the problem he favours is a 'conversational approach', meaning that the social researcher should reflect one's favoured perspective in relation to other strategies, and in this way one's own strategy becomes much clearer (Morgan, 1983). Still, this does not solve the problem of relativism, and Morgan seems to have surrendered in this epistemological problem

> While not necessarily favouring a completely anarchistic theory of knowledge, we are obliged to recognize that no one research strategy or inquiring system can be authoritative or complete and that there is at least some merit in Feyerabend's claim that 'anything goes'. This consideration returns us to the idea that since we cannot find any foundational solution to the problem of knowledge, all we can really do is explore what is possible. The conversational model ... provides an important means of doing this (op. cit., p.381).

Could not it be Both?

The two main approaches in categorizing organizations, as an objective entity with an absolute status of its own, or as a subjective entity constructed in the consciousness of the observer, are often described as two extremes on a one-dimensional scale. In between we can find approaches that utilize more or less the objective and subjective approach respectively. A good example of this way of categorizing the different approaches is found in Burrell and Morgan (1979).[1] Categorizing the objective-subjective approaches on such a one-dimensional scale can make sense, but it is not uncomplicated. For example, they view the objective-subjective dimension as two separate positions at the end of a scale

> ... *whether* the 'reality' is of an 'objective' nature, *or* the product of individual cognition; *whether* 'reality' is a given 'out there' in the world, *or* the product of one's mind (op. cit., p.1, my emphasis).

Seeing the objective-subjective in that manner does in fact reflect some underlying assumptions of reality: that the reality is of an *either/or* nature with regard to the subjective-objective dimension. They run into trouble when they are to categorize the works of people who describe the reality as *both* objective and subjective (see for example their discussion on Silverman, p.199). In other words, the categorization is paradigm-bound, as all other categorizations are.

The objective-subjective problem has its roots in a classical philosophical problem: does matter create consciousness or vice versa? From the standpoint of consciousness and its relation to matter, it is possible to identify three main schools of thought:

1. The objectivists – those who believe that consciousness is generated by neural activity in the brain; thus matter creates consciousness and matter has a status of is own. This view is by far the most widely held among scientists (Eccles, 1980).
2. The subjectivists – those who believe that consciousness is fundamental to matter including the brain; thus consciousness, in a fundamental sense, is the origin of matter. In this school we find old philosophical traditions ranging from Plato, Hegel (1971) and the German idealism (even though the German idealists sometimes are interpreted as seeing consciousness as separate from matter), the ancient Vedic tradition (Maharishi, 1969), to recent quantum physicists (e.g. Hagelin, 1987; Bohm, 1984).
3. Between those two 'extremes' we can place the view of consciousness as separate from and independent of matter, and matter as independent of consciousness. Thus, the third main school of thought would be those who view consciousness and the brain as two separate phenomena (the dualistic approach). Here we find many psychologists (e.g. Bourne *et al.*, 1979; Fancher, 1973) and others (e.g. Popper and Eccles, 1981).

From this perspective the objectivists way of categorizing organization would belong to school no. 1 or 3 above (matter creates consciousness), and the subjectivists would either belong to school 2 or 3. The way Burrell and Morgan (1979) presents the issue (the *either/or* approach to objectivity-subjectivity) indicates that they belong to school 3. However, like all categorizations it is difficult to accurately position ideas in 'square boxes'. We can think of the subjectivist's as extreme solipsists, meaning that matter does not exist at all – it is our minds that create the reality around us. This stance might classify for a school of thought of their own: the classical question of 'mind over matter' is not valid for them – matter just doesn't exist! Or we can think of the subjectivists as dualists: consciousness and matter exist as two separate phenomena, but our cognition of matter is totally dependent on the spectacles of the observer.

To summarize the discussion above, I wanted show that the way we perceive the complex issue of 'organization' is done by categorization. The nature of this categorization is coloured by underlying assumptions, often referred to as 'paradigms'. I also wanted to show that the main ontological question, whether the world is essentially objective or subjective, reflects the classical philosophical question 'mind over matter' or vice versa, and that the present status of this question is mostly of an *either/or* nature, i.e. that the reality is either objective or subjective, as reflected in the most popular contemporary literature on organizations by Gareth Morgan.

I will now discuss an approach to overcome the *either/or* categorization of reality with respect to objective-subjective, which could be called the both perspective. This analysis belongs mainly to school no. 2 above, i.e. the idea that consciousness is the basis of existence. The analysis is mainly based on the ontological assumptions of the Vedic tradition as interpreted by Maharishi Mahesh Yogi, some principles from quantum physics, and the analysis by Rafael Ramirez on 'the beautiful organization' (Ramirez, 1987).[2]

The 'SAMHITA' Approach to Organizational Analysis

Consciousness

I have found that the ancient Vedic notion of consciousness to be a stimulating and fruitful for the understanding of reality. I will only briefly introduce the concept of consciousness here, with a particular emphasis on those aspects related to consciousness and the epistemology of organizations.

Notions of consciousness as the origin of the creation are perhaps most developed in the East, especially India, even though we find many expressions of similar notions in the Western philosophical (such as Plato, Hegel, Kant, Schelling), religious (e.g. Master Eckart), and mythological traditions (e.g. the Edda-tradition). Similar lines of thought can be found in ancient traditions in Africa, South and North America.

Maharishi Mahesh Yogis interpretation of Veda claims that everything in creation has its basis in pure consciousness (1966, 1986a, b), the abstract, non-material, transcendental field which is responsible for successively manifested forms which we experience as matter. Maharishi's favourite analogy to clarify this notion is the 'flower and the sap': the invisible colourless sap in the flower manifests itself in different forms in the flower – as stem, branches, leaves, and petals. The colourless sap in itself is not the flower, but it contains all the characteristics of a flower in seed-form (or rather 'sap-form'); we can say that the totality of the flower is contained in an unmanifest manner in the colourless sap. In a similar manner, the transcendental pure consciousness contains the totality of the creation in an unmanifest, seed-form (ibid.).

Maharishi argues that the human nervous system has the capacity of having an experience of this pure field of consciousness. This is possible trough a natural process (meditation) of refining the mental activity of the mind until the mind eventually experiences the least active state of consciousness, which is described as transcendental, pure, consciousness. Through continued practice of meditation the nervous system can gain the ability of fathoming the entire range of consciousness simultaneously – from the pure consciousness to the most active and gross form of waking state of consciousness. This is referred to as *higher state of consciousness*, and through continued refinement of the senses to appreciate the inner wholeness in the outer creation, the highest possible permanent state of consciousness has been reached, called *unity consciousness*. In that state the person experiences everything in terms of himself, as everything is seen as fluctuations of the underlying field of pure consciousness (Maharishi 1966, 1986a,b; Russell, 1978).

The Loss of Ourselves in the Object

The notion that pure consciousness is the basis of our being has epistemological consequences. 'The Self, in its real nature, is only the silent witness of everything' (Maharishi, 1969, p.98). The pure consciousness is the knower of itself as well as the knower of all events, both subjective and objective, which in ordinary waking-state consciousness are perceived as external to itself. Pure consciousness is described by the adjective 'pure' because it is unqualified, completely general state of consciousness. Any mental event is a qualification of the generality of pure consciousness into some specific state. When we see a rose, pure consciousness as if takes on the quality of the rose and loses its unqualified status. Maharishi calls this loss of pure consciousness *identification* with the objects of awareness (op. cit., p.151). The process can be illustrated by the analogy of a film screen: The screen as such does not have any pictures in it, but when a film is projected onto it, the screen loses its quality-less state and is identified as the pictures that are projected upon it. Pure consciousness has no specific characteristics, but its experience is accurately described as completely general, eternal, and infinite. The specificity of time and space emerges from within the generality of eternity and infinity.

In ordinary waking-state consciousness, the reality of the unity of pure consciousness, underlying the diversity of experience, is lost. This loss gives rise to the experience of oneself (the knower, referred to as 'rishi' in Sanskrit) as moving through the creation (the known, 'chhandas' in Sanskrit), connected to it through processes of knowing ('devata'), an experience that results from not having pure consciousness lively in one's awareness (Orme-Johnson, 1988).

Hence, when pure consciousness identifies with the objects of experience, the knower could be said to be identified with the known – the knower is outside of us. When pure consciousness is lively in ones awareness (described as *higher state of consciousness* above), the object of experience does not overshadow the unqualified status of pure consciousness and the knower remains within the self, while the known is perceived as outside, separate, from the self. In *unity consciousness* the senses can be trained to appreciate the object as emanating from pure consciousness, i.e. from oneself. Here, no objects are external, they are perceived as reverberations of ones own self, and unity of creation is a constant experience. This state of consciousness is described by a famous verse from the Upanishads in the Vedic literature: 'I am That, Thou art That, all this is That' (quoted from Orme-Johnson, 1988).

To summarize, the ontology of the Vedic notion of reality views consciousness as the basis of all of creation. The creation is seen as gradually manifesting from the unmanifest, transcendental state to its most gross and concrete state in the form of matter, including the human being. The human consciousness also has its basis in the same transcendental state of consciousness. The epistemological consequence is that when a person perceives something, the situation can be analyzed into three components: the one who perceives (the subject, the knower, or in Vedic terms, the 'rishi'); the perception process (the perception, the process of knowing, the 'devata'); and the thing perceived (the object, the known, the 'chhandas').

Where does the Organization Exist?

In the Object?

In the light of this three-fold way of analyzing the knowledge process, we can return to the different approaches to science, as discussed above. A branch of the objectivists are those researchers that use *induction* as their main method. The inductionists also treat the object as given and with a status of its own (whether they study physical things or socially constructed behaviour patterns), while the subject is ideally considered as an empty container that needs to be filled with data (school no. 1 above). The direction of the epistemological process is from the object to the subject. The object is seen as a source of incontestable data to bee assembled into descriptive theories of the object. The main focus of the inductionist is the object, as they argue that in order to gain maximum knowledge one must identify with the object as much as possible and at the same time observe and categorize (Glaser and Strauss, 1967).

In the Observation?

The kind of objectivists who are often referred to as positivists could be said to live in a two-piece world: the subject and the object are living in two separate worlds (school 3 above). In its most fundamental sense, positivists regard the object as given and independent of our observation of it. The object has a status of its own and it can be observed in the same way and in the same manner by any observer. The result of the observation will be the same for all observers, and the observed object is not supposed to be influenced by the observation. The subject is viewed as a black box in its own world. The processes of how the subject gains knowledge which is formulated into hypotheses ('the context of discovery'), is not a field of inquiry and subsequently not of interest for the positivist:

> The initial stage, the act of conceiving or inventing a theory, seems to me neither to call for logical analysis nor to be susceptible of it. The question how it happens that a new idea occurs to a man – whether it is a musical theme, a dramatic conflict, or a scientific theory – may be of great interest to empirical psychology; but it is irrelevant to the logical analysis of scientific knowledge (Popper, 1980, p.31).

The positivist is therefore focusing on the process of observation, creating rigorous measuring methods in order to connect the 'black box subject' with the given object.

In the Subject?

The subjectivists, on the other hand, do not consider data as given, nor do they view the object as with a status of its own (school no. 2 above). The object has different values for different observers. In the most extreme sense, from the solipsist view, the objective world does not exist, but is merely our mental projections of it. The object of inquiry must be interpreted in order to become meaningful. The emphasis for the subjectivist is on the subject, the observer

> To the advocates of interpretative research the tolerance is great for theoretical ambitions, influence from the personality of the researcher, his/her subjectivity, for a research process that is more based on intuition, continuing interpretations etc, than on explicit procedure and expressed account of working procedure. To the interpretative, point-catching research the appearance of the outer, empirical reality is always coloured by the researcher himself, the theories, metaphors etc. that he is more or less consciously influenced by, that 'data' is as much a question of construction as neutral reflection of an empirical reality (Alvesson, 1989, p.56).

A graphical representation of the different emphasizes with relation to the subject, the process of observation, and the object in the epistemological process is shown in the Figure 13.1 below:

Subject	**Process of obs.**	**Object**
'The interpre-tivists'	'The positivists'	'The induc-tionists'

Figure 13.1 A Graphical Representation

These different approaches of gaining knowledge all have their different underlying assumptions of the ontology of the reality. The difference might not always be clear-cut and expressed, so the categorizations I have made above more reflect tendencies of different approaches. When studying various research strategies, I have often found that they are focusing on one, at most two, elements in the epistemological process. If one is focusing on only one (or two) elements, problems will arise such as that of relativism (for the subjectivists), the influence of the researcher on the object (for the positivists), and the absolute status given to the object (for the inductivists). From this standpoint I have found the notion of consciousness as a helpful theoretical framework for including all elements in the epistemological process. As related above, this notion claims that all three elements are included in the process: the observer, the process, and the observed. All are but different aspects of the underlying pure consciousness. When all elements are included in the process, when there is unity between the three, the Vedic term is *Samhita*. Is there a way to formulate a research strategy from the *samhita* perspective?

In the Samhita of Knower, Experience, and Known!

Ramirez' (1987) attempts to include aesthetics in the theory of social organization is an example of a direction towards such a strategy. Ramirez claims that he is following a Kantian and neo-Kantian tradition.[2] Here, Kant's famous 'das ding an sich', plays an important part, because, according to Kant, 'the thing in itself' must exist because it is a necessary component of experience, but the precise components of the object cannot be determined by a single perceiver. The experience thus becomes a relativistic one, implying a meeting of 'the thing itself' and the subject.

Ramirez interprets Kant as acknowledging a separate, but relative, existence of the outer world. Things have existence of their own, but this existence is related to the interpreter, the knower (or 'rishi'). In this way he claims that an experience of phenomena is neither entirely subjectivistic (nor solipsistic), nor entirely objectivistic (or a-subjectivistic).

One pre-requisite for an aesthetic experience,[3] according to Ramirez, is that all elements in the experiential process are involved. In other words, we cannot consider an experience complete until all elements in the process are involved. We cannot, as the objectivists do, consider only the object in the experience. On the other hand, neither can only the subject be considered as the subjectivists do. The experience can be illustrated as follows:

In the first stage we consider all three entities as separate. The subject is there, the experience, and that which we call the object (the thing in itself):

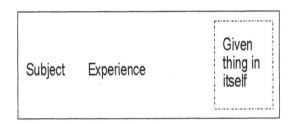

Figure 13.2 'The Thing in Itself'

An objectivist would replace the epithet 'given thing in itself' and use the word 'object' instead. He would claim that the quality sought for is found in the object as such, independent of the subject and the experience.

The next step would be the experience of the subject, irrespective of an object. We can call that the fusion of subject and experience:

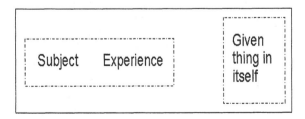

Figure 13.3 Fusion of Subject and Experience

This would be a solipsist's perspective: the experience is not dependent on the object, because all experiences of the world are projected from one's subject ('there is no world, just mental images of it').

In the next step the subject's experience with the thing in itself takes place. It is not until the subject experiences the thing in itself that it becomes an object of experience. Before the subject's experience of the thing in itself, this did not have a status of its own, according to the Kantian tradition as Ramirez interprets it. It is not until the subject and his experience of it takes place that an object is formed in the consciousness of the subject:

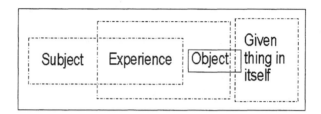

Figure 13.4 Formation of Object in the Consciousness

This would be the '*samhita*' of an experience, the unity of knower, process of knowing, and the known. The conclusion we can make is that an experience of a phenomenon is the dynamic process of the knower, process of knowing, and known, and that nothing is given or absolute in this process.

If we apply this general analysis to the epistemology of organizations, we can conclude that the *samhita* perspective includes the observer, the experience, as well as the observed. This calls for a few comments.

The Subject's Perceptual Ability

The nature of consciousness of the observer is not often discussed when research is being presented. The positivists believe that the subject is irrelevant in the research process and hence there is seldom any discussion regarding the observer, his personality, experiences, convictions etc. Even though such things are sometimes extensively discussed when an interpretative study is being presented, there is seldom or ever any discussion about the qualities of consciousness of the researcher. In the *samhita* perspective consciousness is of vital importance in the research process. Knowledge can be different in different states of consciousness; we know that from our everyday experience. Days when we are tired we perceive the environment in a different manner compared to days when we arrested and alert. It depends on the level of consciousness (the degree of inner wakefulness or to which pure consciousness is lively in our awareness) how we perceive the object and how much wholeness and abstraction we can have in that perception.[4] Thus, the subject and the consciousness of the subject cannot be treated as a black box or as a given in the knowledge process. It is really a question of development of consciousness in order for the subject to have a broader frame of reference in his/her perception.

The Object is not really Objective

When discussing organizations as the objects of an experience, we are dealing with a far more complex and immanent 'thing in itself' than a physical object, such as a painting, a flower etc. Organization is a human concept imbued with ambiguity as discussed in the beginning of this article. When discussing organizations, we are talking about unspecific forms. Depending on the approach, we can perceive the organizations as forms on even subtler levels: as cultures (see for example Frost el al, 1985); or as collective consciousness (Gustavsson, 1992). The notion of organizations as collective forms of transcendental consciousness has led to difficulties in defining the boundaries of the organization. It has even raised questions like 'Do organizations exist?' (Herriot, 1988) These subtler forms of organization might constitute the form of the experience as well as more gross forms.

To experience the 'form' of an object is in other words very important. Ramirez (1987) refers to the perceptual theories of Langer (1953), when he claims that the first thing we register in our perception of a 'thing in itself', is the form. The form of a thing is a sense of wholeness, or *presentational symbol*, which means that the apparent, outer aspects of the thing are fused with all meanings, feelings, sense of belonging to that the thing symbolizes, i.e. in presentational symbolism the symbol and the symbolized are fused and non-separable. The moment we start to analyze or explain our experience, the wholeness gets lost and we enter the *discursive symbolism* mode. Here we are dealing with the parts and their interactions.

This leaves us with the conclusion that the object, in our case the organization, can have many faces. When the objectivist says that the structure is the organization he is right, but also wrong if he claims that it is the whole truth. And if someone claims that organizations do not exist, such as Herriot, he is also right, but only in a partial sense. Obviously the object, the organization, has different 'lives' depending on which level of manifestation one is focusing on. When we as subjects have been trained to identify with the outer reality of an object only, it has led to that we have perceived as the material aspect of the organization. This brings us to the third element in the process, the observation process.

Culture = Collective Perception of Organizations

My analysis has so far been on an individual level, i.e. how the individual perceives the object. The process of observation in the epistemological process is influenced by many sources such as language, context, the observer's background and previous experiences etc. This is an important factor, which can result in many different perceptions of an organization. And yet, on the collective level the experience of the members of the organization is often pretty similar (Ekvall, 1987). With a very general concept this phenomenon has been called corporate, or organizational, culture. In this context, I will focus on the symbolic aspects of culture. It could be argued that the symbolic aspect of culture serves as a direction of the collective consciousness in the organization, and that the corporate culture is the collective perception of an organization.

The dependence of the social environment on our perceptions and cognitions has been pointed out by many sociologists and others. Emile Durkheim introduced in the beginning of the century concepts like collective thoughts: 'How many ideas of sentiments are there which we obtain completely of our own? Very few of us speak a language, which he has not himself created: we find it ready-made' (quoted from Thompson, 1982, p.14). The French philosopher Ludwig Fleck emphasized that 'every epistemological theory is trivial that does not take the sociological dependence of all cognition into account in a fundamental and detailed manner' (quoted from Douglas, 1986, p.12). Fleck argues that the 'thought style' directs any cognition, provides the context and sets the limits for any judgement about objective reality.

Later research into organizational culture has explored this idea further. Linda Smirchich (1983), for example, claims that organizations can be seen as a network of meaning:

> The emergence of social organization depends on the emergence of shared interpretive schemes, expressed in language and other symbolic constructions that develop through social interaction. Such schemes provide the basis for shared systems of meaning that allow day-to-day activities to become routinized or taken for granted' (op. cit., p.160). 'Human actors do not know or perceive *the* world, but know and perceive *their* world, through the medium of culturally specific frames of reference. All forms of human organization, though apparently concrete and real, are in actuality constantly being enacted in this way (p.161).

Broms and Gamberg (1983) exemplify this aspect of culture by studying the role of strategic plans in organizations. Among other things they claim that the strategic plan has a purpose of focusing of mind, goal seeking and generating enthusiasm for an organization. Other examples of symbols influencing the collective perception are leadership. Smirchich and Morgan (1982) argue that leaders often try to enact a particular form of organizational experience to the members in the organization by defining interpretations and meanings so that the members' actions are guided by a common definition of the situation. One example of such interpretation is the leader of an insurance company who always said to his salesmen that 'it is a jungle out there'. He even put posters of jungles on the walls of the company (Turner, 1983). In this way, he was trying to define the meaning for the salesmen as a fight for survival on the market.

Other examples of symbols are buildings and other physical structures (Alvesson, 1989) as a way to define e.g. the communication in the company. Language could also be said to serve as an interpreting symbol for the collective perception, unspoken as well as written and spoken. The 'science' that studies signs and language is called semiotics. Manning (1987) argues that codes and signs communicate social meanings that present complex problems of interpretive understanding.

To summarize my analysis of the perception of organizations, I'm arguing that the organizational culture forms the collective perception of the organization through symbols such as leadership, language, ritual actions (e.g. strategic plans), artefacts etc. We could say that the symbols act as a direction of the collective consciousness in the experience.

The Samhita of Organization = All Elements in the Epistemological Process

Ramirez (1987) argues that there is no absolute ontological status of an organization without taking into account the observer, and hence the perception of an organization is an *interactive process* between the subject and the object. From a theoretical point of view, an experience of an organization must have the *samhita* perspective and include the observer, the observation, and the observed.

The non-specific form of an organization may require more wholeness in the consciousness of the observer than other forms in order to produce a 'full' experience of the organization (whatever a 'full' experience of an organization means). This could be an understanding of why different categorizations limit the perspective to either the object (e.g. structure), or the subject (e.g. emotions), or the observation process (e.g. jungle).

The form is a necessary element in the *samhita* of the experience. If no form is perceived, the experience will not be able to respond to the pattern that connects. This is probably why most experiences of organization are in terms of alienation, or *apart from*. Attempts to overcome this feeling of alienation that many people have of the organizations they are members of, are good in themselves. As mentioned before, one way of achieving less alienation is by decentralizing decisions, at least in some cultures.[5] In that way it is easier for the subject to comprehend the form of the smaller organizational unit he belongs to. In other words, by delimiting the object one can facilitate a *samhita* experience for the organizational members. Other attempts are trying to strengthen the organizational culture, for example by a deliberate use of symbols (see for example Alvesson, 1989, for an analysis of symbols used in a loosely coupled software company). From my perspective, this is a manipulation of the collective perception of the organization in order for the members to make sense out of it, to perceive a form, to get a meaning. On the observer side, the subject, attempts are often made to try to increase the subject's ability to have a broader comprehension of the organization. The employers are sending their managers and employees to all kinds of education at an increasing rate (see for example Ledarskap, 1988). Increasing the intellectual knowledge among the organization members can increase the ability to experience more expanded forms of the organization. But the perception of 'form' is not on the level of discursive symbolism, according to Langer, the form is a matter of presentational symbolism, which is beyond the intellect. Broaden ability of comprehension is rather a matter of expanding the consciousness of the individual. In research on managers meditating the TM-technique, I found an increased holistic thinking, which could be a sign of increased comprehension and thus increased ability to perceive a broader form (Gustavsson, 1992).

My conclusion is that the nature and understanding of organization requires a consideration of the interaction between the subject and the object, and also the process of observation. In this way we can overcome the *either/or* classifications of organizations made by, for example, Burrell and Morgan. We can understand organizations as *both* objective and subjective and go in the direction of more holistic understanding and research of organizations.

The Samhita Research Strategy

I have up until now been discussing the nature and understanding of organizations on a theoretical and abstract level. I would like to take the discussion down to practical implications the '*samhita*-perspective' would have for the researcher on organizations. Can we talk of a specific research theory with this perspective? I will argue that there is a certain difference in terms of both how to do research and how to apply research. I will in this concluding section briefly discuss those two aspects.

Know Thyself!

This research strategy is the main implication of the *samhita* perspective and the most fundamental strategy. It is based on the assumption that the human being is an integrated part of the world and is able to experience its wholeness and abstraction within. By developing our consciousness to fathom greater ranges of inner wholeness, the less alien will the 'outer' be and the more we will recognize in terms of ourselves. The inner and outer reality is nothing but the same.

Meditate! Develop your intuitive understanding! Know thyself! This will give us a subtle but fundamental 'understanding' or intuitive feeling for the 'object' under investigation (which in reality is not an object, it could be said to be an extension of ourselves). Recall that many of the groundbreaking ideas in science have had their basis in a deep and intuitive level of consciousness:

> Scientist often speak of the 'scales falling from their eyes' or the 'lightning flash' that 'inundates' a previously obscure puzzle, enabling its components to bee seen in a new way that for the first time permits its solution. On other occasions the relevant illumination comes in sleep. No ordinary sense of the term 'interpretation' fits these flashes of intuition through which a new paradigm is born (Kuhn, 1970, pp.122-123).

The *Know thyself* strategy is a necessary but not sufficient condition in the research process. It gives us a better[6] basis for understanding the outer world, but the details of that outer world must be studied as well. We might use Bateson's terms and say that knowing ourselves puts us in tune with the pattern that connects. The basis of this idea has also been called the holographic universe metaphor (Morgan, 1980).

Morgan (1980) takes a similar stance in the epistemological process, but the other way around – by knowing the outer world we come to know ourselves:

> The position I have adopted hinges on the argument that the process of knowing involves a process of forming and transforming, and that in knowing our world, we also form and transform ourselves. Approached in this way, the diversity of social research practice presents itself as a realm of choice of central importance to the way we make and remake ourselves, both individually and collectively. This perspective frames social science as an activity that is not just epistemological, but human in the fullest sense (op. cit., p.405).

The principle is basically the same principle as I am proposing: that the inner and outer worlds are different aspects of the same reality. But I am surprised by the emphasis Morgan is putting on the outer world, especially as he consider himself a 'radical humanist' (Burrell and Morgan, 1979), which basically have a subjective approach to science.

To know thyself is the basic research strategy in the *samhita* perspective, a prerequisite for better understanding of the outer world. But this is not enough. The details of the outer world will not be understood be knowing thyself. The strategy for this aspect of the research is

Anything Goes!

This is the famous conclusion of Feyerabend in his work *Against Method* (1975). As one of the strongest critics of modern science, Paul Feyerabend proposes complete anarchism for the scientist in his choice of methods. Otherwise, he argues, the scientist will get trapped within the framework of the present structure of thinking. He maintains that this is an absolute necessity for the growth of knowledge. There is not a single rule in the history of science that is not violated at some time or another. Thus, the rules would have been an obstacle to progress if they had not been violated. 'The only principle that does not inhibit progress is: *anything goes*' (op. cit., p.23). The process of creativity, says Feyerabend, is not guided by a well-defined programme, but rather by a vague urge, by a passion. And here the scientist must be free to develop his vague impulses without the destructive influence of rational methods.

In this way Feyerabend could be said to describe the processes of knowledge: how the knowledge that rises from within very easily gets lost through the binding influence by the predominating paradigm. On this methodological point I fully agree with Feyerabend, but not with the ontological implications that his ideas are said to have. In my discussions on the inherent dangers of relativism in the interpretive approach to knowledge, the relativism is on the ontological level, not epistemological. I believe that the ontology of the *samhita* approach is not a relativistic one.

The reasons why I am favouring Feyerabend's approach are the same reasons as Feyerabend is discussing: method should not be an obstacle to knowledge. By stating that, I am not arguing that method is always an obstacle. Method is also an important way of gaining knowledge. That is why we can use traditional positivistic and induction measures to gain knowledge of the outer aspects of the object in the *samhita* of organization. That is also why we can use interpretive approaches to understand the object from a subjective level. We can actually use any method, as long as we are aware of benefits, limitations and ontological assumptions. A mixture of measures is actually preferred, as the picture of our results will be richer and more fruitful.

With all these different methods we can understand the totality of the subject, the process of observation, and the object; the wholeness of the understanding, the *samhita* of organization. And the *samhita* is formed when the pure consciousness is lively in the awareness of the observer.

Notes

1   They also add another dimension (order-conflict), resulting in four quadrants where they try to position many different social theorists according to their meta-theoretical assumptions. I find this last dimension confusing and arbitrarily chosen and that their main contribution is found in the objective-subjective dimension.
2   Ramirez' interpretation of Kant is obviously different from that of Burrell and Morgan. The latter claim that Kant is an extreme subjectivist.
3   At this general stage of Ramirez' analysis we can include any experience, not necessarily the aesthetic one. Thus, I have excluded the aesthetic aspect from the analysis here.
4   This is also a key element in the aesthetic experience of an organization, according to my analysis of Ramirez' work. Ramirez uses Bateson's definition of an aesthetic experience: 'By aesthetic I mean responsive to the pattern that connects' (1979, p.17). In order to be 'responsive' I'm arguing that this 'pattern' must be lively in one's awareness.
5   Hofstede (1980) argues that theories on motivation, management, and organization have to be considered in relation to the cultural context they have sprung from and applied to, respectively. For example, semi-autonomous groups might work well in the Swedish culture, but might be a disaster in more autocratic cultures.
6   To know oneself is a process, rather than an either/or situation. We already (with individual differences) have a certain degree of ability to fathom deeper level of consciousness.

References

Abravanel, Harry (1983) 'Mediatory Myths in the Service of Organizational Ideology', in *Organizational Symbolism*, Pondy *et al.* (eds), JAI Press, Greenwich, Conn.
Alvesson, Mats (1989) *Ledning av Kunskapsföretag. Fallet Enator* (Managing the Knowledge-company. The Enator Case), Norsteds, Stockholm.

Argyris, Chris (1968) 'Organizations: effectiveness', *International Encyclopedia of the Social Sciences*, vol. 11: Macmillan and the Free press, New York.

Bateson, Gregory (1979) *Mind and Nature, a Necessary Unity*, Bantam Books, New York.

Bohm, David (1984) *Wholeness and the Implicate Order*, Ark, London.

Bourne, L.E.; Dominovsky, R.L.; Loftus, E.F. (1979) *Cognitive Processes*, Prentice Hall, New Jersey.

Broms, Henri and Gahmberg, Henrik (1983) 'Communicating to Self in Organizations and Cultures', in *Administrative Science Quarterly*, no. 28, September.

Burrell, Gibson and Morgan, Gareth (1979) *Sociological Paradigms and Organizational Analysis*, Heineman Educational Books, Portsmouth, N.H.

Chopra, Deepak (1989) *Quantum Healing*, Bantam, N.Y.

Douglas, Mary (1986) *How Institutions Think*, Syracuse University Press.

Eccles, John C. (1980) The Human Psyche – the Gifford Lectures, University of Edingburgh 1978-1979, Springer International, Berlin.

Ekvall, G.; Arvonen, J.; Nyström, H. (1987) Organization och innovation – en studie av fyra divisioner vid EKA Kemi i Bohus, Studentlitteratur, Lund.

Fancher, Raymond (1973) *Psychoanalytic Psychology*, Norton & CO, New York.

Feyerabend, Paul (1975) *Against Method*, New Left Books, London.

Frost, D., *et al.* (eds) (1985) *Organizational Culture*, Sage, Beverly Hills, CA.

Gerth, H.H. and C. Wright Mills (1958) *From Max Weber: Essays in Sociology*, Oxford University Press, New York.

Glaser, Barney G. and Strauss, Anselm L. (1967) *The Discovery of Grounded Theory: strategies for qualitative research*, Aldine, New York.

Gustavsson, Bengt (1992) *The Transcendent Organization*, Akademitryck, Edsbruk.

Hagelin, John S. (1987) 'Is Consciousness the Unified Field?', *Modern Science and Vedic Science*, vol. 1, no. 1, 28-87.

Hegel, Friedrich (1971) *Philosophy of Mind*, transl. by W. Wallace and A.V. Miller, foreword by J.N. Findlay, Oxford at the Clarendon Press.

Herriot, Scott R. (1988) 'Do Organizations Exist?', Paper presented at the conference Towards a Theory of Organizational Consciousness, Maharishi International University, Fairfield, Ia.

Hicks and Gullet (1975) *Organizations: Theory and Behavior*, McGraw-Hill.

Hofstede, Geert (1980) 'Motivation, Leadership and Organization: Do American Theories Apply Abroad?', in *Organizational Dynamics*, summer, 42-63.

Johansson-Lindfors, Maj-Britt (1989) Organizationers Ideologiska Ansikten: Om grundlägg ande föreställningar i mindre företag, Dissertation, Business Dept., University of Umeå, Sweden.

Katz, Daniel and Kahn, Robert L. (1966) *The Social Psychology of Organizations*, Wiley, N.Y.

Kostopoulos, Tryphon (1987) *The Decline of the Market: The Ruin of Capitalism and Anti-Capitalism*, Almquist and Wiksell International, Stockholm.

Kuhn, Thomas S. (1970) 'The Structure of Scientific Revolutions', *International Encyclopedia of Unified Science*, vol. 2, no. 2, The University of Chicago Press, Chicago.

Langer, Susan (1953) *Form and Feeling*, Routledge, Kegan and Paul, London.

Ledarskap (1988) Special issue on corporate education, no. 1-2, February.

Maharishi, Mahesh Yogi (1966) *The Science of Being and Art of Living*, SRM Publications, London.

Maharishi, Mahesh Yogi (1969) *Maharishi Mahesh Yogi on the Bhagavad-Gita: A new translation and commentary*, Chapters 1-6, Penguin, Baltimore.

Maharishi, Mahesh Yogi (1986a) *Thirty Years Around the World – Dawn of the Age of Enlightenment*, MIU Press, Vlodrop, Netherlands.

Maharishi, Mahesh Yogi (1986b) *Life Supported by Natural Law. Lectures by Maharishi Mahesh Yogi*, Age of Enlightenment Press, Washington DC.

Manning, Peter K. (1987) 'Semiotics and Fieldwork', in *Qualitative Research Method Series*, vol. 7, Sage, Newburg Park, CA.

Miller, D. and Friesen, P.H. (1984) *Organizations: A Quantum View*, Prentice-Hall, New Jersey.

Morgan, Gareth (ed.) (1983) *Beyond Method: Social Research Strategies*, Sage, Beverly Hills, CA.

Morgan, Gareth (1986) *Images of Organization*, Sage, Beverly Hills, CA.

Orme-Johnson, David (1988) 'The Cosmic Psyche. An Introduction to Maharishi's Vedic Psychology: The Fulfillment of Modern Psychology', *Modern Science and Vedic Science*, 2, 112-163, MIU Press, Fairfield, Ia.

Plato *The Republic*, transl. Thomas Taylor, The Walter Scott Publishing Co, London (publishing year unknown).

Popper, Karl (1980) *The Logic of Scientific Discovery*, Hutchinson, London.

Popper, Karl R. and Eccles, John, C: (1981) *The Self and Its Brain*, Springer International, Berlin.

Pugh, D.S. (1972) 'Modern Organization Theory', in the *The Modern Business Enterprise*, Michael Gilbert (ed.), Penguin Books.

Ramirez, Rafael (1987) Towards an Aesthetic Theory of Social Organization, Unpublished dissertation, University of Pennsylvania, USA.

Russell, Peter (1978) *The TM-technique*, Routledge, Kegan and Paul, London.

Smirchich, Linda (1983) 'Studying Organizations as Cultures', *Beyond Method: Social Research Strategies*, Gareth Morgan (ed.), Sage, Beverly Hills, CA.

Smircich, Linda and Morgan, Gareth (1982) 'Leadership: The management of Meaning', *Journal of Applied Behavioral Studies*, no. 18, 257-273.

Thompson, J.D. (1967) *Organizations in Action*, McGraw-Hill, N.Y.

Turner, Stephen P. (1983) 'Studying Organization Through Lévi-Strauss' *Structuralism' Beyond Method: Social Research Strategies*, Gareth Morgan (ed.), Sage, Beverly Hills, CA.

Wieland, George F. and Ullrich, Robert A. (1976) *Organizations – Behavior, Design, and Change*, Irwin, Ill.

Åredal, Åke (1989) Den Osynliga Styrningen – en hermeneutisk studie av styrning i svensk tandvård, Dissertation, Business Dept., University of Stockholm, Sweden.

Chapter 14

Human Values in Indian Management

N. Vittal

Management in the final analysis means getting things done. Managers are supposed to make people work for an overall objective and normally managers operate in the set up of an organization. The question is also being raised whether we need today managers or leaders. Jack Welch, the icon for management in the 20th century, has very harsh things to say about management. He associates management with control.

The world of the 1990s and beyond will not belong to 'managers' or those who can make the numbers dance. The world will belong to passionate, driven leaders – people who not only have enormous amounts of energy but who can energize those whom they lead.

I simply dislike the traits that have come to be associated with 'managing' controlling, stifling people, keeping them in dark, wasting their time on trivia and reports. Breathing down their necks. You can't manage self-confidence into people. You have to get out of their way and let it grow in them by allowing them to win, and then rewarding them when they do. The word manager has too often come to be synonymous with control– cold, uncaring, button-down, passionless. I never associate passion with manage, and I have never seen a leader without it.

Somebody who can develop a vision of what he or she wants their business unit, their activity to do and be. Somebody who is able to articulate to the entire unit what the business is, and gain through a sharing of discussion – listening and talking – an acceptance of the vision. And [some on] who then can relentlessly drive implementation of that vision to a successful conclusion.

Too often we measure everything and understand nothing. The three most important things you need to measure in a business are customer satisfaction, employee satisfaction, and cash flow. If you're growing satisfaction, your global market share is sure to grow, too. Employee satisfaction feeds you productivity, quality, pride and creativity and cash flow is the pulse– the key vital sign of a company.

GE leaders always with unyielding integrity create a clear, simple, reality based customer focused vision, and are able to communicate it straightforwardly to all constituencies. They reach, set aggressive targets, recognize and reward progress, while understanding accountability and commitment, they have a passion for excellence, hate bureaucracy, and all the nonsense that comes with it. They have the self confidence to empower others and behave in a boundary less fashion; believe in and are committed to workout as a means of empowerment, are open to ideas from anywhere have, or have the capacity to develop, global brains and global sensitivity, and are comfortable building diverse and global teams. They also have enormous energy and the ability to energize and invigorate others, stimulate and relish change and not be frightened or paralyzed by it, see change as an opportunity, not a threat, possess a mindset that drives quality, cost and speed for a competitive advantage.

Growing productivity must be the foundation of everything we do. We've been chasing it at GE for years. We once thought we could manage it into business operations, with control and hierarchies and vinyl books with charts. All we did was stifle people, sit on them, slow them up, and bore them to death. In the early 80s we fell in love with robots and automation and filled some of our factories with them as our employees looked on sullenly and fearfully. It didn't work. We now know where productivity – real and limitless productivity – comes from. It comes from challenged, empowered, excited, rewarded teams of people. It comes from engaging every single mind in the organization. When a business becomes productive it gains control of its destiny.

What we have done has barely scratched the surface. It turns out that there is, in fact, unlimited juice in that lemon. The fact is, this is not about squeezing anything at all; it is about tapping an ocean of creativity, passion, and energy that as far as we can see, has no bottom and no shores.

Just as surely as speed flows from simplicity, simplicity is grounded in self confidence. Self confidence does not grow in someone who is just another appendage on the bureaucracy ... whose authority rests on the bureaucracy ... whose authority rests on little more than a title ... people who are freed from the confines of their box on the organization chart, whose status rests on real world achievement ... Those are the people who develop self confidence to be simple, to share every bit of information available to them, to listen to those above, below and around them, and then move boldly.

We may, for the purpose of our analysis, look at management as the function that involves making people come together, work for a common objective and achieve that objective. While management, as visualized by Welch, may involve bureaucracy and may not involve drive, I think, today in the competitive environment, one cannot be a successful manager unless one is also a successful leader.

We will look at this whole issue of management from the point of view of getting things done and perhaps we may have to look at both the software aspect of management, which is leadership, and the hardware aspect, which is procedures and systems. Is there anything special about Indian management? At one level, getting any organization to run effectively and get results may involve the same fundamental principles like having a vision, planning for it, motivating people and measuring success. These may be common in the successful management anywhere in the world. These principles may not be specific for any particular country. There is also a very strong aspect of ethos and culture of a place, which has also a bearing on how managements function in the 1980s and 1990s when there was a lot of debate about the success of the South East Asian economic tigers. Lee Kwan Yew articulated the concept of Asian values, which could be distinguished from that of western democratic values. This meant that it was possible for the people working in Asian organizations to accept a certain degree of discipline and regimentation and perform effectively. Religion, ethos and culture of a place have a bearing on how an enterprise or an organization functions. Richard Tawney wrote a book in the 1930s about *Religion and The Rise of Capitalism*. The Protestant work ethic has been behind much of the success of western style management and development. On the other hand, the homogenous culture of Japan, and Buddhist values like the respect for the elders and sacrificing the self for the good of the group have marked the Japanese management. The Chinese are perhaps influenced by the Taoist and Confucian principles where again respect is an important factor. We can look at the Indian management also from the point of view of how the actual functioning of organizations and enterprises in our country is affected by our culture and ethos.

Human values in Indian management would therefore mean that while respect for the individual and the basic principles of motivating a group of human beings may be common elements in any management, when we examine the experience of Indian management, we may find that Indian culture, ethos and values may affect our functioning in certain cases. We can perhaps identify those elements in Indian management where the local ethos prevail and distinguish them from those where universal principles apply.

For the purpose of our analysis, we may confine ourselves only to management in the sense of managing an organization or enterprise. Today, one can talk about management in government also. Generally, when we talk about government, these days the word 'governance' is preferred. The word 'governance' has become so popular that we talk of corporate governance also. In order to keep our focus on the process of management, we may look at enterprises and organizations which are, commercial organization as well as not for profit organization.

We may consider first the issue of the Indian management in the context of the commercial enterprise. The ethos that prevails is of a family. This is because a substantial part of Indian commercial enterprises are family controlled. As pointed out by Prof. Dwijendra Tripathy in the 10th anniversary issue of *Business Today* (January 2002)

> It is significant that as many as 14 business houses occupied centre stage in 1951 (Tata, Birla, Dalmia, Sahu, Jain, Kirloskar, Shri Ram, Lalbhai, Valchand, Thaper, Mafatlal, Mahindra, Bangur and Singhanias). They are still among the top 100 groups according to a list drawn by *Business Today* in 1997.
>
> With the exception of Tatas, all major enterprises in these group are headed by members of the promoting families and the succession of the top leadership of a group is normally synonymous with the succession in the family. No one conversant with the situation in the Indian corporate sector was surprised when a young and still rather inexperienced Kumaramangalam Birla was appointed to the group chairmanship after his father Aditya Vikram passed away a few years ago in the prime of his life.
>
> Similar things happened in the house of Tatas also when a 34-year old JRD Tata was replaced at the top of the Tata organization in 1938. Another Tata, Ratan took over the reigns from him in 1991. But the fact that with somewhat better luck, the post would have gone to a non-Tata tells something about the change that has occurred in the managerial structure of the house during the intervening 53 years.

Prof. Tripathi speculates that family businesses all outgrow family control and management. This has been the experience of the developed world. Practically enterprises that grew into global giants in due course started as family firms.

Dupont and Ford all went through this process. Is Indian business moving in this direction? The culture of any Indian business enterprise is very much shaped by the family of the promoters. According to one estimate, nearly 90 per cent of the Indian business today is still family controlled. As the values of an enterprise are determined by the families which are dominating, we find that broad business strategies are affected by these values. For example, the firms dominated by Jains ensured that they would not get into businesses which will go against the sacred principle of *Ahimsha*. Similarly, it will be difficult to find any enterprise owned by Sikhs which are in the tobacco business. So, at one level, some of the religious taboos may dominate the selection of the area of enterprise itself.

There have been certain communities which have been known for their enterpreneurship. The Gujaratis, Marvaris and the Chettiars come to mind immediately. Each of them also have very strong family culture and tradition. These are reflected in the culture of these enterprises. For example, companies run by the Lalbhai Group with eminent leaders like Kasturbhai Lalbhai had a very high sense of ethical values. During the freedom struggle again, some of the companies like Birlas, Bajajs and Lalbhais also brought in their national sentiments in business. The human values of the Indian management at the enterprise level to a significant extent are determined by the nature of the business community which is running the enterprise.

The post-independence era gave rise to a socialistic approach by the government with the idea that the commanding heights of the economy must be controlled by the government. This, in turn, led to what Rajaji called the permit licence raj. In this licence raj period, I think the majority of the Indian business enterprises had to sacrifice, to some extent, whatever values and ethics they may have had because ultimately the whole exercise of business became an exercise in contact management. Liaison men flourished. The permit licence raj also gave rise to other evils the most important of which is corruption. The enormous extent of black money in the system which is estimated at 40 per cent of the GDP is another consequence of this culture of licensing and corruption. Many business enterprises therefore would have found that they cannot continue to be in business unless they come to terms with the powers that be. It may be worthwhile to have a research on this issue about how, when it comes to corporate governance whether many Indian enterprises would be able to score high because of the legacy of the permit licence raj. In any discussion on human values in Indian management, we must realize that while there may be a fundamental influence of values dictated by tradition and religion, there is also a continuous reshaping of the values of the enterprise because of the prevailing business environment.

One of the negative aspects of our Indian ethos is supreme sense of tolerance and also the concept of *prayashchita*. We are probably more patience and tolerance than many people in the world and therefore we find that many of our organizations are inefficient but still somehow they survive. They are always given a second chance. Secondly, the concept of *prayashchita* means that a person can commit a large crime but by making a small token repentance, he can be excused. Perhaps this is the reason why we are reluctant to punish anybody and the reward and the punishment system in our country is not as well developed. It may also be because the public sector plays an important role in the economy and the public sector does have a very effective reward and punishment system. The private sector may still have a reward and punishment system but even there the laws relating to lack of flexibility in labour etc. may perhaps made it even difficult for even the private sector to have a very effective reward punishment system. I wonder whether this characteristics of the Indian management can be traced only to the socialistic policies or also there is an atavistic impact of our Hindu concept of extreme tolerance and the principle of *prayashchita*.

In fact, the post-liberalization period 1991 has brought the issue of values back into the centre stage and today we talk about corporate governance. Behind every human action there is ultimately a value. Positive values like altruism, helping others, love, friendship etc. create the basis for a happy united community. Negative values like hatred, anger etc. work in the opposite direction. Values ultimately are evolved for smooth operation of any human activity. Business is one of the important functions of any modern society. As the civilization progresses, business also progresses. For each business and profession, ultimately there are certain values which are adopted and honoured because without such coherence of values, it is not possible to have orderly, smooth and positive developments.

The concept of values got crystallized in the Hindu thinking in the form of *Dharma*. The *Bhagavad Gita* says that it is better to die than give up one's own *dharma*. *Swadharme nidhan shreya para dharmo bhayapaha.*

In the context of today's knowledge economy and the world which has become a global village, so far as business is concerned, what are the values that are worth observing? As the Central Vigilance Commissioner, I am constantly looking at the issue of corruption which is a manifestation of dishonesty. The World Bank defines corruption as the use of public office for private gain. In business, the value of trust is important. If trust is not honoured, then there is breach of trust. Business is supposed to be a win-win exercise. It ceases to be so if there is no trust. Honesty is the best policy. The world is rediscovering this value thanks to globalization.

In 1994, I went to Bangkok. I was told that there was corruption both in Bangkok and in India. But in Thailand they had honest corruption whereas in India we had dishonest corruption. Honest corruption was a contradiction in terms. I was told that what was meant by honest corruption was that there was a bribe to be paid for every activity in Thailand and if the bribe was paid, the work would be done and if the work was not done, the bribe would be returned. In India on the other hand, when the bribe is paid and if the work is not done, the bribe was also not returned. This was dishonest corruption. Perhaps even in this cynical story, one can find that ultimately in business, delivering on promises is an important value.

The collapse of the South East Asian economies highlighted the need for integrity in business. If there is crony capitalism and corruption in the financial sector, to act against a country is perceived to be corrupt. This is what the World Bank says

> For operational purposes, the World Bank defines corruption as the abuse of public office for private gain. While this definition does not include wholly private sector corruption, it does include the interface between private and public sectors without

which much private sector corruption could not occur. Some of the examples are Bribery in purchasing government contracts, benefits, licenses, judicial decisions, evading customs duties, taxes and other regulations; theft or misappropriating budgetary funds and public assets; patronage, nepotism and cronyism; influence peddling like election or party financing in exchange for influence.

Corruption is not likely ever to be fully eliminated but the objective is to minimise it so that it becomes and exception and not the rule, by turning it from a low risk and high return activity into a high risk and low return activity. The World Bank's approach therefore focuses on an economic analysis of the conditions conducive to corruption based on rents, discretion and accountability. Corruption is a function of all three. Corruption has the potential to flourish where rents are high, discretion extensive, and reporting and monitoring are poor.

In combating corruption, it is useful to focus on minimising the extent to which these factors can influence behaviour, rather than relying solely on prosecution of corrupt individuals. Prosecuting the guilty is important but can do little to reduce the opportunities and incentives for corruption 'upstream'. To do this, it will be necessary to focus on rents, discretion and the efficiency of monitoring and accountability mechanisms in the political, administrative and other structures of the state. At the same time, it is important to ask why there have not been more successful prosecutions of corruption. This highlights the importance of including judicial, prosecutorial and police bodies among the state organizations to be scrutinised. The analysis based on high potential rents, extensive discretion and low transparency is also relevant to them.

Corruption undercuts the macroeconomic, efficiency, equity and institutional functions of government. It is helpful to distinguish these four types of costs imposed by corruption:

Macro-fiscal: lost revenues (from tax, customs duty and privatisation) and excessively high expenditure (through corruption loadings on state contract);

Reduction in productive investment and growth: through abuse of regulatory powers, misprocurements and other costs imposed by corruption. International evidence indicates that countries with higher incidence of corruption systematically have lower investment and growth rates and that public safety can be compromised by unsafe infrastructure.

Costs to the public and to the poor in particular: via higher taxes than necessary, bribe extraction in delivery of services and poor quality of and access to services. Bribe are frequently a higher proportion of income of the poor even though they do not pay the highest bribes.

Loss of confidence in public institutions: corruption can undermine the rule of law, tax compliance, respect for contracts, civil order and safety, and ultimately the legitimacy of the state itself.

The importance of values in business is also underlined by the increasing emphasis on corporate governance. This is an index of the increasing awareness about the need for having a proper moral, value and ethical framework for taking decisions in business. Good corporate management is using the financial, physical and human resources of an enterprise to get the best results in terms of productivity, profitability, market capitalization etc. Corporate governance would mean having a proper ethical framework before taking business decisions.

As I see it, in good corporate governance ultimately the focus is on transparency. This transparency is assured by having professional part time directors in the Board of Directors. They also head committees like ethics committee and finance committee of the Board. These ensure that the process of decision making is transparent.

Transparency is needed because the next important value in business is accountability. Once the system is transparent, accountability can readily be fixed because responsibility for decisions and action taken are known. That brings us finally to the question of what is the accountability for? This is related to value added to the stakeholders. For example, in the case of investors it is return on investment and for customers, quality of goods and services and so on.

While delivering the 10th JRD Tata oration on Ethics in Business at XLRI Jamshedpur recently, Dr. Robert T. Drinan drew attention to two important sources of corporate ethics. Dr. Drinan pointed out that business schools, corporate leaders and political officials around the globe are following closely the interwoven forces that want to make a better place of a market-driven world: after the horrors of the 40 years of the Cold War how to foster a system that will bring economic decency and political stability to the world's poor and vulnerable. He said

Citing two important sources of corporate ethics-the Caux Principles and the Interfaith Declaration of 1993 – he pointed out that the intense worldwide emphasis on business ethics since the demise of the Cold War is unprecedented. The Caux Principles (named after the place in Switzerland where world business leaders deliberated and drew up a code) is aptly subtitled 'Business behaviour for a better world'. It emphasis the Japanese concept of 'Kyosei' (living and working together for the common good) along with the more Western concept of human dignity. Even its preamble states that 'laws and market forces ... are necessary but insufficient guides for comfort'. Business can be a powerful agent of positive social change and hence a 'commitment to shared prosperity' is essential in the operation of the corporation.

The Caux Declaration affirmed the 'centrality of moral values' in economic decision making. Its cardinal principles are the corporation should (a) share the wealth created with all its employees, shareholders and customers in order to improve their lives; (b) be responsible citizens from whom competitors can expect 'a spirit of honesty and fairness'; (c) contribute to human rights, education and welfare; (d) protect and wherever possible improve the environment; (e) in the exercise of its vast power be guided not by the law alone but by the 'centrality of moral values' in economic decision making; (f) pledge to support human rights and democratic institutions and to cooperate with those forces that are dedicated to raising standards of health, education and work place safety.

In 1993 the Interfaith Declaration having the core values of the Abrahamic religions in mind sought to give a distinctly spiritual flavour to the issue. Central to those religious – indeed to all the world's great religions – are traits such as justice, fairness, love for others, stewardship for natural resources and honesty and integrity.

A significant conclusion after perusing both Caux Principles and Interfaith Declaration is that an ethic for the global village may need more than secularistic approach. Two other developments keeping pace with the evolution of ethics and effectively complementing it have been (1) a move to promote honesty and openness in governments and (2) a global commitment to human rights. Across the globe there is felt need for stable and hones governments. The literature on the subject is enormous. Key issues here are (a) how corporations can preserve integrity while operating in a corrupt environment. (b) Is the dominant purpose of the corporation to return profits to its shareholders? Or are there larger purposes going beyond the maximisation of profits? (cd) how to set higher ethical standards for business – government interaction and especially in tackling corruption, money laundering and so on.

How do we operationalize the concept of values in business? The best advice I have come across is in a small book by Norman Vincent Peale and Kenneth Blanchand called the 'Power of Ethical Management'. The authors have articulated what has been called the three way ethical check. The ethical check questions are as follows:

- Is it legal?
- Will it be violating either civil or company policy?
- Is it balanced?
- Is it fair to all concerned in the short-term as well as in long-term?
- Does it promote win-win relationship?
- How will it make me feel about myself?
- Will it make me proud?
- Would I feel good if my decision was published in the newspaper?
- Would I feel good if my family knew about it?

These ethical check questions provide a good reference point to decide on ethical issues, which arise in the contemporary Indian management. The authors have also provided the following five principles of ethical power for organizations.

Purpose: The mission of our organization is communicated from the top. Our organization is guided by the values, hopes and a vision that helps us to determine what is acceptable and unacceptable behaviour.

Pride: We feel proud of ourselves and of our organization. We know that when we feel this way, we can resist temptations to behave unethically.

Patience: We believe that holding to our ethical values will lead us to success in the long-term. This involves maintaining a balance between obtaining results and caring how we achieve these results.

Persistence: We have commitment to live by ethical principles. We are committed to our commitment. We make sure our actions are consistent with our purpose.

Perspective: Our managers and employees take time to pause and reflect, take stock of where we are, evaluate where we are going and determine how we are going to get there.

I think the experience of excellent companies and visionary companies shows that in the ultimate analysis values do matter, ethics does matter. In their book, *In Search Of Excellence* by Peters and Waterman, the authors pointed out how one of the characteristics of excellent companies was 'hands on value driven'. While the managements are hands on and decide on day to day matters, they have also not forgotten their values. Similarly in their book, *Built To Last*, Jeremy Porrass and James Collins pointed out that ultimately the visionary companies, the companies which lasted much longer 50 to 100 years compared to the normal lifetime of 15-20 years of the standard companies, one main characteristic was their core values which irretrievably linked with their company practices and procedures. In other words, the long-term basis for success appears to be internalization of ethical values and ensuring that these are woven irretrievably into the company policies and practices.

We have seen so far the dynamics of how human values in Indian management may be affected. In the context of today's globalization, is it possible to draw inspiration from our ethos and arrive at the most effective strategies for development. After all, business enterprises, whether for profit or not for profit enterprises, exist with certain objectives. So when we talk about values, we will have to judge them in the context of to what extent these values help in achieving the results. Poised as we are at the beginning of a new century, we may perhaps look at the prevailing global scene and see to what extent Indian management can draw inspiration from our culture and ethos and particularly the all time guide for life, the *Bhagawat Gita*.

As Jack Welch points out leadership is most important in today's management. The importance of leadership is also stressed by the *Bhagawat Gita*. *Yad yad acharati shreshtas, tat tat deve itrojanaha, sayat pramanam kurute lokostat anuvartate*. The influence of leaders in ensuring the followers adopt their techniques is spelt out and we will find that the responsibility of leaders is spelt out in this shloka. The responsibility of leaders is not only to show techniques and methods that can be adopted for achieving success, they must also maintain the professional conduct. *Dharmo rakshate rakshataha*, it is said. If the leaders are able to observe the right conduct then the conduct itself will protect them. Leaders, in other words, must lead by example.

The first requirement in today's globalized context is the focus on the customer and satisfying his needs. It has been proved that in a competitive environment nobody can survive unless one is able to have quality goods? Margaret Thatcher was asked: 'What is the difference between a company that produces quality goods and one that does not produce quality goods?' She said: 'The answer was simple. If the company produces quality goods, the customers will come back but if the company does not produce quality goods, the product will come back.' In our Indian concept, the quality is nothing but a quest for perfection. This is spelt out in the famous shloka. *Om purnamadap, purnamidam, purnat purnaam udachyate Purnasya purnamadaya purnamevavashishyate*

The quality can be looked upon as a commitment for perfection and this concept of perfection is also articulated in other shlokas. For example, Vallabhacharya's Madurashtakam described how every aspect of Lord Krishna is beautiful. Every aspect of Lord Krishna is beautiful and sweet, and the entire world is sweet. This is nothing but a culture of quality pervading the entire environment and total quality management is one aspect of this concept of all pervading perfection which includes sweetness and beauty also.

Adharam madhuram, vadanam madhuram,
nayanam madhuram, hasitam madhuram
hridayam madhuram, gamanam madhuram
madhuratipate akhilam madhura

In other words, there is also an underlying principle of joy and this in turn reflects the very high morale. So in an enterprise which is dedicated to quality, we can also expect a high employee morale and arising from a pride in achievement and a pride in perfection.

The basic resource of any organization today is human capital. This is all the more so in the era of knowledge economy and intellectual property rights. The question therefore arises of respecting the dignity of the individual. It is here that the Gita teaches us that every person is has his own strong points and every person cannot but act according to his nature. In the third chapter, Lord Krishna says '*nahi kaschit kshnamapi, jatu tishtya karmakrith, karyate yavasha, karmasarvaha prakatijaigunehi*'. In other words, every person has to act according to his nature and even for a second he cannot remain without acting according to that character. For any good management, it will be necessary to study the nature of the people and see that there is match between their nature and their function assigned to them.

In the era of competition, it will also mean that we will have to think innovatively. Innovation provides the cutting edge in competition today. This is also highlighted by Lord Krishna in the Second Chapter of the *Bhagawat Gita* where one of the characteristics of the *Sthithapragnya* is a capacity to take a contrarian view, a capacity to think of the unthinkable, the capacity to swim against the current. While others are sleeping, *Sthithapragnya* is awake and vice versa. *Ya nisha sarva bhutanam tasyam jagriti samyami Yasyam jagrati bhutani sa nisha pashyato munehe.* We can look at the classics like *Bhagawat Gita* to find out how we can evolve strategies for innovation and developing competitive edge through innovation.

One of the major concerns in today's world is the environment. The question of sustainable development or industries having green technologies becoming increasingly important. For any management, therefore, to manage the environment in such a way that while the business does not suffer and flourishes, it also at the same time does not damage the environment. This balance may be maintained between achievement and success or enjoyment on the one side and at the same time ensuring that the damage is not caused to the environment is reflected in the fine balancing between the sacrifice and enjoyment articulated in the very first shloka of the Ishavashi Upanishad. *Ishavashyam, idham sarvaham, yatkinchit jagatyam jagat Tena taktena bhunjitaha, magradha kalashayastati dhanam*

The strategy to be adopted for an eco friendly management is spelt out in this shloka. After all, the process of mobilizing people, the process of management has also been spelt out in some of the *vaakyas* of Upanishads. They give us guidelines about how to go in for effective thinking. The Chandokya Upanishad says: 'If we apply our knowledge with faith and conviction and also with deep analysis, then our action becomes strong and to that extent, then we are ready for success'. *Yadaiva Vidyaya Karoti Shradhaya Upanishada Tadeva Viryavattaram Bhavati!*

Again in the Taitreya Upanishad, there is the standard formula given about how people can come together, enjoy together, bring their skills together, move from darkness to light and avoid the poison of misunderstanding or hatred to achieve success. *Sahanavavatu sahanaubhunaktu sahaviryam kara va vahai Tejasvinam aditamastu ma vid visha vahai, om shanti shanti shanti!*

Perhaps the most important aspect of value is the professional ethics and doing one's duty. Here the two gems from *Bhagawat Gita*, which are very well-known and are worth recalling. The first is that one should do one's job thoroughly in a detached manner and not look for the results. It may look odd that in the era when we want management as an activity to get results, how can working without looking for results be a solution. This only highlights the need for dedication in carrying on one's duty and performing. *Karmanyevadhikaraste mafaleshu kadachanaha Makarmaphalheturbyo, matesangusukarmanahi.*

At the same time, the need for maintaining professional integrity is highlighted in the Third Chapter of the Gita where Lord Krishna says: Death is preferable to giving up one's *dharma*. *Swadharme nidhanam shreya, paradharmo bhayapaha.*

Ultimately, the whole set of values needed for management can be summed up in the words of *dharma* and *dharma* is the code of right conduct. In these days when corporate governance is emerging as a significant factor, we find that Indian management can emerge successfully in the market place if it is able to draw on its route for good corporate governance which are available in our culture and tradition. But then the question may arise, how many of us are aware of the scriptures, Upanishads, culture and so on. Though one may not be consciously aware, one learns about basic principles from our childhood, from our parents and from our religion. All religions have highlighted the need for being truthful and kind and helpful. Ultimately, perhaps the universal principle and human value that honesty is the best policy.

Chapter 15

Moral Consciousness and Communicative Action: From Discourse Ethics to Spiritual Transformation

Ananta Kumar Giri

In his stress on performative competence Habermas consistently privileges speaking over hearing or listening. In The Theory of Communicative Action, a categorical distinction is drawn between 'cognitive-instrumental' and 'communicative rationality' but the distinction is dubious given that both are modes of formal reasoning. (Fred Dallmayr, 1991: 24, 11) The speculative employment of reason with respect to nature leads to the absolute necessity of some supreme cause of the world: the practical employment of reason with a view to freedom leads also to absolute necessity, but only of the laws of the actions of a rational being as such. Now it is an essential principle of reason, however employed, to push its knowledge to a consciousness of its necessity. It is however an equally essential restriction of the same reason that it can neither discern the necessity of what is or what happens. ... [Reason] cannot enable us to conceive the absolute necessity of our unconditional practical law. (Immanuel Kant, 1987: 101) In the wake of metaphysics, philosophy surrenders its extraordinary status. Explosive experiences of the extraordinary have migrated into an art that has become autonomous. Of course, even after this deflation, ordinary life, now fully profane, by no means becomes immune to the shattering and subversive intrusion of extraordinary events. Viewed from without, religion, which has largely been deprived of its world-view functions, is still indispensable in ordinary life for normalizing intercourse with the extraordinary. For this reason, even post-metaphysical thinking continues to coexist with religious practice and not merely in the sense of the contemporaneity of the non-contemporaneous. This ongoing coexistence even throws light on a curious dependence of a philosophy that has forfeited its contact with the extraordinary. Philosophy, even in its post-metaphysical form, will be able neither to replace nor to repress religion as long as religious language is the bearer of a semantic content that is inspiring and even indispensable, for this content eludes (for the time being?) the explanatory force of philosophical language and continues to resist translation into reasoning discourses. (Jurgen Habermas, 1992: 51)

The Problem

The contemporary moment is characterized by unmet challenges both in theory and practice. Processes of change at work in individual social systems as well as interaction among different societies in the global economy bring to the fore the unfinished task lying before us with regard to moral consciousness and communicative action. Now because of globalization, as 'moral issues stemming from cultural diversity that used to arise mainly between societies now increasingly arise within them' (Geertz, 1986: 115), the nature of interaction between different cultures with widely variant moral standards and the development of a critical reflective consciousness on the part of the actors where moral issues are not easily disposed of either through a convenient relativism or through universalism is an epochal challenge before us. Similar is the task when we come to individual social systems as they are characterized by pervasive structural differentiations and as in these societies' morality gets no clear status in the construction of a structurally 'differentiated life world' (Habermas, 1987a: 92). A related issue here is the unprecedented crisis of institutions that characterizes individual social systems to cope with the contemporary dynamics of change in self, society and culture. For many insightful critics, our contemporary dilemmas are also significantly institutional, inasmuch as they spring from the irrelevance of existing institutions and the lack of availability of new institutions to guide our private lives and the public sphere. These institutional dilemmas are primarily 'moral dilemmas' (Bellah *et al.*, 1991: 38), and call for a new moral language in which to think about our institutions, as they are now ridden with 'unprecedented problems' (Bellah *et al.*, 1991: 42). For instance, reflecting on contemporary American society Robert Bellah and his colleagues argue that in the face of the challenge of the present and the dislocations of the post-industrial transition there is an urgency to think of 'democracy as an ongoing moral quest', not simply as a political process 'as an end state' (Bellah *et al.*, 1991: 20). They are emphatic in their proposition that we currently need a new 'moral ecology' to think creatively about institutions – their predicament and possibility since the decisions that are made about our economy, our schools, our government, or our national position in the world cannot be separated, from the way we live in practical terms, the moral life we lead as a 'people' (Bellah *et al.*, 1991: 42; emphasis added). The imperative for a moral grounding of institutions in contemporary practice is paralleled by reflective developments in theory as well. This is most evident in the restructuring of theory from structure to reflective self in thinking through moral consciousness and communicative action. Most important sign of this restructuring is the theory of 'post-conventional' morality developed by psychologist Lawrence Kohlberg. In Kohlberg's theory of moral development one's moral consciousness is not a mere appendix to social conventions and one is able to differentiate oneself 'from the rule and expectation of others' and one's 'values in terms of self-chosen ethical principles' (Cortese, 1990: 20). The idea of post-conventional morality rescues moral consciousness from unreflective sociologism, where morality is looked upon as an extension of social norms and cultural expectations, and brings critical reflection to its very core. In this move from unreflective sociologism to critical reflection, the self-justificatory systems of society and culture are critically lived, analyzed and transcended by seeking actors in quest of justice, well being and freedom.

The current idea of post-conventional morality has a long pedigree in critical and transformation-seeking social theory, which can be drawn back at least as far as John Dewey's insightful distinction, made at the turn of the century, between customary and reflective morality. For Dewey (1960: 29), 'the question of what ends a man should live for does not arise as a general problem in customary morality. It is forestalled by the habits and institutions which a person finds existing all around him.' He goes on: 'There can, however, be no such thing as reflective morality except where men seriously ask by what purposes they should direct their conduct and why they should do so; what it is which make their purposes good' (Dewey, 1960: 30). The fact that reflective morality is accompanied by a scheme of critical evaluation is clearly stated by Dewey: 'Reflection has its normal function in placing the objects of desire in a perspective of relative values so that when we give up one good we do it because we see another which is of greater worth and which evokes a more inclusive and more enduring desire' (1960: 35). The work of Jurgen Habermas is a significant contribution to both the idea of post-conventional morality and the contemporary discourse of moral transformation of institutions. It reflects the challenge of theory and practice outlined above. His *Moral Consciousness and Communicative Action* is an important contribution to the idea of post-conventional morality, given his distinction between critical moral reflection and ethical substantialism. He is also a systematic and transformation-seeking critic of institutional life under late capitalism where his political criticism employs not only the familiar variables of class and power but also the less familiar moral consciousness and communicative action. Habermas has written extensively on specific issues in the history and development of Germany, as well as on the wider questions of the history and discourse of modernity.

Though Habermas is too easily categorized as the most prominent member of the contemporary European Left, his agenda has always involved a wider critical engagement, critiquing the conventional theories and methods of Marxism as well. In that sense, he has always pursued his task as a critic of the existing methods and systems. In his recent work, Habermas has championed the cause of radical democracy, one important aspect of which is the moral renewal of individuals and the public sphere (Habermas, 1990b, 1994). Habermas argues that the task of human emancipation today requires a moral approach along with the familiar models of political action. Consider, for instance, the persistent question of poverty and disadvantage in advanced industrial societies. For Habermas, while in the classical phase of capitalism capital and labour could threaten each other for pursuing their interests, today 'this is no longer the case' (Habermas, 1990b: 19). Now the underprivileged can make their predicament known only through a 'protest vote' but without the electoral support of a majority of citizens. Problems of this nature do not even have enough driving force to be adopted as a topic of broad and effective public debate (Habermas, 1990b: 20). In this situation, for Habermas, a moral consciousness diffusing the entire public sphere is crucial for tackling the problem of poverty and disadvantage. As Habermas argues: 'a dynamic self-correction cannot be set in motion without introducing morals into the debate, without univerasalizing, interests from a normative point of view' (1990b: 20). The same Imperative also confronts us In addressing contemporary global problems such as environmental disaster, world poverty and the North-South divide. For Habermas, in addressing these problems we also need a moral perspective, as he writes:

> ... these problems can only be brought to a head by rethinking topics morally, by universalizing interests in a more or less discursive form. The moral or ethical point of view makes us quicker to perceive the more far-reaching, and simultaneously less insistent and more fragile, ties that bind the fate of an individual to that of every other, making even the most alien person a member of one's community. (1990b: 20)

In this article, I strive to make a critical assessment of the work of Habermas with regard to his own stated goal of transformation. I begin with Habermas' own assumptions such as 'linguistification of sacred' in the field of moral consciousness and strive to look into incoherence in his project considered in accordance with its own norms. In other words, what I am interested in, to begin with, is an internal critique of the Habermasian agenda of transformation. In this way, I share a similarity of goal with the noted Habermas school. Thomas McCarthy who sums up the objective of this as critical engagement: 'Rather than confronting Habermas' ideas with objections from competing theoretical traditions, I hope to bring out tensions in those ideas themselves' (McCarthy, 1992: 52). But while I am interested in bringing out tensions in Habermas' ideas I am also engaged in interrogating Habermas' agenda from outside its own frame of reference precisely because the issues that these tensions raise cannot be resolved within its own frame. Thus, the tradition towards which I move from Habermas' own frame of reference is the tradition of spiritual criticism and spiritual transformation. While Robert J. Antonio, the Habermas scholar, argues that the 'secular and inter-subjective turn in critical theory begun by Habermas can be completed by encouraging a broader dialogue with pragmatism' (Antonio, 1989: 74), I submit that it is the question pertaining to inter-subjectivity that requires an opening towards processes of spiritual transformation and criticism. What I argue is that critical theory now must make a dialogue with critical and practical spirituality in order to achieve its own stated objective of transformation.

Moral Consciousness and Communicative Action: Habermas' Agenda

Habermas argues that at the contemporary juncture where the sacred no longer has the unquestioned authority that it once had, morality can no longer be grounded in religion. Rather it has to emerge out of and be anchored in a process of rational argumentation where the actors participate in undistorted communication as members of a community of discourse. For Habermas, the rise of the public sphere of rational argumentation and rationally motivated communicative action goes hand in hand with the relocation of the sacred from the domain of the 'Unspeakable' to our everyday world of language, making it both an object and a medium of our ordinary conversation. Habermas' moral theory has to be understood in his evolutionary framework of the 'linguistification of the sacred' (Habermas, 1987a) and the 'structural transformation of the public sphere' (Habermas, 1989). Habermas believes that morality, anchored in and emerging out of the rational arguments of participants in discourse, can fill the void created by the demise of the sacred order. The idea of a rational society and an 'ideal communication community' is central to Habermas' agenda of morality. In his emphasis on rationality, Habermas is 'closest to the Kantian tradition' (McCarthy in Habermas, 1987a: vii). Both for Kant and Habermas, 'calculations of rational choice generate recommendations relevant to the pursuit of contingent purposes in the light of given preferences'. Like Kant, Habermas understanding of practical reason as universal in import: 'it is geared to what everyone could rationally will to be a norm binding on everyone else' (1987a: vii). Habermas' discourse ethics, however, 'replaces Kant's categorical imperative with a procedure of moral argumentation', shifting 'the frame of reference from Kant's solitary, reflecting moral consciousness to the community of moral subjects in dialogue' (McCarthy in Habermas, 1990a: vii). For Habermas, 'the projection of an ideal communication community serves as a guiding thread for setting up discourses' (Habermas, 1990a). Those who participate in this communication community have an urge to participate in not only communication but also a discursive transformation, where 'in the relationship between the *Self and the Other*, there is a basic moment of insight' (1990a). Habermas quotes George Herbert Mead, whose work he values a lot and whom he considers as one of the main inspirations behind his theory of communicative action, programmatically: 'What is essential to communication is that the symbol should arouse in oneself what it arouses in the other individual' (Habermas, 1987a: 15). Habermas tells us: 'I think all of us feel that one must be ready to recognize the interests of others even when they run counter to our own, but the person who does that *does not really sacrifice himself, but becomes a larger self*' (Habermas, 1987a: 94; emphasis added). For Habermas, an urge for justification of norms that guide individual action is very much part of being human. Though Habermas is dismissive of, questions of ontology he proceeds with two basic assumptions about man, namely that he has a need for communication and an urge for justification. Habermas argues: 'From the perspective of first persons, what we consider justified is not a function of custom but a question of justification or grounding' (Habermas, 1990a: 20). This universal need for justification has a special manifestation in modern societies where all norms have now 'at least in principle lost their customary validity' (Habermas, 1988: 227). In this context, the procedure of rational argumentation, which is the other name of 'discourse ethics', fulfils this need for justification and provides the 'discursive redemption of normative claims of validity' (Habermas, 1990a: 103). Habermas argues that the realization of moral consciousness is based upon our ability to take a hypothetical attitude to the 'form of life and personal life history' that has shaped our identities (Habermas, 1990a: 104). But those who are uncritical about their socialization by and immersion in the society and culture to which they belong are incapable of taking a hypothetical attitude towards these since they fail to realize that though every form of life presents itself as the best possible form of 'good life', it is the task of moral consciousness to go beneath such taken-for-granted assumptions and self-proclaimed truths. It is here that participation in the procedure of practical discourse functions as a redeeming process. First of all, it breaks the illusion of the 'good life' that has been associated with a particular form of life by the force of custom and habit. While the 'formal' ethics of a society binds us to its order and scheme of evaluation, discourse ethics breaks this bondage and enables us to understand our own self as well as the validity of our culture from the point of view of justice. Habermas (1990a: 104) tells us that 'the universalization principle of practical discourse acts like a knife that makes razor-sharp cuts between evaluative statements, and strictly normative ones, between the good and the just'. It is this concern for justice that creates an incessant thrust towards problematization, laying bare the moral problems within our taken-for-granted cultures. For Habermas, a 'thrust towards problematization' is essential for moral consciousness to emerge and to be at work in the context of the life world (Habermas, 1990a: 107). Habermas tells us how in the normal circumstances of what he calls 'ethical formalism' this problematization possible. But participation in discourse ethics enables the participants to look at one's own culture critically, where criticism means discovering whether the 'suggested modes of togetherness genuinely hang together' or not (see Neville, 1974: 189). Habermas argues that 'for the hypotheses-testing participant in a discourse, the relevance of the experiential context of his life world tends to pale' (Habermas, 1990a: 107). Habermas believes that 'under the unrelenting moralizing gaze of the participants in discourse. Familiar institutions can be transformed into so many instances of problematic justice' (1990a: 108).

Discourse Ethics: Habermas' Self-Criticism

Habermas argues that the abstractive requirements in discourse ethics provide actors with a cognitive advantage, a capacity for distantiation. But this cognitive distantiation is not enough either for the practice of discourse ethics or for the realization of moral consciousness. It calls for parallel emotional maturity, adequate motivational anchoring and growth. He argues that 'cognition, empathy, and agape' must be integrated in our moral consciousness especially when we are engaged in the 'hermeneutic activity of applying universal norms in a context-sensitive manner' (Habermas, 1990a: 182). Thus he argues, reminding us of Christian imperatives for love and care, that 'concern for the fate of one's neighbour is a necessary emotional pre-requisite for the cognitive operations expected of participants in discourse' (1990a: 182). This integration of cognitive distantiation and emotional care is particularly required when the initial separation between morality and ethical life is to be overcome. He is aware of the difficulties that this separation poses for the practice of morality. Thus he is not content to leave his agenda only at the 'deontological level' like Kant. He is interested in bringing back 'morality' as a guide for action and reflection into practice. Habermas himself writes

> Moral issues are never raised for their own sake; people raise them by seeking a guide for action. For this reason the demotivated solutions that post-conventional morality finds for decontextualized issues must be reinserted into practical life. If it is to become effective in practice, morality has to make up for the loss of concrete ethical life that it incurred when it pursued a cognitive advantage. (Habermas, 1990a: 179)

This opening has to be achieved through 'an integration of cognitive operations and emotional dispositions and attitude' that characterizes 'the mature capacity for moral judgement' (Habermas, 1990a: 182). Though a notion of 'universal human justice is central to Habermas'.

Moral Consciousness and Communicative Actions

Perspective on moral consciousness, Habermas himself takes great care to emphasize that morality must obey both the principles of justice and solidarity; it must achieve an integration of 'the ethics of love and ethics of justice'. While the first 'postulates equal respect and equal rights for the individual', the second 'postulates empathy and concern for the well-being of one's neighbour' (Habermas, 1990a: 200). For him 'morality cannot protect the rights of the individual without also protecting the well-being of the community to which he belongs' (1990a: 200). Thus criticism of the taken-for-granted ways of life must be accompanied by a concern for the community. What is important to note is that both of these concerns, for him, should flow from an adequate description of the 'highest stage of morality itself' (Habermas, 1990a: 182).

Discourse Ethics and Moral Consciousness: The Limits of the Habermasian Approach

But though Habermas speaks of the need for 'adequate description of the highest stage of morality itself', he himself does not inquire into the nature and height of this stage. For him, it is the public sphere that constitutes this highest stage. Habermas speaks of appropriate emotional development and reflective engagement for the project of critical moral reflection to have its desired effect on individuals in society. But he does not look into the issue of how far his own rational approach can facilitate this. Participation in mutually transforming dialogue, which is the key feature of Habermas' discourse ethics, raises the question of inter-subjectivity – the mode of relationship between the self and the other. But the whole question of inter-subjectivity – its realization and its needed rich description for a project of morality to succeed is missing from Habermas˙ The question for us here is what kind of relationship between the self and the other is envisaged in discourse ethics – whether the self and the other are just talking to each other in discourse ethics, or the non-self is also part of the self. In this context, McCarthy argues that Habermas' agenda refers only to ethical self-clarification and that 'ethical self-clarification itself cannot get us beyond the value differences that may result from it' (McCarthy, 1992: 62). It is perhaps for this reason that Zygmunt Bauman (1993: 84) writes: a post-modern ethics would be one that readmits the other as a neighbour into the hard core of the moral self, an ethics that recasts the other as the crucial character in the process through which the moral self comes into its own. But the process of this dialectic between self and other is not only rational but also spiritual. As Robert Bellah *et al.* argue, paying attention to the needs of the other is a spiritual process. In their words: 'as in the religious examples, we mean to use attention normatively in the sense of 'mindfulness' as the Buddhists put it, an openness to the leadings of God, as the Quakers say' (Bellah *et al.*, 1991: 256).

The problem with the Habermasian discourse ethics is also its strength, namely its emphasis on rationality. Rationality is an important starting-point but there are problems when it is made the be-all or end-all in life, as it is in the approach of Habermas. In Habermas' strongly held belief, a rational philosophy of science that is not scientists holds the key to the overcoming of the confusion in which moral science finds itself today (Habermas, 1981). But though Habermas distinguishes between instrumental reason and communicative reason and is an ardent critic of modern positivism, his communicative rational agenda still has its limits in coming to terms with the challenge of transforming moral awareness into a basis of transformative communicative action. Bernard Williams' argument in *Ethics and the Limits of Philosophy* is of crucial significance here: How truthfulness to an existing self or society is to be combined with reflection, self-understanding and criticism is a question that philosophy itself cannot answer. It is the kind of question that has to be answered through reflective living. (Williams, 1985: 200) To be fair, Habermas himself is aware of the need for reflective living but not sensitive to its manifold dimensions. Moral issues raise questions that are not merely rational but also spiritual. This is a point argued by two important interlocutors of our times, namely Charles Taylor (1989) and Govind Chandra Pande (1989, 1991), who, incidentally, come from two different traditions. For Taylor, to speak of moral consciousness is to speak of the qualitative distinction between the higher and the lower desire or scheme of things, a realization that is dependent on spiritual enlightenment. Moral questions inevitably raise matters of ontology the nature of the actor and the quality of that actor's depth dimension.

Though Habermas makes a distinction between ego identity and role identity and speaks of self-reflection in the context of the therapeutic dialogue of the actors (Habermas 1972a, 1979), he does not address the question of ontology, *vis-à-vis* moral consciousness. In this he seems to be carried away by the modernist preference for epistemology to ontology. But Taylor (1989: 7) here urges us to proceed cautiously. For Taylor, 'the whole way in which we think, reason, argue and question ourselves about morality supposes that our moral reactions' are 'not only 'gut' feelings but also implicit acknowledgments of claims concerning their objects'.

The various ontological accounts try to articulate these claims. The temptations to deny this, which arise from modern epistemology, are strengthened by the widespread accepting of a deeply wrong model of practical reasoning, one based on an illegitimate extrapolation from reasoning in natural science. (Taylor, 1989: 7) Moral ontology is not confined to spiritual ontology alone but is an important part of it. Moral notion requires a reflective self whose source is spiritual. For Taylor, an inquiry into the sources of the self 'is not only a phenomenological account but an exploration of the limits of the conceivable in human life, an account of its transcendental conditions' (Taylor, 1989: 32). Govind Chandra Pande also makes a similar argument. For him ... it is only a self which is conscious of its ideal universality that can distinguish values from appetites, pleasures and selfish interests and can become the moral subject. It is the question of the ideal self, which is the source of the moral law on which social unity, and coherence depends. The ideal self is not an abstract transcendental subject in which immediacy and coherence or non-contradiction both coalesce. (Pande, 1982: 113) Pande's ideal self is spiritual in its source, actualization and imagination. Pande draws on the concept of man in Indian tradition where it is believed that spirituality is an important dimension of self and identity (see Pande, 1985, 1989, 1991, 1992).

But this is also true in traditions of spirituality in the West, which, as Taylor argues, have encouraged 'detachment from identities given by particular historical communities' (Taylor, 1989: 37). Habermas takes it for granted that the sacred has become part of modern rational language; he calls this 'the linguistification of the sacred'. But this view of the modern condition is coloured by Protestant religious experience where religious engagement is subservient not only to the process of rationalization at work in society but also to the power of the word. Habermas' theory of linguistification of the sacred is based upon the Protestant style of tradition, which privileges words over silence in religious engagement. But this may not be so in the Catholic tradition and is certainly not so in the Buddhist and Hindu traditions where silence is very much part of reflection; in fact, silence is the source of critical reflection and transforming utterances in acts of discourse.

Habermasian discourse ethics is based upon a very naive view of religion and religious evolution in the modern societies. In this context, Robert Antonio's critique of Habermas is particularly true of his notion of linguistification of the sacred: 'the problem of formalism can be overcome, and the true limits of immanent critique clarified, only after all the pseudo-historical baggage is left behind' (1989: 741). Habermas' discourse ethics is procedural but is not serious about the preparation required of participants to take part in the procedure and also does not address the question of normative direction. Habermas does not deal with the ontological preparation required if actors are to listen and hear in the process of conversation. It is perhaps for this reason that even such a sympathetic critic of Habermas as McCarthy argues that arguments in which actors are engaged in discourse ethics 'themselves remain tied to specific contexts of action and experience and thus are not able wholly to transcend the struggle between Max Weber's warring gods and demons' (1992: 58). This problem can be overcome by opening oneself to spiritual awareness, which would enable the actors to 'transcend the struggle between warring gods and demons'. Participation in spiritual practice or what is called *sadhana* can and does facilitate this. As a prelude to arguments to follow, at this point it may be helpful briefly to point out the meaning of spiritual engagement referred to here. It is seen as a process of multi-dimensional critical movement. First, it is a process of discovering a higher self within oneself – a self that is characterized by more intimate subjectivity. If ethics has to do with the challenge of the other, then spirituality as a transformative seeking of values in both inner freedom and in more genuine bonds of inter-subjectivity helps us to invite the other into the self. If each dialectic inevitably has a process of self-reflection, this is also true of the dialectic of self and the other, and spiritual transformation of the consciousness of actors makes this dialectic more reflective.

As Taylor argues of the spiritual point of view, *vis-à-vis* St Augustine, 'radical reflexivity takes on a new status, because it is the space in which we come to encounter God, in which we affect the turning from lower to higher' (1989: 140). Spiritual transformation also involves transforming the base or infrastructure of society. It requires transforming the structures of a society that subjects human beings to indignity and exploitation. Spirituality has a dimension of institutional criticism as well, which is most evident in traditions of prophetic criticism and martyrdom, and in the *Bhakti* movements (Giri, 1996; Uberoi, 1996; Walzer, 1988).

From Discourse to Spiritual Transformation

Though Habermas pleads for post-metaphysical orientations in our moral engagement, a careful reading of him shows that he is deeply aware of the limitations of his agenda. He recognizes that his agenda is anthropocentric but does not explore ways of overcoming the limits of anthropocentrism. Furthermore, while the question of justice is central to his agenda of morality, Habermas does not address whether the pursuit of justice is a question of socio-political-legislation only or involves, as Agnes Heller (1987) argues, a 'profound anthropological revolution'. For Heller, pursuit of justice almost always involves an engagement with a 'Beyond' (see also Giri, 1997; Dallmayr, 1993, 1995, 1996; and Laclau, 1992). By 'Beyond' Heller refers to something beyond and deeper than mere socio-political-legislation. She states quite clearly that 'Beyond has the connotation of higher and not only of being different' (Heller, 1987: 325-6). But it is this intimation of the 'Beyond', this matter of a transcendental height, that is missing from Habermas, which has grave consequences for the realization of some of his own objectives such as the realization of justice and the overcoming of anthropocentrism.

Habermas speaks of 'linguistification of the sacred' but does not explore the critical potential that a transcendental sacred has in rethinking existing social arrangements and transforming our conventional institutions, which chain human dignity in many guises. In this context, the work of Robert M. Unger (1987) calls for our attention. For Unger (1987: 576), there are two kinds of sacred reality: 'The first is a fundamental reality or transcendent personal being; the second, the experiences of personality and personal encounter that, multiplied many times over, make up a social world'. Though human beings have a tendency to reduce the first sacred reality to the logic of the societal sacred, the transcendental sacred still continues its autonomy and acts as a source of criticism, creativity and transformation. For Unger, when people are bound only to the sacredness of the existing social contexts, 'nothing is left to them but to choose one of these words and to play by its rules' (Unger, 1987: 577). These rules, though 'decisive' in their influence, are ultimately 'groundless' (1987: 577). Unger argues that when the decisiveness of the present social world, presenting itself as a sacred order, 'arises precisely from its lack of any place within a hierarchy of contexts' then 'there is no larger defining reality to which it can seem as the vehicle or from whose standpoint it can be criticized' (Unger, 1987: 577). Habermas' agenda of linguistification of the sacred suffers from this problem as well.

It is perhaps for these reasons that Dallmayr does not look at Habermas' 'discourses ethics' as a categorical shift from the Kantian deontological morality. 'Discourse ethics', Habermas writes, 'picks up the basic intent of Hegel's thought in order to redeem it with Kantian means' (quoted in Dallmayr, 1991: 117). But for Dallmayr there is no scope for genuine redemption in the Habermasian agenda. For Dallmayr (1991: 126), Habermas 'makes reference to the alleviation of suffering or of 'damaged life' but only as a marginal gloss not fully integrated in his arguments'. Dallmayr argues that in order to address the questions of justice, suffering, moral responsibility and the self-justification of inhuman social systems as the sacred order, discourse ethics needs a spiritual opening (see Dallmayr, 1995, 1996).

The Spiritual Foundations of Moral Consciousness: The Agenda of Sri Aurobindo

Habermas uses rational argumentation as the key to the realization of moral consciousness. But in traditions of spiritual criticisms there is a much more inclusive approach to rationality and morality, which is illustrated in the work of a critic such as Sri Aurobindo (1871-1950). Aurobindo is a multi-dimensional critic of the human condition and is noted for his works such as *The Human Cycles, The Life Divine, The Synthesis of Yoga* and *The Future Poetry*. He does not discount the significance of reason for the origin and growth of morality but wants us to have a proper perspective regarding 'the office and limitations of reasons' (Sri Aurobindo, 1962). Much like Habermas, he argues that reason and rational development have played a key role in our being human. Aurobindo himself argues, reminding us of Habermas, that 'an attempt to universalize first of all the habit of reason and the application of intelligence and the intelligent will to life' has played a crucial role in the shift from the 'infrarational' to the 'rational' age (Sri Aurobindo, 1962: 179).

He also wants us to appreciate the crucial significance of reason in understanding the validity of traditions like Habermas' plea for undistorted communication. Aurobindo also sensitizes us to the distortion that power can introduce in the working of a rational discourse and the realization of even its inherent emancipatory potential. But for Aurobindo even though reason is so important for moral development and evolution (both phylogenetic and ontogenetic) it cannot be a sole foundation of morality. Aurobindo accords this role to spirit, not to reason. For him, both order and evolution in life involve 'interlocking of an immense number of things that are in conflict with each other' and discovering 'some principle of standing-ground of unity' (Sri Aurobindo, 1962: 201). Reason cannot perform this function because 'The business of reason is indeterminate. In order that it may do its office, it is obliged to adopt temporarily fixed viewpoints' (1962: 201). When reason becomes the sole arbiter of life and morality, 'every change becomes or at least seems a thing doubtful, difficult and perilous. While the conflict of view points, principles, systems leads to strife and revolution and not to basis of harmonious development' (1962: 201). For Aurobindo, harmony can be achieved only when the soul discovers itself in its highest and completest spiritual reality and effects a progressive upward transformation of its life values into those of the Spirit; for they will all find their spiritual truth and in that truth their standing-ground of mutual recognition and reconciliation. (1962: 201)

For Aurobindo, the inadequacy of reason to become the governor of life and morality lies in man's transitional nature – half animal and half divine. He believes that 'the root powers of human life, its intimate causes are below, irrational, and they are above, suprarational'. It is for this reason that 'a purely rational society could not come into being and, if it could be born, either could not live or sterilize or petrify human existence' (Sri Aurobindo, 1962: 114). He argues: ... if reason were the secret, highest law of the universe. It might be possible for him by the power of the reason to evolve out of the dominance of the infrarational Nature that he inherits from the animal. But his nature is rather transitional; the rational being is only a middle term of Nature's evolution. A rational satisfaction cannot give him safety from the pull from below nor deliver him from the attraction from above. (Sri Aurobindo, 1962: 206) Aurobindo uses reason but unlike Habermas does not take it as the be-all and end-all of life. For him, 'The solution lies not in reason but in the soul of man, in its spiritual tendencies. It is a spiritual; an inner freedom that alone can create a perfect human order. It is spiritual, *a greater than rational enlightenment*, that can alone illumine the vital nature of man and impose harmony on its self-seeking, antagonisms and discord' (Sri Aurobindo, 1962: 206; emphasis added). An ideal society, for Aurobindo is not a mere 'rational society ' but a 'spiritual society'. A society founded on spirituality is not one governed by religion as a mere social, one that uses religion 'to give an august, awful and eternal sanction to its mass of customs and institutions' (Sri Aurobindo, 1962: 211). It is not a theocratic society. Rather, a spiritual society is one guided by the quest of the spirit.

Sri Aurobindo's idea of the highest stage of morality is close to the Kohiberg-Habermas idea of the post-conventional stage of moral development. Like the Habermasian idea of the post-conventional stage of morality, Aurobindo's idea of morality is not an extension of the collective egoism of a particular society. But what distinguishes his idea of morality is its invocation of God not only as a tertiary factor but also as a constituting factor in the dyadic relationship between the self and the other. For him (1962: 136), 'the seeking for God is also, subjectively, the seeking of our highest, truest, fullest, largest Self'. He argues that 'ethics is not in its essence a calculation of good and evil in action of a laboured effort to be blameless according to the standards of the world – these are only crude appearances – it is an attempt to grow into divine nature' (1962: 143). Let us hear him in his own words about the probably more reassuring route towards moral consciousness and communicative action: ethics only begins by the demand upon [man] of something other than his personal preference, vital pleasure or material self-interest; and, this demand seems at first to work on him through the necessity of his relations with others. But that this is not the core of the matter is shown by the fact that the ethical demand does not always square with the social demand, nor the ethical standard always coincide with the social standard. His relations with others and his relations with himself are both of them the occasions of his ethical growth, but that which determines his ethical being is his relations with God, the urge of the Divine whether concealed in his nature or conscious in his higher self or inner genius. He obeys an inner ideal, not to a social claim or a collective necessity. The ethical imperative comes not from around, but from within him and above him. (Sri Aurobindo, 1962: 141)

Beyond the Technology of Power: Spirituality and the Technology of Self

In his *The Imperative of Responsibility*, Hans Jonas (1984: 141) argues: 'it must be understood that we are here confronted with a dialectic of power which can only be overcome by a further degree of power itself, not by quietest renunciation of power.' This more power, in Jonas's own view, has to emanate from society and supposedly can break the tyrannical automation of power. Jonas is articulating a point of view towards ethical responsibility, which is more widely shared among interpreters and actors today. The crux of this approach lies in the belief that by having more power we can solve the ethical problems confronting us today. But such politicization of morality removes the 'inner life from the sphere of the moral', making it impossible to articulate proper moral concepts (Edelman, 1990: 53). But a spiritual approach to ethics and morality, as Aurobindo's work shows, brings the 'inner life' of the actors to the heart of their moral consciousness and communicative action. Spirituality not only retrieves the inner life of the actors and juxtaposes it to their outer life but also continuously strives to scrutinize: critically the structure of desire of the inner life and to subject it to transformative criticism. This transformed inner life becomes a source of transformational criticism of the logic of power in society.

Habermas' discourse ethics shares the above-mentioned problems of an approach to morality where the logic of power reigns supreme over the creative desire and the devotional dynamics of the self. Though Habermas makes a distinction between technology of power and technology of self (see, for instance, Habermas, 1987b), his critical theory in general and his perspective on discourse ethics in particular scarcely scratch the surface of technology of self. To be fair to him, Habermas is deeply concerned with the need for self-reflection on the part of the actors but he limits this to the context of therapeutic dialogue between the patient and the analyst. Habermas does not explore the possibility of autonomous self-discovery without the mediation of the therapist – Spirituality here suggests a different route. Spiritual traditions stress that self-knowledge and self-reflection go together. Aurobindo (1950: 2), for instance, proposes yoga as a synthetic mechanism where 'Yoga is a methodological effort towards self-perfection by the expression of the potentialities latent in the being and a union of the human individual with the universal and Transcendent Existence'. Yoga is a practical psychology of self-perfection to help God complete her unfinished task of creation. Its objective is trans-formation and the making possible of a higher stage of evolution here on Earth, not individual *moksha* (salvation). Yoga helps us to overcome our 'separative ignorance' (Sri Aurobindo, 1950: 618). The practice of Yoga helps us to go beyond altruism and egoism, good and evil, where we are able to 'take a wider psychological view of the primary forces of our nature' (1950: 618).

Through the practice of Yoga there grows an immediate and profound sympathy and immixture of mind with mind, life with life, a lessening of the body's insistence on separateness, a power of direct mental and other intercommunication and effective mutual action which helps out now the inadequate indirect communication and action. (Sri Aurobindo, 1950: 615). Yoga enables individuals to have a right relation with the collectivity where the individual does not 'pursue egoistically his own material or mental progress or spiritual salvation without regard to his fellows', nor does he 'maim his proper development' for the sake of the community, but sums up in himself 'all [the community's] best and completest possibilities' and pours them out 'by thought, action and all other means on his surroundings so that the whole race may approach nearer to the attainment of its supreme potentialities' (Sri Aurobindo, 1950: 17). A spiritual approach to self-reflection, for instance, such as that of Yoga, proceeds with a different relationship between knowledge and human interest or knowledge and power. In the spiritual traditions of practice and inquiry, the aim of knowledge – whether of self or other, or of both – is not to have power over the other but to become an instrument of service and creativity in the genuine growth and development of the other. This creative service begins with enhancing the 'functioning' and 'capability' of the other and aims at the spiritual transformation of their consciousness. The urge of the seekers within traditions of spiritual practice and inquiry, as Rabindra Nath Tagore puts it in one of his poems, is to fulfil one's life through self-sacrifice and presenting oneself as a gift to the other.

The idea of discourse in the traditions of spiritual transformation is different from the over-politically determined view of discourse in modernity. Discourse here is not confined to politically significant utterances nor is it full only of speech acts. In spiritual traditions, silence is also an important part of discourse. It is undoubtedly true that the discourse that the participants in Habermasian discourse ethics are engaged in is not confined to the political; in fact its critical significance lies in the fact that it is carried out in the life world. But in order to realize the search for multi-dimensional criticism, such as the therapeutic criticism and aesthetic criticism that the participants in discourse ethics are engaged in, there is a need for them to participate in the spiritual dialectic of silence and utterances as well. It is an integral part of spiritual realization that money and power are not the sole measures of a good life; they must be provided with normative direction by the quest for meaning in discovering the depth dimension of one's being and creating bonds of inter-subjectivity (see Bellah *et al.*, 1991). This realization affects the technology of self that the actors seek to cultivate. Robert Bellah and his colleagues describe some of these ideally imagined modes of practices and criticism (Bellah *et al.*, 1991). The following critique of consumerism, which Bellah and his colleagues provide, is an instance of spiritual criticism that bears a lot of suggestions for transformation for the participants in discourse ethics: 'Consumerism kills the soul as any good Augustinian can see because it places things before the valuing of God and human community' (Bellah *et al.*, 1991: 211). Bellah and his colleagues also suggest a pattern of cultivation as an appropriate mode of being in the world today a pattern characterized by a spiritual attentiveness to the need of the others).

By Way of Conclusion: From Practical Discourse to Practical Spirituality

Habermas does not 'tie the criterion of rationality to the idea of self-constituting subject of history, he locates it in the basic context of action, in talk between subjects' (Wagner and Zipprian, 1989: 103). This is the problem with the Habermasian approach to rationality and morality. The key question is can we have such a view of rationality or what he calls communicative rationality and realize the ends that he sets for himself; adequate motivational development of actors for them to be able to act upon their moral realization as critics and transformers? Can his procedure of rational argumentation actualize his worthy expectation that participants in discourse ethics realize that one who recognizes the interests of others 'does not really sacrifice himself, but becomes a larger self' (Habermas, 1987 a: 94)? Realizing these goals requires a wider view of rationality where it is part of the consciousness of actors – a consciousness that is simultaneously rational and supra-rational, rational and spiritual.

Habermas (1979: 93) believes that at the highest stage of moral development internal nature is moved into a 'utopian perspective'. At this stage, internal nature is not subject to the 'demands of ego autonomy; rather through a dependent ego it obtains free access to interpretive possibilities' (1979: 93). He also hopes that moral consciousness as a kind of critique would terminate in a 'transformation of the affective-motivational basis' of actors (Habermas, 1972a: 234). But my argument in this article has been that his rational approach is incapable of realizing these worthy ideals; it has to be supplemented by spiritual praxis. Habermas speaks of practical discourse. Communicative interaction is the most important part of this practical discourse. This practical discourse can be part of a practical spirituality (Metz, 1970; Vivekananda, 1991). Practical spirituality, as Swami Vivekartanda argues, urges us to realize that 'the highest idea of morality and unselfishness goes hand in hand with the highest idea of metaphysical conception' (1991: 354). This highest conception pertains to the realization that man himself is God: 'You are that Impersonal Being: that God for whom you have been searching all over the time is yourself not in the personal sense but in the impersonal' (Vivekananda, 1991: 332). The task of practical spirituality begins with this realization but the watchword of all well-being of all moral good is not 'I' but 'thou'. Who cares whether there is a heaven or a hell, who cares if there is an unchangeable or not? Here is the world and it is full of misery. Go out into it as Buddha did, and struggle to lessen it or die in the attempt. (Vivekananda, 1991: 353) What practical spirituality stresses is that the knowledge that one is Divine, one is part of a Universal Being, facilitates this mode of relating oneself to the world. This knowledge, however, is not for the acquisition of power over the other; rather it is to worship her as God. In the words of Vivekananda: 'Human knowledge is not antagonistic to human well being. On the Contrary, it is knowledge alone that will save us in every department of life, in knowledge as worship' (Vivekananda, 1991: 353). This plea for practical discourse being part of a practical spirituality has to as a distinct caste of solitary individuals and folded into the political fabric be understood in the context of the emergent contours of religious evolution of our times, which point to a new direction. In this direction exists not only religious fundamentalism but also an urge for spiritual realization on the part of the believers, which is not confined to the religions to which they belong (Giri, 1994). People of faith also now realize that spiritual realization is possible only through addressing the concrete problems of man and woman who live in their midst. As E. H. Cousins (1985: 7) tells us in his *Global Spirituality:* 'people of faith now rediscover the material dimensions of existence and their spiritual significance.' The realization of practical spirituality in the dynamics of self, culture and society is as much a normative ideal as the building of a rational society or the realization of a state of undistorted communication. The coming of a spiritual society requires both the 'reflexive mobilization of self' (Giddens, 1991) and also the building-up of alternative communities that are founded on the principles of practical spirituality. According to Aurobindo, the coming of a spiritual society begins with the spiritual fulfilment of the urge to individual perfection but ends with the building of a 'new world, a change in the life of humanity or, at the least, a new perfected collective life in the earth-nature' (Sri Aurobindo, 1950: 1031).

This calls for the appearance not only of isolated evolved individuals acting in the uninvolved mass, but of many gnostic individuals forming a new kind of beings and a new common life superior to the present individual and common existence. A collective life of this kind must obviously constitute itself on the same principle as life of the gnostic individual. (1950: 1031) These gnostic individuals are seekers and bearers of the multi-dimensional transformation of practical spirituality. But these gnostic individuals are not the Nietzschian supermen driven by the will to power; they are animated by a will to serve and by a desire to transform the contemporary condition and to build a good society. They do not form a type or a caste of chosen people to dominate this world and interpret its urge for meaning. What Connolly writes below aptly sums up the spiritual seekers who are going to carry forward the task of moral consciousness and communicative action well into the future. But this typological differentiation between man and overman no longer makes much sense, if it ever did. For the overman constituted as an independent, detached type, refers simultaneously to a spiritual disposition and to the residence of free spirits in a social space relatively insulated from reactive politics. If there is anything in the type to be admired, the ideal must be dismantled as a distinct caste of solitary individuals and folded into the political fabric of late modem society. The 'overman' now falls apart as a set of distinct dispositions concentrated in a particular caste or type, and its spiritual qualities migrate to a set of dispositions that may compete for presence in any self. The type now becomes (as it actually was to a significant degree) a voice in the self-contending with other voices including those of resentment. (1991: 187)

References

Antonio, Robert J. (1989) 'The Normative Foundations of Emancipatory Theory: Evolutionary Versus Pragmatic Perspectives', *American Journal of Sociology*, 194 (4): 721-48.

Baldamus, William (1992) 'Understanding Habermas's Method of Reasoning', *History of the Human Sciences*, 5(2): 91-115.

Bauman, Zygmunt (1993) *Post-modern Ethics*, Oxford: Blackwell.

Beck, Ulrich (1992) *Risk Society: Towards a New Modernity*, London: Sage.

Bellah, Robert *et al.* (1991) *The Good Society*, New York: Alfred A. Knopf.

Bidney, David (1967) *Theoretical Anthropology*, New York: Schocken.

Connolly, William E. (1991) *Identity/Difference: Democratic Negotiation of Political Paradox*, Ithaca, NY: Cornell University Press.

Cortese, Anthony (1990) *Ethnic Ethics: The Restructuring of Moral Theory*, Albany: State University of New York Press.

Cousins, E.H. (1985) *Global Spirituality*, Madras: University of Madras Press.

Dallmayr, Fred (1991) *Life World, Modernity and Critique: Paths between Heidegger and the Frankfurt School*, Cambridge: Polity Press.

Dallmayr, Fred (1993) *The Other Heidegger*, Ithaca, NY: Cornell University Press.

Dallmayr, Fred (1995) ''Rights' Versus 'Rites': Justice and Cultural Transformation', University of Notre Dame, IN, paper.

Dallmayr, Fred (1996) *Beyond Orientalism: Essays on Cross-Cultural Encounter*, Albany: State University of New York Press.

Dewey, John (1960/1908) *Theory of the Moral Life*, New York: Holt, Rinehart and Winston.

Edelman, John T. (1990) *An Audience for Moral Philosophy?*, London: Macmillan.

Geertz, Clifford (1986) 'The Uses of Diversity', *Michigan Quarterly Review*, (Winter): 105-23.

Giddens, Anthony (1991) *Modernity and Self-Identity: Self and Society in the Late Modern Age*, Cambridge: Polity Press.

Giri, Ananta (1994) 'Religious Resurgence in Contemporary United States: a View from India', *Sociological Bulletin*, 43(2): 177-92.

Giri, Ananta (1996) 'Social Criticism, Cultural Creativity and the Contemporary Dialectics of Transformations: A Poser', introductory statement at the workshop on 'Social Criticism, Cultural Creativity and the Contemporary Dialectics of Transformations', Madras Institute of Development Studies, Madras, 4-7, December 1996.

Giri, Ananta (1997) 'Well-Being of Institutions: Problematic Justice and the Challenge of Transformation', Madras Institute of Development Studies, working paper.

Habermas, Jürgen (1972a) *Knowledge and Human Interests*, Cambridge: Polity Press.

Habermas, Jürgen (1972b) *Theory and Practice*, Cambridge: Polity Press.

Habermas, Jürgen (1979) *Communication and the Evolution of Society*, Cambridge: Polity Press.

Habermas, Jürgen (1981) *Philosophical-Political Profiles*, London: Heinemann.

Habermas, Jürgen (1987a) *A Theory of Communicative Action, vol. 2: Life World and System: A Critique of Functionalist Reason*, Cambridge: Polity Press.

Habermas, Jürgen (1987b) *The Philosophical Discourses of Modernity*, Cambridge: Polity Press.

Habermas, Jürgen (1988) 'Law and Morality', in S.M. McCurrin (ed.) *The Tanner Lectures on Human Values*, vol. VII. Cambridge: Cambridge University Press and Salt Lake City: University of Utah Press.

Habermas, Jürgen (1989) *The Structural Transformation of the Public Sphere*. Cambridge: Polity Press.

Habermas, Jürgen (1990a) *Moral Consciousness and Communicative Action*, Cambridge: Polity Press.

Habermas, Jürgen (1990b) 'What Does Socialism Mean Today? The Rectifying Revolution and the Need for New Thinking in the Left', *New Left Review* 183: 183-321.

Habermas, Jürgen (1992) *Postmetaphysical Thinking*, Cambridge: Polity Press.

Habermas, Jürgen (1994) 'Overcoming the Past: Interview with Adam Michnik', *New Left Review*.

Heller, Agnes (1987) *Beyond Justice*. Cambridge, MA: Basil Blackwell.

Hosle, Vittorio (1992) 'The Third World as a Philosophical Problem', Social Research 59(2): 227-62.

Jonas, Hans (1984) *The Imperative of Responsibility: In Search of an Ethics for the Technological Age*, Chicago, IL: University of Chicago Press.

Kant, Immanuel (1987[1781]) *Fundamental Principles of the Metaphysics of Ethics*, Delhi: Orient Publications.

Laclau, Ernesto (1992) 'Beyond Emancipation', in Jan N. Pieterse (ed.) *Emancipations, Modern and Postmodern*. London: Sage.

McCarthy, Thomas (1992) 'Practical Discourse: On the Relation of Morality to Politics', in Craig Calhoun (ed.) *Habermas and the Public Sphere*, Cambridge, MA: MIT Press.

Metz, Johannes B. (1970) 'Does our Church Need a New Reformation? A Catholic Reply', *Concilium*, 4(6): 81-91.

Neville, Robert C. (1974) *The Cosmology of Freedom*. New Haven, CT and London: Yale University Press.

Pande, Govind Chandra (1982) 'On the Nature of Social Categories', in Ravinder Kumar (ed.) *Philosophical Categories and Social Reality*, Delhi: Allied Publishers.

Pande, Govind Chandra (1985) *Aspects of Indian Culture and Civilization*, Varanasi: BHU Press.

Pande, Govind Chandra (1989) *The Meaning and Process of Culture as Philosophical of History*, Allahabad: Raka Prakashan.

Pande, Govind Chandra (1991) 'Two Dimensions of Religion: Reflections Based on Indian Spiritual Experience and Philosophical Traditions', in Eliot Deutch (ed.) *Culture and Modernity*. Honolulu: University of Hawaii Press.

Pande, Govind Chandra (1992) 'Sri Aurobindo: Cultural Perspectives', paper presented at the National Seminar on Sri Aurobindo at Pondicherry.

Rorty, Richard (1989) *Contingency, Irony and Solidarity*, Cambridge: Cambridge University Press.

Sacks, Jonathan (1991) *The Persistence of Faith*, London: Weidenfeld and Nicolson.

Sen, Amartya (1987) 'The Standard of Living', in Geoffrey Hawthorn (ed.) *The Standard of Living*, Cambridge: Cambridge University Press.

Sri Aurobindo (1950) *The Synthesis of Yoga*, Pondicherry: Sri Aurobindo Ashram.

Sri Aurobindo (1953) *The Future Poetry*, Pondicherry: Sri Aurobindo Ashram.

Sri Aurobindo (1962) *The Human Cycles, The Ideal of Human Unity, War and Self-Determination*, Pondicherry: Sri Aurobindo Ashram.

Sri Aurobindo (1970) *The Life Divine*, Pondicherry: Sri Aurobindo Ashram.

Taylor, Charles (1989) *Sources of the Self*, Cambridge, MA: Harvard University Press.

Uberoi, J.P.S. (1996) *Religion, Civil Society and State: A Study of Sikhism*, Delhi: Oxford University Press.

Unger, Roberto M. (1987) *False Necessity: Anti-Necessitarian Social Theory in the Service of Radical Democracy*, Cambridge: Cambridge University Press.

Verma, Roop Rekha (1991) 'The Concept of Progress and Cultural Identity', in Eliot Deutch (ed*.) Culture and Modernity*, Honolulu: University of Hawaii Press.

Vivekananda, Swami (1991) *Complete Works of Swami Vivekanada*, Calcutta: Advaita Ashrama.

Wagner, G.R. and Zipprian, H. (1989) 'Habermas on Power and Rationality', *Sociological Theory*, 7(1): 102-9.

Walzer, Michael (1988) 'Interpretation and Social Criticism', in S.M. McCurrin (ed.) *The Tanner Lectures on Human Values*, vol. VII. Cambridge: Cambridge University Press and Salt Lake City: University of Utah Press.

Williams, Bernard (1985) *Ethics and the Limits of Philosophy*, London: Fontana.

Chapter 16

Effective Leadership: Human Values Perspective

C. Panduranga Bhatta

Introduction

Leadership is the sum essence of personality, character, motivation and sacrifice. Effective leadership is the capacity to frame plans that will succeed, and the faculty to persuade others to carry them out, in the face of all difficulties. It is the leader who shapes destiny of an organization and not the other way around. The hard fact is that there is no 'easy short cut' or the 'latest finding' about effective leadership because it has always stood majestically on the foundation of character, and it will be so even in the future. To be a person of character and to act without any selfish motive is the starting point of responsible and effective leadership. A leader's conduct should be above reproach. Self-restraint, humility, righteousness and straight forwardness are essential for his success.

The true leader will listen carefully, assess prudently and act confidently. Effective leaders take responsibility as an obligation that needs to be fulfilled and cannot be wished away. When they exercise responsibility they automatically gain the trust of their subordinates. Responsibility means that the individual is willing to face the consequences of his acts. It also implies that the individual is in harmony with his surroundings and wants to bring about a better future for those in his charge.[1]

There are no bad organizations, only bad leaders. Organizations fail only when the leaders fail to manage their external and internal environment. The ancient Indian wisdom has pithily expressed the paramount importance of leadership and the profound influence a leader has on his followers through Bhisma's advice to Yudhishira in the *Mahabharata*. Bhisma says, 'whether, it is the leader (ruler) who is the maker of the age or the age that makes the leader is a question about which there is no room for doubt. The leader is undoubtedly the maker of the age: *raja kalasya karanam*.[2] The effective leadership depends on motivating the organizational members to a high pitch, towards achievement of professional excellence besides depending on the capacity to pool in the expertise and experience of many and act on the collective wisdom in decision making process.

This paper explores the ingredients of effective leadership such as character, based on human values, selflessness, self-effacement, leading by example etc. through classical and contemporary writings besides holding mirror to a few corporate examples for the sake of helping future leaders to develop their full potential for good and effective leadership.

Leadership Effectiveness through Human Values

When people in leadership positions compromise their moral values, they do great harm to themselves as well to the organizations, which they lead. Their callous neglect or compromise of moral values tends to create an atmosphere of moral cynicism, which, like a cancer, corrodes the moral health of an organization.[3] The quality of an organization depends on the moral calibre of its members. In addition to the leaders' ethical qualities, the organization's moral environment is equally important, if leaders are to be effective. However, its leaders largely shape the moral fibre of an organization's members.

Almost all the outstanding leaders have a few qualities of character and knowledge that are universal. Character and knowledge support one another. Mere knowledge, without strength of character, makes a person indecisive. Mere character, not supported by knowledge, puts a ceiling on a leader's potential. On the strength and balance of this structure depends the effectiveness of a leader. Self-confidence makes a leader proactive, which means that we are responsible for our own lives.

Our behaviour is a function of our decision, not our condition. We can subordinate feelings to values. We have the initiative and responsibility to make things happen.[4]

According to Lord Buddha, the founder of Buddhism certain basic human values are essential for anyone to become a good leader. The human values listed by him for this purpose are shown in the following exhibit.[5]

Exhibit 16.1

Human Values Propagated by Lord Buddha
• Charity, generosity and liberality
• Moral character
• Sacrificing everything for the good of the people
• Honesty, integrity and sincerity
• Kindness, gentleness,
• Austerity, self-control, simple life,
• Freedom from hatred, ill will and anger
• Non-violence and promoting peace
• Patience, forbearance, tolerance and understanding
• Ruling in harmony

All those who those who hold leadership positions in government, such as the head of the State, ministers, political leaders, legislative and administrative officers, corporate heads etc. should practice these values. The first condition for good leaders is that they should not have craving and attachment to wealth and property, but should use it for the welfare of the people. Besides possessing a high moral character, they must be prepared to give up all personal comfort, in the interest of the people. They must be free from fear or favour in the discharge of their duties, must be sincere in their intentions, and must not deceive the public. They must be kind and gentle in their speech, thought and actions. Leading a simple life, and not indulging in a life of luxury based on self-control is a must.

Freedom from hatred, ill will, enmity and bearing no grudge against anybody makes them good leaders. Patience, forbearance, tolerance, understanding, and ready to bear hardships and difficulties are again the hallmarks of good leadership as pointed out by the Buddha.

The ancient Indian King Ashoka the Great tried to operationalize these ideals of the Buddha and therefore, he could provide an efficient and effective administration, which may appear to be utopian for the present day leaders. A set of human values promoted by Ashoka in the name of *dhamma* may be described as moral law independent of any caste or creed based on the essence of all religions. His *dhamma* included the least amount of sin and the greatest amount of good done to others. Ashoka's *dhamma* not only addressed itself to a large spectrum of opinions but also drew its inspiration from an equally large body of ethical doctrine. The fundamental human values promoted by the king Ashoka are shown in the following exhibit.[6]

Exhibit 16.2

Human Values Promoted by King Ashoka
• Kindness
• Generosity
• Truthfulness
• Purity of thought
• Proper behaviour towards servants and employees
• Self-Control
• Gratitude

Ashoka wanted the people to cultivate and control certain virtues and vices in order to become good citizens. Ashoka's *dhamma* is both negative and positive. It is negative in terms of calling on people to refrain from evil, by pointing out its psychological consequences of fury, cruelty, anger, pride and envy. It is positive in terms of asking people to practice kindness, liberality, truthfulness, inner and outer purity, gentleness, moderation in spending and saving, self-control and gratitude etc.[7]

Exhibit 16.3   Acting with Partiality

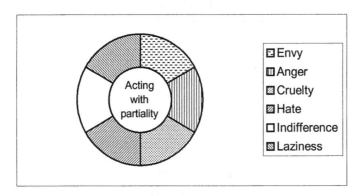

A leader becomes ineffective because of favouritism, prejudices, mutual hatred and subjectivity in decision-making process and all these lead to situations of frustration and inefficiency. King Ashoka had thoroughly understood this problem and hence in one of his inscriptions he tells the administrators to overcome the influence of certain dis-values because they prevent leaders from taking impartial decisions. Therefore, he says that leaders should take concrete steps to see that these dis-values do not enter them. The disvalues that make a leader act with partiality while making decisions, mentioned by Ashoka, are shown in the exhibit 3 given above.

A mere knowledge of *dharma* (righteous conduct) does not enable an individual to practice it. This aspect is forcefully brought-forth in the character of Duryodhana in the great epic *Mahabharata*. He says, 'I know what is righteous conduct, but I have no tendency to act accordingly, I know what is unrighteous conduct, but I cannot abstain from doing it'.[8] The author of the *Mahabharata* laments with upraised arms over the fatal greed of men who ignore integrity and fellow feeling in the insatiable pursuit of power and pleasure. He says, 'with uplifted arms I am crying aloud but nobody hears me. From righteous conduct originate profit and pleasure. Why should not righteous conduct, therefore be sought?'[9]

All virtues like responsibility, moral and spiritual peace, universal benevolence originate from proper view of *dharma*. *Dharma* evokes the sense of duty, of social and global co-operation, since it is the reflection of universal and cosmic order, in which there is no individual claim or right. *Dharma* as an ethical value signifies the cultivation of virtues such as non-injury, sincerity, honesty, cleanliness, control of the senses, clarity. Self-restraint, love and forbearance. Therefore, those who are guided by *dharma* will have necessarily to eliminate the ego sense, which belongs to the empirical plane and which nurtures greed, acquisitiveness, violence, and socio-political exploitation of others. There is an eternal relation between goodness and *dharma* and therefore, to speak of a person as devoted to *dharma* is to imply that he is of a virtuous character.

It is the possible postponement of the result to an indefinite future that explains the common indifference of men towards righteous conduct, not withstanding their awareness of its excellence. It is a fact that men do pursue virtue i.e. they want to conform to the laws of virtue, but this impulse may not be as strong or widespread as the impulse to seek profit and pleasure. Hence the need to emphasis that virtue has to be, ought to be followed.[10]

It is not enough that leaders are intelligent, industrious and competent in their respective fields. Despite these admirable qualities they are ineffective when they lack ethical qualities. They should be pure, good, truthful, and universally beneficent in their attitudes and acts. Leaders should adopt a code of ethics in their decisions and behaviours so that they can fulfill the missions of uplifting the moral climate of their organizations. For this purpose, the leaders must develop morally as persons and also assist in the moral development of their followers by promoting and encouraging suitable activities. The leaders' moral development results from character formation through the practice of virtue in private as well as in public life. When the leaders' moral integrity is in doubt, then their words-however noble and well articulated will lose their vigour and are incapable of inspiring their followers.

Management of senses[11] is a pre-requisite for effective leadership. For, since the outgoing tendencies habitually create a riot of confusion at the discursive level, one can neither acquire a synthesizing insight into complicated problems; nor can one muster the sustaining power of unshakable conviction to clinch and stick to a course of action dictated by such insight. The great stress laid on character and discipline on the part of leaders applies with equal force to all persons who come to exercise organizational power under public or private enterprises. They are the internal check, which automatically control the evil propensities of men in power and position and prevent them from swerving from the path of righteousness. These in-built traits are more effective than all the external constitutional and legal checks, inquiry commissions, though their importance cannot in any way be minimized.

As a matter of fact, a leader is more liable to err and fall than ordinary men, as he is exposed to greatest temptations; he should, therefore, take greater precautions to see that he does not become a prey to different vices and calamities that arise our of passion (*kama*), anger (*krodha*) and greed (*lobha*).[12] Just as an ordinary stone requires a beautiful design and long and continued effort of an expert sculptor in chiseling and engraving in order to make it a beautiful idol, a proper blue print or scheme and a constant and vigilant and untiring efforts of all those concerned is necessary, to make an individual born with all the frailties of a human being, into a responsible person.

A leader has to make great sacrifices for the effectiveness of his role. There is no escape from it. This feature has been instanced both in classical and contemporary leaders who have made tremendous impact on their teams and organizations. N.R. Narayana Murthy,[13] the founder Chairman of Infosys says, 'A true leader is one who leads by example and sacrifices more than anyone else, in his or her pursuit of excellence'. This is echoed in a famous Sufi proverb, which says, 'What is to give light must endure burning'. One instance for leadership effectiveness based on sacrifice is cited here from the leadership style of Alexander the Great.

> Alexander, at the head of 30,000-foot soldiers, with cavalry in the rear, was crossing the dreaded Gedrosian Desert in Asia Minor. It was mid summer and the yellow sands stretched to the horizon, with a few rocks jutting out here and there. It was hot like a furnace. They had completely run out of water. Alexander, like everyone else, was tormented by thirst, yet he kept on marching on foot, leading his men. It was all he could do to keep going, but he did so, and the result as always was that the men were better able to endure their misery, whey they saw it as equally shared. As they toiled on, a party of light infantry, which had gone off looking for water found some, just a wretched little trickle collected in a shallow gully. They scooped up with difficulty what they could and hurried back, with their priceless treasure, to Alexander; then, just before they reached him, they tipped the water into a helmet and gave it to him. Alexander, with a word of thanks for the gift, took the helmet and, in full view of his troops, poured the water on the ground. So extraordinary was the effect of this action that the water wasted was as good as a drink for every man in the army. I cannot praise this act too highly; it was a proof, if anything was, not only of his power of endurance, but also of his genius for leadership.[14]

As a general rule, the empires and organizations built mainly by rude force, bloody strife, and violation of the universal moral imperatives have been short-lived and disastrous. Moderate also has been the life span of organizations built by moderately selfish economic interests. The average life span of small business organizations like drug or hardware stores is only about four years, while the average life span of the big business firms listed on the stock market is only 29 years. The largest existing organizations have been those animated by spiritual and altruistic forces for realization of the supreme values of God, Truth, Goodness, and Beauty. Such are the great ethico-religious organizations.[15]

The Taoist, Confucianist, Hindu, Buddhist, Jainist, Judaist, Christian, Mohammedan, and other religious and ethical organizations have already lived one, two, or three millennia; and so far they do not show any clear sign of irretrievable disintegration.[16] This means that the really, fruitful and constructive policy of any leader, anxious to build a durable organization, is that of scientifically-competent and wise realization of the moral values of love, friendship, mutual help and compassion, and not the policy motivated by unlimited egoism, hate, nihilism and carried on by coercion, fraud, hypocrisy and other anti-moral and ugly means.

Effective Leadership Based on Selflessness

It needs very deliberate reflection on the part of potential leaders to understand that the effectiveness of a leader does depend on selflessness. Self-interest is the most powerful factor in the life of everyone. No one is dear to another unless there is some gain involved.[17] 'To be selfish is human, to be selfless is divine'. A leader must be fully aware of this basic psychological fact. It will help him to understand the importance of one of his key functions, to meet the needs of the men in his team to keep them motivated. Unless a leader can sublimate this weakness and rise above self-interest, he cannot soar to the lofty heights of his innate potential.[18] The overarching motive for good leadership is the leader's altruistic intent as opposed to egotistic intent. Leaders are truly effective only when they are motivated by a concern for others, when their actions are invariably guided primarily by the criteria of 'benefit to others even if it results in some cost to self'. Leader's helping concern for others is prompted without any consideration of self-interest. This behaviour can be categorized as genuine or moral altruism.[19] Moral altruism or *selfless generosity is possible only if a leader is benevolent from within*. This makes him to hear not the spoken grievances of all those who come under him, but the unspoken desires, and the unspoken wishes of all those who are associated with his organization externally and internally. For only when a leader has learned to listen closely to people's hearts, hearing their uncommunicated feelings, unexpressed pains, and unspoken complaints, he hope to inspire confidence in his people, understand when something is wrong, and meet the true needs of his people. Organizations perish when leaders listen only the spoken words and do not penetrate the soul of the people to hear their true opinions, feelings and desires.

Two examples for selfless generosity are cited here to make it clear that it not only exists in literature but also in practice. The action of the ancient Indian king Ashoka who went to the extent of importing and growing the medicinal herbs useful to human beings and animals wherever they were not available is the first example.[20] The second example is from the contemporary India. The CEO of Dharmasthala, a temple town in Karnataka Sri Veerendra Heggade took the initiative of purchasing and installing a machine from Japan costing several lakhs to clean the rice that is used to feed the pilgrims coming to the place. This is an exemplary case in Total Quality Management because the pilgrims never demand anything at the sacred places and whatever they get they accept it with great reverence because it is *prasada* (God's grace).

Selflessness means soaring higher to an ideal and anyone who achieves this becomes a dynamic go-getter because selflessness or unselfishness is based on a loftier goal. Higher goal, higher the degree of selflessness, thus, higher the potential for becoming an effective leader. There is a very perceptive observation about this reality by Swami Vivekananda who said: 'I cannot ask everybody to be totally selfless; it is not possible. But, if you cannot think of humanity at large, at least think of your country. If you cannot think of your country, think of your community. If you cannot think of your community, think of your family. If you cannot think of your family, at least think of your wife. For heaven's sake do not think merely of yourself.[21] At the lowest end is I and me and mine; and, at the highest, humanity'.

Exhibit 16.4　Selfishness and Selflessness Indicator

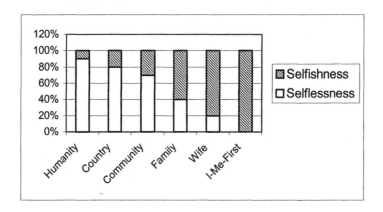

Selflessness is also the repository of all that is noble in a human being i.e. truth, right conduct, honesty, integrity, loyalty etc. A selfless person is neither greedy nor looking for shortcuts to success; hence, his integrity never wavers. He seeks no unfair advantage over others; hence, honesty comes naturally to him. He is not a self-seeker; hence loyalty is steady and strong. When a leader has these virtues then his thoughts, words and deeds become pure and well integrated. He says what he thinks and does what he says. There is no 'double speak' or 'double standard' in his nature. That establishes his credibility, and he is trusted. A trusted person alone can become an effective leader.[22]

The great Chinese philosopher Lao Tza[23] presents the case of a self-effacing leader. This self-effacing leader effectively meets the needs of the organization and its members.[24]

Exhibit 16.5

Self-effacing Leader Presented by Lao Tza
When the Master governs, the people are Hardly aware that he exists. Next best is a leader who is loved. Next, one who is feared. The worst is one who is despised. If you don't trust the people, You make them untrustworthy. The Master does not talk, he acts. When his work is done, The people say, 'Amazing: We did it, all by ourselves!'[25]

In the highly evolved organization, each member senses his role, responds intuitively to the needs of the organization. Each individual acts with high autonomy while respecting the needs of the overall system. As the members learn, the leader can become more of a coach, a mentor, a teacher. And ultimately in the evolved organization, the leader's role as leader becomes tacit-such a person will inevitably move to emulate Lao Tzu's Taoist description of a leader.

Coordinating Leader

An organization cannot thrive only on intellectual or spiritual power, or physical power or money-power or labour. A harmonious combination of all these is needed to create an ideal organization. An organization needs thinkers, planners, executives, financiers and labourers. All are equally necessary, equally important, but not equal. A leader is he who can harmoniously co-ordinate all these men and women of different turns of mind, different capabilities and tastes and belonging to different strata of society so that they can co-exist harmoniously in an organization. This harmonious co-existence is the unfailing test of leadership. Everyone feels at home with such a leader. All differences melt and each one blooms in a unique way. No suppression, no forced duty, but freedom, love, self-expression, self-expansion. A joint 'unlimited' company where everyone is a leader in unison with others, each one's individuality blooming to infinity, caressing each other's.[26] There is a general saying in Sanskrit literature that 'There is no individual who is useless, but there is dearth of an able leader who could utilise the individual effectively' (ayogyah purusho nasti yojakah tatra durlabhah).

Exhibit 16.6   Visionary Leader

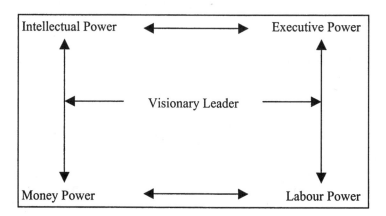

The coordinating leader creates participants by means of coordinating activity. This presupposes the delegation of tasks and responsibilities and, thereby, the creation of independent co-workers. Employees who merely keep to the rules and perform their duties are probably not in a position to solve problems or complete tasks on their own. The independent solution of tasks presupposes the ability to take initiatives. The delegation of tasks and the autonomizing of co-workers involve power sharing. This creates a far more active and reciprocally stimulating contact area between colleagues. The coordinating leadership is a dialogical style of leadership. The delegation of the tasks and responsibilities is always a delegation to independent co-workers within given aims and goals. It is the goals, which integrate all the activities and create a whole out of the enterprise's various parts. But it is only a powerful communication and community culture, which can guarantee the maintenance of this culture of integration. Delegation and enhancing the independence of co-workers leads to a large degree of decentralized power, and in this decentralizing style of leadership, it inheres that the leader succeeds best by helping others to succeed. The reason is that in this communication model, everybody acts on behalf of a paramount aim or a specification of this aim.[26]

Reins of leadership should be placed not in the ordinary intellectual, executive, industrialist or worker, but it should be placed in the hands of the visionary, who can be an intellectual, or executive, or industrialist or worker, by inclination. It does not matter at all. A visionary is an awakened man, the leader par excellence. In any problem concerning leadership, we have to seek the guidance of a visionary who is a seer of totality. A visionary sees the whole, whereas an ordinary man-however efficient or skilled or qualified he may be-sees only a part, partial solutions are temporary. They lead to other problems ad infinitum. The visionary has a total comprehension.

The coordinating style of leadership may be compared with hierarchically oriented leadership because they express respectively two fundamentally different views of what is to be human. For the one, employees are considered to be no more than means to an end in the process of production. For the other, employees are participants in a wider sense in which the quality of cooperation by which to achieve certain goals is based upon more inclusive interpersonal relations, a rich community culture, than merely relations between professionals. These two types of leadership are presented clearly in the following exhibit.

Exhibit 16.7   Two Models of Leadership

The hierarchical leadership	*The coordinating leadership*
Directs/Commands	Delegates
	- tasks and jobs
	- responsibility
• Controls	Encourages independence
• Often discriminates	Integrates
• Centralization of power	Coordination and consideration of welfare
• Lacks flexibility	Is flexible
• Ethics of duty and obedience	Ethics of co-creativity
• The leader must succeed	The leader's task: to help others succeed

The role of the leader concerns the ability to create an organic and adaptive system in which all participants can realize their potentials as creators of their future lives. For this purpose coordination becomes more important than control. Co-evolution (evolution with one another) must replace evolution. Satisfying the needs of all must replace the search to satisfy leaders' own singular needs. This becomes the ultimate challenge for leaders in the new context of globalization.

Leading People for Organizational Excellence

The most important resource of a leader in any profession, enterprise or activity, is the 'Human Resource'. Getting the best out of men is obviously the main function of leadership and forms the major function of his capability. Even though, professional knowledge is only a small proportion of leadership capability, it is so vital that without it, appropriate to the level of command, a leader cannot lead effectively. Leadership and management are not the same nor are they interchangeable. It is well to remember that: we manage inventories, things, and schedules. However, when it comes to people we have to lead them. The following exhibit informs the difference in the role of leader and manager.

Exhibit 16.8

Leader Vs. Manager	
Leader	**Manager**
• Formulates vision	• Makes Plan
• Focuses on Long-term	• Focuses on Short-term
• Aligns	• Organizes
• Inspires	• Directs
• Generates Ideas	• Implements policies
• Empowers	• Controls
• Transforms	• Transacts
• Activates	• Stabilizes
• Encourages diversity	• Enforces uniformity

A leader should inspire people in his organization to get best out of them by caring for them, with no thoughts of pleasing himself, subordinating his own wishes and desires to those of his people. He should guard them as a mother guards her child. There is an interesting finding by the Stan ford Research Institute in the U.S.A., which has a bearing on this issue. During the Eighties, many scholars in the U.S.A. began to investigate why the Japanese were forging ahead of the Americans in almost every economic enterprise and activity. This was happening in spite of the Japanese not having many colleges to teach business management in their country, whereas, the Americans have some of the best business management institutions in the world. The finding of the Stanford Research Institute pinpointed the area the Americans had ignored. It virtually sums up the composition of good leadership, which has to be rediscovered. The study concluded that: Twelve per cent of effective management (i.e. leadership) is knowledge and eighty-eight per cent is dealing appropriately with people.[27] A good leader knows his people better than their mothers do and cares even more'

Exhibit 16.9   Effective Management

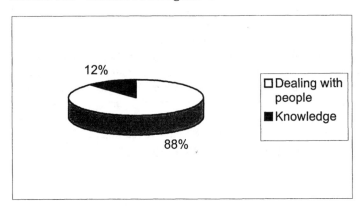

This interesting finding informs us that dealing with people is most important for leadership effectiveness. To become effective, leaders must believe in the primacy of human resources and know how to utilize time, resources and potentials of their people. It is the human resources, which ultimately bring to reality, the dream and vision of leaders and deliver satisfaction to all stakeholders. A verse composed by the famous Sanskrit poet Bhartrihari is of considerable value in this matter. It says, O King, if you wish to milk this cow-like earth, then first nourish (enrich) the people as they do the calf. When the people are constantly enriched, the earth, like the wish-granting tree, yields a variety of fruits.[28] This is a very sound advice to leaders interested in securing the prosperity of their organizations. Mr. Keval Nohriya, who is largely responsible for the corporate turnaround of the Crompton Greaves Ltd. says,[29] 'I believe in the primacy of human assets over all other resources. It is the human resources, which ultimately bring to reality the dream, and vision of leaders, and deliver satisfaction to other stakeholders'.

Sumantra Goshal, Gita Pirmal and Christpher A Bartlett[30] are of the opinion that companies, which have achieved international best practices, excel in managing their people and creating a working environment that satisfies the employee's intellectual and emotional needs. In the companies studies by them, one distinguishing factor was the systematic process by which employees were given a sense of involvement with corporate decisions and targets, creating emotional feeling of empowerment and at the same time enabling employees to take local level decisions. The CEOs of these companies proudly say, 'The kind of freedom one enjoys in this company is something unique', 'We have the right kind of environment for people to perform to their full potential', 'We let our staff do things which in most organizations would not be allowed', 'There is much scope here for a person to show initiative' etc. No organization can be successful without the active involvement of the majority of its employees. Having good people is not enough, a company needs to create the context in which good people can become the best they can be and perform at the highest level.[31] This is perhaps the most difficult to quantify in any meaningful manner. Yet successful companies have developed their own unique work culture for this purpose and are zealous in maintaining it. Sustaining competitive advantage has a lot to do with innovating work culture. It requires a mindset, which reflects the belief that it is a tough world, and everyone has to contribute towards success. Mr. Keval Nohriya says, 'I coined a slogan that as CEO, I would like the nearly 10,000 employees working 'in' the company start working 'for' the company'.[32]

Delegation and Empowerment

An effective leader is one who gets things done through his subordinates. It is the prowess to delegate effectively, which differentiates the good leader from the bad. The leader who utilises the skill, aptitude and commitment of his subordinates thereby enabling them to enrich their leadership qualities as well as broaden their professional experience is undoubtedly earmarked for success in all his endeavours. An effective leader would comply with the three essential aspects of delegation namely, responsibility, authority, and accountability. When a subordinate is entrusted with a job, it is his responsibility to carry it out, and complete it in line with the terms and conditions stipulated by the leader. Authority is the power invested in the subordinate to enable him to discharge the responsibility assigned to him. Authority and responsibility always go hand in glove, both in terms of quantity and quality. The subordinate is authorized to use whatever resources are required, and take whatever decisions are necessary to accomplish the task. Leaders must have the capacity to own the responsibility for their subordinates' failures, and the confidence to give them the credit for their success.[33] A leader can delegate authority not responsibility. If he delegates responsibility, then he must build competence to enable them to handle it. Delegating responsibility without building competence is abdication of responsibility. Delegating responsibility after building competence is empowerment, and the empowered people rarely fail.[34] Good and effective leaders have used the human urge for appreciation and recognition with telling effect, to foster interpersonal bonds with their people and to motivate them. They have scrupulously used the principle of 'praise in public and reprimand in private', to create an organizational culture, in which people work 'much beyond the call of duty' to maintain excellence in their organization.

Leading by Example

Dealing appropriately with people is the crux of the entire leadership process. Personal example is the most potent factor in the technique to inspire people to do what they are expected to do. Personal example in punctuality, integrity, honesty, frugality, courage, persistence, initiative, unselfish love for the people or whatever is infectious. To do oneself what one preaches is the secret of leading people. The leadership effectiveness depends on TO BE, TO DO, TO SEE and TO TELL.[35]

- TO BE is composed of leader's values, his qualifications and his knowledge. TO BE is the largest component in the leadership process. The major proportion of TO BE of a leader, is his character.
- TO DO indicates that the best style of leadership is to lead by personal example: to practice what one preaches. Personal example can be set only if the TO BE of the leader is worthy of emulation.
- TO SEE implies that a leader must be in complete touch with the realities of the environment in which he is working. He should have the fullest possible information regarding the problem or the task to be handled. Only then can he evaluate the options that he has, make a sound decision and evolve a realistic plan of action to get a feel of things on the spot. One should not sit in an air-conditioned office and make decisions.
- TO TELL means conveying to his team what the leader wants to be done. This happens when the channel of communication is through hearts. This depends entirely on the strength of TO BE and TO DO of the leader. If he has good qualities and sound knowledge, and he leads by personal example, then very few words are necessary to convey what a leader wants to be done. Character communicates more eloquently than anything leader says or does. This is what Emerson wanted to convey in his famous words, 'What you are, shouts so loudly in my ears that I cannot hear what you say'.[36]

Exhibit 16.10 Leadership Effectiveness

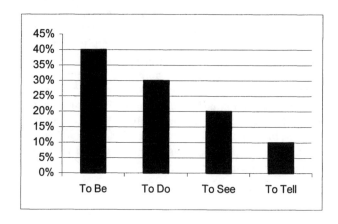

The famous police commissioner of India Kiran Bedi firmly believes in leading by example. She wanted to make the leading process tacit. This is very clear in her statement 'I didn't have to say, 'I am walking, so you walk'. I did it by example. And they felt compelled to follow. After that it became a habit. And they became leaders themselves. My job was to create leadership and not remain a leader'.[37] This approach of leading by example inspires great changes in the behaviour of subordinates. The statement of the vision, mission, and policies however numerous, well crafted, and articulated, are futile if the leader's actions and behaviour are inconsistent with these statements. Actions speak louder than words; what the leader does and values sets the ethical tone and creates the moral environment of the organization.[38]

Conclusion

Before ending the paper it is to be reiterated that effective leadership is based on the foundation of the personality of a person and his ability to transform into a leader by imbibing those explicit qualities that are associated with a great leader. Since leadership is exercised by the mind (reflected in character), it is the mind that has to be trained, to develop qualities, which add up to the total leadership potential. The future leaders should examine themselves in respect of attributes of leadership, which they learn about; and try to adjust themselves, first in behaviour, and subsequently, to the ideal attitude.

Exhibit 16.11

Test of an Effective Leader
The first test of an effective leader is that he leaves behind him The conviction and will to carry on. The genius of a good leader is to leave behind him a situation which, common sense, without the grace of genius, can deal with successfully.[39]

The survival of an idea or a set of values indicates that a leader has made a profound contribution to the longevity of the organization itself.[40]

There is no doubt that wisdom backed up by a desire to learn, can effect great changes in ability to lead other men.[41] Leaders must be ever conscious of the dynamic of learning and teaching, the yin and the yang of receiving knowledge and giving knowledge. The Chinese wise men, setting off on a pilgrimage at the age of 60, declares: 'If I meet a three year old Child on the path who knows more than I do, I will learn from him. If I meet an 80-year old sage who knows less, I will teach him'.[42]

A leader who practices human values is the seer and practitioner of eternal truth, and holism. He lives in and works for the world. He has overcome selfishness, greed, vanity and the other dis-values, and has the clear, undistorted, authentic grasp of anything and everything. Possessing pure intuitive consciousness or insight, he is able to manage the affairs with increasing infallibility. This composite leadership model is very much in need for leaders in every field of human activity, including business. Tendencies of the leaders in just sermonizing for the others and not caring for their own thoughts and actions, will lead organizations to a situation where ideals and norms of behaviour will become only the field for talking and not for action. It will create a situation of 'leadership crisis'. The effective leaders are capable of maintaining harmony between thoughts, speech and action. It is the duty of the leader to sacrifice his self-interest and set ideals for others. Leaders should command respect from their personality and idealized actions.

The Indian cultural tradition talks of five primary elements namely earth, water, fire, air and space, which sustain the universe. Each one of these has some special characteristics of its own as mentioned in following exhibit.

Exhibit 16.12 Leadership Effectiveness Based on Five Primary Elements

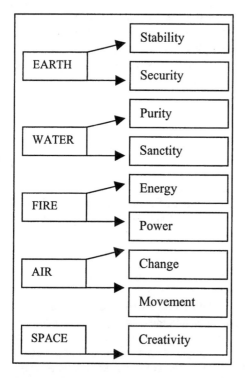

The paper concludes by saying that to become an effective a leader one has to assimilate all the special characteristics of these five elements in one's personality. Devils and crooks do not make effective leaders. They lead organizations astray, rather than down the path of righteousness and rarely achieve long-term success. Potential leaders will have positive values and benevolent motives.[43]

Notes

1   Kamath, M.V. (2000) *The Pursuit of Excellence*, Rupa and Co, New Delhi, 63.
2   Mahabharata *Shantiparva*, Chapter 69, verse 79.
3   Kanungo, R.N. and Mendonca, M. (1998) 'Ethical Leadership in Three Dimensions', *Journal of Human Values*, 4 (2), 137-39.
4   Stephen Covey, (1990) *The 7 Habits of Highly Effective People*, Simon and Schuster, New York.
5   Jatakas, I. 260, 399; II. 274, 320; V.119, p.378.
6   Pillar Edict XII.
7   Kalinga Roack Edict I; (2001) See also Dhammika, S., 'An English Rendering of the Edicts of Ashoka', *Ashoka 2300*, The Bengal Buddhist Association, Calcutta, p.53.
8   Mahabharata.
9   Mahabharata, XVIII *Parva*, Chapter 5, verse 75.
10   Hiriyanna, M. (1960) *The Quest After Perfection*, Kavyalaya Publishers, Mysore, 105.
11   Manusmriti, VII. 17.
12   Manusmriti, VII. 45.
13   Narayana Murthy's speech at the Inauguration of Infosys Leadership Institute, Mysore.
14   Recorded by Arian, the historian of Alexander's conquests.
15   Sorokin and Lunden (1994) *Power and Morality*, Bharatiya Vidya Bhavan Bombay, p.177.
16   Ibid.
17   *Leadership* (1999) published by Army Training Command Shimla, p.50.
18   Ibid.
19   Kanungo, R.N. and Conger, J., 'Promoting Altruism as a Corporate Goal', *Academy of Management Executive*, 1993, 7(3), 37-48.
20   Rock Edict II.
21   Quoted by Vaghul, N. (1998) in 'Raja Ramdeo Anandi Lal Podar Sixteenth Memorial Lecture' at Jaipur on December 10.
22   Leadership, op. cit., 47.
23   The Sterven Mitchell (1991) translation of the *Tao Te Ching*, Harper Perennial.
24   Ibid.
25   Guttorm Floistad (2000) *Leadership, Ethics and Creativity*, University of Oslo, Norway, p.47.
26   Ibid., p.49.
27   Kochler Berret (1993) *Power of Dharmic Management*, San Francisco.
28   Nitishataka, 46.
29   Keval Nohriya (1999) *Painless Transformation*, Macmillan India Ltd, p.52.
30   Sumantra, Ghoshal, Gita Piramal and Christopher, A. Bartlett, (2000) *Managing Radical Change*, Penguin Books India, p.284 ff.
31   Sumantra Ghoshal and others, op. cit., p.194.
32   Keval Nohriya, op. cit., p.33.
33   Panduranga Bhatta, C., 'Leadership Values from Ashoka's Inscriptions, *Journal of Human Values*, vol. 6, no. 2, p.106.
34   Keval Nohriya, op. cit., p.52.
35   Leadership, op. cit., pp.19-21.
36   Ibid., p.33.
37   Kiran Bedi's interview with T.K.V. Desikachar published in *The Hindu*.
38   Kanungo and Mendonca, op. cit.
39   Walter Lippmann (1945) 'Roosevelt is Gone', *New York Herald Tribune*, April 14.

40 Ibid.
41 Edwin Boring, C. (1973) *Psychology of Armed Services*, Harvard University Press printed in India by Natraj Publishers, Dehradun.
42 Robert J. Allio (2000) *Leadership Myths and Realities*, Tata McGraw-Hill Publishing Company Limited, New Delhi.
43 Ibid., p.200.

Chapter 17

Stakeholder Thinking:
Beyond Paradox to Practicality

Kenneth E. Goodpaster, T. Dean Maines and Michelle D. Rovang

Clarification of 'Stakeholder Thinking'

Many believe that 'stakeholder thinking' is important because it is through this
kind of thinking that specifically *ethical* values enter management decision-
making. On this view, business ethics is really about setting aside more
conventional management frameworks in favour of a stakeholder framework. It is
our belief that this idea, while it contains an important truth, can be very
misleading.[1] To understand why, we will first define the term 'stakeholder' and
then distinguish between two very different ideas with which it can be associated:
analysis and *synthesis*.

The term 'stakeholder' appears to have been invented in the early 1960s
as a deliberate play on the English word 'stockholder' to signify that there are other
parties who have a 'stake' in the decision-making of the modern, publicly held
corporation besides those holding equity positions. Professor R. Edward Freeman
(1984:46) defines the term as follows: 'A stakeholder in an organization is (by
definition) any group or individual who can affect or is affected by the
achievement of the organization's objectives.' Examples of stakeholder groups
(other than stockholders) are employees, customers, suppliers, communities and
even competitors.

Decision-making: Stakeholder Analysis and Stakeholder Synthesis

Any rational decision-making process includes such steps as: (i) gathering
information, (ii) sorting, (iii) weighing, (iv) integrating and eventually, (v) acting
on the processed information. 'Stakeholder analysis' as we shall use the phrase,
includes the first two of these steps in relation to information about stakeholders,
but does not go beyond them. In a stakeholder analysis of several options available
to a decision-maker, the affected parties for each available option can be identified
and the positive and negative implications for each stakeholder group can be
clarified. But questions having to do with weighing and integrating this
information in order to make a choice remain to be answered. These latter steps are
not a part of decision *analysis* but of decision *synthesis*.

Analysis, then, is simply the first stage of a process that eventually calls upon the moral (or non-moral) values of the decision-maker. To be told that someone regularly makes stakeholder analysis part of his or her decision-making is to learn very little about such a person's values. We learn that stakeholders are identified in relation to proposed courses of action and even that the implications for each stakeholder are identified, but we do not learn *why and by what criterion a decision will be made.* Stakeholder analysis, as a decision-making process, is incomplete and for the most part, morally neutral.[2]

The idea of 'stakeholder synthesis', on the other hand, includes the remainder of the decision-making steps, weighing the significance of the available options for the affected stakeholders and making a normative judgement that integrates this information into a decision. The key point is that stakeholder synthesis goes beyond simply *identifying* various affected stakeholder groups. It makes a normative response to this information, assigning relative weights to stakeholder interests and rights.

Stakeholder Synthesis: Prudential and Impartial

A 'stakeholder synthesis', however, may not be *ethically* motivated. A politician or a management team, for example, might be careful to consider positive and (especially) negative stakeholder impacts for no other reason than offended stakeholders might resist or retaliate. This kind of stakeholder thinking is not really done out of ethical concern. It simply manifests a concern about possible impediments to one's objectives. It is what we might call a *prudential* synthesis. On such a view, negative effects on relatively *powerless* stakeholders (those who cannot retaliate) may be ignored or discounted in the synthesis and eventual decision. Machiavelli is often interpreted as recommending discounting of the least powerful.[3]

So we can see: (i) that 'stakeholder analysis' is not a complete decision-making process to begin with; and (ii) that moving from stakeholder analysis to stakeholder synthesis is not necessarily moving towards *ethics*, especially if it amounts to treating merely prudentially the interests and rights of stakeholder groups other than stockholders. Suppose we go beyond a prudential synthesis, however, treating all stakeholders *non-instrumentally*, just like stockholders? Would we then arrive at a more ethically satisfactory form of stakeholder synthesis? The answer, we believe, leads to some conceptual puzzles.

What Makes a Synthesis Ethical?

In contrast to taking a prudential approach in stakeholder thinking, we can imagine a management team giving the same care to the interests of, say, employees, customers and local communities as to the economic interests of stockholders. This kind of synthesis might involve trading off the economic advantages of one group against those of another: for example, in a decision having to do with a plant closing or product safety.

Using this type of synthesis, the interests and rights of stakeholders would be treated equally, though 'equally' would be interpreted along utilitarian lines (the greatest good for the greatest number of stakeholders) or along more 'contractarian' lines (maximizing the well being of the least-advantaged stakeholders).

Unlike the prudential or 'partial' view of stakeholder synthesis, such an 'impartial' view considers stakeholders apart from their instrumental, economic or legal clout. Here the word 'stakeholder' carries with it, by the deliberate modification of a single phoneme, a shift in managerial outlook. Some would say a shift from amoral to moral. Others, however, would disagree.

Problems with Impartiality

Unfortunately, an *impartial* approach to stakeholder synthesis may be as incompatible in its way with our convictions about the nature of morality as the *partial* approach, leaving conceptual disarray. The underlying issues have to do with:

1. The special fiduciary obligations owed by management to stockholders
2. The nature of the 'common good' as more than a mere summation of numerous private goods Behind (1) lies the belief that the obligations of agents (managers) to principals (stock holders) are either stronger or different in kind from those of agents to other (stakeholder) parties. Behind (2) lies the belief that simply adding up individual (or constituent) interests and rights is relevant but ultimately inadequate to discerning the 'common good' towards which organizations are expected to order their behaviour.

There are, then, *two* ways in which the idea of an 'ethical synthesis' can be problematic. One has to do with the way in which the interests and rights of stockholders are treated in relation to other stakeholders. The other has to do with the way in which the interests and rights of the full complement of stakeholders are combined into a unified whole.

It is hard to imagine that a practitioner who is looking to 'stakeholder thinking' for a decision procedure would find much encouragement in the face of these problems. Such a practitioner could, of course, simply ignore the two problems by (i) treating stock-holders as having no more claim on management than any other stake-holder; and (ii) treating the 'common good' as simply the aggregate or sum of constituency goods weighted by the number of individuals affected. But we believe this is a significant price to pay to achieve stakeholder synthesis.

Stakeholder Paradox I

Practitioners who would simply pursue an *impartial* stakeholder synthesis first must come to terms with a strong moral intuition about the *legitimacy* of treating stockholders impartially, given the economic mission and legal constitution of the modern corporation. This anomalous situation has been referred to as the *stakeholder paradox* (but we will call it *stakeholder paradox I, since* there is a second, related paradox to be taken up below).

> Stakeholder paradox I. It seems essential, yet illegitimate, to guide corporate decisions by ethical values that go beyond prudential or instrumental stakeholder considerations to impartial ones.[4]

The issue arises from management's *fiduciary* duty to the stockholder, essentially the duty to keep not a profit-maximizing promise but a promise of 'most-favoured' stake-holder consideration. An impartial stakeholder synthesis, in the eyes of some, cuts managers loose from certain well-defined obligations of accountability to stockholders and could lead to a betrayal of trust. If corporate responsibility is modelled on public-sector institutions with impartiality towards all constituencies, the provider of capital seems to lose status.

Stakeholder paradox I seems to call for an account of corporate responsibility that: (i) avoids surrendering moral relationships between management and multiple stakeholders as the prudential view does; while (ii) interpreting obligations to stockholders as fiduciary obligations (thus protecting the uniqueness of the principal-agent relationship between management and stockholders).

The responsibilities of management towards stakeholders can best be understood as extensions of the obligations that *stockholders themselves* would be expected to honour in their own right. No one can expect of an *agent* behaviour that is ethically less responsible than that expected of him or herself. I cannot (ethically) have done on my behalf what I should not (ethically) do myself.

This guiding principle does not, of course, resolve the synthesis for business decision makers. But it does suggest that such conflicts are of a piece with those that face us all.

It urges a form of stakeholder thinking different from the prudential and the impartial approaches, one that both managers and institutional investors might apply to policies and decisions.[5]

Stakeholder Paradox II

All this being said, practitioners face a second stakeholder paradox, in addition to the first puzzle about special fiduciary obligations to stockholders. This second paradox stems not from accommodating stockholders properly in the synthesis but from approaching the synthesis as an aggregation problem. Behind the idea of stakeholder synthesis as an aggregation lies a view of the common good that many would question.[6] In the words of David Braybrooke and Arthur Monahan, the common good as an ideal in the history of ethics

> is clearly incompatible with the individualistic reckoning required by contractarianism. It takes as settled, moreover, a question that utilitarianism deliberately leaves open to determination by contingent facts ... Theorists of the common good refuse, for purposes of working out an ethics, to contemplate the possibility that human beings might be

fully happy apart from subordination [to the common happiness] (Braybrooke and Monahan 1992:175).

The relevance of each stakeholder category to the common good is not in question but the idea that individual destinies are first arrived at and then added to make an optimal common destiny is seen as backwards. The seeds of synthesis are planted in the analytical soil ahead of time, so to speak. A stakeholder group – for example, employees – may be called upon to make sacrifices for the common good (in wages or even lay-off arrangements) which would, from a more individualistic point of view, be difficult to defend. The situation is similar for customers in the context of acceptable risk in product safety debates. The concept of the common good invites a form of stakeholder thinking that looks at synthesis in a more organic or holistic way.

The conventional idea of stakeholder synthesis tends to view management as a trustee charged with balancing the diverse claims of a broad set of constituencies. Each constituency has its own special set of interests. Each seeks its own advantage, however enlightened its view of this advantage might be. What the stakeholder model describes is less a community than an assembly of fragmented interests. Stakeholder synthesis is supposed to *maximize* or *optimize the sum of these interests*. But, in the words of Naughton *et al.* (1996:222): 'Because the stakeholder approach focuses on individual claims as its starting point, it has tremendous difficulty pursuing a collective notion of a common life in which goods are shared to enhance human development'.

The ideal of the *common good* is neither the particular good of one stakeholder group, 'the good of the community in which people develop' (Naughton *et al.* 1996: 221). This unitary good includes, yet transcends, the particular goods of each stakeholder group. It does not provide managers with a detailed blueprint for organizational life. But it does suggest a *normative orientation* for the firm's activities.[7] Companies are called to contribute to human development through the products and services they offer, the working environment they create and the collaborations and partnerships they form (Naughton *et al.* 1996: 208). The upshot is that there appears to be a second barrier to the straightforward application of a synthesis-producing calculus for stakeholder thinking – a second 'paradox' Stakeholder paradox II. It seems essential, yet problematic, to guide corporate decisions by a view of the common good arrived at by simply aggregating separate stakeholder costs and benefits. While ethical responsibility clearly has something to do with impartial concern for affected parties, it is not at all clear that the pursuit of the common good is equivalent to the maximization or optimization of the separately calculated interests of various stakeholder groups. And if this equivalence fails, then impartial stakeholder synthesis faces a second barrier, as puzzling as the barrier indicated by *stakeholder paradox I*.

Stakeholder Thinking: Beyond the Paradoxes?

We now find ourselves in uncomfortable territory. Clearly multiple 'stakeholders' have a morally significant relationship to management, but that relationship (except in one case)is different from a fiduciary one. Management may never have promised customers, employees, suppliers, etc. a 'return on investment', but management is nevertheless obliged to take seriously its extra-legal obligations not to injure, lie to or cheat these stakeholders *quite apart from* whether it is in the stockholders' interests. Clearly, too, the interests and rights of multiple 'stakeholders' are relevant to an organization's understanding of the 'common good'. But corporate responsibility to customers, employees, suppliers and stockholders might involve asking certain of these stakeholder groups to make sacrifices for the sake of the common good that do not maximize the satisfaction of their interests, viewed *apart* from the common good. What, then, is a practitioner to do? Motivated to think in stakeholder terms, but faced with paradoxes in any decision-making synthesis, the practitioner appears to be left with either a calculus of questionable legitimacy or business as usual. Is there any other way — a way beyond the conceptual paradoxes? We think the answer is yes. Understanding that stakeholder analysis is different from stakeholder synthesis and that stakeholder synthesis can take many forms, some of which are more ethically plausible than others, but most of which face significant obstacles, may help us to clarify the challenge facing the responsible corporation. In the next section we shall examine in some detail an approach to stakeholder thinking that business leaders from around the globe have found persuasive: the Caux Round Table Principles for Business and their accompanying implementation guidelines, the Self-Assessment and Improvement Process (SAIP). Later, we shall reflect on how this approach may take us *beyond* the stakeholder paradoxes.

A Stakeholder-Based Process for Self-Assessment

The acknowledgement that a business enterprise has responsibilities towards multiple stakeholders is an acknowledgement of the validity for corporations of the idea of conscience. Conscience generates what philosopher Josiah Royce once referred to as the 'moral insight'; 'the realization of one's neighbour, in the fullest sense of the word *realization*; the resolution to treat him unselfishly'. He also noted that human frailty clouds this insight after only a short time.

We see the reality of our neighbour, that is, we determine to treat him as we do ourselves. But then we go back to daily action and we feel the heat of hereditary passions and we straightaway forget what we have seen. Our neighbour becomes obscured. He is once more a foreign power. He is unreal. We are again deluded and selfish. This conflict goes on and will go on as long as we live after the manner of men. Moments of insight, with their accompanying resolutions; long stretches of delusion and selfishness: That is our life (Royce 1885:155). Surmounting the barriers to ethical awareness and action identified by Royce is no small task for individuals. For business organizations, it requires an *institutionalization* of conscience. Institutionalization facilitates the translation of ideals into action. It also sustains their presence within the firm as a source of moral suasion.

The Caux Principles: Institutionalizing Conscience

Integral to the process of institutionalization is the *progressive articulation* of ethical standards. By crystallizing ethical values into principles, we capture and convey vital dimensions of human moral experience. Articulating principles helps overcome what Royce called the 'obscuring of neighbours' to which organizations are prone by making moral wisdom explicit, so that it can guide future decisions and actions. Furthermore, by explicating standards with specific measures, companies are better able to judge whether their behaviour truly embodies their ideals. Progressive articulation helps an organization to assess the 'fit' between the demands of conscience and its deeds. Any discrepancy between aspiration and action then serves as a point for organizational reflection and learning, as well as a spur to improvement.

The Caux Round Table Principles for Business

This process can be illustrated through one of the best-known sets of transcultural ethical principles available today. The Caux Round Table Principles for Business were officially launched in July 1994 (see Appendix).These principles emerged from discussions among Japanese, European and American executives and were fashioned in part from a document called the Minnesota Principles.[8] The Caux Principles (as they are called) articulate a comprehensive set of ethical norms that could be embraced by a business operating internationally and in multiple cultural environments. To meet this challenge, the Caux Principles had to formulate core values in such a way that both Eastern and Western mind-sets could find them intelligible and acceptable. The Caux Principles rest on two broad ethical ideals: human dignity and the Japanese concept of *kyosei*. The former witnesses to the significance of each person as an end. It implies that a person' s worth can never be reduced to his or her instrumental utility or value as a means to the fulfilment of another's purpose. The ideal of *kyosei* was defined by Ryuzaburo Kaku, the late chairman of Canon, Inc., as 'living and working together for the good of all' (Kaku 1997:55). *Kyosei* is a subtle and complex concept that tempers individual, organizational and even national self-interest with concern for more embracing 'common goods' (Goodpaster 1998:530). These two ideals emphasize distinct yet complementary aspects of Royce's moral insight. Human dignity underscores the moral reality of our neighbour, the innate worth he or she has by virtue of being human. It establishes our neighbour as deserving of our concern. In contrast, *kyosei* heralds behaviour that recognizes and honours our resolve to treat our neighbour as ourselves. The realization of our neighbour is achieved by pursuing in solidarity the good we have in common – through co-operative action that promotes justice, prosperity and community.

The Caux Principles express these ideals in a format that progresses towards greater specificity. The document's Preamble establishes the vital need for corporate conscience in a world that is interdependent and an economy that is increasingly transnational. The next section outlines seven General Principles;

these begin to clarify how the values of human dignity and *kyosei* inform business practice within a global context. The third and final section of the Caux Principles utilizes a stakeholder framework to supplement these general norms with more detailed guidelines. The 'Stakeholder Principles' specify how the ideals of human dignity and *kyosei* may be activated practically in a company's relationships with customers, employees, investors, suppliers, competitors and communities. The Stakeholder Principles thus function as a battery of more detailed aspirations that point executives and managers towards specific practices. The implementation of these practices helps bring the ideals of the Caux Principles for Business to life within an enterprise. A further development in this progressive articulation, the SAIP, will be discussed below.

The Caux Principles give meaning to the phrase 'principled business leadership'. The progressive articulation of standards for responsible business conduct, however, must continue. What is needed is a more direct assessment of the fit between the Principles and a company's operations. Managers would then be able to identify behaviour inconsistent with the Principles and to craft new initiatives in keeping with the Principles' letter and spirit (see Figure 17.1).

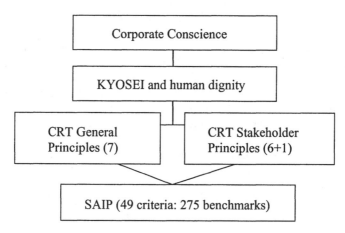

CRT= Caux Round Table; SAIP=Self Assessment Improvement Process

Figure 17.1   Progressive Articulation

Corporate Self-Awareness

An individual conducts a journey towards self-awareness by discovering meaning and values. A corporation proceeds on a similar quest – finding self-awareness in its cultural identity and shared values. In his classic book on leadership, Philip Selznick wrote that

There is a close relation between 'infusion with value' and 'self-maintenance'. As an organization acquires a self, a distinctive identity, it becomes an institution. This involves the taking on of values, ways of acting and believing that are deemed important for their own sake. From then on self-maintenance becomes more than bare organizational survival; it becomes a struggle to preserve the uniqueness of the group in the face of new problems and altered circumstances (Selznick 1957:21-22).

Selznick describes a search for self-awareness that transforms an organization into an institution. Clearly, a necessary first step towards this self-awareness is articulation of responsible business standards. Rather than merely espousing values and standards, an institution must find ways to transform its initial principled commitment into a progressively more specific self-assessment process. The Caux Principles may serve as an expression of a company's goals for conduct, or as a template for assessing a company's current norms. More importantly, the progressive articulation of these Principles suggests an organizational cycle of communication, which includes educating, listening, reflecting and learning (Goodpaster 1998:534).

The idea of self-awareness is reminiscent, on an organizational level, of Plato's famous cave allegory (Jowett 1920:514-17), which depicts an underground cave that eventually opens towards the light of the sun. People are chained within the cave, forcing them to see only its back wall, illuminated by a fire projecting shadows of objects before them. Truth and reality for the prisoners consist only of shadowy images and darkness because they know nothing else. If one of the inhabitants left the cave, however, he would realize the more profound reality outside. If this enlightened cave dweller were then to return to the cave, he would not be able to view the situation as before. Plato suggests further that if the enlightened escapee attempted to share his new knowledge with the rest of the prisoners, they might feel a heightened sense of intimidation and danger about his new convictions. Thus, the cave represents the world of appearances and shadows, while the journey outside stands for the ascent to knowledge and transparency.

A Newly Developed Tool for Organizational Self-Awareness

Corporations need objective criteria, or self-awareness benchmarks, to assist them in escaping the cave. The Caux Round Table recently initiated the development of the Self-Assessment and Process (SAIP), a tool designed to progressively articulate the Caux Principles. The SAIP is ultimately dialogical, focused on internal conversation and positive change. It offers a pathway towards enhanced corporate self-awareness, translating the aspirations articulated by the Caux Principles into detailed questions about company practices.

The SAIP allows senior leaders to 'score' the firm's conduct in relation to an acknowledged global standard for responsible behaviour. It helps the company to identify past patterns of behaviour and areas of strength and weakness. It also facilitates awareness of emerging concerns and issues, thus functioning as an early warning system for senior leaders. By promoting internal disclosure and effective oversight, the SAIP assists with such critical management tasks as communications, corporate control and strategic planning.

The net effect of the process is to strengthen confidence in management on the part of groups affected by the company's decisions and activities. The specific benefits that can accrue include enhanced loyalty on the part of customers and employees, and improved relationships with shareholders, union representatives, government officials and community leaders. Another benefit can be a positive assessment of the firm's stock price by analysts.

Perhaps even more vital, however, is the transformative journey that such self-appraisal represents. By pursuing self-awareness in this way, executives become more informed and enlightened. They are then in a position to undertake improvements in the spirit of the Caux Principles that will benefit corporate stakeholders.

The SAIP is structured around the Caux Principles. A company's performance against each of the seven general Caux Principles is evaluated from seven distinct perspectives: how well the firm has fulfilled the fundamental duties that flow from a principle, and how well it has realized the aspirations articulated by that principle in its relations with six stakeholders customers, employees, owners, suppliers, competitors and communities. The result is a 7-by-7 matrix of assessment criteria (see Table 17.1).

Table 17. 1 SAIP Assessment Criteria

Category	1 Funda- mental duties	2 Cust- omers	3 Empl- oyees	4 Owners /Investors	5 Suppliers /Partners	6 Compet- itors	7 Comm- unities
1. Responsibil- ities of business	Criterion 1.1	Criterion 1.2	Criterion 1.3	Criterion 1.4	Criterion 1.5	Criterion 1.6	Criterion 1.7
2. Economic and social impact of business	Criterion 2.1	Criterion 2.2	Criterion 2.3	Criterion 2.4	Criterion 2.5	Criterion 2.6	Criterion 2.7
3. Business behavior	Criterion 3.1	Criterion 3.2	Criterion 3.3	Criterion 3.4	Criterion 3.5	Criterion 3.6	Criterion 3.7
4. Respect for rules	Criterion 4.1	Criterion 4.2	Criterion 4.3	Criterion 4.4	Criterion 4.5	Criterion 4.6	Criterion 4.7
5. Support for multilateral trade	Criterion 5.1	Criterion 5.2	Criterion 5.3	Criterion 5.4	Criterion 5.5	Criterion 5.6	Criterion 5.7
6. Respect for the environment	Criterion 6.1	Criterion 6.2	Criterion 6.3	Criterion 6.4	Criterion 6.5	Criterion 6.6	Criterion 6.7
7. Avoidance of illicit operations	Criterion 7.1	Criterion 7.2	Criterion 7.3	Criterion 7.4	Criterion 7.5	Criterion 7.6	Criterion 7.7

To illustrate the use of the SAIP, let us consider a company's self-assessment regarding the general principle 'The Economic and Social Impact of Business' and a critical stakeholder group: customers. To perform this appraisal, the company must reflect on the assessment criterion contained in Table 17.1 and the five specific questions ('benchmarks') that amplify and elaborate this criterion (see Exhibit 17.1).

The SAIP identifies the maximum possible score a company can receive for its performance against these interrogatories. By comparing relevant data against a set of quantification guidelines, the firm can generate a score characterizing its current level of performance for this general principle and stakeholder group. By totalling the scores for all 49 cells, the company can generate an overall indication of its performance against the requirements of the Caux Principles.[9]

Exhibit 17.1 Company Score

Customers
How does the company contribute to the social well-being of its customers through its marketing and communications?
2.2.1 How does the company respect the integrity of the culture of its customers?
2.2.2 How does the company address situations where prevailing evidence deems a product harmful in any country? What role does disclosure play in this strategy?
2.2.3 How does the company provide remedies for customer dissatisfaction? Describe applicable mechanisms for redress through recalls, warranties, and claims procedures.
2.2.4 How does the company follow relevant consumer codes to protect vulnerable consumer groups?
2.2.5 What are the company's current levels and trends in key measures of product/service performance and applicability?

Box 1 some sample SAIP questions

The SAIP is modelled after the Malcolm Baldrige National Quality Award, a comprehensive and flexible process for measuring total quality. The Baldrige process represents some of the best thinking available today on self-assessment, incorporating feedback from business leaders, academics and corporate observers. The SAIP attempts to capture and capitalize on this thinking.

Self-knowledge Through Sharing

As corporations complete self-assessment journeys, journeys mapped by stakeholder co-ordinates, something much more than a 'score' will be the result.

For during such a process, if it is done honestly and carefully, a new kind of corporate mind-set is likely to emerge. Just as Plato's cave dweller found a less shadowy, more three-dimensional world at the conclusion of his upward trek, the company will come to see its policies and their implementation, as well as its measurements of progress, in a 'new light'.[10] Also, like the escapee from the cave, such a company may eventually want to share its experience with others.

We have seen how stakeholder thinking can be translated into a set of aspirational principles for guiding corporate conduct worldwide. And we have seen further (in the previous section) how a corporate self-assessment process (SAIP) using benchmarks can help to make aspirational principles more specific and more 'actionable'. Indeed, self-assessment based on credible benchmarks and measures can be a culturally transformative process-strengthening ethical integrity in organizations that undertake such an effort.

The significance of the self-awareness to which the SAIP gives rise can hardly be overstated. It gives senior leaders and employees throughout the organization a dispassionate, empirical and consciousness-raising profile of the company's ethical culture, rooted in policies, their implementation and their measurable results. Beyond consciousness-raising, such a self-assessment provides a platform for whatever future interventions may be necessary to improve the culture. Now, one of the key attributes of the SAIP is its *privacy* or company *confidentiality*. This attribute has many benefits, but it also has some costs that may lead organizations to pursue something less private – thereby changing *self-awareness* into something more, what we will call *self-knowledge*.

Benefits of a Private SAIP

The fact that the SAIP is conducted *privately* and *confidentially* by the companies that choose to use it is beneficial in many ways:

- It lowers the threshold of risk for companies to undertake the SAIP in the first place, because it does not involve revealing any negative findings that might publicly embarrass the company.[11]
- It encourages the use of otherwise confidential data in the assessment, increasing its candour and reliability.
- It allows for comparisons and contrasts between business units within a company, as well as between the same business units at different times, so long as the application of criteria and scoring are handled consistently.
- It systematically identifies areas in need of improvement and intervention by senior company leadership and/or the board.

Such benefits lower the risk and enhance the utility of the SAIP, leading to significant self-awareness. What (if anything), therefore, might encourage a corporation to consider an approach to this process that was less than fully private or confidential?

Costs of a Private SAIP

Such a question has an analogue in the lives of individuals: What, if anything, would encourage a person to consider less than fully private or confidential treatment of candid ethics-related information about himself or herself? The traditional answers to this question include:

- That sharing such information with others (or a least one other, such as an impartial counsellor or confessor) improves one's *perspective* on both the data and on underlying causes (think again of the cave allegory)
- That exchanging such information with others through dialogue allows one to benefit from the *experiences* of those others
- That self-assessment measures, if they are to have genuine *validity* and provide a basis for improvement, call for comparability across persons

These traditional observations about the 'downside' of privacy in the context of individual persons (loss of perspective, experience and validity) apply to organizations in natural ways. Corporations, like individuals, can lose perspective and exaggerate both positive and negative self-assessments. Without a counsellor or consultant familiar with other company self-assessments, it is difficult to get beyond the subjectivity of the self-scoring process. How a company stands ethically is difficult to discern unless there is some impartial quality control on the methods of measurement used. Privacy, while it may allow for comparability between old and new assessment scores for a given company, does not allow for comparability in scoring *across* companies.

Corporations, like individuals, can benefit enormously from sharing in the experiences of other corporations. Such 'best practices' dialogues benefit all parties, not only by providing a marketplace of ideas for improvement but also by providing motivation to 'stay the course'. How a company stands ethically in relation to other companies may influence its decisions about what and how to change over time.

Finally, corporations, like individuals, often benefit from third-party scrutiny in the conventional arenas of market competition and government regulation. Why should it be different in the arena of principled business conduct? But such third-party scrutiny, if it is to have any validity, depends on comparable, minimally subjective measures of corporate responsibility.

The fact that one company achieves a certain score and another company achieves a lower or higher score cannot, because of the subjectivity involved in the scoring process, reliably be used to draw any ethical comparisons between the two companies. And being able to demonstrate how it stands ethically in relation to other companies can be helpful to a company trying to defend itself against unreasonable charges of wrongful behaviour. So we can see that, if the SAIP is conducted privately and confidentially by the companies that choose to use it, there are certain benefits – and certain costs. The benefits have a lot to do with achieving self-awareness while lowering publicity risks and enhancing the completeness of the information base. The costs, as with personal privacy, are primarily opportunity costs – *perspective*, shared *experience* and third-party *validity*.[12]

It is our belief that, in the near term, most companies will value the benefits of privacy over its opportunity costs, but, in the long run, especially as the number of companies doing such self-assessment increases, they (and their investors) will become less interested in these benefits and more interested in what *shared* assessments make possible. The trend will be from corporate self-awareness to a more 'transparent' corporate self-knowledge.[13]

While we have not attempted here to explore the logic in the 'trend' just hypothesized (from privacy and corporate self-awareness to transparency and corporate self-knowledge), we believe it is consistent with and a natural outgrowth of developmental patterns in human behaviour. Moral maturity seems to carry with it a willingness for greater self-disclosure, once it becomes clear that such disclosure is a significant asset to the individual (or organization) involved.[14] Taking one's own 'moral inventory' leads naturally to a desire for feedback from (at least some) others, if only to gain perspective and insight into strategies and tactics for *responding* to the inventory (self-improvement). Research in social psychology would be required to support this hypothesis, of course.

From Decision Procedure to Cultural Discipline

It should be clear from the foregoing that the SAIP is not intended to be a decision procedure for business leaders. Rather, it is a transformative activity. It fosters greater ethical self-awareness and self-knowledge through internal and (ultimately) external dialogue and catalyses actions that strengthen and invigorate the conscience of the corporation. Using the SAIP, senior leaders and employees embark on a reflective journey that offers the possibility of changing not just how they view their own company, but how they understand the nature of business. A manager's conception of the human value added by the enterprise may shift as a result of insights garnered from the SAIP.

This returns us to a question implicit at the end of the first section: How is it possible, *if* it is possible, to avoid the paradoxes associated with stakeholder synthesis while still acknowledging the central importance of 'stakeholder thinking' in business ethics? Our excursion in the second section into the realm of organizational self-assessment promised certain benefits which in Plato's time would have been called *enlightenment*. But does the enlightenment fostered by the SAIP *remove* the paradoxes of stakeholder synthesis? In our view, the answer to this last question is *no*. The silver lining of this cloud may be that at the end of the day, the paradoxes do not *need* to be removed.

A Path Around Paradox

When we originally introduced the ideas of stakeholder analysis and synthesis, we said that any rational decision-making process included such steps as: (i) gathering information, (ii) sorting, (iii) weighing, (iv) integrating and, eventually, (v) acting on the processed information. The assumption behind the scenes was that, if stakeholder thinking was to enter into the decision-making of business executives, the most obvious point of entry was a *decision-making process*, a guideline invoked or applied whenever significant options presented themselves.

We saw fairly quickly, however, that the demands of a decision-making process included not only analysis but synthesis – and that the challenge of synthesis carried with it some barriers (paradoxes). We were not optimistic about finding an algorithm that gave proper weight to the interests and rights of *stockholders* and which then combined the weights of all stakeholders into some approximation to the *common good* in an increasingly global community.

We are now in a position to appreciate that the paradoxes emerge only if we insist that 'stakeholder thinking' be parsed as a decision-making process. But what if 'stake-holder thinking' entered into the ethical outlook and behaviour of an organization in a different way? What if, instead of providing a decision-making process, 'stakeholder thinking' was undertaken as a cultural discipline in a company, much as a periodic moral inventory is often part of the discipline of individuals? (See Figure 17.2)

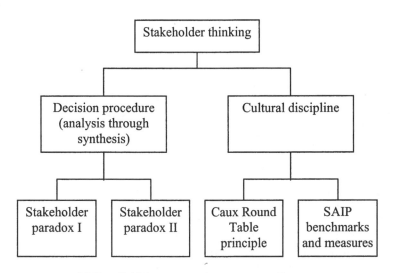

SAIP = Self Assessment Improvement Process

Figure 17.2   Perspectives on Stakeholder Thinking

Stakeholder Thinking as a Cultural Discipline

This is in fact the interpretation of 'stakeholder thinking' that permeated our discussion of the Caux Principles and the SAIP in the second section. The SAIP is not offered as a decision-making process. Instead, it functions as a cultural audit, a systematic review of a company's stakeholder awareness. Based on such a review, the company's leader ship can encourage informed dialogue aimed at improvement.

It has often been remarked that ethics in the modern (not to mention postmodern) period is preoccupied with decision-making, in contrast to the Greek and Mediaeval emphasis on character and virtue. The organizational analogue to this observation hints at why 'stakeholder thinking' might instinctively be interpreted as a decision procedure today. But the more classical approach to ethics, epitomized in a remark attributed to St Augustine – 'Love and do what you will!' – offers an alternative interpretation. Perhaps a cultural discipline aimed at stakeholder awareness provides a company's source of character or virtue, *without* a decision-making formula. Perhaps stockholders are properly served by companies with a fiduciary discipline, and perhaps the common good in an increasingly global community is also properly served.

Summary and Conclusion

We began this paper in search of an interpretation of 'stakeholder thinking' that might both clarify the idea and make it practical. Instead, we discovered that there were some significant barriers (paradoxes) to both clarification and practicality. We then offered an account of a transcultural set of ethical principles (the Caux Principles) for business organizations, along with a Self-Assessment and Improvement Process that enables a company to understand very concretely how it measures up to these principles.

The SAIP actually served two purposes at once. It helped us to institutionalize the idea of conscience or 'moral insight' through a progressive articulation of general ethical principles. And it offered us an alternative interpretation of 'stakeholder thinking' as a cultural discipline, less vulnerable to paradox, through a Socratic process reminiscent of Plato's cave allegory.

The direction of business enterprise in the 21st century is clearly towards globalization, which means that the concept of corporate citizenship is undergoing fundamental change. We know that citizenship, to be meaningful, presupposes a *community* with a *common good*. Business ethics in this new century, therefore, calls for a culture of corporate citizenship with a *global* perspective on the common good. We hope our pursuit of 'stakeholder thinking' beyond paradox to practicality helps respond to this call.

Appendix

The Caux Round Table Principles: Business Behaviour for a Better World

Section 1: Preamble

The mobility of employment, capital, products and technology is making business increasingly global in its transactions and its effects. Laws and market forces are necessary but insufficient guides for conduct. Responsibility for the policies and actions of business and respect for the dignity and interests of its stakeholders are fundamental. Shared values, including a commitment to shared prosperity, are as important for a global community as for communities of smaller scale. For these reasons, and because business can be a powerful agent of positive social change, we offer the following principles as a foundation for dialogue and action by business leaders in search of business responsibility. In so doing, we affirm the necessity for moral values in economic decision-making. Without them, stable business relationships and a sustainable world community are impossible.

Section 2: General Principles

Principle 1. The responsibilities of corporations: beyond shareholders towards stakeholders

The value of a business to society is the wealth and employment it creates and the marketable products and services it provides to consumers at a reasonable price commensurate with quality. To create such value, a business must maintain its own economic health and vitality, but survival is not a sufficient goal. Businesses have a role to play in improving the lives of all of their customers, employees and shareholders by sharing with them the wealth it has created. Suppliers and competitors as well should expect businesses to honour their obligations in a spirit of honesty and fairness. As responsible citizens of the local, national, regional and global communities in which they operate, businesses share a part in shaping the future of those communities.

Principle 2. The economic and social impact of corporations: towards innovation, justice and world community

Businesses established in foreign countries to develop, produce or sell should also contribute to the social advancement of those countries by creating productive employment and helping to raise the purchasing power of their citizens. Businesses should also contribute to human rights, education, welfare and vitalization of the countries in which they operate. Businesses should contribute to economic and social development not only in the countries in which they operate but also in the world community at large, through effective and prudent use of resources, free and fair competition, and emphasis on innovation in technology, production methods, marketing and communications.

Principle 3. Corporate behaviour: beyond the letter of law towards a spirit of trust

While accepting the legitimacy of trade secrets, businesses should recognize that sincerity, candour, truthfulness, the keeping of promises, and transparency contribute not only to their own credibility and stability but also to the smoothness and efficiency of business transactions, particularly on the international level.

Principle 4. Respect for rules: beyond trade friction towards co-operation

To avoid trade frictions and promote freer trade, equal conditions for competition, and fair and equitable treatment for all participants, businesses should respect international and domestic rules. In addition, they should recognize that some behaviour, although legal, may still have adverse consequences.

Principle 5. Support for multilateral trade: beyond isolation towards world community Businesses should support the multilateral trade system of the World Trade Organization and similar international agreements. They should co-operate in efforts to promote the progressive and judicious liberalization of trade and to relax those domestic measures that unreasonably hinder global commerce, while giving due respect to national policy objectives.

Principle 6. Respect for the environment: beyond protection towards enhancement

A business should protect, and, where possible, improve the environment, promote sustainable development, and prevent the wasteful use of natural resources.

Principle 7. Avoidance of illicit operations: beyond profit towards peace

A corporation should not participate in or condone bribery, money-laundering and other corrupt practices; indeed, it should seek co-operation with others to eliminate them. It should not trade in arms or materials used for terrorist activities, drug traffic or other organized crime.

Section 3: Stakeholder Principles

Customers. We believe in treating all customers with dignity, irrespective of whether they purchase our products and services directly or otherwise acquire them in the market. We therefore have a responsibility to

- Provide our customers with the highest-quality products and services consistent with their requirements

- Treat our customers fairly in all aspects of our business transactions, including a high level of service and remedies for customer dissatisfaction
- Make every effort to ensure that the health and safety of our customers, as well as the quality of their environment, will be sustained or enhanced by our products or services
- Assure respect for human dignity in products offered, marketing and advertising
- Respect the integrity of the culture of our customers

Employees. We believe in the dignity of every employee and in taking employee interests seriously. We therefore have a responsibility to

- Provide jobs and compensation that improve workers' living conditions
- Provide working conditions that respect employees' health and dignity
- Be honest in communications with employees and open in sharing information, limited only by legal and competitive constraints
- Listen to and, where possible, act on employee suggestions, ideas, requests and complaints
- Engage in good-faith negotiations when conflict arises
- Avoid discriminatory practices and guarantee equal treatment and opportunity in areas such as gender, age, race and religion
- Promote in the business itself the employment of differently abled people in places of work where they can be genuinely useful
- Protect employees from avoidable injury and illness in the workplace
- Be sensitive to the serious unemployment problems frequently associated with business decisions, and work with governments, employee groups, other agencies and each other in addressing these dislocations

Owners/investors. We believe in honouring the trust our investors place in us. We there fore have a responsibility to

- Apply professional and diligent management in order to secure a fair and competitive return on our owners' investment
- Disclose relevant information to owners/investors subject only to legal and competitive constraints
- Conserve, protect and increase the owners'/investors' assets
- Respect owners'/investors' requests, suggestions, complaints and formal resolutions

Suppliers. Our relationship with suppliers and subcontractors must be based on mutual respect. We therefore have a responsibility to

- Seek fairness and truthfulness in all our activities including pricing, licensing and rights to sell

- Ensure that our business activities are free from coercion and unnecessary litigation
- Foster long-term stability in the supplier relationship in return for value, quality, competitiveness and reliability
- Share information with suppliers and integrate them into our planning processes
- Pay suppliers on time and in accordance with agreed terms of trade
- Seek, encourage and prefer suppliers and subcontractors whose employment practices respect human dignity

Competitors. We believe that fair economic competition is one of the basic requirements for increasing the wealth of nations and ultimately for making possible the just distribution of goods and services. We therefore have a responsibility to

- Foster open markets for trade and investment
- Promote competitive behaviour that is socially and environmentally beneficial and demonstrates mutual respect among competitors
- Refrain from either seeking or participating in questionable payments or favours to secure competitive advantages
- Respect both tangible and intellectual property rights
- Refuse to acquire commercial information by dishonest or unethical means, such as industrial espionage

Communities. We believe that as global corporate citizens we can contribute to such forces of reform and human rights as are at work in the communities in which we operate. We therefore have a responsibility in those communities to

- Respect human rights and democratic institutions, and promote them wherever practical
- Recognize government's legitimate obligation to the society at large and support public policies and practices that promote human development through harmonious relations between business and other segments of society
- Collaborate with those forces in the community dedicated to raising standards of health, education, economic well being and workplace safety
- Promote and stimulate sustainable development and play a lead role in preserving the physical environment and conserving the Earth's resources
- Support peace, security, diversity and social integration
- Respect the integrity of local cultures
- Be a good citizen through charitable donations, educational and cultural contributions, and employee participation in community and civic affairs

Acknowledgement

For this paper permission has been taken from the Editor, *Journal of Corporate Citizenship*, vol. 7, Greenleaf Publishing, England, Autumn 2002.

Notes

1   The inadequacy, as will become apparent, stems from several sources: (a) mistaking stakeholder analysis and stakeholder synthesis; (b) mistaking partial and impartial stakeholder synthesis; (c) mistaking fiduciary and non-fiduciary responsibility; and (d) mistaking constituency-based thinking and moral reflection based on the common good.

2   It is therefore a mistake to see it as a substitute for normative ethical thinking.

3   Were this kind of synthesis to be adopted in a business organization, stakeholders (or at least those outside the stockholder group) would be viewed instrumentally, as factors that might advance the corporation's interests. *Moral* concern would avoid injury or unfairness to those affected by one's actions because it is wrong, regardless of the retaliatory potential of the aggrieved parties.

4   See 'Stakeholder Paradox' in the revised and expanded 2001 edition of Lawrence Becker and Charlotte Becker (eds.), *The Encyclopedia of Ethics* (Becker and Becker 2001).

5   The way out of the paradox seems to lie in understanding the conscience of the corporation as a logical and moral extension of the consciences of its principals. It is not an *expansion* of the list of principals, but a gloss on the principal–agent relationship itself. Whatever the structure of the principal–agent relationship, neither principal nor agent can claim 'moral immunity' from the basic obligations that apply to any human being (or human organization) towards other members of the community.

6   'Putting together the clues that St Thomas [Aquinas] has left ... shows that the common good specifically rules out a number of prospects licensed by utilitarianism and insists on things that contractarianism at best brings in as contingent super additions to the basic plan of justice' (Braybrooke and Monahan 1992:175).

7   For a more thorough discussion of this point and a description of a model of the firm based on the concept of the common good, see Chapter 2 of Helen J. Alford and Michael J. Naughton, *Managing as if Faith Mattered* (Alford and Naughton 2001).

8   In language and form, the Minnesota Principles provided the substantial basis for the Caux Round Table Principles for Business. To obtain a copy of the Minnesota Principles, contact the Center for Ethical Business Cultures (CEBC), Minneapolis, Minnesota, http://www.cebcglobal.org.

9   The maximum possible score of the SAIP is 1,000 points. The SAIP scorecard indicates how this total is allocated across the General Principles and, within a given principle, to each stakeholder. In other words, it highlights the

maximum possible score that a company can receive for its performance against each principle and how these points are distributed across the seven distinct perspectives represented within the self-assessment. These allocations involve differential weightings of the criteria.

10 To quote Plato again: '[M]y opinion is that in the world of knowledge the idea of good appears last of all and is seen only with an effort; and, when seen, is also inferred to be the universal author of all things beautiful and right, parent of light and of the lord of light in this visible world and the immediate source of reason and truth in the intellectual; and that this is the power upon which he who would act rationally either in public or private life must have his eye fixed' (Plato, *The Republic*, Book VII:517).

11 It may also lower the risk of involuntary exposure due to legal discovery interventions, since the process is carried on with some degree of attorney–client privilege.

12 To return to Plato's *Allegory*, the way out of the cave involved dialogue and discovery, eventually a more substantial kind of knowledge than the shadows on the wall permitted.

13 The litigation environment, of course, could negatively influence this trend.

14 Within Cummins Engine Company, one time-honoured guideline for addressing ethical problems states that 'facts are friendly'. It suggests that an accurate and fair description of the situation in question, however painful or embarrassing, will help the company resolve such matters consistent with its ethical obligations. The maxim indicates a level of moral maturity where self-disclosure is embraced as a virtue, one the organization should exercise and cultivate.

References

Alford, H.J. and M.J. Naughton (2001) *Managing as if Faith Mattered*, Notre Dame, IN: University of Notre Dame.

Becker, L.C. and C.B. Becker (eds) (2001) *The Encyclopedia of Ethics*, (New York: Garland Publishing, rev. edn.

Braybrooke, D. and A. Monahan (1992) 'Common Good', in L.C. Becker and C.B. Becker (eds), *The Encyclopedia of Ethics*, New York: Garland Publishing: p.175.

Freeman, R.E. (1984) *Strategic Management: A Stakeholder Approach*, Boston, MA: Pitman Publishing: pp.52-82.

Goodpaster, K.E. (1998) 'Bridging East and West in Management Ethics: Kyosei and the Moral Point of View', in K.E. Goodpaster, L.L. Nash and J.B. Matthews (eds), *Policies and Persons: A Casebook in Business Ethics*, New York: McGraw-Hill, 3rd edn.: pp.529-39.

Jowett, B. (1920) *The Republic, The Dialogues of Plato, Book VII*; New York: Random House: pp.773-800.

Kaku, R. (1997) 'The Path of Kyosei', *Harvard Business Review*, 75(4) July/August: 55-63.

Naughton, M., H. Alford and B. Brady (1996) 'The Common Good and the Purpose of the Firm: A Critique of the Shareholder and Stakeholder Models from the Catholic Social Tradition', in J. Donahue and M.T. Moser (eds), *Religion, Ethics and the Common Good*, Mystic, CT: Twenty-Third Publications: pp.206-35.

Royce, J. (1885) *The Religious Aspects of Philosophy: A Critique of the Bases of Conduct and of Faith*, Gloucester, MA: Peter Smith: pp.131-70.

Selznick, P. (1957) *Leadership in Administration: A Sociological Interpretation*, New York: Harper and Row: pp.21-22.

Chapter 18

Re-placing People in Organizational Activity

David Crowther and Miriam Green

Creating Shareholder Value

One of the principal foci, in recent years, of organizational activity has been a concern with the creation of shareholder value. This concern has been predicated in the rationale, based upon the legal position, that organizations are actually owned by their shareholders and therefore owe a duty to them and to no-one else. Essentially this is a removal of people from the concern of the organization, as the only concern has become shareholder value. This is not of course a new concept, as finance theory has long assumed that the primary objective of the firm is to maximize shareholder wealth, and that a firm will seek to achieve this by making decisions which create shareholder value.

In doing so companies, however, often pay lip-service to a concern for other stakeholders while acting as if their only concern is for the creation of shareholder value, no matter how it is created. Indeed in recent years, there has been a shift towards a more explicit shareholder value oriented approach to managing a business, which has become known as Shareholder Value Management (SVM) or Value-Based Management (VBM). VBM has been defined as

> ... an approach to management whereby the company's overall aspiration, analytical techniques and management processes are all aligned to help the company maximise its value by focusing on the key drivers of value. (Copeland, Koller and Murrin, 1996, p.96)

SVM is an approach to managing an organization which requires a change in the way decisions are made from the way they are normally made. It is for this reason that it has been classed as a programmed change initiative – not because it is a way of managing change but rather because it is a way of managing a business which results in change. It is based simply upon the premise that all actions within the organization must be made based upon the desire to maximize shareholder value. Thus it requires the application of appropriate measures of value to provide a 'shareholder value' perspective for all key internal planning and control systems: strategic decision-making, resource allocation, performance measurement and control and managerial compensation.

The proponents of shareholder value techniques would argue that the use of the techniques by an organization will inevitably lead to better performance by that organization, both for shareholders and for other stakeholders. Thus this implies a different approach to management and therefore a change in organizational behaviour as it also requires the application of appropriate measures of value to provide a 'shareholder value' perspective for all key internal planning and control systems: i.e. strategic decision-making, resource allocation, performance measurement and control and managerial compensation. An important, if not fundamental, feature of all VBM approaches is this alignment of objectives, measures, and rewards intended to promote shareholder value creation at all levels of the business. Advocates of VBM techniques have advanced strong claims on its behalf, the chief of which is that its use will lead to the creation of shareholder value.

As stated above, finance theory suggests that the primary objective of the firm is to maximize shareholder wealth. It has been argued that the pursuit of this objective not only benefits shareholders but also maximizes, through the natural workings of the free market, the value created in a business for other stakeholders. There has been, however, increasing debate on the validity of this argument and it has been suggested that shareholder value is in fact actually maximized through an expropriation of value from the other stakeholders to the business. This is to say that if shareholder value is maximized then this must be at the expense of the other stakeholders such as employees, consumers, government, and community / society. If this latter view is accepted then it has been further argued that firms are behaving unethically. There has therefore been an increased interest in ethics and stakeholder management theory as a result, which suggests that the firm should be managed with reference to the needs of all of the different stakeholders. However, despite the attention stakeholders have received in theory, there appears to be limited work, which has suggested how stakeholder management can be achieved and would work in practice.

Theorizing Organizational Behaviour

Most organizational theory takes the view, as far as an organization is concerned, that the only activities with which the organization should be concerned are those which take place within the organization, or between the organization and its direct stakeholders – employees, suppliers or customers. This view places the organization at the centre of its world and the only interfaces with the external world take place at the beginning and end of its value chain. These interfaces comprise of, at the commencement of the organizational processing cycle, resources acquisition (raw materials, labour capital etc) and, at the end of the cycle, selling its wares (goods or services) and distributing a share of the value created through its transformational process to its owners (ie shareholders). This view is essentially concerned with the transformational process within the organization, and the management of that transformational process.

A growing number of writers (see Crowther 2002a) however have recognized that the activities of an organization impact upon the external environment. Such a suggestion first arose in the 1970s and a concern with a wider view of company performance is taken by some writers who evince concern with the social performance of a business, as a member of society at large. This concern was stated by Ackerman (1975) who argued that big business was recognizing the need to adapt to a new social climate of community accountability but that the orientation of business to financial results was inhibiting social responsiveness. McDonald and Puxty (1979) on the other hand maintain that companies are no longer the instruments of shareholders alone but exist within society and so therefore have responsibilities to that society, and that there is therefore a shift towards the greater accountability of companies to all participants.

Alongside this recognition that corporations are accountable to their stakeholders has come a development of the principles upon which this demonstration of accountability should be based. Inevitably this is predicated in accounting as a mechanism by which such action can be measured and reported. In generic terms this has come to be called either social or environmental accounting. The objective of environmental accounting is to measure the effects of the actions of the organization upon the environment and to report upon those effects. In other words the objective is to incorporate the effect of the activities of the firm upon externalities and to view the firm as a network which extends beyond just the internal environment to include the whole environment (see Crowther 2000b, 2002a). In this view of the organization the accounting for the firm does not stop at the organizational boundary but extends beyond to include not just the business environment in which it operates but also the whole social environment. Environmental accounting therefore adds a new dimension to the role of accounting for an organization because of its emphasis upon accounting for external effects of the organization's activities. In doing so this provides a recognition that the organization is an integral part of society, rather than a self contained entity which has only an indirect relationship with society at large. This self-containment has been the traditional view taken by an organization as far as their relationship with society at large is concerned, with interaction being only by means of resource acquisition and sales of finished products or services. Recognition of this closely intertwined relationship of mutual interdependency between the organization and society at large, when reflected in the accounting of the organization, can help bring about a closer, and possibly more harmonious, relationship between the organization and society. Given that the managers and workers of an organization are also stakeholders in that society in other capacities, such as consumers, citizens and inhabitants, this reinforces the mutual interdependency.

It is apparent that any actions which an organization undertakes will have an effect not just upon itself but also upon the external environment within which that organization resides. In considering the effect of the organization upon its external environment it must be recognized that this environment includes both the business environment in which the firm is operating, the local societal environment in which the organization is located and the wider global environment. This effect of the organization can take many forms, such as

- the utilization of natural resources as a part of its production processes;
- the effects of competition between itself and other organizations in the same market;
- the enrichment of a local community through the creation of employment opportunities;
- the distribution of wealth created within the firm to the owners of that firm (via dividends) and the workers of that firm (through wages) and the effect of this upon the welfare of individuals;
- transformation of the landscape due to raw material extraction or waste product storage.

It can be seen from these examples that an organization can have a very significant effect upon its external environment and can actually change that environment through its activities. It can also be seen that these different effects can in some circumstances be viewed as beneficial and in other circumstances as detrimental to the environment. Indeed the same actions can be viewed as beneficial by some people and detrimental by others.[1] This is why planning enquiries or tribunals, which are considering the possible effects of the proposed actions by a firm, will find people who are in favour and people who are opposed. This is of course because the evaluation of the effects of the actions of an organization upon its environment are viewed and evaluated differently by different people.

The Principles of Environmentalism

There are three basic principles to environmentalism – sustainability, accountability and transparency.

Sustainability

Sustainability is concerned with the effect which action taken in the present has upon the options available in the future. If resources are utilized in the present then they are no longer available for use in the future, and this is of particular concern if the resources are finite in quantity. Thus raw materials of an extractive nature, such as coal, iron or oil, are finite in quantity and once used are not available for future use. At some point in the future therefore alternatives will be needed to fulfil the functions currently provided by these resources. This may be at some point in the relatively distant future but of more immediate concern is the fact that as resources become depleted then the cost of acquiring the remaining resources tends to increase, and hence the operational costs of organizations tend to increase.[2]

Sustainability therefore implies that society must use no more of a resource than can be regenerated. This can be defined in terms of the carrying capacity of the ecosystem (Hawken 1993) and described with input – output models of resource consumption. Thus the paper industry for example has a policy of replanting trees to replace those harvested and this has the effect of retaining costs in the present rather than temporally externalizing them. Similarly motor vehicle manufacturers such as Volkswagen have a policy of making their cars almost totally recyclable. Viewing an organization as part of a wider social and economic system implies that these effects must be taken into account, not just for the measurement of costs and value created in the present but also for the future of the business itself.

Measures of sustainability would consider the rate at which resources are consumed by the organization in relation to the rate at which resources can be regenerated. Unsustainable operations can be accommodated for either by developing sustainable operations or by planning for a future lacking in resources currently required. In practice organizations mostly tend to aim towards less unsustainability by increasing efficiency in the way in which resources are utilized. An example would be an energy efficiency programme.

The Development of Stakeholder Approaches

Implicit in a concern with the effects of the actions of an organization on its external environment is the recognition that it is not just the owners of the organization who have a concern with the activities of that organization. Additionally there are a wide variety of other stakeholders who justifiably have a concern with those activities, and are affected by those activities. Those other stakeholders have not just an interest in the activities of the firm but also a degree of influence over the shaping of those activities. This influence is so significant that it can be argued that the power and influence of these stakeholders is such that it amounts to quasi-ownership of the organization. Indeed Gray, Owen and Maunders (1987) challenge the traditional role of accounting in reporting results and consider that, rather than an ownership approach to accountability, a stakeholder approach, recognizing the wide stakeholder community, is needed.[3]

The desirability of considering the social performance of a business has not always however been accepted and has been the subject of extensive debate. Thus Hetherington (1973: 37) states

> There is no reason to think that shareholders are willing to tolerate an amount of corporate non-profit activity which appreciably reduces either dividends or the market performance of the stock.

While Dahl (1972: 18) states

> ... every large corporation should be thought of as a social enterprise; that is an entity whose existence and decisions can be justified insofar as they serve public or social purposes.

Nevertheless the performance of businesses in a wider arena than the stock market and its value to shareholders has become of increasing concern. Gray, Owen and Maunders (1987) consider social reporting in terms of responsibility and accountability. Gray (1992) argues that there is a need for a new paradigm with the environment being considered as part of the firm rather than as an externality and with sustainability and the use of primary resources being given increased weighting. Rubenstein (1992) goes further and argues that there is a need for a new social contract between a business and the stakeholders to which it is accountable.

Environmentalism provides an explicit recognition that stakeholders other than the legal owners of the organization have power and influence over that organization and also have a right to extend their influence into affecting the organization's activities. This includes the managers and workers of the organization who are also stakeholders in other capacities. Environmentalism therefore provides a mechanism for transferring some of the power from the organization to these stakeholders and this voluntary surrender of such power by the organization can actually provide benefits to the organization. Benefits from increased disclosure and the adoption of environmental accounting can provide further benefits to the organization in its operational performance, beyond this enhanced relationship with society at large.

Accountability

Accountability is concerned with an organization recognizing that its actions affect the external environment, and therefore assuming responsibility for the effects of its actions. This concept therefore implies a quantification of the effects of actions taken, both internal to the organization and externally. More specifically the concept implies a reporting of those quantifications to all parties affected by those actions. This implies a reporting to external stakeholders of the effects of actions taken by the organization and how they are affecting those stakeholders. This concept therefore implies a recognition that the organization is part of a wider societal network and has responsibilities to all of that network rather than just to the owners of the organization. Alongside this acceptance of responsibility therefore must be a recognition that those external stakeholders have the power to affect the way in which those actions of the organization are taken and a role in deciding whether or not such actions can be justified, and if so at what cost to the organization and to other stakeholders.

Accountability therefore necessitates the development of appropriate measures of environmental performance and the reporting of the actions of the firm. This necessitates costs on the part of the organization in developing, recording and reporting such performance and to be of value the benefits must exceed the costs. Benefits must be determined by the usefulness of the measures selected to the decision-making process and by the way in which they facilitate resource allocation, both within the organization and between it and other stakeholders. Such reporting needs to be based upon the following characteristics:

- understandability to all parties concerned;
- relevance to the users of the information provided;
- reliability in terms of accuracy of measurement, representation of impact and freedom from bias;
- comparability, which implies consistency, both over time and between different organizations.

Inevitably however such reporting will involve qualitative facts and judgements as well as quantifications. This qualitativeness will inhibit comparability over time and will tend to mean that such impacts are assessed differently by different users of the information, reflecting their individual values and priorities. A lack of precise understanding of effects, coupled with the necessarily judgmental nature of relative impacts, means that few standard measures exist. This in itself restricts the inter-organization comparison of such information.

Transparency

Transparency, as a principle, means that the external impact of the actions of the organization can be ascertained from that organization's reporting and pertinent facts are not disguised within that reporting. Thus all the effects of the actions of the organization, including external impacts, should be apparent to all from using the information provided by the organization's reporting mechanisms. Transparency is of particular importance to external stakeholders as these users the background details and knowledge available to internal users of such information. Transparency therefore can be seen to follow from the other two principles and equally can be seen to be a part of the process of recognition of responsibility on the part of the organization for the external effects of its actions and equally part of the process of transferring power to external stakeholders.

The Development of Social Accountability

Recognition of the rights of all stakeholders and the duty of a business to be accountable in this wider context therefore has been largely a relatively recent phenomenon.[4] The economic view of accountability only to owners has only recently been subject to debate to any considerable extent.

The performance of businesses in a wider arena than the stock market and its value to shareholders has become of increasing concern. Fetyko (1975) considers social accounting as an approach to reporting a firm's activities and stresses the need for identification of socially relevant behaviour, the determination of those to whom the company is accountable for its social performance and the development of appropriate measures and reporting techniques. Klein (1977) also considers social accounting and recognizes that different aspects of performance are of interest to different stakeholder groupings, distinguishing for example between investors, community relations and philanthropy as areas of concern for accounting. While these writers consider, by implication, that measuring social performance is important without giving reasons for believing so, Solomons (1974) considers the reasons for measuring objectively the social performance of a business. He suggests that while one reason is to aid rational decision making, another reason is of a defensive nature.

Social Responsibility and Organizational Performance

There have been many claims that the quantification of environmental effects and costs, and the inclusion of such costs into business strategies, can significantly reduce operating costs by firms; indeed this was one of the main themes of the 1996 Global Environmental Management Initiative Conference. Little evidence exists that this is the case but Pava and Krausz (1996) demonstrate empirically that companies which they define as 'socially responsible' perform in financial terms at least as well as companies which are not socially responsible.[5] Similarly in other countries efforts are being made to provide a framework for the quantification of environmental effects (Abreu and David 2003) and the certification of accountants who wish to be considered as environmental practitioners and auditors.[6] Azzone, Manzini and Noci (1996) however suggest that despite the lack of any regulatory framework in this area a degree of standardization, at least as far as reporting is concerned, is beginning to emerge at an international level. If this is the case then it can be expected to become reflected in the regulatory frameworks at national levels in due course. It can equally be argued that firms which regard themselves as successful can afford to devote more effort towards being socially responsible as they progress upwards through a form of Maslow's hierarchy.

Jones (1996) suggests that any method of managing for biodiversity should be based upon the concept of stewardship rather than ownership. Similarly Ranganathan and Ditz (1996) state that when environmental issues are quantified they are more likely to be included in the business decision-making process and can therefore help to improve the performance of firms. As well as a concern with environmental effects from the point of view of the internal use of such information for decision making purposes, of equal concern is the use of environmental information for external reporting purposes. In this respect it can be argued that the incorporation of environmental information into the annual reports of firms reflects the concern with the wider scope of organizational activity. Such concern can be seen to be reflected in the discourse concerning environmental issues which is taking place in society at large and is reflected in the media. Equally however it can be argued that the inclusion of such information into the corporate reporting system, as manifest in the annual reports, is a reflection of the desire of firms, and their managers, to address a wider audience through their reports. This wider audience can be considered to be those members of society at large who are concerned with the environment and with environmental issues. This will include environmental pressure groups and their individual members as well as other individual members of society. At one level it can be argued that this reflects a recognition by the firm and its managers that the wider external stakeholder community has an interest in the firm and the effect of its actions upon the environment.

At another level however it can be argued that these individual members of society, whether members of environmental pressure groups or not, also may be stakeholders in the firm in other roles; for example they may well be customers, or potential customers, or suppliers or employees. As stakeholders may well have multiple roles in their interaction with an organization it becomes impossible to separate out the reasons for an organization desiring to increase the extent of its environmental concern Nevertheless, as Jones (1996) reports, the extent of environmental reporting, in terms of the number of firms engaged in such reporting, has grown rapidly since 1990 and continues to grow. Similarly KPMG (an internationally known management consultancy firm) (Management Accounting 1996) confirm this growth in environmental reporting but state that it differs considerably in terms of just what is reported. They argue that a lack of standards, coupled with an uncertainty as to whom such reporting is directed, has led to this wide variation in environmental reporting. Gamble, Hsu, Jackson and Tollerson (1996) on the other hand argue, based upon empirical research, that environmental reporting is not increasing in coverage but that there are national differences. Beaver (1989) however has identified some changing trends in reporting and highlights a rapid growth in reporting requirements and changes in existing requirements, while Eccles (1991) concurs.[7]

Corporate Social Responsibility

There appears to have been a resurgence of public interest and concern about the environment in recent years. These concerns have led to the general opinion that there is something different about environmental information which deserves reporting in its own right rather than being subsumed within the general corporate reporting and lost in the organization-centric norm of corporate reporting. This opinion is based upon a recognition that

> The environment (which is a free resource to individual businesses) is increasingly being turned into a factor that does carry costs. Primarily as a result of requirements imposed by current or probable future government regulation on pollution control, but also to some extent because of the wider concern of the public, who can affect a business's profitability by their behaviour as consumers, employees, and investors, there is a financial impact that needs to be accounted for. (Butler, Frost and Macve, 1992: 60)

This general concern with social and environmental effects of organizational activity has recently become known as Corporate Social Responsibility (CSR). CSR has gained prominence in recent years (Abreu *et al.* 2003) in practically every sector of society: this includes business, civil society, and other areas. Actually defining CSR is however difficult as it is a broad and elastic concept. The concept continues to expand to embrace new problems associated with corporate activities.

For example, some topical problems which are today associated with corporate activities (e.g. global warming) were virtually unknown to the corporate world in the early days of the concept. The fragmented and elastic nature of CSR means that any problems that are remotely connected with corporate activity can properly be brought within the ambit of the concept. Thus, not only is CSR concerned with the company's relationship with its employees, its consumers and others in close proximity with the company, as might have been thought in the early days of the concept, but it also encompasses such new corporate problems as the exploitation of child labour, which implicates corporate activity located thousands of miles away from the problem.

From Social Accountability to Corporate Social Responsibility

In recent years the concept of corporate social responsibility (CSR) has gained prominence to such an extent that the concept seems ubiquitous in popular media and is gaining a increasing attention among academics from a wide range of disciplines. There are probably many reasons for the attention given to this phenomenon not least of which is the corporate excesses of recent times. For many people, particularly in the Western world the year 2002 was the one in which corporate misbehaviour was exposed by the collapse of some large corporations. In particular the spectacular collapse of Enron and the subsequent fallout among the financial world – including the firm which Arthur Andersen himself founded in 1913 – will have left an indelible impression among people that all is not well with the corporate world and that there are problems which need to be addressed (Crowther and Rayman-Bacchus 2003a). This will be particularly the case amongst those adversely affected by this collapse, not least of whom are the former employees of the company who have lost their jobs, their life savings and their future pensions. Equally remembered however in other parts of the world are other events such as the Union Carbide incident in Bhopal, India – the worst pollution incident in the history of the world. This incident killed thousands, left thousands permanently injured and an even greater number living a life of misery in the area surrounding the former plant. To date not one penny has been paid in compensation to those whose lives have been blighted by an incident caused by the lack of safety precautions which would be required in the Western world and which any socially responsible organization would implement as a matter of course.

Issues of socially responsible behaviour are not of course new and examples can be found from throughout the world and at least from the earliest days of the Industrial Revolution and the concomitant founding of large business entities (Crowther 2002a), and the divorce between ownership and management – or the divorcing of risk from rewards (Crowther 2003). But corporate social responsibility is back on the agenda of corporations, governments and individual citizens throughout the world.

This raises the question as to what exactly can be considered to be corporate social responsibility. According to the EU Commission [(2002) 347 final: 5]

> ... CSR is a concept whereby companies integrate social and environmental concerns in their business operations and in their interaction with their stakeholders on a voluntary basis.

The Social Contract

All definitions of CSR seem to be based upon a concern with more than profitability and returns to shareholders. Indeed involving other stakeholders, and considering them in decision making is a central platform of CSR. Stakeholder management is based upon a consideration of all stakeholders. Numerous definitions of a stakeholder have been provided within the literature and Sternberg (1997) demonstrates that Freeman (1984)[8] has used multiple definitions. A stakeholder managed organization therefore attempts to consider the diverse and conflicting interests of its stakeholders and balance these interests equitably. The motivations for organizations to use stakeholder management maybe in order to improve financial performance or social or ethical performance howsoever these may be measured. In order to be able to adequately manage stakeholder interests it is necessary to measure the organization's performance to these stakeholders and this can prove complicated and time-consuming.

One issue which arises from this concern for stakeholders is the extent to which we can assess the accountability of organizations to a broader constituency by reference to an implicit or hypothetical social contract. In the process it is attempted to show how social contract theory also helps bind the relationship between corporate social responsibility and ethical behaviour. This raises questions about the scope and depth of commitment among corporate leaders to social responsibility. Assessing this commitment is difficult given what appears at present to be an unrestricted free market ideology: a belief system that seems to be elevating the corporation above the nation state, and is being transmitted through corporate global expansion and USA led government sponsorship. This can be developed in the context of the globalizing process by considering the extent to which corporate and social exploitation of Internet technology is helping both corporate bodies and consumer and citizens transform our world into a global village and then broadened to consider the broader relationship between technological innovation and social change. In examining this relationship it can be shown that technological development is underpinned by a utilitarian perspective, and at the same time technological change is unavoidably bound up with making moral choices.

The broadest definition of corporate social responsibility is concerned with what is – or should be – the relationship between the global corporation, governments of countries and individual citizens. More locally the definition is concerned with the relationship between a corporation and the local society in which it resides or operates. Another definition is concerned with the relationship between a corporation and its stakeholders. For us all of these definitions are pertinent and represent a dimension of the issue. All involve re-placing people in the concerns of organizations. A parallel debate is taking place in the arena of ethics – should corporations be controlled through increased regulation or has the ethical base of citizenship been lost and needs replacing before socially responsible behaviour will ensue? In the UK at the present the government seems to believe that citizenship needs teaching to our school children, presumably in the belief that this will manifest itself in the behaviour of corporations in the future. However this debate is represented it seems that it is concerned with some sort of social contract between corporations and society.

Replacing People

This social contract implies some form of altruistic behaviour – the converse of selfishness. Self-interest connotes selfishness, and since the Middle Ages has informed a number of important philosophical, political and economic propositions. Among these is Hobbes's world where unfettered self-interest is expected to lead to social devastation. A high degree of regulation is prescribed in order to avoid such a disastrous outcome, but in the process we sacrifice our rights. Self-interest also reappears in the utilitarian perspective of Bentham, Locke and J. S. Mill. The latter for example advocated as morally right the pursuit of the greatest happiness for the greatest number. Similarly Adam Smith's free-market economics, is predicated on competing self-interest. These influential ideas put interest of the individual above interest of the collective. Indeed from this perspective, collective interests are best served through self-interest. At the same time this corporate self-interest has come to draw disapproval in modern times and the moral value of individualism has all but vanished.

The increasing concern being given to social responsibility is a reaction against the individualistic ethos of the 1980s. Individualism, which led to the greed of this era, is based upon the philosophy of Classical Liberalism. Classical Liberal Theory started to be developed in the seventeenth century by such writers as John Locke as a means of explaining how society operated, and should operate, in an era in which the Divine Right of Kings to rule and to run society for their own benefit had been challenged, and was generally considered to be inappropriate for the society which then existed. Classical Liberalism is founded upon the two principles of reason and rationality: reason in that everything had a logic which could be understood and agreed with by all, and rationality in that every decision made was made by a person in the light of what their evaluation had shown them to be for their greatest benefit. Classical Liberalism therefore is centred upon the individual, who is assumed to be rational and would make rational decision, and is based upon the need to give freedom to every individual to pursue his/her own ends. It is therefore a philosophy of the pursuance of self interest. Society, insofar as it existed and was considered to be needed, was therefore merely an aggregation of these individual self interests. This aggregation was considered to be a sufficient explanation for the need for society. Indeed Locke argued that the whole purpose of society was to protect the rights of each individual and to safeguard these private rights.

There is however a problem with this allowing of every individual the complete freedom to follow his/her own ends and to maximize his/her own welfare. This problem is that in some circumstances this welfare can only be created at the expense of other individuals. It is through this conflict between the rights and freedoms of individuals that problems occur in society. It is for this reason therefore that de Tocqueville argued that there was a necessary function for government within society. He argued that the function of government therefore was the regulation of individual transactions so as to safeguard the rights of all individuals as far as possible.

Although this philosophy of individual freedom was developed as the philosophy of Liberalism it can be seen that this philosophy has been adopted by the New Right governments throughout the world, as led by the UK government in the 1980s. This philosophy has led increasingly to the reduction of state involvement in society and the giving of freedom to individuals to pursue their own ends, with regulation providing a mediating mechanism where deemed necessary. It will be apparent however that there is a further problem with Liberalism and this is that the mediation of rights between different individuals only works satisfactorily when the power of individuals is roughly equal. Plainly this situation never arises between all individuals and this is the cause of one of the problems with society.

While this philosophy of Liberalism was developed to explain the position of individuals in society and the need for government and regulation of that society, the philosophy applies equally to organizations. Indeed Liberalism considers that organizations arise within society as a mechanism whereby individuals can pursue their individual self-interests more effectively that they can alone. Thus firms exist because it is a more efficient means of individuals maximizing their self interests through collaboration than is possible through each individual acting alone. This argument provides the basis for the Theory of the Firm (Coase 1997), which argues that through this combination between individuals the costs of individual transactions are thereby reduced and efficiency is thereby increased. The doctrine of the Free Market is based upon the notion that this efficiency in combinations will be increased and businesses will thereby benefit. The notion that this will benefit all individuals is of greater concern however because the doctrine ignores the inequalities in power relations between individuals which led to the corporate greed causing a renewed concern with social responsibility.

The concept of Utilitarianism was developed as an extension of Liberalism in order to account for the need to regulate society in terms of each individual pursuing, independently, his or her own ends. It was developed by people such as Bentham and John Stuart Mill who defined the optimal position for society as being the greatest good of the greatest number. They argued that it was government's role to mediate between individuals to ensure this societal end. In Utilitarianism it is not actions which are deemed to be good or bad but merely outcomes. Thus any means of securing a desired outcome was deemed to be acceptable and if the same outcomes ensued then there was no difference, in value terms, between different means of securing those outcomes. Thus actions are value neutral and only outcomes matter. This is of course problematical when the actions of firms are concerned because firms only consider outcomes from the point of view of the firm itself. Indeed accounting as we know only captures the actions of a firm insofar as they affect the firm itself and ignores other consequences of the actions of a firm. Under Utilitarianism however if the outcomes for the firm were considered to be desirable then any means of achieving these outcomes was considered acceptable. In the nineteenth and early twentieth centuries this was the way in which firms were managed and it is only in more recent times that it has become accepted that all the outcomes from the actions of the firm are important and need to be taken into account. The development of Utilitarianism led to the development of Economic Theory as means of explaining the actions of firms. Indeed the concept of Perfect Competition is predicated in the assumptions of Classical Liberal Theory. From Economic Theory of course accounting developed as a tool for analysis to aid the rational decision making assumed in Economic Theory.

During the era of individualism in the 1980s however a theoretical alternative was developed in the USA, which became known as Communitarianism, although the concept goes back to the earlier work of such people as Tonnies (1957) and Plant (1974). Communitarianism is based upon the argument that it is not the individual, or even the state, which should be the basis of our value system. Thus the social nature of life is emphasized alongside public goods and services. The argument is that all individuals, including corporations have an obligation to contribute towards the public nature of life rather than pursuing their own self interests. Underpinning the theories of communitarianism is the assumption that ethical behaviour must proceed from an understanding of a community's traditions and cultural understanding. Exponents argue that the exclusive pursuit of private interest erodes the network of social environments on which we all depend, and is destructive to our shared experiment in democratic self-government. A communitarian perspective recognizes both individual human dignity and the social dimension of human existence and that the preservation of individual liberty depends on the active maintenance of the institutions of civil society where citizens learn respect for others as well as self-respect where we acquire a lively sense of our personal and civic responsibilities, along with an appreciation of our own rights and the rights of others.

Corporate vs Public Self-Interest

Many would argue that currently there is too great a concern with encouraging corporate self-interest at the expense of the public interest and that people are very much absent from the equation of concern regarding the effects of corporate activity. Indeed the continuing conversion of public service provision to market testing by many governments suggests a strengthening belief that the two interests are not in conflict. Self-interest and altruism (promoting the welfare of others over self) need not be in conflict. There is ample evidence that encouraging corporate self-interest (and risk taking) does benefit society (albeit unequally from a Marxist perspective). Some of that evidence is contested, as in the case of genetically modified foods. Nevertheless, during the last two decades most of the world's nations have set about creating anew, or refining, (capitalist) economic and political institutions that encourage corporate self-interest.

While governments and consumers alike look to business to continue delivering economic and social benefits, many observers remain concerned about corporate self-interest; a self-interest that is synonymous with those of the managers. Managerial self-interest is unavoidably driven by a combination of shareholder interests (backed up by markets for corporate control and managerial talent), and occupational rewards and career opportunity. The public interest is easily sacrificed on the altar of these managerial motivators (or constraints). Moreover, public interest is not homogeneous and therefore cannot be simply represented. Public interest has become factionalized into constituencies and stakeholder groupings, each concerned with their particular interests.

Perhaps one reason for corporate self-interest being such a mixed blessing is that we are overly reliant on evaluating the consequences of corporate action, especially our fixation with the bottom line. Nothing concentrates the managerial mind like performance targets and outcomes. Self-interest encompasses however not just consequences and results (Wilbur 1992), but also requires freedom of choice and consistency. From this perspective the pursuit of corporate (self-interested) activity should be guided by structured alternatives and consistency, in order to ensure that the self-interest of others is not undermined by selfish action. Sensing that we cannot rely on corporate altruism we the public are demanding our governments to initiate more legislation and tighter regulation. However, even this move has shown important weaknesses. Self-interest is even here, and it is not acceptable to us. These arguments casts doubt on the extent to which we are able to arrange our economic and political institutions in order to harness self-interest to the benefit of society. The functioning of a civilized society includes putting the interests of others before self-interest – the re-placing of people in the organization. As Baron *et al.* (1992) and Mansbridge (1990) observed, altruism is part of social, political and economic life. However, the exploitative nature of capitalism sits uncomfortably with Kant's (1959) ideal of mutual respect for the interests of others, and even less with Rawls's (1971) desire to see a strong form of egalitarian liberalism. These tensions (between capitalism and liberalism, and between meeting unconditional social obligations and the pursuit of economic value), drives the need for constant vigilance of corporate activity. Since we are unlikely to abandon capitalism, nor escape from the fixation on performance measurement, managerial commitment to upholding the interests of others could straightforwardly be included in the managerial performance appraisal (Crowther and Rayman-Bacchus 2003b).

Crowther and Rayman-Bacchus (2003a) have argued that the corporate excesses, which are starting to become disclosed and which are affecting large numbers of people, have raised an awareness of the asocial behaviours of corporations. This is one reason why the issue of corporate social responsibility has become a much more prominent feature of the corporate landscape. There are other factors which have helped raise this issue to prominence and Topal and Crowther (2003) argue that a concern with the effects of bioengineering and genetic modifications of nature is also an issue which is arising general concern. At a different level of analysis Crowther (2000a, 2002b, 2002c) has argued that the availability of the World Wide Web has facilitated the dissemination of information and has enabled more pressure to be brought upon corporations by their various stakeholders.

Conclusion

There is therefore a general assumption that CSR is recognized globally as an issue which will have equal concern throughout the world, albeit with differing emphases according to the perspectives of the countries concerned. Although Abreu and David (2003) demonstrate that this is an issue of concern throughout the countries of the European Union (EU), but with diverse aspects being focused upon in different countries, the reality is that the impetus for this concern stems from the Anglo-Saxon world and is arguably predicated in the corporate misbehaviour manifest within this world. Arguably it is only within the Cartesian world of Anglo-Saxon hegemony – which is increasingly dominating the global market – that the separation of rights from responsibilities (Crowther 2003) has allowed such corporate misbehaviour to occur and thereby necessitates this concern with CSR. One of the dominant discourses concerning CSR is concerned with accountability and this accountability implies reporting to the various stakeholders of the corporation. Thus responsible behaviour for organizations requires the re-placing of people within the management of organizations.

Notes

1   See Child (1984) and Crowther (1996) regarding the different dimensions of performance.
2   Similarly once an animal or plant species becomes extinct (Topal and Crowther 2003) then the benefits of that species to the environment can no longer be accrued. In view of the fact that many pharmaceuticals are currently being developed from plant species still being discovered this may be significant for the future.
3   The benefits of incorporating stakeholders into a model of accountability have however been extensively criticized. See for example Freedman and Reed (1983), Sternberg (1997, 1998) and Hutton (1997) for details of this ongoing discourse.
4   Mathews (1997) traces its origins to the 1970s although arguments show that such concerns can be traced back to the Industrial Revolution.
5   It is accepted however that different definitions of socially responsible organizations exist and that different definitions lead to different evaluations of performance between those deemed responsible and others.

6   For example the Canadian Institute of Chartered Accountants is heavily involved in the creation of such a national framework.
7   These changes are principally concerned with the use of a broader range of measures of performance together with an increasing recognition of the social implications of organizational activity.
8   This work is very often referred to as the seminal work in the area of stakeholder management.

References

Abreu, R., Crowther, D., David, F. and Magro, F. (2003) 'An Overview of Corporate Social Responsibility in Portugal', *The Corporate Citizen*, vol. 3, no. 2, 7-15.

Abreu, R. and David, F. (2003) 'Corporate Social Responsibility: Exploration inside experience and practice at the European Level' in D. Crowther and L. Rayman-Bacchus (eds) *Perspectives on Corporate Social Responsibility*, Aldershot; Ashgate, pp.109-139.

Ackerman, R.W. (1975) *The Social Challenge to Business*, Cambridge, Ma; Harvard University Press.

Azzone, G., Manzini, R. and Noci, G. (1996) 'Evolutionary trends in environmental reporting', *Business Strategy and Environment*, 5 (4), 219-230.

Baron, L., Blum, L., Krebs, D., Oliner, P., Oliner, S. and Smolenska, M.Z. (1992) *Embracing the other: Philosophical, Psychological, and Historical Perspectives on Altruism*, New York: New York University Press.

Beaver, W. (1989) *Financial Reporting: an Accounting Revolution*, Englewood Cliffs, NJ; Prentice-Hall.

Butler, D., Frost, C. and Macve, R. (1992) 'Environmental Reporting' in L.C.L. Skerratt and D.J. Tonkins (eds) *A Guide to UK Reporting Practice for Accountancy Students*; London; Wiley.

Coase, R.H. (1997) 'The Nature of the Firm' in Putterman and Kroszner (eds.) *The Economic Nature of the Firm*, Cambridge; Cambridge University Press.

Child, J. (1984) *Organization: A Guide to Problems and Practice*, London; Harper and Row.

Copeland, T., Koller, T. and Murrin, J. (1996) *Valuation: Measuring and managing the value of companies*, 2nd edn, John Wiley & Sons, New York.

Crowther, D. (1996) 'Corporate performance operates in three dimensions', *Managerial Auditing Journal*, 11 (8), 4-13.

Crowther, D. (2000a) 'Corporate reporting, stakeholders and the Internet: mapping the new corporate landscape', *Urban Studies*, vol. 37, no. 10, 1837-1848.

Crowther, D. (2000b) *Social and Environmental Accounting*, London; Financial Times Prentice Hall.

Crowther, D. (2002a) *A Social Critique of Corporate Reporting*, Aldershot; Ashgate.

Crowther, D. (2002b) 'Psychoanalysis and auditing' in S. Clegg (ed.), *Paradoxical New Directions in Management and Organization Theory*, Amsterdam; J. Benjamins; 2002 pp.227-246.

Crowther, D. (2002c) 'The psychoanalysis of on-line reporting'; in L. Holmes, M. Grieco and D. Hosking (eds); *Distributed technology, distributed leadership, distributed identity, distributed discourse: organizing in an information age*, Aldershot; Ashgate pp.130-148.

Crowther, D. (2003) 'Limited liability or limited responsibility' in D. Crowther and L. Rayman-Bacchus (eds) *Perspectives on Corporate Social Responsibility*; Aldershot; Ashgate, pp.42-58.

Crowther, D. and Rayman-Bacchus, L. (2003a) Perspectives on corporate social responsibility; in D. Crowther and L. Rayman-Bacchus (eds) *Perspectives on Corporate Social Responsibility*, Aldershot; Ashgate, pp.1-18.

Crowther, D. and Rayman-Bacchus, L. (2003b) 'The future of corporate social responsibility' in D. Crowther and L. Rayman-Bacchus (eds) *Perspectives on Corporate Social Responsibility* Aldershot; Ashgate, pp.229-249.

Dahl, R.A. (1972) 'A prelude to corporate reform', *Business and Society Review*, Spring 1972, 17-23.

Eccles, R.G. (1991) 'The performance evaluation manifesto', *Harvard Business Review*, 69 (1), 131-137.

Fetyko, D.F. (1975) 'The company social audit; Management Accounting', 56 (10), 645-647.

Freedman, R.E. and Reed, D.L. (1983) 'Stockholders and stakeholders: a new perspective on corporate governance', *California Management Review*, XXV (3), 88-106.

Freeman, R.E. (1984) *Strategic management: A stakeholder approach*, Pittman, Boston.

Gamble, G.O., Hsu, K., Jackson, C. and Tollerson, C.D. (1996) 'Environmental disclosure in annual reports: an international perspective', *International Journal of Accounting*, 31 (3), 293-331.

Gray, R., Owen, D. and Maunders, K. (1987), *Corporate Social Reporting: Accounting and Accountability*, London; Prentice-Hall.

Hawken, P. (1993) *The Ecology of Commerce*, London; Weidenfeld and Nicholson.

Hetherington, J.A.C. (1973) *Corporate Social Responsibility Audit: A Management Tool for Survival*, London; The Foundation for Business Responsibilities.

Hutton, W. (1997) *Stakeholding and its Critics*, London; IEA Health and Welfare Unit.

Jones, M.J. (1996) 'Accounting for biodiversity: a pilot study', *British Accounting Review*, 28 (4), 281-303.

Kant, I. (1959) *Foundations of the Metaphysics of Morals*, trans. L.W. Beck, New York: The Liberal Arts Press.

Klein, T.A. (1977) *Social Costs and Benefits of Business*, Englewood Cliffs, NJ; Prentice-Hall.

Mansbridge, J. (1990) *Beyond Self-Interest*, Chicago: University of Chicago Press.

Mathews, M.R. (1997) Twenty-five years of social and environmental accounting: is there a silver jubilee to celebrate?; paper presented at the British Accounting Association National Conference, Birmingham, March 1997.

McDonald, D. and Puxty, A.G. (1979) 'An inducement – contribution approach to corporate financial reporting', *Accounting, Organizations and Society*, 4 (1/2), 53-65.

Pava, M.L. and Krausz, J. (1996) 'The association between corporate social responsibility and financial performance: the paradox of social cost', *Journal of Business Ethics*, 15 (3), 321-357.

Plant, R. (1974) *Community and Ideology*, London; Routledge, Kegan and Paul.

Ranagnathan, J. and Ditz, D. (1996) 'Environmental accounting: a tool for better management', *Management Accounting*, 74 (2), 38-40.

Rawls, J. (1971) *A Theory of Justice*, Cambridge, Mass: Harvard University Press.

Rubenstein, D.B. (1992) 'Bridging the gap between green accounting and black ink; Accounting', *Organizations and Society*, 17 (5), 501-508.

Solomons, D. (1974) 'Corporate social performance: a new dimension in accounting reports?' in H. Edey and B.S. Yamey (eds), *Debits, Credits, Finance and Profits*, London; Sweet and Maxwell; pp.131-141.

Sternberg, E. (1997) 'The Defects of Stakeholder Theory', *Corporate Governance: An International Review*, vol. 5, no. 1, 3-10.

Sternberg, E. (1998) *Corporate Governance: Accountability in the Marketplace*, London; Institute of Economic Affairs.

Tonnies, F. (1957) *Community and Society*, Trans. Loomis C.P.; Harper and Row; New York.

Topal, R.S. and Crowther, D. (2003) 'Bioengineering and corporate social responsibility' in D. Crowther and L. Rayman-Bacchus (eds), *Perspectives on Corporate Social Responsibility*; Aldershot; Ashgate, pp.186-202.

Wilbur, J.B. (1992) *The Moral Foundations of Business Practice*, Lanham: University Press.

Epilogue

In order to summarize all the papers included in this volume, first of all, we have to look into the essentials of the Indian Moral System. Indian outlook is spiritual and the Indian moral system is oriented towards that spiritual goal. The spiritual goal is generally known as 'moksa' and morality in any of its form is a means to that goal. So morality in India is thoroughly spiritualistic. There is one materialists system of thought also in the Indian tradition, which neither believes in the spiritual foundation of the world nor in spiritual goal. But the tone of the system to be so meagre in the overall spiritualistic atmosphere, that it has hardly any impact on the Indian moral system.

Indian moral system has a metaphysical basis. In the West, ethics is autonomous and it does not need to have a metaphysical or religious foundation. It is a social affair and therefore the ought-questions of morality are to be decided simply on social and rational considerations. It does not need to have any transcendental basis. Moreover, metaphysics purports to deal with factual (although of a fundamental nature) questions and purely factual considerations can never become a foundation of deciding ought-questions. For, from mere 'is', there is non-passage to 'ought'. If, however, we make such a passage, we become victim of a fallacy popularly known as 'naturalistic fallacy'. The two distinguished features of Indian concept of morality are as follows: (1) Authority has the basis for deciding what is moral and what is immoral and (2) Morality refers not only to the social obligations but also to obligations related to one's own self.

In the Indian context, man's own nature furnishes a justification for his being moral. Perhaps this is why most Indian systems prove to be deontological in nature. According to them, '*dharma*' is to be followed because it is its own justification. 'Moksa' has been brought forth as a motivation in the sense that one who will follow '*dharma*' will automatically pave his way for that, but 'Moksa' has never been taken as a justification for being moral. Morality is involved in the nature of man. This can find an apt solution in solving the corporate ethical dilemmas.

On the other hand, we find that the 'modern' western conception of morality is a successor to the Judaeo-Christian notion of a divine law that binds all souls. Another is that the moderns accept the empirical methods of modern science and want to achieve an understanding of ethics that is consistent with the worldview of modern science. Next is the rise of the idea of the liberal democratic state, and the idea that the state must be justifiable to its citizens on equal terms without any premise that some lives are inherently better and more noble than others.

Mill is something of an exception to this because of his doctrine of quality, but generally the utilitarian tradition treats each person's preferences equally and does not take a view about which preferences are really worth satisfying and which are not. And morality, for the utilitarian, has the goal of promoting the greatest happiness of all, counting each person for one and no more than one. Kant's theory has something of the same 'liberal' structure. All ends other than the distinctively moral end of rational nature itself are merely 'non-moral' and can generate no categorical imperatives. They are all ultimately reducible to the agent's own happiness. Morality, on the other hand, is constituted by an equal regard for all as rational autonomous agents, and this end, and this end only, is fully obligatory.

Aristotle, on the other hand, writes as though a consensus on what matters in life is much likelier, at least among those he is willing to take seriously. The modern conception of morality plays no apparent role in Aristotle's thought. The word 'moral' certainly appears in our translation of Aristotle's text, but it simply carries the meaning of anything relating to character in the broadest sense.

Aristotle's major question in the 'Nicomachean Ethics' is what is the good, or the chief good? The modern distinction between moral and non-moral good plays no role in his thought. He is simply concerned to discover the good.

Against these two moral backgrounds that is from the East and the West, we have included, for this volume, inputs from a number of reputed and established academicians who are spiritually inclined and have amalgamated new era principles in management. The recurrent theme we discerned was that business and ethics can coexist.

Indeed, this synthesis is imperative for long-lasting success and societal well being. Corporate-houses have realized that the pursuit of self-interest will not only destroy the environment, but our social fabric as well. The era of shortsighted corporate autocracy is gradually coming to an end. If our country, our planet has to survive, it cannot be otherwise.

This being the 'zeitgeist', more corporate-houses are practicing New Era management principles, with the multinationals fast catching up. Which should mean a field day in the years to come for corporate social practices and precepts.

The whole set of values needed for management can be summed up in the words of *dharma* and *dharma* is the code of right conduct. In these days when corporate governance is emerging as a significant factor, we find that Indian management can emerge successfully in the market place if it is able to draw on its route for good corporate governance, which are available in our culture and tradition. But then the question may arise, how many of us are aware scriptures, culture and so on. Though one may not be consciously aware, one learns about basic principles from our childhood, from our parents and from our religion. All religions have highlighted the need for being truthful and kind and helpful. Ultimately, perhaps the universal principle and human value is that honesty is the best policy.

Ananda Das Gupta

Index